"An exciting, meticulously researched spy story. . . . This book functions marvelously as a history of science, detailing the research, engineering, and policy decisions behind the U-2 and Corona, but it's also an excellent social history of the Cold War in the 1950s and early '60s. It's a page-turner as well, notably with Taubman's narratives of the first U-2 flight, *Sputnik*, and the downing of Francis Gary Powers's U-2 over the Soviet Union."

—*Publishers Weekly* (starred)

"A compelling book of Cold War history. . . . Philip Taubman adds new luster to Eisenhower's growing reputation for greatness. . . . The author unabashedly sings of unsung heroes, the men of courage, tenacity, and above all, patriotism who brought Eisenhower's vision into reality. The result is uplifting and inspirational."

—*Austin American-Statesman*

"Lively and engaging."

—Alex Roland, *The New York Times Book Review*

"An expertly related, accessible account of a turning point in American intelligence. . . . Absorbing throughout, and meaty stuff for intelligence and aviation buffs."

—*Kirkus Reviews*

"Taubman delivers an excellent history of the nation's spy-in-the-sky program and does so in a sprightly fashion."

—Jim Barlow, *Houston Chronicle*

"What is new and different about Taubman's book is that it presents, in a single volume written in accessible prose, a comprehensive history of overhead reconnaissance from the camera-carrying balloons of the early Cold War to the electro-optical, near-real-time eyes in orbit relied upon by American strategists in the current Gulf War. And unlike other books on what espionage cognoscenti like to call 'technical collection,' Taubman focuses on some memorable characters."

—Gregg Herken, *The Boston Globe*

"A bracing, well-timed book."

—Richard Reeves, Universal Press Syndicate

"With the help of recently declassified government documents, Taubman has taken an oft-told tale of U.S. government spying and enhanced it greatly. . . . He is a fine stylist, making even the technical portions of the story relatively easy going."

—Steve Weinberg, *The Denver Post*

"One of the joys of outliving proscriptions against the release of sensitive government information is that at some point you are given insight into what was really happening in your youth. Such is the case with *Secret Empire*. . . . If you have an interest in spying, the space race or the burgeoning post–World War II government, you will enjoy *Secret Empire*."

—Michael L. Ramsey, *The Roanoke Times & World News*

"Taubman, a veteran reporter and now an editor at the *New York Times*, covered the intelligence beat for his paper and displays an impressive familiarity with the shadow world. In addition, he deals with matters that were not declassified until the 1990s, so the story he tells will be new— at least to readers who are not specialists in the field—and gripping in the bargain."

—Paul Gray, *The New Leader*

"Should find a prominent place on the shelf of important Cold War reference works."

—Jeff Stein, *The New York Times*

"Philip Taubman . . . makes a good case that we got our money's worth out of the CIA in the Eisenhower years."

—Bob Hoover, *Pittsburgh Post-Gazette*

PHILIP TAUBMAN

SIMON & SCHUSTER

NEW YORK · LONDON · TORONTO · SYDNEY

SECRET EMPIRE

Eisenhower, the CIA, and the Hidden Story of America's Space Espionage

FOR FELICITY, MICHAEL, AND GREGORY

SIMON & SCHUSTER
Rockefeller Center
1230 Avenue of the Americas
New York, NY 10020

First Simon & Schuster trade paperback edition 2004

SIMON & SCHUSTER and colophon are registered trademarks
of Simon & Schuster, Inc.

For information about special discounts for bulk purchases,
please contact Simon & Schuster Special Sales:
1-800-456-6798 or business@simonandschuster.com.

Manufactured in the United States of America

1   3   5   7   9   10   8   6   4   2

The Library of Congress has cataloged the hardcover edition as follows:
Taubman, Philip.
Secret Empire : Eisenhower, the CIA, and the hidden story of America's
space espionage / Philip Taubman.
p.   cm.
Includes bibliographical references and index.
1. Aerial reconnaissance, American—History—20th century.
2. Space surveillance—United States—History—20th century. 3. United
States. Central Intelligence Agency—History—20th century.
4. U-2 (Reconnaissance aircraft). 5. Cold War. I. Title.
UG763.T38 2003
327.1273'009'045—dc21   2002042937

ISBN 0-684-85699-9
0-684-85700-6 (Pbk)

"It was as if an enormous floodlight had been turned on in a darkened warehouse."

—ALBERT D. "BUD" WHEELON,
DEPUTY DIRECTOR FOR SCIENCE AND TECHNOLOGY,
CENTRAL INTELLIGENCE AGENCY, 1962–1966

CONTENTS

VAULTING INTO SPACE
1956–1976

PREFACE

THE GATHERING AT George Washington University on May 23, 1995, could have been mistaken for a college reunion. Several hundred participants, mostly men of retirement age, swapped stories about the past and compared notes about their careers. The tales they recounted, however, had nothing to do with school. The visitors had come to mark the official public disclosure of one of the great secret spy enterprises of the twentieth century—the creation by the United States of reconnaissance satellites in the late 1950s and early 1960s. The engineers, scientists, businessmen, and former government officials who assembled in Washington that fine spring day had designed, built, and launched the first satellites. Yet due to the airtight secrecy that cloaked the project, many of the men who had worked on different components at sites around the country had never met prior to the declassification conference. Some had never seen the remarkable pictures of Soviet military bases, shipyards, and munitions factories that the satellites snapped from more than 100 miles out in space. Suddenly freed from the oaths of secrecy that had sealed their stories for decades, they talked late into the night, poignantly aware that their service to the nation would finally be recognized.

This book is the chronicle of these pioneers and their work, including the groundbreaking science and backbreaking failures that marked the swift passage of America's aerial espionage from the lower atmosphere to the stratosphere to outer space during the presidency of Dwight D. Eisenhower. Faced with the danger of a surprise Soviet nuclear attack in the 1950s—the gravest military threat the United States had ever confronted—the Eisenhower administration forged a creative partnership with science and industry to produce new spy planes and satellites that could see behind the Iron Curtain to measure the strength of Soviet military forces and detect preparations for a surprise attack.

In reconstructing this hidden chapter in American history, I encountered a singular group of people and sequence of events that transformed the nature of espionage, and in so doing, profoundly changed the national security apparatus of the United States in ways that continue to affect the nation today. The earliest satellites served as the building blocks for the powerful space-based systems the United States employs today to gather intelligence, direct combat operations, and guide warplanes and precision missiles and bombs to their targets in foreign wars.

The story told in these pages unfolded in a simpler but no less perilous era than the one the United States faces today. It was a time when the nation was frightened by the emergence of a new and powerful foreign enemy. At first, we knew little about the exact dimensions of the Soviet threat, and feared the worst. Unable to see how many warplanes and missiles the Kremlin was building, we assumed the numbers were great and growing larger every day. The only way to answer such an unfathomable threat, it seemed, was to devote the national treasure to building ever greater and more expensive defenses, even at the risk of damaging the American economy and creating what Dwight Eisenhower described as a garrison state. That debilitating path was largely skirted, due in no small measure to the ingenuity and industry of the architects of the new espionage technologies.

Looking back at the Eisenhower era, it is clear that a rare combination of circumstances encouraged innovation in defense and intelligence technologies. Whether that environment can be replicated today to help deal with new threats is unclear.

The Eisenhower presidency (1953–1961) has often been depicted as a time of muddled leadership, but I found in the area of military and intelligence technology that Dwight Eisenhower was a visionary leader with a high tolerance for risk. In these fields, Eisenhower was confident in his judgments, open to new ideas, respectful of the contributions science could make, and wary of the Pentagon's conventional thinking and stifling bureaucracy. Throughout his presidency, Eisenhower repeatedly bet on daring new defense technologies, often rejecting the recommendations of cabinet members and the established institutions of

Washington, including the military services. When things went wrong, which they often did during the development and testing phase of new projects, he didn't flinch. The result was a formidable array of new spy systems and weapons, including exotic spy planes and satellites, nuclear-powered submarines and aircraft carriers, intercontinental ballistic missiles and nuclear warheads compact enough to fit atop missiles. All in all, it was a time of landmark advances in defense, a record unequaled by nine subsequent presidents.

Eisenhower, unlike most of his successors, gave high-powered scientists frequent access to the Oval Office and invited them to provide independent advice and a fresh perspective on research and development projects. He paid close attention to what they told him. When the Pentagon or other government agencies failed to produce inventive ideas, or neglected the ones they had, men like James R. Killian, the president of the Massachusetts Institute of Technology, and Edwin Land, the creator of instant photography, urged Eisenhower to look at unconventional proposals like the plans for the ungainly U-2 spy plane or a no-frills spy satellite that returned its exposed film to earth. The productive collaboration between government and science, which carried over into the Kennedy administration, was sundered by the Vietnam War. It has never been fully rebuilt.

Once Eisenhower settled on a spy project, even one that involved airplanes or rockets, he turned it over to the CIA to manage, figuring the Pentagon was too cumbersome to handle it and too porous to keep it secret. Only a retired five-star general could get away with that, or know instinctively that it was the smart thing to do. As the World War II supreme commander in Europe and a national hero, Eisenhower had the clout and nerve to give the CIA the leading role in the creation of reconnaissance planes and spy satellites. The projects would not have been possible without the help of the Air Force, including the loan of top officers to help run the programs, but Eisenhower understood that the armed services were too bureaucratic and cautious to develop heretical new technologies on their own.

At the CIA, Eisenhower found an unexpectedly agile partner for his spy pursuits. Though Allen Dulles, the director of central intelligence at the time, was not technology minded, the agency sprang into action once the White House made clear the CIA was going into the aircraft and satellite business. Under the direction of Richard M. Bissell Jr., who is better known for his stewardship of the failed Bay of Pigs invasion of Cuba in 1961, the agency proved to be an effective manager of advanced technology projects. By today's more exacting standards, Bissell's operation would probably be closed down after a few days for lack of administrative controls and a failure to micromanage contractors such as Lockheed and General Electric that had signed on to build the new machines. There were few rules, little paperwork, and accounting procedures that would doubtless give congressional committees a fit today, but it all somehow worked smoothly, and in the case of the U-2, ahead of schedule and under budget. The big defense contractors themselves seemed more supple and inventive than they are today.

Unfortunately, the gusher of espionage innovation during the Eisenhower years, and another burst of creativity in the 1960s and 1970s, were not followed by a similar period of technological advancement in the 1990s that might have helped the Central Intelligence Agency and Federal Bureau of Investigation home in on Mohammad Atta and his fellow hijackers as they prepared for their assault on the World Trade Center and the Pentagon on September 11, 2001.

Ironically, one of the reasons Washington was unprepared for Osama bin Laden was that over the years it had come to rely heavily on spy satellites and other sophisticated hardware. The machines, which were made for tracking Soviet missiles and tanks, were not as adept at monitoring terrorist plots. The high cost of building and operating satellites also consumed such a large chunk of the intelligence budget that more conventional espionage activities tended to be shortchanged. This included the maintenance of a worldwide corps of experienced field officers who might have a chance to penetrate terrorist groups. And the giant intelligence organizations which grew up around spy satellites were hobbled by senseless bureaucratic rivalries and independent reporting channels that impeded efforts to pull together signs of terrorist activity when they were detected by different agencies.

My interest in the development and impact of spy satellites was stirred shortly after I began covering the CIA and its fellow spy agencies for the *New York Times* in 1979. One day I got a call from an official in the Carter administration. He told me the president of South Korea, Park Chung-hee, had been assassinated during a bloody coup d'état that day. When I checked the news wires there was nothing about the incident. Nor had the foreign desk of the *Times* heard anything from a correspondent who happened to be in Seoul, the South Korean capital. As a newcomer to the intelligence beat, and the *Times*, I began to worry that I had raised a false alarm. Soon the paper was preparing to order up three or four stories about a news event that had yet to be confirmed or reported anywhere. Several hours later, news of the assassination finally flashed across the wire services.

I later learned that the original information about the killing had come from the interception of South Korean military communications channels by sophisticated American listening devices and that top Carter administration officials had been notified as soon as word reached Washington. As months passed and I developed sources at the CIA and other agencies, I found that the great preponderance of critical intelligence data flowing into Washington came from satellites and other technological devices. The massing of Soviet forces on the Afghan border in 1979—the indication that an invasion was imminent—had been tracked by spy satellite. When Soviet troops assembled for a possible invasion of Poland in December 1980, satellite photographs helped to alert Washington. When I learned of sensitive information about American collection systems, the CIA and the White House were quick to ask the *Times* to delay publication, a request we sometimes honored to prevent the exposure of operations that seemed vital to American national security. Even the fact that the United States possessed spy satellites was considered a state secret and the existence and name of the organization that managed them—the National Reconnaissance Office—were classified, and remained so until 1992.

As I learned about the satellites and their companion systems, and realized how they had eclipsed traditional forms of espionage, I wanted to know more about their origins. So began the search that led to this book.

As the United States struggles today to overcome the new threats to its security, and to devise new methods of watching its enemies, it may find useful guideposts in the Eisenhower years. The ambition of Dwight Eisenhower's espionage endeavors was exceedingly high—to overcome a terrifying blindness that left the nation vulnerable to surprise attack and to defeat an acute fear of the unknown threatening to disfigure American society. He succeeded.

CAST OF CHARACTERS

Henry H. "Hap" Arnold: commander of the Army Air Corps (later renamed the Army Air Forces), 1938–1946. He recognized the role science could play in developing military technologies and built a network of scientists and businessmen who studied photography and flight.

Harold R. "Hal" Austin: reconnaissance pilot with the Strategic Air Command. His May 8, 1954, overflight of the Soviet Union in a conventional plane helped convince Washington to develop better reconnaissance equipment after he was nearly shot down.

James G. Baker: Harvard optics expert and lens designer. He designed cameras that provided high-resolution photos from the U-2 spy plane, 13 miles above the earth, and the Corona reconnaissance satellites, 100 miles out in space.

Richard M. Bissell Jr.: joined the CIA in 1954. Served as deputy director of central intelligence, 1959–1962. He assembled and ran the highly efficient management teams that directed the development of the U-2 spy plane, the supersonic A-12 spy plane, and the Corona spy satellites.

Merton B. Davies: researcher at the California-based RAND Corporation. He championed the creation of spy satellites and did some of the early design work on them.

Allen W. Dulles: director of Central Intelligence, 1953–1961. He reluctantly added complex technological development projects to the work of the CIA.

John Foster Dulles: secretary of state, 1953–1959. He supported the use of new espionage systems to gather information about Soviet military forces.

Dwight D. Eisenhower: president of the United States, 1953–1961. His faith in science and openness to new ideas led to the development of revolutionary new espionage and military technologies.

Trevor Gardner: special assistant for research and development to the secretary of the Air Force, 1953–1955. Assistant secretary of the Air Force, 1955–1956. He helped prod the Eisenhower administration into action to prevent a surprise Soviet nuclear attack.

Gen. George W. Goddard: chief photographic officer in charge of aerial photographic research, Wright Field, 1936–1944. He was a pioneer in aerial reconnaissance.

Gen. Andrew J. Goodpaster: Eisenhower's staff secretary. He served as the president's gatekeeper and confidant on military and intelligence matters.

Clarence L. "Kelly" Johnson: gifted and prolific airplane designer for the Lockheed Corporation, 1933–1975. He designed the U-2 and A-12 spy planes, shattering aeronautical conventions in the process.

Lyndon B. Johnson: Democratic senator from Texas, 1949–1961; vice president of the United States, 1961–1963; president of the United States, 1963–1969. As a senator, he led hearings in the late 1950s on Soviet bomber and missile threats.

John F. Kennedy: president of the United States, 1961–1963. The first president to benefit extensively from intelligence information provided by spy satellites.

Nikita S. Khrushchev: first secretary of the Soviet Communist Party, 1953–1964. His efforts to strengthen Soviet military power led to fears in Washington that the Soviet Union could launch a surprise nuclear attack on the United States.

James R. Killian Jr.:   president of MIT, 1948–1959. As a science adviser to Eisenhower, he pushed for the development of new spy technologies.

Martin Knutson: one of the first U-2 pilots.

Edwin H. Land: inventor of instant photography and founder of Polaroid Corporation. As an adviser to Eisenhower and the CIA, he promoted the choice of the U-2 over competing spy plane proposals favored by the Air Force and encouraged the creation of other new espionage systems.

Richard S. Leghorn: Army Air Forces pilot and Kodak research scientist. He recognized the need to gather intelligence about America's enemies in peacetime to help prevent a surprise attack and pressed for the development of a new, high-flying spy plane in the years immediately following World War II.

Gen. Curtis E. LeMay: head of the Strategic Air Command, 1948–1957. Air Force chief of staff, 1961–1965. He resisted the development of the U-2.

Tony LeVier: Lockheed's top test pilot. He was the first pilot to fly a U-2.

Arthur C. Lundahl: the CIA's top photo analyst, 1953–1973. He built and directed the nation's primary photo interpretation center in the 1950s to handle pictures produced by the U-2 and the first spy satellites.

James W. Plummer: program manager for the Corona satellite project at Lockheed Missile Systems Division; director of the National Reconnaissance Office, 1973–1976. He guided the novel satellite program through crippling problems with booster rockets, guidance systems, film, and cameras.

Francis Gary Powers: pilot of the final U-2 overflight of the Soviet Union on May 1, 1960. He survived the downing of his plane, was captured and put on trial by the Soviet government, and spent two years in prison there before being released in a prisoner exchange.

Donald A. Quarles: assistant secretary of defense for research and development, 1953–1955; secretary of the Air Force, 1955–1957; deputy secretary of defense, 1957–1959. He supported the development of new military technologies.

Gen. Osmond J. "Ozzie" Ritland: vice commander, Western Development Division, 1956–1959. He worked as Richard Bissell's deputy during development of the U-2 and the Corona satellite system and worked alongside Gen. Bernard Schriever, who ran the Air Force's missile development programs.

Gen. Bernard A. Schriever: commander, Western Development Division, 1954–1958; commander, Air Research and Development Command, 1959–1966. As director of missile development programs, he led the Air Force into space in the 1950s and pushed for the development of both the U-2 and the Corona satellite system.

Harold E. Talbott: secretary of the Air Force, 1953–1955. He favored alternatives to Lockheed's proposal for a high-altitude reconnaissance plane but eventually endorsed development of the U-2.

Harry S Truman: president of the United States, 1945–1953. He approved the first cold war overflights of Soviet territory in 1948.

Gen. Nathan F. Twining: Air Force chief of staff, 1953–1957; chairman of the Joint Chiefs of Staff, 1957–1960. He thought aerial reconnaissance operations should remain under the purview of the Air Force.

Albert D. "Bud" Wheelon: deputy director of the CIA for science and technology, 1962–1966. He consolidated the scientific and technological programs of the CIA in a directorate of science and technology and began the work that led to the creation of a new generation of advanced spy satellites in the 1970s, including the first near-real-time photoreconnaissance satellites, which transmitted photographs back to earth electronically.

PART ONE

Reimagining Reconnaissance
1946–1954

CHAPTER ONE

"Racing Toward Catastrophe"

H AL AUSTIN HAD always assumed that the first time he flew an American warplane into Russian airspace, Moscow and Leningrad would be burning, incinerated by an American nuclear attack. This was no Strangelovian fantasy. It was his job description.

As a reconnaissance pilot in the Strategic Air Command (SAC), he had standing orders in the early 1950s to join the initial wave of American bombers over Moscow if the cold war turned hot. He would activate high-powered cameras to record the damage below. Every week, no matter where he was based, Austin would carefully review his role under the Emergency War Order, the top-secret plan for SAC operations in the opening hours of World War III. Though his day-to-day work was training other pilots in flight techniques, Austin knew his ultimate responsibility, however unthinkable it might seem, was to guide his aircraft through the nuclear firestorm to determine what was left of the targets around the Soviet capital that the bombers were supposed to destroy.

His assumptions were overturned on May 8, 1954. As first light faintly illuminated the rolling English countryside west of London that Saturday morning, Austin and his two-member crew were summoned to an unscheduled meeting at Fairford Royal Air Force Base, where they were temporarily stationed. The three men, dressed in their flight suits and anticipating another uneventful day of flying, were separated from the other American crews by their wing commander, Col. Joe Preston, and directed to a small, simply furnished conference room. There, two SAC colonels whom they had never seen before—one an operations officer, the other an intelligence officer—invited them to be seated, then gave them startling news.

That day, the airmen were told, they were to fly over the Soviet Union to photograph military airfields on Russia's northern frontier. They would be hundreds of miles from friendly airspace, under orders to maintain radio silence. If they were shot down, the U.S. government would disavow their mission and make no effort to rescue them.

Any doubt that they were about to venture along the most hazardous front lines of the cold war was eliminated when one of the colonels unfurled a long, narrow map and placed it on the table. It showed a corridor starting over the Barents Sea and running southeast from the Soviet port of Murmansk across the Kola Peninsula and White Sea to Arkhangel'sk. The remote Arctic area was studded with Soviet air and naval bases and air defense forces.

The three men, part of the 91st Strategic Reconnaissance Wing, stood up to get a closer look at the map. Nine airfields were marked along the flight plan. The two colonels did not explain why these bases had been selected for photographing, but Austin surmised that the war planners at SAC wanted fresh targeting information. As Vance Heavilin, the navigator for the flight, examined the thin strip of paper, he learned there was a reason for its diminutive dimensions. If the plane was forced down in Soviet territory, his duty was to crumple the map into a small ball and swallow it before the Americans were captured.

In the chilling, cold war calculus that prevailed at the time, the mission was a necessary intelligence-gathering task. The United States had to update its war plans frequently, and monitoring the picket line of airfields along the northwest Soviet border would show whether the Russians were gathering their forces for a surprise attack. Knowing what aircraft were in the area would also help SAC figure out how to suppress Soviet air defense units so American bombers could reach their assigned targets over the Russian heartland. Austin's high-flying RB-47E, a six-engine jet that could cruise above 40,000 feet at better than 600 mph, would be well above the range of the Soviet MiG-15 fighters that were thought to be based in the region. The crew was told that the most advanced Soviet fighter, the MiG-17, was still being tested and none of the new planes would likely be stationed along their route. The new fighter was designed to fly higher and faster than the MiG-15, and might be able to intercept the American plane.

In truth the flight plan was a high-risk gamble, a cold war roll of the dice that might well end up killing Austin and his crew or depositing them in a Siberian prison camp. Once the American plane crossed into Soviet airspace, there was no guarantee it would ever get out. There was even a chance that the flight could ignite a wider conflict with the Soviet Union.

Under international law and the rules of war, the planned violation of Soviet airspace would be an act of aggression, potentially reason enough for the Kremlin to retaliate by attacking the United States. President Dwight Eisenhower well understood the danger, and kept a tight rein on flights over Soviet territory, insisting that most missions be cleared in advance by him. Later in his presidency, he would tell the Pentagon's top civilian and military leaders that nothing would send him more quickly to Congress to request authority to declare war than the violation of American airspace by Soviet aircraft.

Harold R. Austin, a native of Sweetwater, Oklahoma, was twenty-nine years old, a quintessential SAC warrior immersed in the unforgiving business of preparing to wage nuclear war. Flying was his life and passion, and he was skilled at it. His commanders had placed him among the elite group of pilots selected to make sure other airmen met the SAC standards for handling of the RB-47E jets that had recently been acquired for reconnaissance work.

As Austin surveyed his aircraft on the morning of May 8, 1954, it seemed well suited to his daring mission. The streamlined plane with swept-back wings was equipped with six General Electric J47 engines, each capable of producing 7,200 pounds of thrust. With a maximum speed of 610 mph, a range of 3,500 miles, and a cruising ceiling above 40,000 feet, it was ideal for high-altitude, long-distance reconnaissance flights.

The reconnaissance model was built to carry cameras, not bombs. The bomb bay, which would normally hold one nuclear bomb, was instead configured to house cameras for photographing ground installations. Other cameras on board would make a record of the plane's radarscope during the flight. The combination would allow SAC not only to study the Soviet bases and combat aircraft in the Arctic region, but would also provide a sequence of radar images that could later help to guide pilots to the same targets at night or in bad weather.

Like most 1950s bombers, Austin's RB-47E was only lightly armed. Two M-24 20mm cannons were located in the tail. They could only be operated by remote control by the co-pilot if he swiveled around to face the rear. Bomber crews knew the guns were unreliable and would offer only a feeble defense against far more agile and heavily armed fighters.

Austin entered the hatch at the belly of the plane and climbed a short ladder to the cockpit, where he took his accustomed place in the front seat. Carl Holt, the co-pilot, was from Pittsburgh. He settled in behind Austin, divided by the co-pilot's instrument panel. A bubble canopy would cover them in flight. Heavilin, an Ohio native, descended a step to the navigator's quarters, a windowless space in the nose that was crammed with navigational instruments, a radar screen, and other equipment. There was just enough room in a cramped aisle alongside the pilots for the crew members to move about during the flight.

Austin powered up the engines, and with a deafening rumble, the plane rolled down the taxiway to await takeoff clearance from the control tower. The English countryside was a lush green from the spring rains. As the plane climbed into the sky shortly after 7 A.M., the tidy little village of Lechlade was visible below. The plane crossed over the meandering Thames River, which stretched east toward Oxford and on to London.

As agreed in advance with the other two crews that were flying with Austin that day, he took the lead as the three aircraft headed out over the North Sea. The flight plan called for the planes to refuel off the Norwegian coast, then proceed around the northern tip of Norway to a point 100 miles north of Murmansk, where the other two crews believed all three planes would turn back.

The tankers, also from the 91st Strategic Reconnaissance Wing, were waiting when Austin reached the preset rendezvous point off Stavanger, a port city on the southwest coast of Norway. In a delicate piece of aerial choreography that he had practiced dozens of times, Austin guided his plane under and slightly behind the tanker and slowed his speed. The long refueling boom was lowered from the plane toward Austin and into the RB-47E's receptacle. Once the connections were secure, thousands of gallons of jet fuel streamed into fuselage tanks.

From Stavanger, Austin proceeded northeast along the Norwegian coast for more than an hour, passing by Bergen and Trondheim. He soon crossed the Arctic circle. The northernmost region of Europe was now visible, a desolate, windblown landscape at the top of the world. At the far tip, Norway, Finland, and the Soviet Union coexisted uneasily by the Barents Sea. Murmansk was less than 150 miles down the coast from the Norwegian-Soviet border.

The moment to part company with the two other SAC aircraft had come. Heavilin checked the map and the aircraft heading, plotting a course toward Murmansk. He relayed the information to Austin, who then banked the plane to the right on a southeast flight path. As the plane slowly wheeled toward the Russian mainland, Austin could see the pilot and co-pilot of one of the other planes twist around and look at him in disbelief. Jimmy Valentine, the other pilot, was a good friend, and Austin waited tensely to see if he would break the radio blackout. He didn't, though he was mystified and alarmed by Austin's unexpected maneuver.

Within minutes, the Soviet coastline loomed in the distance, and, with it, the invisible dividing line between international and Soviet airspace. Austin was right on course. But after flying through the morning without generating contrails, the plane entered a new air mass, and its progress across the cloudless sky was clearly marked by a white ribbon stretching back to the horizon. The Russians didn't need a radar system to see that an unidentified intruder was coming their way.

They were waiting, on high alert. Unbeknownst to Austin, ten days earlier three British crews, using American RB-45C airplanes temporarily based at Sculthorpe Royal Air Force Base on England's east coast, had made a nighttime flight over the western Soviet Union. Soviet air defense forces around Kiev had unsuccessfully tried to shoot down one of the planes with antiaircraft fire. The two other aircraft were pursued by Soviet fighters, but escaped untouched. Commanders in Moscow were furious at the ineffectual performance, and the entire air defense system had been placed on heightened alert.

Heavilin switched on the cameras and Austin leveled the plane as it coasted in over Murmansk, a gritty seaport that served as the Soviet Union's main fishing and naval hub in the Arctic region. Directly below were the shipyards and concrete-block buildings that the Russians had erected in the inhospitable terrain to take advantage of the ice-free waters, warmed by the remnants of the Gulf Stream. One of Russia's most sensitive military installations, the submarine base at Severomorsk, was located not far up a narrow inlet that leads to the open sea.

As instructed, Austin had climbed to 40,000 as he neared the Soviet coast, even though the plane was carrying the fresh load of fuel it had picked up off Stavanger. The combination of weight and altitude reduced the plane's speed to about 510 mph. Austin had questioned the assigned altitude at the morning briefing, concerned that he would lose airspeed just as he penetrated Soviet airspace. There was no sign of Russian resistance as the RB-47 passed over its first targets, two airfields outside Murmansk. But as the crew completed the photographing of the second base, Holt spotted three fighters rising toward the American aircraft. The planes approached but made no effort to attack. They had apparently been scrambled into the air to get a better look at the intruder.

Austin, Holt, and Heavilin were determined to complete their mission, believing that their altitude and airspeed provided protection against any attack. The first group of Soviet planes dropped back toward their base. A second and then a third set appeared, but remained out of attack range below the Americans. Austin continued over the White Sea to Arkhangel'sk, where the crew photographed several other airfields. At that point, six new fighters roared into view, climbing rapidly toward the reconnaissance plane. As they got closer, Austin concluded that they were MiG-17s.

Austin ordered Holt to unbuckle himself from his seat so he could swivel around to see what the Russian planes were doing and get the guns ready for firing. Holt was just turning when Austin saw tracer rounds streaking above and below. Any illusions about invulnerability vanished instantly. "We had been identified as foe, and they were going to shoot us down if they could," he said.

He told Holt to return fire with the cannons, warning that the next attack run would come right up their tailpipes. The co-pilot got off two or three shots before the guns jammed. But the brief burst forced the pursuing jets to pull away from the prime firing position behind the American plane. Firing from 30 to 40 degrees to the side, the Russian pilots would not have as good a shot at disabling or destroying the plane.

Austin hollered, "The hell with this 40,000-foot bit. I'm gonna let down." Since the altitude wasn't proving any defense against the high-performance Russian planes, he wanted to descend to 37,000 feet, where he would pick up speed. "I pushed the nose over," he recalled. In an effort to outrun the Russians, he rammed forward the six throttles that controlled the plane's engines.

The plane accelerated to 550 mph as it descended, and Austin momentarily thought he might have eluded the pursuing jets. He turned toward the next airfield. As he was making the 45-degree turn to the left, the plane shuddered as a shell smashed into the top of the port wing, about 8 feet from the fuselage. It exploded on impact, knocking a jagged hole in the top of the wing and piercing the fuselage in a dozen spots in the area of the forward main wheel well and the number one main fuel tank. The largest hole was big enough for a football to fit through. Austin and Holt, seated forward of the wing, couldn't see the damage, but they knew the plane had been hit when the intercom system suddenly went dead. The Russian planes, possibly short on fuel and struggling to keep pace with the RB-47 as it picked up speed, broke off pursuit. Heavilin quickly calculated that the final airfield on their list was located along their escape route toward Finland, so Austin headed southwest toward that target. They got the photographs they wanted, then raced for the border.

Flying time to Finland would be about twenty minutes, the last part of it over Karelia, a land of lakes, pine forests, and wooden churches that had been contested for centuries by Finland and Russia. The Russians had time for another attack before the Americans crossed into Finnish airspace. It came just as the plane neared the border. Three fighters swooped into view. The leader came up alongside, on the right wing, close enough that Austin could clearly make out the head of the pilot. For several minutes—to Austin it seemed like an eternity—the planes flew in formation, side by side, the American and Russian pilots periodically gazing at one another. The Soviet pilot chased him well into Finnish airspace before dropping down and out of sight.

After hooking up with a tanker off England just as his plane was about to run out of fuel, Austin made it back to Fairford. As he brought his battered plane to a stop and killed the engines, he saw all the men in the detachment had assembled to welcome them back. He was more than ninety minutes behind schedule. One of the ground crewmen, spotting the large hole in the wing, said, "My God, you must have hit a big bird."

The next day, the Swedish Defense Ministry complained about the unauthorized appearance of several planes in its airspace the preceding day. The ministry reported that the aircraft had crossed into Sweden at high altitude, flying west out of Finland. The planes had not been identified. On May 15, a Helsinki newspaper reported there had been an air battle over northern Finland on May 8, possibly involving Russian and American planes.

The U.S. Air Force firmly denied that there had been any such incident. It insisted that no American planes had been in the area. Jimmy Valentine, the pilot who had watched in astonishment as Austin guided his plane toward the Soviet coastline, knew better, but could only guess what had actually happened to Austin and his crew. He was still shaken by the incident when he and Austin met for a drink at a Fairford pub not long after the flight. "What the hell happened to you guys?" he asked Austin. Then, as the men sipped their drinks, he said, "Don't ever do that to me again."

Valentine didn't know it, but he might as well have been speaking for Dwight Eisenhower as well. It was getting too dangerous to send conventional airplanes over the Soviet Union to gather information on Russian military forces. There had to be a safer way.

Back in Washington, Trevor Gardner didn't need the example of Hal Austin's flight to know that the United States had to move quickly to invent new techniques for collecting intelligence about the Soviet military. In 1954, Gardner was a thirty-nine-year-old special assistant to Secretary of the Air Force Harold E. Talbott. No one in Washington was more abrupt and abrasive than Gardner, and no one worried more about the possibility that the United States might fall dangerously behind the Soviet Union in devising new military technologies like intercontinental ballistic missiles and ever smaller yet more powerful nuclear weapons. Gardner was a tireless, sometimes punishing proponent of the need to accelerate American efforts to produce its own advanced weapons and spy systems. By the time of Austin's narrow escape, Gardner was doing his best to kick the Eisenhower administration into increased action.

Born in the seaside city of Cardiff, Wales, on August 24, 1915, Gardner emigrated to the United States when he was twelve and grew up in Southern California. He studied engineering at the University of Southern California, where he was an Olympic-class water polo player. He picked up a business degree at USC, and after working briefly for several industrial companies, signed on in 1942 as a research administrator at the California Institute of Technology. At the elite Pasadena school he became involved in rocket designing, and in World War II worked on the Manhattan Project, the secret American program to produce an atomic bomb. After the war he was hired by General Tire and Rubber Company as a senior executive. He quit three years later, in 1948, to found Hycon Manufacturing Company, an electronics and optical firm located in South Pasadena not far from the Rose Bowl.

Gardner's energy and profanity were legendary, and by the time he joined the Eisenhower administration in 1953, he had a well-earned reputation as a cold, headstrong engineer, business executive, and evangelical champion of new technologies. Not intimidated by the Air Force high command or the Pentagon bureaucracy, Gardner started pushing almost immediately to upgrade missile-development programs, which were poorly organized, insufficiently funded, and generally neglected by generals who were fixated on airplanes and saw no need for the Air Force to get into space. The young, pugnacious Gardner, who dressed in impeccably tailored suits and always sported a neatly folded handkerchief in his breast pocket, thought nothing of lecturing three-star generals about their benighted views and using his influence in Secretary Talbott's office to overcome their resistance. It wasn't long before the sight of Gardner in Pentagon corridors elicited whispers about that "bastard" and "son-of-a-bitch."

Gardner was troubled by Washington's inability to reliably track Soviet progress in designing and building new weapons, including missiles and jet-powered, long-range bombers. Like a growing number of other officials, he believed Moscow might be developing the means to launch a surprise nuclear attack against the United States. For those in the Eisenhower administration who studied the evidence that suggested such an assault might soon be possible, and knew American defenses were hopelessly inadequate, the threat became a consuming fear.

Gardner's concerns had crystallized a few months after he moved to Washington, when he received a highly secret report from RAND, the Air Force research center, on the vulnerability of SAC bases in the United States. The Air Force had commissioned the study to determine how damaging a Soviet nuclear air attack would be to America's primary offensive strike force. Based on the best estimates of growing Soviet power, RAND experts looked at the likely consequences of a Soviet sneak attack in 1956. They examined high- and low-altitude attack paths, reviewed American radar operations, and calculated the warning time the Pentagon might get once Soviet aircraft were detected and what kind of defensive actions might be initiated against the Soviet bombers.

The report, published on April 15, 1953, stunned Gardner and other officials in Washington. The lightly defended SAC bases, with their concentration of airplanes, hangars, fuel depots, and crew housing, were ideal targets for atomic attack. If Russian bombers swept through America's porous air defenses before dawn on a summer Sunday morning, a time of maximum exposure, they could conceivably deliver a knockout blow. "The enemy will have the capability of destroying a major part of the SAC potential in a surprise attack at relatively low cost in bombs and aircraft," the report said. With just fifty atomic bombs, RAND estimated, the Soviet Union could wipe out two thirds or more of SAC's bombers and reconnaissance aircraft.

The import was clear and breathtaking: For the first time in its history, the United States was vulnerable to a crippling attack from overseas, and would find it difficult, if not impossible, to retaliate after being struck. Even in the bleakest days of World War II, with Europe slipping under Nazi control and Japan ascendant in the Pacific, the continental United States seemed safe from foreign invasion or a disabling military strike. The advent of nuclear weapons and long-range bombers had erased that reassuring margin of safety. A surprise attack of unimaginably destructive force was possible. If it came, it would make Pearl Harbor seem like a pinprick.

Gardner was so alarmed, he flew out to SAC headquarters in Omaha to talk with Gen. Curtis E. LeMay, the top commander. From there he traveled to Pasadena for an unconventional homecoming at Caltech. Gardner wanted to see Lee DuBridge, the school's president and head of a White House Scientific Advisory Committee. The panel, composed of scientists and engineers, had been formed during the Truman administration to advise the government on technology issues. But it had done little to push the Truman or Eisenhower administrations into new technological ventures. Though DuBridge was an eminent figure in American science, Gardner did not mute his message. Vincent Ford, an aide to Gardner, later recalled his boss's words to DuBridge: "You're abnegating your responsibility to science and the country, sitting on your dead asses in fancy offices in Washington, wasting your time and the taxpayers' money going through a lot of goddamn motions on a lot of low-level, shitty exercises—all in the name of science." Gardner urged DuBridge to study the threat of surprise attack and the nation's ability to meet it. He wanted an honest report, "the true story, not that shit Washington is feeding the American people."

Gardner's language may have been intemperate, but his analysis was correct. The Soviet Union appeared to be gaining on the United States, and Washington was misleading the American people with confident assurances about the nation's military and scientific superiority. Americans were only dimly aware that traditional concepts of war and defense were rapidly being overtaken by new technologies. Bombers powered by jet engines were compressing time and distance between the Soviet

Union and the United States. Scientists in both countries, taking advantage of the explosive power of the hydrogen bomb, were starting to design smaller nuclear weapons that would be easier to transport between continents. American and Soviet refinements of rocket technology promised before long to produce missiles that could deliver nuclear warheads to distant targets in a matter of minutes.

By 1954, the combination of cold war hostility, advances in military technology, and huge gaps in intelligence had reached a critical state. The Soviet Union possessed atomic weapons and the United States had no safe, reliable way to spy on its enemy or to gauge its military strength. This was a breeding ground for fear and instability. The uncertainty could lead Washington into unnecessary and excessive defense spending, draining resources needed for domestic programs and creating a garrison state, a possibility that weighed heavily on Eisenhower after he moved into the White House in January 1953. Even worse, it could make the tripwire for war so taut that a small miscalculation or misunderstanding would trigger a nuclear exchange. Sensing the rising danger, Eisenhower wrote in his diary at the end of 1953, "As of now the world is racing toward catastrophe."

The makings of a cataclysm dated back to World War II and the inauguration of the nuclear age on July 16, 1945, when J. Robert Oppenheimer and his fellow scientists in the Manhattan Project detonated the first atomic bomb in the New Mexico desert. In an instant, the nature of warfare was transformed. The bombing of Hiroshima and Nagasaki a few weeks later demonstrated the annihilating power of atomic weapons. John Hersey's harrowing account of the Hiroshima attack and its aftermath, printed by the *New Yorker* on August 31, 1946, and published as a book later that year, made clear to readers around the world that mankind had set loose elemental forces that, if wantonly used, could not just win wars but erase entire civilizations.

Americans might be proud of the technological achievement of creating the bomb or ashamed of the devastation they inflicted in Hiroshima and Nagasaki, they might be thankful for the American lives saved by the quick surrender of Japan or appalled at the loss of Japanese lives, but there was no escaping the implications of the atomic era. Once the Soviet Union ended America's nuclear monopoly and built bombers capable of carrying atomic weapons over great distances, the oceans that had effectively protected the United States from foreign enemies would no longer shield it from a disabling attack. All it would take was a small arsenal of Soviet atomic weapons and a few dozen bombers capable of reaching Washington, New York, Boston, Chicago, and a handful of other population centers.

The collapse of the wartime alliance with the Soviet Union was swift and jarring to a nation weary of conflict and eager to see a realization of the Wilsonian ideals embodied in the establishment of the United Nations. Though it seems clear today that maintaining America's wartime partnership with the Soviet Union in the postwar era was implausible, given the two countries' opposing ideologies and economic systems, the idea did not seem so outlandish in the optimistic days immediately after the end of World War II.

Eisenhower himself was infected by the euphoria that followed the German surrender in April 1945 and the capitulation of Japan four months later. In his role as supreme commander of Allied forces in Europe, he flew to Moscow in August as the guest of Marshal Georgi Zhukov, the top Soviet general, to celebrate the victory. Eisenhower was received warmly, met with Joseph Stalin, and stood atop Lenin's Tomb in Red Square alongside Stalin as thousands of Russians paraded across the cobblestone plaza, passing below the towering walls of the Kremlin and the ornate onion domes of St. Basil's Cathedral. Spirits were high, the personal chemistry between Eisenhower and Zhukov was good, and the future looked promising. As he prepared to depart, Eisenhower declared, "I see nothing in the future that would prevent Russia and the United States from being the closest of friends."

Looking back in 1953 at those days of promise, Eisenhower would say in sorrow, "This common purpose lasted an instant and perished."

Debate over the origins of the cold war persists today, often colored by political convictions. It is tempting to look for miscalculation and ill-will both in Washington and Moscow, and certainly both countries contributed to the demise of the friendship that Eisenhower described. But efforts to apportion blame equally misrepresent history. The Soviet

Union, driven by an expansionist ideology, long-standing grievances against the West, and the decisions of a demented dictator, was incapable of sustaining the wartime partnership with the United States and Britain.

The power vacuum in Europe after the defeat of Nazi Germany was an invitation to trouble. Stalin was not content to rely on benign forces like trade, geographic proximity, and cultural affinity to extend Russia's influence in Eastern Europe. As John Lewis Gaddis notes in his wise 1997 reassessment of cold war history, *We Now Know*, Stalin's approach was based on "equating security with territory."

This was inimical to the notions of collective security imbedded in the U.N. charter, signed on June 26, 1945, and the postwar expectations of American leaders. Washington was determined to defend its political and economic interests by supporting democracy and free markets in Europe and preventing renewed military aggression on the continent. That attitude was bound to collide with Soviet aspirations to extend Moscow's influence, but an intense rivalry rather than a volatile cold war might have evolved if Stalin had not moved so ruthlessly to impose Soviet control in Eastern Europe.

The most charitable explanation is that history, geography, and ideology compelled him to defend the Soviet Union's interests by installing the Communist regimes. Invasions from the west—led by Napoleon and Hitler—had reached the outskirts of Moscow, and Russia had suffered horrific losses in two world wars during Stalin's lifetime. Leninism taught that imperialism was a natural and inevitable dynamic of capitalism. But these justifications, however much Stalin may have subscribed to them, cannot excuse what was essentially a brazen move to establish a Soviet empire in Eastern Europe.

By early 1946, less than a year after the defeat of Germany, idealism was in retreat. On February 9, Stalin delivered his first broad policy statement since the end of the war. It was a grim analysis that talked of the incompatibility of Communism and capitalism and the inevitability of war between the two systems. Even allowing for some rhetorical excess in addressing Communist Party leaders in Moscow, the speech was alarming. On February 22, George Kennan, the American ambassador in Moscow, sent an extended cable, later known as "The Long Telegram," to Secretary of State James Byrnes, bluntly describing the Soviet Union's inherent hostility toward the United States.

"We have here," Kennan said, "a political force committed fanatically to the belief that with the United States there can be no permanent modus vivendi, that it is desirable and necessary that the internal harmony of our society be disrupted, our traditional way of life be destroyed, the international authority of our state be broken, if Soviet power is to be secure."

Kennan's proposed response, recapitulated by him in an anonymous article in *Foreign Affairs* in 1947, was to help shape American foreign policy for the next four decades. Kennan called for Washington to resist Soviet expansion by maintaining a global balance of economic and political power that would discourage Moscow from trying to extend its influence in Western Europe and Asia. Over time, Washington transformed the Kennan strategy into a doctrine that emphasized the role of American and Western European military power in checking the Soviet Union. This approach came to be known as the policy of containment.

A few weeks after Kennan's telegram arrived in Washington, Winston Churchill, Britain's redoubtable wartime leader, distilled the unfolding conflict into an iconic phrase. On March 5, speaking at Westminster College in Fulton, Missouri, Churchill declared, "From Stettin in the Baltic to Trieste in the Adriatic, an iron curtain has descended across the Continent."

A year later, faced with the possibility of Communist gains in Greece and Turkey, President Truman formally committed the United States to help free peoples around the world resist Soviet-inspired efforts to impose totalitarian regimes in their countries. The enunciation of the Truman Doctrine on March 12, 1947, was followed three months later by the unveiling of the Marshall Plan, the inspired American program to strengthen the development of democracy in Europe by providing money for economic reconstruction. Czechoslovakia, the only Eastern European country that still had a freely elected government, was eager to participate in the plan, but Stalin blocked Czech involvement. A Communist coup in February 1948 erased the last vestiges of democracy in Prague.

At this stage, the Communist threat in Europe was primarily political rather than military, and the United States still seemed secure from attack. The Soviet Union had emerged from the war with its economy badly weakened and its western cities in ruins. Nearly 27 million Soviet men and women had been lost in the war, a staggering blow to a nation already shaken by Stalin's terror and bloody purges. Moscow's military forces were victorious but battered. With a standing army of 4.5 million men after postwar demobilization, the Soviet Union remained the preeminent land power in Europe. But it was not an air or naval power, and lacked the long-range bombers needed to threaten the continental United States. Though its scientists were working frantically to build an atomic bomb, the Soviet Union had not yet tested one.

The next few years changed all that. First came the Berlin blockade in June 1948, the initial military crisis of the cold war. By closing down road, rail, and river access to Western sectors in the divided city of Berlin, the old German capital that was now locked inside Soviet-controlled territory, Moscow hoped to dissuade the United States, Britain, and France from establishing a separate West German state. A Western airlift supplied the city with food and fuel for nearly a year, and the crisis only accelerated Washington's efforts to consolidate its position in Europe. Unprepared for war, Stalin backed down by lifting the blockade in May 1949. By then, the United States and its allies had created the North Atlantic Treaty Organization (NATO), a military alliance that would guarantee American defense of Western Europe and put a quarter of a million American troops on the continent for the next forty years.

On August 29, 1949, the Soviet Union ended the American atomic monopoly. The first Russian atomic bomb was tested at Semipalatinsk, a remote site in the Kazakhstan steppe on the southern rim of the Soviet Union. The blast leveled buildings in a 4-mile radius. In a preview of the intelligence problems that were to haunt Washington in the years ahead, the United States did not learn of the test until September 19, when an Air Force reconnaissance plane detected unusually high levels of radiation in the atmosphere as it flew from Japan to Alaska. Other planes confirmed the finding, and on the evening of September 19, David Lilienthal, the head of the U.S. Atomic Energy Commission, returned to his vacation home on Martha's Vineyard to find Gen. James McCormack, a commission official, waiting for him in the fog. In a room illuminated by a kerosene lamp, McCormack informed Lilienthal of the Soviet test. The next morning Lilienthal flew to Washington to tell President Truman.

The danger of a Soviet surprise attack on the United States was beginning to gather. Two weeks after Washington's belated discovery of the Russian atomic test, the Chinese Communists completed their revolution and proclaimed the establishment of the People's Republic of China. The potential for cold war combat was realized on June 25, 1950, when Communist North Korea used its armored divisions to invade South Korea, easily overcoming the South's weak defenses. Truman had just settled down for the evening at his home in Independence, Missouri, when Secretary of State Dean Acheson called from Washington to give him the news. Truman feared the invasion was the beginning of World War III.

Three days later, the South Korean capital of Seoul was occupied. A shaken but determined Truman ordered American air and naval forces to come to the defense of South Korea. The United Nations voted the same day to authorize the use of armed force to oppose the North Koreans. Braced by a bleak assessment from Gen. Douglas MacArthur, the American commander in Asia, Truman approved the use of American ground troops on June 30. The North Korean onslaught was halted far to the south, outside the port of Pusan, which became the staging area and resupply center for American forces on the peninsula. In mid-September, 70,000 men of the Tenth Corps made an amphibious landing at Inchon on the North Korean coast, carrying out MacArthur's audacious plan to attack behind enemy lines. The landing was successful and within days more than half the North Korean army was encircled and Seoul was liberated. The war seemed to be won, but MacArthur pressed his luck by pushing deep into North Korea. The day after

Thanksgiving, China unexpectedly entered the conflict with an initial force of 260,000 men.

The Americans were driven back across the 38th parallel, the prewar dividing line between North and South Korea, but neither side could gain a decisive advantage in battle and the war soon settled into a costly, demoralizing stalemate. Though Stalin had pressed the Chinese to enter the war, he refrained from committing Soviet ground troops. An armistice was finally signed on July 27, 1953, six months after Dwight Eisenhower became president and four months after Stalin's death.

The Korean War ended any illusions Americans may have had about the new world order. The cold war was going to be protracted and brutish. There might be other armed clashes in Asia and Europe. Most ominously, the Soviet Union in 1953 was building a fleet of new high-speed, long-range bombers that could reach targets in the United States and had demonstrated that it had matched the United States in the design of advanced nuclear weaponry.

On July 30, a military attaché at the American embassy in Moscow spotted a new Russian bomber on the tarmac at Ramenskoye airfield, south of the capital. The airfield was attached to the Myacheslav Aviation Design Bureau, an incubator of new Soviet warplanes. The large aircraft was notable for several reasons: It was Moscow's first jet-powered heavy bomber, and its swept-back wings and other aerodynamic features demonstrated more advanced Soviet design skills than American experts had anticipated. After years of building military aircraft based on the designs of American and British planes that had been left behind in the Soviet Union during and after the war, Moscow now had its first homegrown jet-powered bomber, and it appeared to be on a par with the latest American bomber.

The new aircraft was far different from anything previously seen in the Soviet bomber fleet. Moscow had accelerated its production of turboprop bombers in the early 1950s. The Tupolev-16, designated the Badger by NATO, was built for medium-range missions over Europe and could not reach the United States. The Tupolev-95, or Bear, had better range—7,800 nautical miles, more than enough to reach Boston,

New York, and Washington—but like all turboprop planes, it was slow; its flying time to American targets would be better than fifteen hours.

The new plane, the Myacheslav-4, or Bison, was roughly the equivalent of the American B-52, which was just going into production at the big Boeing Aircraft plant in Seattle. Equipped with four jet engines, the Bison had a top airspeed of 560 mph, could carry a bomb load of 10,000 pounds, and cruise over 7,000 nautical miles without refueling. This was more than enough distance and heft to deliver two atomic bombs to any site on the American east coast.

On August 12, 1953, the Soviet threat grew exponentially. Moscow tested its first hydrogen, or thermonuclear, bomb. Barely nine months had passed since the initial American test of a similar weapon at Eniwetok Atoll in the South Pacific. The speed of Soviet progress astonished American officials, who had not expected to see the first Soviet H-bomb test for at least three or four more years.

Andrei Sakharov, one of the architects of the Soviet H-bomb, described the menacing blast at the Kazakh test site. "We saw a flash, and then a swiftly expanding white ball lit up the whole horizon. I tore off my goggles, and though I was partially blinded by the glare, I could see a stupendous cloud trailing streamers of purple dust. The cloud turned gray, quickly separated from the ground and swirled upward, shimmering with gleams of orange. The customary mushroom cloud gradually formed, but the stem connecting it to the ground was much thicker than those shown in photographs of fission explosions. More and more dust was sucked up at the base of the stem, spreading out swiftly. The shock wave blasted my ears and struck a sharp blow to my entire body; then there was a prolonged, ominous rumble that slowly died away after thirty seconds or so. Within minutes, the cloud, which now filled half the sky, turned a sinister blue-black color."

The development of fusion weapons by Washington and Moscow sharply escalated the potential devastation of a nuclear war. In creating explosive energy, fusing two atoms together was three to four times more efficient than splitting the atoms apart, the technique used in atomic or fission bombs. The design and engineering of hydrogen weapons also theoretically made it possible to generate the greater explosive power from bombs that were much smaller and lighter than their atomic cousins.

The practical result was astounding. The explosion that Sakharov witnessed, and the earlier American tests, represented a revolution in weapons since the final conventional air raids of World War II that was almost beyond comprehension. In less than a decade, the explosive power of a 10,000-pound bomb had gone from 5,000 pounds of TNT to more than 10 billion pounds of TNT. Yet the actual weight of the bomb was no different.

Even more powerful yet smaller weapons were thought to be possible. Initial estimates that the minimum weight of a hydrogen bomb would be a backbreaking 9,000 pounds were quickly erased. By the end of 1953, the Strategic Missile Evaluation Committee, a panel of scientists and engineers appointed by Trevor Gardner to review the state of American missile technology, reported that nuclear warheads weighing no more than 1,500 pounds could someday be built, small enough to be carried between continents by a missile.

The notion of placing a compact but powerful nuclear weapon atop a missile that could streak through space, crossing the North Pole in thirty minutes, was stunning. Any nation that mastered that technology would have a tremendous military advantage. Though the prospect of coupling nuclear warheads with intercontinental ballistic missiles still seemed remote in 1953, there were already signs that the Russians were breaking ahead of the United States in rocket technology.

As the Red Army advanced westward in the spring of 1944, the Russians had captured the Nazi V-2 rocket center at Peenemünde, located on an island just off the Baltic Sea coast of eastern Germany. In October 1946, more than five thousand German technicians and twenty thousand family members were brought to Moscow to jump-start Soviet rocket projects. The Russians, led by several gifted scientists, including Sergei Korolyov, had done pioneering work in rocket science in the 1930s and had founded the Rocket Research Development Center in Moscow in 1932. The Kremlin launched its first rocket in August 1933. Indeed, some of the earliest thinking about rockets had come from a

Russian, Konstantin Tsiolkovsky, a schoolteacher born in 1857 who had been inspired by reading Jules Verne. In a 1903 article that was not translated and published outside Russia, Tsiolkovsky described how a rocket could be built using liquid oxygen and liquid hydrogen as fuel—nearly two decades before Robert H. Goddard, an American, came up with the same idea. But Moscow's efforts to produce reliable rockets, and use them in warfare, were disabled temporarily by the arrest and imprisonment of Korolyov in 1937 on charges that he was involved in anti-Soviet activities.

The Soviet program was reassembled after the war with the release of Korolyov and the arrival of the Germans. In 1947, a missile test site was opened at Kapustin Yar, in the Soviet republic of the Ukraine. Not long after it opened, Washington learned about the missile base from Britain's intelligence services. More detailed information arrived in the early 1950s when some of the German engineers who had been moved to Moscow were repatriated to East Germany and fled to the West. Though the Russians had carefully excluded the Germans from the most advanced aspects of the missile program, the Germans knew about Kapustin Yar and filled in British and American intelligence officials in September 1952. A month later, the Air Force brought some of the German engineers to Wright-Patterson Air Force Base in Ohio to be debriefed.

An incomplete but disturbing picture of the Soviet program was pieced together by the British and Americans and presented to policymakers in July 1953 as a joint intelligence report. The Russians, building on the V-2 technology acquired from the Germans, were trying to produce a medium-range missile that could reach any site in Europe. By 1956, the report said, Moscow was likely to have a missile with a range of 2,275 nautical miles—enough to hit London. It was clear that it would only be a matter of a few more years before the Soviet Union came up with a missile that could strike Washington.

To get a closer look at the Soviet test site, the British modified an RAF B-2 Canberra bomber for a spy flight over Kapustin Yar. The plane could not be refueled, but with extra gas tanks installed in the bomb bay, it had the range to fly from West Germany across Eastern Europe and the Ukraine. In late August 1953, the airplane, outfitted with reconnaissance cameras, took off from Giebelstadt in West Germany in daylight, which was necessary for photographing the missile base but left the plane vulnerable to Soviet air defenses. The Canberra was hit by gunfire as it dodged Soviet fighters, but managed to get pictures of the missile complex and then fly on to Iran, where it landed. The mission, however, was a failure. Vibrations produced by the damage to the plane made the pictures so blurred they were all but useless.

The muddy photographs were a perfect metaphor for the intelligence problems Washington faced as Eisenhower and his aides tried to assess and respond to the rising Soviet threat, especially the danger of surprise attack. No one in Washington could be certain how much progress the Russians were making, but it was apparent from everything that was known that Moscow was working feverishly to build an offensive nuclear strike force.

Looking back at this period years later, Lawrence Houston, the general counsel of the CIA in the 1950s, said the lack of reliable intelligence information "was just appalling."

"We just didn't have it—any real information," he explained. "We just didn't know what was going on."

Richard Helms, then a rising young CIA intelligence officer, remembered how little he and his colleagues knew about the Soviet military. "There was an extraordinary absence of knowledge," he recalled in an interview in 1999. "It was totally frustrating trying to learn anything, no matter how hard we tried or how imaginative we were. Eisenhower was sorely pressed to know what his enemy was about."

The intelligence vacuum was intolerable. Gardner knew it when he went to see Lee DuBridge at Caltech. The May 1954 flight of Hal Austin and his crew was just another measure of the desperate need for better intelligence about Soviet armaments. The American government was essentially unable to pry open the "Iron Curtain" to learn more about the state of Soviet military forces. Airmen like Austin were risking their lives to fly near or over the Soviet Union, and others, less fortunate than Austin, had been killed when their planes were shot down during flights along the Soviet border. Aside from modified bombers like the RB-47E, Washington's most exotic overhead reconnaissance system at the time was a fleet of camera-carrying helium balloons that the Air Force launched into the jet stream, hoping they would drift over the Soviet Union, take pictures of military installations, and be recovered when they reached the western Pacific. Most were shot down or fell to earth in Siberia.

Espionage operations on the ground were no better. The suffocating security apparatus of the Soviet police state made it exceedingly difficult to recruit spies in Russia or to plant agents in the Soviet military and intelligence services. The Central Intelligence Agency, which had been established by President Truman in 1947, learned what little it could about Russian military forces by interviewing thousands of Soviet citizens who had emigrated to the West after World War II. Their accounts were spotty and unreliable. Nazi photographs of Soviet factories and military bases, shipped to Washington after the German surrender, were useful but dated. The Agency's best information about the Soviet rocket and missile programs came from the German rocket engineers, and was already badly outdated.

After taking office in January 1953, Eisenhower had complained often and sometimes angrily about the lack of hard intelligence information about the Soviet Union, whether the issue was Kremlin politics or Russian military power. The European battles of World War II had taught him about the risks of operating without information about enemy forces. Gen. Andrew J. Goodpaster, Eisenhower's staff secretary during most of his years in the White House, said, "Eisenhower's experience at the Battle of the Bulge, where the Germans secretly amassed a major force unbeknownst to Allied intelligence, deeply impressed upon him the value as well as the limitations of intelligence, together with the dangers of being caught off guard."

When he convened his cabinet on March 6, 1953, the day after Stalin's death, Eisenhower was in a testy mood. "Ever since 1946," he said, "I know that all the so-called experts have been yapping about what would happen when Stalin dies and what we, as a nation, should do about it. Well, he's dead. And you can turn the files of our government inside out—in vain—looking for any plans laid. We have no plan. We are not even sure what difference his death makes."

At the end of April, Eisenhower told his cabinet, "There can be no accurate prediction as to when, if ever, the enemy will attack."

The absence of reliable intelligence about Soviet military forces was maddening and unsettling. Divining the intentions of foreign leaders was nearly impossible, and always had been among the hardest objectives of any intelligence service. But counting the number of bombers at an airfield, or warships at a naval base, and determining the state of the Soviet missile program seemed more reasonable goals. Yet in 1954 they were largely unattainable through conventional espionage methods.

The CIA ground out reports about the strength of Soviet forces, but these top-secret papers, known as National Intelligence Estimates (NIEs), often sounded much more authoritative than they actually were. In truth, the numbers in them were soft, not much better than educated guesses about how many nuclear bombs or long-range bombers Moscow possessed or was expected to have on hand in the years ahead. The analysts who prepared the reports were working with almost no hard facts.

Not surprisingly, the absence of reliable information led to a wide variety of predictions about Soviet military strength, with the CIA usually on the conservative side and the Air Force at the high end, warning that Moscow was overtaking Washington in airpower and might soon achieve clear superiority. General LeMay had been sounding the alarm for several years, and other concerned Air Force officials, mindful of supporting their requests for budget increases, were providing congressional leaders with frightening estimates about the size and reach of a growing Soviet air force.

The implications were unnerving. Eisenhower did not know whether the Soviet Union was preparing to attack the United States. He expected to get little, if any, warning if an assault were imminent, and he had no solid information about how many nuclear weapons and delivery systems Moscow could direct at American targets. The dismaying conclusion of a high-level 1951 study of American defenses remained true:

"The problem of defense of the United States against air attack is characterized above all by lack of knowledge of what we have to defend against. The enemy has the initiative. Our intelligence tells us essentially nothing about his plans; informs us only partially about his present capabilities; and, as to his future capabilities, leaves us essentially dependent on assumptions that he can, if he chooses, do about as well in any aspect as we expect to do ourselves."

In the nuclear age, such ignorance was untenable. Americans had discovered the cost of intelligence failure at Pearl Harbor in 1941. Eisenhower knew that a surprise nuclear attack by the Soviet Union would be far more damaging to the nation and its military forces than the Japanese attack on Pearl Harbor. In March 1954, Eisenhower told aides he was "haunted" by the threat of surprise attack. A year later, addressing a summit of world leaders in Geneva, he said, "Surprise attack has a capacity for destruction far beyond anything which man has yet known."

The level of expected destruction was unfathomable. A nuclear attack would obliterate cities, kill millions of Americans, destroy a large portion of the nation's industrial base, poison its food and water supplies, and cripple its financial institutions. More than half the population was likely to require medical care. Economic collapse and government decapitation were likely. The detonation of a single 10-megaton bomb over Washington would kill or injure more than a million people and reduce the capital to rubble, requiring the states to form a new federal government.

Even if an attack never came, the fear of one, fueled by the absence of intelligence, was potentially debilitating to the United States. Faced with such a severe threat, the White House had no choice but to do everything possible to defend the country. Yet in the absence of reliable information about the precise nature of Soviet forces, both offensive and defensive, there was a high risk that the country would build defenses and weapons that did not match the threat, or invest in military programs that were unnecessary. The drain could be great not only on the federal treasury but on the entire economy and health of American democracy.

Eisenhower anguished over this possibility. He had articulated his concerns on April 16, 1953, a month after Stalin's death, in a speech to the American Society of Newspaper Editors.

"The worst to be feared and the best to be expected can be simply stated," he told the news executives, who had gathered at the Statler Hotel.

"The worst is atomic war.

"The best would be this: a life of perpetual fear and tension; a burden of arms draining the wealth and the labor of all peoples; a wasting of strength that defies the American or the Soviet system or any system to achieve true abundance and happiness for the peoples of this earth.

"Every gun that is made, every warship launched, every rocket fired signifies, in the final sense, a theft from those who hunger and are not fed, those who are cold and not clothed."

"The cost of one modern heavy bomber is this: a modern brick school in more than 30 cities.

"It is two electric power plants, each serving a town of 60,000 population.

"It is two finely equipped hospitals.

"It is some 50 miles of concrete highway.

"We pay for a single fighter with a half million bushels of wheat.

"We pay for a single destroyer with new homes that could have housed more than 8,000 people.

"This, I repeat, is the best way of life to be found on the road the world has been taking.

"This is not a way of life at all, in any true sense. Under the cloud of threatening war, it is humanity hanging from a cross of iron."

Better intelligence was the key to easing these pressures. Edwin Land, the prolific inventor and creator of instant photography who came to play a pivotal role in the development of new spy technologies, later summed up the equation nicely. "We simply cannot afford to defend against all possible threats," Land said. "We must know accurately where the threat is coming from and concentrate our resources in that direction. Only by doing so can we survive the cold war."

Thanks in part to Trevor Gardner, the gateway to a new era in intelligence gathering was being pushed open by the White House as word of

Hal Austin's narrow escape was flashed back to Washington on May 8, 1954. After the harsh lecture from Gardner, Lee DuBridge invited him to address the next meeting of the Science Advisory Committee. Gardner impressed the panel members and DuBridge soon spoke with Arthur Flemming, the head of the Office of Defense Mobilization, a White House office that supervised the work of the committee. Flemming, in turn, suggested that the advisory panel meet with Eisenhower.

The meeting was held at 9:30 on Saturday morning, March 27, 1954, in the Cabinet Room of the White House. DuBridge was accompanied by thirteen other members of the committee, among them some of the leading scientists and science administrators in the country, including Detlev W. Bronk, the president of the National Academy of Sciences; Oliver E. Buckley, the head of Bell Laboratories; and I. I. Rabi, a physicist at Columbia University. In addition to Eisenhower, Donald A. Quarles, the assistant secretary of defense for research and development and a champion of new military technologies, attended from the administration.

Eisenhower told the committee about the discovery the previous year of the new Soviet intercontinental bomber, the jet-powered Bison. He warned that the new aircraft might eventually be used to attack America. James R. Killian Jr., the president of the Massachusetts Institute of Technology and a member of the science committee, later recalled the conversation: "Eisenhower directed the discussion to the danger of a surprise attack on the United States and stressed the high priority he gave to reducing the probability of military surprise. Modern weapons, he warned, had made it easier for a hostile nation with a closed society to plan an attack in secrecy and thus gain an advantage denied to the nation with an open society."

Eisenhower told the group, "To anyone bearing the responsibility for the security of the United States, the situation was highly unsatisfactory." He asked the committee to advise him on how to deal with the threat of surprise attack.

A fresh look at the problem and ways to ameliorate it seemed advisable. DuBridge asked Killian to meet as soon as possible in Cambridge with committee members who lived in the Northeast. On Thursday,

April 15, a small group of men including Oliver Buckley and Edwin Land assembled in Killian's Cambridge office. They agreed a special task force should be appointed to conduct an intensive review of America's vulnerability to surprise attack, and to recommend steps to lessen the danger. The recommendation, which Eisenhower would soon approve, was awaiting presidential action on the day Hal Austin flew over Murmansk.

The day before, Vietminh forces had overrun the French garrison in Dien Bien Phu after a fifty-five-day siege, ending France's colonial role in Vietnam. Few Americans could have imagined that the victory of Ho Chi Minh's forces would open a long, tortured path to an American war in Indochina, but the French defeat did increase fears in Washington of a Communist advance in Southeast Asia. Before going to the Burning Tree Club in suburban Maryland to play golf, Eisenhower had summoned his top national security aides to the Cabinet Room to review the developments in Vietnam.

Closer to home, the capital and nation were riveted by Senator Joseph McCarthy's reckless assault on the loyalty of the leadership of the U.S. Army, the latest front in his demagogic hunt for Communists in the government. Eisenhower was belatedly but forcefully challenging the Wisconsin senator; even some of McCarthy's allies in Congress, including Senator John McClellan of Louisiana, were questioning his tactics.

Most Americans were only beginning to awake to the danger of surprise attack in the spring of 1954. On Saturday, May 1, a week before Austin's mission, the Bison bomber had made its public debut by flying over Red Square during the annual May Day parade. Though only one bomber joined the air show over Moscow, its appearance was startling, since word of the plane's initial sighting in 1953 had not circulated widely outside the government. The appearance of the giant bomber was page-one news in the United States the next day. A few days later, the *New York Times* for the first time printed a photograph of the plane as it passed over Red Square. An accompanying news story, based on photographs that had been published on Sunday by *Pravda*, the Communist Party newspaper, noted that "The new craft is believed to be an intercontinental bomber similar to the United States B-52 and capable of delivering nuclear weapons to distant targets."

The American people were hardly oblivious to the dangers of the cold war. Fifty-five thousand had died fighting in Korea. The threat of nuclear war produced a constant sense of anxiety that was like a low-grade fever that the nation could not shake. It was reflected in growing efforts to promote the construction of fallout shelters and other civil defense projects. On December 18, 1950, *Life* magazine had published a long article entitled "How U.S. Cities Can Prepare for Atomic War."

Yet for all the uncertainty about the future, American life in 1954 was good and getting better. Prosperity was spreading, the middle class was growing, suburbs were springing up around the cities, and the dislocation and sacrifices of World War II were starting to fade into memory. The nation's population was 162 million, an increase of nearly 20 percent since 1940. The unemployment rate was 5.5 percent. More than half of American households had a television set, three times as many as in 1946, and two-thirds of American families owned a car, compared to just over half in 1948.

Just a month before Austin's flight, *Newsweek* captured the ambivalent mood of the nation with a cover photograph of two attractive young women driving a convertible covered with stickers of vacation destinations. The shot called attention to the issue's special report on "Spring-Summer Travel." But printed across the top of the cover was a reference to another special section in the same issue: "The Bomb: What Odds for Survival Now?"

Trevor Gardner and Jim Killian knew the odds of preventing a nuclear war would improve if the United States knew more about the Soviet Union's military strengths and weaknesses and could manage relations with Moscow accordingly. But as the Eisenhower administration gathered itself in the spring and summer of 1954 to face the threat of surprise attack, the obstacles to gaining that knowledge were immense.

The idea of developing less vulnerable, more effective ways of photographing Soviet military installations had been kicking around Washington for years. In fact, the first scheme for placing a satellite in space was dreamed up for the Pentagon in 1946 by the engineering division of the Douglas Aircraft Company in Santa Monica. This research shop, later detached from Douglas and rechristened the RAND Corporation, became a vital source of ideas for the Air Force. By the time of Hal Austin's narrow escape, detailed work was under way to design a spacecraft that could take pictures of the Soviet Union and relay them electronically back to earth. The Air Force was also trying to produce a reconnaissance airplane that could fly high enough to elude Soviet interceptors and missiles. But none of these efforts had the support of the White House or the financial backing needed to overcome the technological barriers that confronted scientists and engineers.

The challenges seemed nearly insurmountable. No one had yet come close to firing a rocket into space, much less a sophisticated surveillance system. Even if a powerful enough rocket could be built, it was unclear whether a camera system could survive the jolting ride into space and function in the hostile conditions there, including temperatures of 455 degrees below zero Fahrenheit. If useful pictures could be taken from space, relaying the images back to earth would require either a new means of transmission or the development of a film-return capsule that would not burn up during the scorching reentry through the atmosphere. As for new spy planes, the upper reaches of the atmosphere remained an unknown zone filled with potentially lethal dangers for any man or machine that ventured to such heights. Jet engines would flame out for lack of oxygen above 70,000 feet, and fluids in the human body would vaporize at that altitude.

Fortunately, the first concrete steps were being taken to develop the revolutionary new technologies that were required. Kelly Johnson, the top aircraft designer at Lockheed, was pitching the Air Force on his latest proposal for a new spy plane that could cruise over the Soviet Union at 70,000 feet. Lockheed was also working with the Air Force on plans for a photoreconnaissance satellite. Though much of the Air Force high command had little interest in either idea, a young general named Bernard Schriever recognized the potential importance of both and was using his influence to press for their development.

Two other talented men would soon be drawn into pivotal leadership roles in the effort to upgrade America's intelligence operations. One of them was Edwin Land. The weekend Hal Austin was penetrating Soviet airspace, Land was indulging one of his periodic impulses to break with the conventions of business and science. He was in Hollywood, where he had taken up temporary residence to work with Alfred Hitchcock on making 3-D movies. The other person was Richard M. Bissell Jr., a brilliant, eccentric economist who had recently started work at the Central Intelligence Agency as a special assistant to its director, Allen W. Dulles.

Thanks to these men and others who believed that the preservation of democracy and freedom required the creation of radically new technical systems for collecting intelligence, the leap was made. Before the year was out, the Eisenhower administration set in motion a series of secret studies and projects that over the short span of the next six years would revolutionize the intelligence business and profoundly alter the course of the cold war.

In this period of explosive innovation, the nation would produce the U-2 spy plane, which could cruise at 75,000 feet, and started work on a successor aircraft so advanced that it would be considered a startling engineering feat if proposed today. In the late summer of 1960, the United States placed the first successful reconnaissance satellite in orbit. Along the way, the scientists, engineers, businessmen, and government officials who worked on these highly classified programs rewrote the book on airplane design and performance and led the nation into space. They transformed the world of espionage by building machines that in a day could collect more information about a foreign enemy than an army of spies could assemble in a decade, and opened the way to a sea change in warfare made possible by the development of space-based reconnaissance, mapping, communications, and targeting systems. Altogether, it was a triumph of American ingenuity and technology, the cold war equivalent of the Manhattan Project.

Like the invention of the bomb, and the development of intercontinental ballistic missiles that also raced ahead in the late 1950s, the creation of new spy systems reshaped the political, bureaucratic, and budgetary landscape in Washington in both constructive and destructive ways that continue to be felt half a century later. Huge new government organizations were created to manage and exploit the new technologies, billions of dollars were diverted to fund them, and bitter debates were joined over how to manage the systems and how much to rely on them. The struggle for control provoked a boiling conflict between the Central Intelligence Agency and the Pentagon that has yet to be resolved.

But the immediate payoff from the reconnaissance advances was a stream of new, reliable information about Soviet military forces. The photographs provided by the U-2 and, later, the first satellites gave Washington its first real look at Moscow's military machine, including air and naval bases, bombers, missile test sites, submarines, and radar systems. As Albert D. "Bud" Wheelon, one of the men who developed the new generation of spy systems, later said, "It was as if an enormous floodlight had been turned on in a darkened warehouse."

CHAPTER TWO

The Origins of
Strategic Intelligence

No one person can fairly be called the progenitor of the reconnaissance revolution, but Richard S. Leghorn comes as close as anyone to fitting the description. He vividly remembers the day when his thoughts about the future of reconnaissance crystallized. It was July 25, 1946.

Leghorn was a twenty-seven-year-old tactical reconnaissance pilot, one of the best in the U.S. Army Air Forces. As commander of the 30th Photo Reconnaissance Squadron (67th Photo Reconnaissance Group) during the war, he had seen the consequences of combat during many missions over Nazi-occupied Europe. A few days after the Allied landing at Normandy on June 6, 1944, he walked among the dead and wounded at Omaha beach. Yet none of this prepared him for the sobering scene he witnessed on that summer day in 1946.

The sun was already scalding as Colonel Leghorn boarded a B-29 aircraft at Kwajalein Atoll in the Marshall Islands, an archipelago of twenty-nine atolls and five islands scattered across the central Pacific, just above the equator. Leghorn, along with hundreds of other American soldiers, sailors, and airmen, had been dispatched to the area to help test the country's latest nuclear weapons. Washington knew what destruction had been caused at Hiroshima and Nagasaki, but the nuclear age was still in its infancy and the Pentagon wanted to measure the power of atomic bombs in more controlled circumstances and specifically to learn how effective they might be against naval vessels.

The Marshall Islands had been picked as a nuclear proving ground because of their remote location, small population, and status as an American protectorate. The 167 residents of Bikini Atoll had reluctantly agreed in February to evacuate their homes after Commodore Ben H. Wyatt, the military governor of the islands, told them the United States needed to test nuclear weapons there "for the good of mankind and to end all world wars."

Operation Crossroads, the code name for the tests, commenced on July 1 when a bomb, roughly as powerful as the one that had been dropped over Hiroshima, exploded in the air over Bikini Lagoon. A floating junkyard of warships, including surplus American cruisers, destroyers, and submarines, as well as vessels captured from Japan and Germany during the war, was arrayed in the translucent waters of the bay.

Leghorn had returned to active duty in April to serve as deputy commander of Task Force 1.52, the group of more than five hundred officers, enlisted men, and civilians responsible for photographing the tests. The unit had more than three hundred cameras of various sizes. Leghorn and his colleagues manned a B-29 bomber and a C-54 transport plane that had been modified to carry cameras and a variety of measuring devices. The explosion of the first bomb, called Able, buffeted these planes, and the fireball and mushroom cloud that punctuated the Pacific sky were sights he would never forget. But it was the second test, an underwater explosion on July 25, that led Leghorn to revise his views on the nature and consequences of war, an epiphany that would come to play a major role in the development of new reconnaissance technologies.

Leghorn peered down from the B-29 cockpit window as the bomb, called Baker, was detonated 90 feet below the surface of the lagoon. The sea heaved, as though lifted from the ocean floor by some elemental force. As Leghorn watched in disbelief, the vessels still afloat in the lagoon after the earlier test were tossed into the air like beach balls. A Japanese cruiser, the *Nagato*, levitated clear of the water, and a Japanese battleship was thrown 400 yards. When they settled back into the water, eight of the vessels slowly sank below the waves.

"I knew at that moment we couldn't have another war," Leghorn recalled many years later, seated at his home on a mountain ridge in southwestern New Mexico.

The explosion in Bikini Lagoon spurred Leghorn to reflect on ways aerial reconnaissance could help the Pentagon and White House keep the peace. In the weeks before the atomic tests, Leghorn had read a summary of the *United States Strategic Bombing Survey*, which examined the damage that Allied bombers had inflicted on Germany during the war. Leghorn could see that better reconnaissance information would have been invaluable in directing the bombing campaign—the survey noted that there had never been a systematic effort to knock out the Nazi electric grid. Because war planners were primarily interested in pinpointing Nazi troop concentrations and the location of tanks and artillery, insufficient attention had been given to German steel factories and other industrial sites shown in the thousands of reconnaissance photos that might have helped guide the bombing campaign.

As Leghorn studied the report and discussed it with colleagues, he also realized that better intelligence could help prevent a new war by eliminating the fear of surprise attack. The bombing survey report underscored the dangers posed by new technologies of warfare in a concluding section that said, "The combination of the atomic bomb with remote-control projectiles of ocean-spanning range stands as a possibility which is awesome and frightful to contemplate."

Drawing on his experience as a reconnaissance pilot, Leghorn concluded that the best way to avoid a nuclear war was to give the White House and Pentagon as much information as possible about potential aggressors well in advance of any attack on the United States. This could be done by monitoring the military forces and industrial installations of potential enemies on a sustained basis so that Washington would fully know the strength of its opponents and could detect preparations for war in time to head off a conflict or at least be ready to retaliate in kind.

The concept, which came to be known as strategic reconnaissance, was quite different from the more familiar notion of tactical or combat reconnaissance, which military commanders had employed for centuries to gain an advantage in war. Tactical reconnaissance involved the collection of information about enemy forces for use in preparing and directing a battle. Leghorn himself had flown numerous missions along the French coast in the weeks before D-Day to determine where German troops were positioned and to see if reinforcements were being sent to the area. He made additional flights during and after the invasion to monitor the fighting and to alert Allied commanders to the movement of German units.

His new idea called for peacetime, or prehostilities, reconnaissance, an idea alien to most military commanders, who were accustomed to making use of intelligence information primarily in wartime. Indeed, the idea challenged some of the basic rules of military intelligence operations. It was fair game, for example, to send spy planes over enemy territory during a war. But doing so in peacetime was considered an act of aggression that could itself provoke a war.

Leghorn was well aware of the difference, and realized that his approach would require the invention of new high-altitude aircraft that could elude detection. As an MIT-trained physicist, he saw no reason why specialized spy planes could not be designed to fly high enough to avoid air defense forces, or even be coated or fabricated with materials that would make them invisible to radar.

When the nuclear tests in the Pacific ended, Leghorn returned to the United States and retired from the Army Air Forces, but remained in the reserves. He didn't stop thinking about the need for strategic reconnaissance, and set to work to convert the Pentagon. He spent the fall of 1946 assembling his ideas, and then presented them in Boston on Friday, December 13, at a symposium that marked the opening of the Boston University Optical Research Laboratory.

The occasion was well chosen. Much of the most inventive and important work in designing high-quality lenses for aerial photography during the war had been done for the Army Air Forces at Harvard University, under the direction of James G. Baker, a brilliant young astronomer and lens maker. When the war ended, Harvard president James Conant wanted to return the university to purely civilian research and ordered the optical lab closed and its vibration-resistant brick building dismantled. Fearing the loss of the country's most creative optical research center, several of Leghorn's wartime colleagues had helped arrange for Boston University to house it. Baker remained at Harvard, but his assistant, Duncan E. MacDonald, moved to BU to direct the work. MacDonald, a lens designer, had served with Leghorn on Task Force 1.52 during the atomic tests, as had a number of other gifted photographic specialists who attended the Boston dedication ceremony.

Leghorn outlined his ideas in a speech he titled "Objectives for Research and Development in Military Aerial Reconnaissance." Though it received little public notice, the address was one of the most visionary documents of the cold war and laid the basis for a new era in overhead intelligence.

"The nature of atomic warfare," Leghorn told the audience, "is such that once attacks are launched against us, it will be extremely difficult, if not impossible, to recover from them and counterattack successfully. Therefore, it obviously becomes essential that we have prior knowledge of the possibility of an attack, for defensive action against it must be taken before it is launched."

"For these reasons," he continued, "it is extraordinarily important that a means of long-range aerial reconnaissance be devised which cannot be detected. . . . The accomplishment of this objective is not as technically difficult as it might first appear. Extremely long-range aircraft, capable of flying at very high altitudes, are currently on the drawing boards, and in some cases prototypes have been constructed. Effective means of camouflaging them at high altitudes against visual observations are well known. It is not inconceivable to think that means of preventing telltale reflections of other electromagnetic wave lengths, particularly of radar frequency, can be developed."

Leghorn was looking so far beyond the horizon that most military officials dismissed his proposals. In 1946, the Army Air Forces, which would become the U.S. Air Force in 1947, were more interested in building new bombers and fighters than in designing exotic spy planes that could fly at the upper edge of the atmosphere. Aerial reconnaissance, in their terms, primarily meant overflying enemy territory in wartime to select targets for bombing and to identify air defense threats.

Fortunately, Leghorn was not the only person who understood the need to expand the frontiers of overhead reconnaissance. Several of the men he had worked with before and during the war had come to a similar conclusion, including two of the country's aviation pioneers and top air commanders, Gen. Henry H. Arnold and Brig. Gen. George W. Goddard.

General Arnold, the chief of the Army Air Forces during World War II, recognized the intelligence demands of a new and uncertain age in November 1945, less than four months after the end of the war. He told Secretary of War Robert Patterson that henceforth Washington would need "continuous knowledge of potential enemies," including all aspects of their "political, social, industrial, scientific and military life" if America's leaders were to have advance "warning of impending danger." Presaging Leghorn's comments a year later, Arnold, who was soon to retire, advised Patterson that such information could not be obtained through traditional spying methods.

Indeed, it was the fortuitous intersection of the careers of Arnold, Goddard, and Leghorn, and of other men in the Army Air Corps in the 1930s and 1940s, that created the theoretical and practical foundation for the overhead reconnaissance revolution of the 1950s. (The name of the air groups was changed to the Army Air Forces in 1941.)

The wartime incubator of the most advanced overhead camera systems was the Aeronautical Photographic Laboratory at Wright Field, near Dayton, Ohio. This small, obscure workshop was the birthplace of modern aerial reconnaissance. George Goddard, no relation to the American rocket designer Robert H. Goddard, ran the lab during the war, combining bold ideas and a fine eye for talent to create a research center that bubbled with innovation.

Goddard and Arnold, who as Army Air Forces commander was effectively owner of the lab, were well matched. Though they come from very different backgrounds—Goddard was born an Englishman, the son of an insurance agent; Arnold came from a family that traced its military service back to the Revolutionary War—they were ardent believers in aerial reconnaissance and wholeheartedly committed to the development of new technologies.

Almost as soon as he learned to fly, Henry Harley Arnold, better known as "Hap" Arnold, started experimenting with airplanes as platforms for photography. As he worked his way up the Army hierarchy, he was constantly looking for ways to advance aviation technology. Long before most military colleagues, he recognized the assistance that outside scientists and engineers could provide. Arnold eventually became impatient with the glacial pace of the Army's research and development efforts. In 1930, the Army's latest observation plane, the Douglas O-38, would fly no faster than 130 mph. "What the hell have we gained in twenty years?" he complained to his son, Hank. "Nothing." Arnold's response was to build his own research network among scientists and businessmen, including the aerodynamicist Theodore von Karman and airplane builders like Glenn Curtiss, Elmer Sperry, Donald Douglas, and Larry Bell.

By the time he assumed command of the Army's air units in 1938, Arnold had forged ties with Caltech, which had the best wind tunnels on the West Coast. Arnold had gotten to know von Karman, who was director of the Guggenheim Aeronautical Laboratory at Caltech and the master of the wind tunnels and other aviation research operations at the campus. Together, Arnold and von Karman deepened the collaboration between the Army and the college, leading to creation of the Jet Propulsion Laboratory.

It was a mutually beneficial arrangement and a model of things to come in other areas of military technology, including the Manhattan Project and the invention of new spy technologies. For von Karman and Caltech, the stream of funding from the Army was like an intravenous line to the U.S. Treasury that supported rocket and electronic research at the school. For Arnold, Caltech was a bountiful source of new ideas and technologies for his air force.

George Goddard was another innovator, though his work was more narrowly focused on aerial reconnaissance and drew more directly on his own technical creativity. Goddard made his first aerial reconnaissance flight in 1918, not long after the end of World War I. Aerial work in those early years was hair-raising. The photographer would stand up in the open rear cockpit of a plane, held in place by a single leather strap.

As the pilot guided the plane over the target area, usually at an elevation of 12,000 to 15,000 feet where breathing became difficult, the operator would point a 10-pound camera earthward and activate the shutter. Goddard went aloft for the first time on a windy, overcast day in Rochester, New York. As the 80-horsepower Curtiss Jenny gained altitude, he discovered life in the slipstream was not as fine as he had imagined. "I had no idea the air could be so rough and unpleasant," he recalled in his autobiography. Goddard spent most of the flight just holding on, hoping he would not be pitched out of the plane.

In the early 1920s, Goddard began to build an impressive record in reconnaissance work, photographing a bombing test on captured German ships, surveying the Tennessee River basin, and taking pictures of archaeological sites near St. Louis. Dissatisfied with the available reconnaissance cameras, he worked with Eastman Kodak in Rochester to produce lenses with long focal lengths. He took the first nighttime aerial photo in November 1925 by dropping a flash powder bomb over Rochester and shooting pictures by the artificial light it created. In 1934, he accompanied Arnold on a photographic mapping mission over Alaska.

With tensions mounting in Europe in 1936, Goddard, sensing a potential demand for reconnaissance flights at higher altitudes where they could escape antiaircraft fire, revived his earlier effort to develop a 36-inch telephoto lens that would take clear pictures of distant objects. His thinking at the time was a preview of Leghorn's later ideas. "If you could fly high enough to be out of range of the enemy's antiaircraft fire and at the same time get photographs that were as clear and detailed as those taken at lower altitudes, you'd have a built-in safety factor," he recalled.

Early in 1939, Arnold summoned Goddard to Washington for consultations. Both men knew war was likely in Europe and that America might become involved. Goddard made a bold proposal: build a special high-performance reconnaissance aircraft. "It must be fast, it must fly high, it must have long range and it must have defensive armament," he told Arnold. The idea was prescient, but Arnold could not afford to devote resources to a plane that would not add to American offensive firepower.

In 1940, during a visit to Eastman Kodak in Rochester, Goddard met Richard Leghorn, who had recently started doing research and development work at the company. Goddard had come to Kodak to talk with the company's top research executive, Kenneth Mees. With Europe at war, Goddard knew he could no longer count on buying high-quality lenses from Germany. Figuring that the United States might get drawn into the war, he anticipated an urgent demand for long-focal-length lenses that were small and light enough to be used in aerial reconnaissance cameras. His conversation with Mees that December day played a pivotal role in shaping the future of American reconnaissance. Mees told Goddard the answer to his lens problem was James G. Baker, a young astronomer and lens designer at Harvard whom he had hoped to recruit to work at Kodak. He urged Goddard to travel to Cambridge to meet Baker. Mees also suggested that Goddard get together with one of Kodak's newest researchers, Dick Leghorn.

Leghorn was from the Boston area. His father, George, was an auto distributor; his mother, Agnes, a housewife. Leghorn, a compact, dashing man with dark hair and a thin mustache, was born on February 7, 1919, in Brookline, just west of Boston, and went to high school in nearby Winchester. He graduated from MIT in 1939 with a degree in physics and a keen interest in photography.

Not long after moving to Rochester to work at Kodak in the summer of 1939, he developed a passion for flying, rising many mornings at 4 A.M. to learn to fly a Waco biplane at Rochester Airport. "I've been a risk-taker," Leghorn said. "Once I learned how to fly, I'd take girlfriends up to show off by doing loops and rolls."

For Leghorn, who yearned to be an airman and had been commissioned as a reserve officer during his undergraduate years at MIT, the introduction to Goddard was perfectly timed. Goddard could transfer Leghorn's commission from the Ordnance Corps to the Army's air command, putting him on the career path he wanted. By March 1941, Leghorn was on his way to Dayton.

When Goddard got to Cambridge in January 1941, he met Baker on a snowy day at the Harvard Observatory. Baker, who was from Louisville, had come to Harvard as a graduate student in 1935. In Cambridge he turned his attention to the design of new long-focal-length lenses that would allow astronomers to peer deeper into space. When Goddard entered Baker's cluttered attic workshop and spotted a young man dressed in coveralls, he at first mistook the astronomer for a graduate student. As soon as he examined some of Baker's designs, he knew Mees had done him a great favor. "I could see that there was an originality to his ideas that was not bound to old concepts," Goddard recalled.

He told Baker that the Army needed novel camera systems with lenses that would not go out of focus at high altitudes, where temperature and air pressure changes made a lens contract and expand. The problem was especially acute in the large glass elements used in long-focal-length cameras. Goddard wanted a 40-inch optical system that would remain in focus by automatically correcting for the changes—a leap in design that no one in the field had even tried to make. Baker, as Goddard remembered, "didn't bat an eye." Goddard, who by this time was receiving plenty of financial support from Washington, offered Baker $25,000 for the project, an uncommonly high fee for a research project in those days. After gaining the assent of Dr. Harlow Shapley, the director of the Harvard Observatory, Baker agreed to set up and direct an optical lab for the Army at the university.

Baker said he would need the help of a shutter specialist to produce the new camera system Goddard had in mind. Fortuitously, several months earlier, Goddard had recruited Amrom H. Katz, a precocious physicist who was working at the Census Bureau. Katz had rattled the camera world by showing that the shutter speeds on all cameras made in the United States were miscalculated because of flaws in the calibration devices used in manufacturing. Katz, a cheerful, cherubic dynamo, went to work with Baker, a laconic, taciturn scientist, in an incongruous but productive collaboration that, with the help of other equally talented experts, yielded ever more advanced reconnaissance cameras over the next three decades.

By the late 1940s, Goddard, working with the Boston University lab, had come up with a 48-inch lens. Pictures taken by the camera as it passed over a golf course in Fort Worth, Texas, at 34,000 feet clearly showed two oversized golf balls on one of the putting greens. It was a photographic feat, even though the balls were three inches in diameter. But Goddard wanted even higher resolution pictures, aiming for a 240-inch system that could distinguish individual aircraft on the ground from a range of 100 miles. The potential uses for such a camera were not obvious to most photoreconnaissance specialists, for space flight still seemed a distant possibility.

Many of the men who worked for Goddard at the Dayton lab in the early 1940s were reunited after the war in the Marshall Islands for the atomic tests, including Leghorn, Katz, and Walter Levison, another bright photographic engineer. Duncan E. MacDonald, who had served as Baker's assistant at the Harvard optical lab, also reported to Kwajalein Atoll to work with the group. During the long, tropical evenings at Kwajalein, Leghorn tested out his reconnaissance ideas with these men in conversations at the officers club.

The group gathered again a few months later at the dedication of the Boston University lab. The most creative minds in aerial reconnaissance were there: Goddard, Leghorn, Baker, Katz, Levison, and Mac-Donald. The audience also included a roster of top Army Air Forces officers, including Lt. Gen. Curtis LeMay, and executives from many of the nation's top photographic companies, including Eastman Kodak, Fairchild Camera, Chicago Aerial, Bausch & Lomb, and Perkin-Elmer. Few of the people who listened to Dick Leghorn spell out his ideas for peacetime reconnaissance that afternoon could have imagined how prophetic his words would be. Fewer still could have realized that many members of the audience would help make his ideas a reality.

Dick Leghorn's vision of an invulnerable, high-flying reconnaissance airplane was brilliant. The only problem was that nothing remotely like it existed in 1946. The jet age was just dawning and the space age still seemed the stuff of science fiction. The idea of operating an airplane 70,000 feet above the earth looked technologically improbable, if not impossible. An entirely new kind of plane would have to be designed and built that could cruise safely in the thin atmosphere, radical changes in fuel chemistry would be needed to keep the jet fuel from boiling off in the extremely low air pressure, and crew members would require pressurized flight suits to keep their blood from vaporizing. By the aeronautical engineering standards of 1946, Leghorn might as well have been hallucinating.

As American and British leaders began to realize that they faced an ominous new military threat from the Soviet Union, the spy hardware at their disposal was anything but invulnerable. If they wanted to peer into the Soviet Union, they would have to use conventional military aircraft with all the dangers that entailed, including the possibility that planes would be shot down, airmen might be captured or killed, and even the chance that the Kremlin would seize on the violation of its airspace to initiate a war. Harry Truman and Dwight Eisenhower, and a series of British prime ministers, including Winston Churchill, reluctantly decided they had to take that risk. To minimize the prospect that spy flights might provoke an explosive conflict, they cloaked them in such great secrecy that the real purpose of the missions remained unknown to the public—and even the families of the men who flew them—for more than four decades.

The first spy flights began in late 1946 along the coast of northeast Siberia, across the Bering Strait from Alaska. They quickly drew protests from Moscow. The Peacetime Airborne Reconnaissance Program, as the campaign was called, aimed at collecting photographic and electronic intelligence without entering forbidden foreign airspace. A good deal of intelligence about Soviet air defenses, including radar and communications systems, could be gathered by reconnaissance planes flying along or near the Soviet frontier. Electronic sensors installed in modified bombers and other warplanes identified Soviet radar sites and analyzed their signals as Soviet defenders scanned the skies, giving war planners in Washington some idea of the resistance American planes would encounter in an attack. Oblique-angle photographs taken from off the Soviet coast provided limited but useful information about air bases and other military sites on the fringe of Soviet territory. Flights like Hal Austin's, which deliberately crossed deep into Soviet territory, began in the early 1950s.

As the secrecy has lifted in recent years, the full dimensions of the reconnaissance campaign have become clear. It was one of the most daring and dangerous elements of the cold war, and the only one that involved frequent military clashes between Soviet and American forces. The costs linger, including grieving families that still do not know if long-missing husbands, fathers, and brothers were killed when their planes were attacked or if the men were captured and lived for years in Soviet captivity. The history of the spy flights is filled with heroism and patriotism, bonds of fellowship that endure to this day, and achievements for which an unknowing nation never gave proper thanks. Hundreds of men in the Air Force and Navy risked their lives flying along or across the Soviet frontier in an effort to learn about Russian air defenses and military forces.

Sadly, there is also no exact accounting of what happened to the men who never made it back to base. At least 252 air crewmen were shot down on spy flights between 1950 and 1970, most directed against the Soviet Union. (China was also a target, as were some Soviet bloc nations.) It is certain that 90 of these men survived, for they were either rescued by American forces or their capture by the Soviet Union or another country was confirmed. But the fate of 138 men is unknown. It is possible, even likely, that some of them survived for years in captivity, while Washington made little effort to determine if they were alive and to make arrangements for their repatriation.

But the secrecy afforded little comfort to the presidents and prime ministers who sent their countrymen into harm's way. As the need for intelligence increased, flights became more frequent and more hazardous. Every time a plane was intercepted or attacked by Soviet forces, inevitably producing a rash of embarrassing headlines and misleading statements by American officials about the purpose of the flights, pressure mounted in Washington to come up with a safer way to do aerial reconnaissance. This dynamic became one of the great engines of invention in the cold war. "We knew Americans were dying on these missions," Leghorn recalled. "It created a real sense of urgency to come up with new aircraft and to think about moving into space."

For years research and design work for a new reconnaissance plane was halting and poorly coordinated, the neglected stepchild of a military establishment wedded to traditional combat aircraft and unwilling to invest in new reconnaissance technologies. But Leghorn and other visionary men kept pushing, and as the Soviet threat intensified and the toll of lost airmen rose, they gained powerful allies in the Pentagon and the White House, as well as in science and industry.

After leaving military service in September 1946, Leghorn had returned to work for Kodak and was sent to London in 1947 to manage distribution operations in Europe. He returned to Kodak headquarters in Rochester in late 1948 and quickly resumed proselytizing for high-altitude reconnaissance flights. His former commander, Brig. Gen. Paul T. Cullen, invited Leghorn to address a reconnaissance symposium in December at Topeka Air Force Base in Kansas (later renamed Forbes AFB). Without missing a beat, Leghorn picked up where he had left off in Boston two years earlier, emphasizing the urgent need to fly unde-tectable intelligence missions over the Soviet Union. He told the audi-ence of Air Force officers that he believed the United States already had the planes, cameras, and camouflage techniques to do the job, and pre-dicted it would not be long before stealth aircraft could be developed that would flummox Soviet radar.

The Korean War gave Leghorn the chance to carry his crusade di-rectly to the high command of the Air Force. As a reservist, he was re-called to active duty in April 1951 and given command of the Reconnaissance Systems Branch of the Wright Air Development Cen-ter back in Dayton. The center was the Air Force's primary internal source of ideas for new aircraft or the reconfiguration of old airplanes for new missions, and Leghorn's department was responsible for com-ing up with spy planes.

Leghorn quickly prepared a five-page memo outlining his ideas on how the Air Force should tackle reconnaissance demands in the coming decade. To collect intelligence on Soviet forces in peacetime, he said in the July 1951 paper, reconnaissance aircraft would need to minimize the risk of detection and interception. Leghorn then discussed half a dozen reconnaissance vehicles, including satellites—which he thought were too far-fetched at the time to warrant much attention—and balloons, which he favored. He also recommended the use of guided missiles and unmanned aircraft and once again underlined the need to develop high-altitude manned planes.

Impatient with the pace of Air Force research work, which had suffered from lack of attention and money after the retirement of Hap Arnold in March 1946, Leghorn soon proposed grabbing the best plane available and modifying it for reconnaissance duty. He wanted to build an aircraft that could cruise above 45,000 feet, higher than the operational limit of the Soviet Union's most advanced fighter planes, and fly fast enough to outrun Russian planes and travel over the Soviet interior without running out of fuel. "It was the first real attempt to get a specialized plane for overflights of the Soviet Union," recalled Harold F. "Bud" Wienberg, a Leghorn colleague at Wright Field and later at the Pentagon.

The available answer was the Canberra, a new British twin-engine jet bomber. Its performance specs were ideal: a service ceiling of 48,000 feet, a maximum speed of 540 mph, and a range of about 3,600 miles. The new bomber, built by the British Electric Company, made its maiden flight in May 1949, and a reconnaissance model, the Canberra PR3, made its debut in March 1950.

Leghorn figured that by extending the wings, adding more powerful Rolls-Royce Avon-109 engines, eliminating one of the two pilots, and dumping the armor plating and other combat hardware that weighed down the plane, a Canberra would be able to cruise at 63,000 feet with a full load of fuel and ascend to 67,000 feet as the fuel burned off during flight. British Electric would produce the customized reconnaissance model.

"We felt as if we were pioneering in aviation," Wienberg said.

If not the plane of Leghorn's dreams, this was certainly a vast improvement over the aircraft Washington was using for spy flights. Leghorn wanted to order twelve of the modified Canberras and proposed setting up a special reconnaissance unit to fly them. He worked closely with the Royal Air Force liaison officer at Wright Field, bypassing the usual bureaucratic channels and paperwork. He sold the idea to his commanders, who submitted it to the Pentagon for approval and funding. But it was blocked by the Air Research and Development Command which, in a spasm of conventional thinking, ruled that the plane must meet combat specifications, including a heavier airframe.

Leghorn also ran into resistance when he presented his plan to General LeMay. "He was dismissive," Leghorn said. The SAC commander wanted nothing to do with a special reconnaissance unit that operated outside his control, nor did he see the need for such a specialized aircraft. That was especially ironic, since Leghorn was proposing to use the plane in part to photograph Soviet military bases that LeMay and his bombers might someday be called upon to attack.

While Leghorn was wrestling unsuccessfully with the Air Force in 1951, Washington was preparing for the riskiest reconnaissance flights yet—missions deep into Soviet airspace. Peripheral operations gave Washington little intelligence about forces based farther inland, let alone in the Russian heartland, where most of the Soviet Union's military and industrial power was located. The pressure to venture deeper into Soviet airspace increased with the advent of the Korean War in June 1950. With many records still classified, it is difficult to know with certainty when the first American plane was ordered to do so. R. Cargill Hall, who did extensive research on the subject when he served as an Air Force historian, found that Truman first approved deep overflights in December 1950, not long after Chinese troops entered the Korean War. Truman acted on the recommendation of the Joint Chiefs of Staff, who feared that Russian long-range TU-4 bombers equipped with nuclear weapons were being assigned to bases on the Chukotskiy Peninsula, just across the Bering Strait from Alaska. From there, the bombers could reach Seattle.

The Korean War, though limited to the Far East, heightened fears in Washington that Moscow was preparing to attack Western Europe. The Air Force feared that if the order came to bomb Soviet targets, American pilots would practically be flying blind, uncertain about the precise location of military and industrial targets and dangerously unaware of interior air defenses. That would be especially true for night or bad weather flights, when navigators could not rely on visual sightings and would need to guide their aircraft to targets by radar. Unless they knew just what terrain and physical features they had to track on radar, and could recognize specific targets on their radar screens, the navigators would have difficulty directing accurate bombing runs. The only answer was to send planes over the western regions of the Soviet Union to record radar images that could be used later if hostilities commenced. Because radar reconnaissance did not require light, the missions could be flown at night, when it would be harder for Soviet forces to spot the aircraft.

The pace of reconnaissance work picked up through 1952, despite the loss of two American aircraft to Soviet attack in the Far East, the first on June 13 over the Sea of Japan, the second on October 7 over the Pacific Ocean north of Japan. Both flights were coastal intelligence-gathering missions. A total of nineteen American airmen were aboard the two planes. All were presumed to have died, but only one body was recovered. Before the year was out, American spy planes were swarming along the Soviet Pacific and Baltic coasts.

By this time, Leghorn had moved to Washington, where he had at last found an Air Force patron who appreciated his concept for a thoroughbred spy plane and knew how to overcome the institutional resistance to it. His new ally and boss was Col. Bernard Schriever, an assistant to the Air Force deputy chief of staff for development. "Benny had big balls," recalled Bud Wienberg. "He may have been a colonel, but he didn't act like one. Even when he was a lieutenant, he behaved like a general. I saw him tell generals what to do. He was a real visionary. He knew we needed new ideas."

Schriever had heard about Leghorn's Canberra proposal and other fresh ideas and was looking for an imaginative officer who could help plan for the Air Force's future reconnaissance needs. In the six months that Leghorn and Schriever worked together in the Air Force planning office—from August 1952 to January 1953—they gave the Pentagon a jolt of fresh thinking about reconnaissance techniques. As conventional American spy planes were being shot out of the sky by the Soviet Union, the two men pushed tirelessly for the development of less vulnerable intelligence-gathering systems.

Schriever was no ordinary Air Force officer. He had a master's degree in aeronautical engineering from Stanford and was a protégé of Hap

Arnold. "I had the good fortune of serving under Hap Arnold when I was a reserve officer just out of flying school in the early thirties at Wright Field, and I got to know him quite well there," Schriever said.

Schriever had emigrated to the United States from Germany in 1917 at age seven with his mother to be reunited with his father, an engineer for a German steamship company. Schriever's father had been marooned in New York on April 6, 1917, when the United States declared war on Germany and his ship was impounded. The family settled in Texas, where Schriever developed an affinity for flying after watching biplanes taking off and landing at Army airfields outside San Antonio. In 1932, when he was twenty-two, he entered the Army Air Corps flying school at Kelly Field in Texas.

The tall, trim pilot, whose passion for aviation was exceeded only by his love of golf, met Arnold soon after graduating from flying school. He learned from Arnold the importance of using new technologies to bolster American airpower and the advantages of working closely with outside scientists and engineers. Through Arnold, Schriever met Theodore von Karman at Caltech, Arnold's chief link to the scientific community. Schriever was impressed by Arnold's interest in von Karman's experiments with jet propulsion and rocket motors, and could see that the scientist offered the Army Air Forces a chance to break free of conventional thinking about its research and development projects. In 1944, while Schriever was based in the Far East, Arnold enlisted von Karman to direct a panel of scientific advisers to look ahead to a new generation of airplanes and weapons. Arnold stressed the critical value of new technologies when he addressed the first meeting of the Scientific Advisory Group at the Pentagon on January 9, 1945: "I have worked with von Karman the last twenty years, and I was sometimes scared by the knowledge he had that we weren't using. . . . I don't want ever again to have the United States caught the way we were this time."

When the war ended, Schriever, by then a colonel, asked to be assigned to the Pentagon, in part to work with Arnold, who was nearing retirement. Schriever's job title was a mouthful—chief of the scientific liaison branch in the office of the deputy chief of staff for matériel—but his duties were a perfect fit. He was the main contact point between the

Army Air Forces and von Karman, whose panel was reconstituted after the war and renamed as the Scientific Advisory Board. Schriever took full advantage of the role to befriend a host of scientists and engineers, some of whom were later instrumental in the development of missiles and satellites. He discovered for himself just how helpful it was to get advice from independent experts whose judgment was not warped by political or financial turf battles in the Pentagon.

Unfortunately for the nation, Arnold's immediate successors did not share his enthusiasm for scientific advice, and von Karman's board of consultants temporarily receded in influence as the Defense Department was reorganized and the U.S. Air Force was created, in 1947, as a separate service. Demobilization and the nation's understandable desire to turn inward after the war left all the military services scrambling to stay in fighting shape as they competed for dwindling resources. The postwar environment did not encourage investments in untested new military technologies, especially in specialized fields like aerial reconnaissance. American airmen paid the price for this inertia when they were dispatched on spying missions in lumbering piston-engine planes that all but invited Soviet attack.

Schriever and Leghorn were determined to change that, and were in a position to exercise considerable influence. Schriever, by the summer of 1952, had left his scientific liaison job to become one of the Air Force's top planners. Part of his job was to imagine the Air Force of the future and the weapons it would need to defend the nation. He had a small staff and encouraged his aides to think creatively. He gave Leghorn responsibility for exploring future intelligence and reconnaissance needs and instructed him to prepare a blueprint—known in Air Force lingo as "development planning objectives"—for the decade ahead. Leghorn was assisted by two men who were also fervent believers in high-altitude photoreconnaissance, Bud Wienberg and Eugene P. Kiefer, both of whom had worked with him at Wright Field.

"We knew American reconnaissance planes were going down," Wienberg said. "That spurred us to work faster to produce a new aircraft."

The Washington arrangement was improvised. Leghorn had worked back channels at the Pentagon to sell his approach to Schriever, including the core idea that Schriever should add intelligence and reconnaissance to his planning office. Schriever, in turn, had gotten Leghorn, Wienberg, and Kiefer assigned to Washington on temporary duty rather than transferring them to Washington permanently. Every week or so the temporary assignment expired, cutting off the government's modest subsidy for living away from home. "It was crazy," Wienberg said. "We had to keep going back to Wright Field to get our orders recut so we could collect our $10 per diem for expenses in Washington."

The men worked in cramped offices without administrative support. Leghorn complained bitterly to Schriever about the conditions. "Present circumstances are so trying that it is difficult to believe that the Air Staff is really serious about this activity," he said in a letter. "In any event I am certain that under present working conditions it is impossible to prepare a development planning objective by the end of the year."

Thanks to Leghorn's and Schriever's outside connections, Leghorn and his associates could call on a group of distinguished consultants for advice, including Edwin Land from Polaroid; James Baker, the Harvard astronomer and lens designer; Edward Purcell, a Harvard physicist and Nobel laureate; and Allen F. Donovan from the Cornell Aeronautical Laboratory.

A year before Leghorn's arrival in Washington, Schriever, partly at Leghorn's urging, had contracted with MIT to add intelligence and reconnaissance problems to "Project Lincoln," a highly classified study of American air defenses that the institute had previously agreed to conduct for the Air Force. Beginning in January 1952, the fifteen members of the reconnaissance study group, drawn from the academic and business worlds, made an intensive examination of Air Force reconnaissance programs. Leghorn, still at Dayton at the time, was assigned to be the liaison officer to the study from Wright Field. Land, Purcell, and Baker were among the panel members who traveled to air bases around the nation and heard from dozens of Air Force officers and academic experts, including Schriever and Leghorn. The group set up shop above a secretarial school located in Beacon Hill in Boston and became known as the Beacon Hill Study Group.

Their report, summarized for the Air Force in April and formally submitted in June, just before Leghorn moved to Washington, gave new energy to the search for high-performance spy planes and other inventive methods of peeking into the Soviet Union. Using language that Leghorn might have drafted himself, the panel said, "We have reached a period in history when our peacetime knowledge of the capabilities, activities and dispositions of a potentially hostile nation is such to demand that we supplement it with the maximum amount of information obtainable through aerial reconnaissance. To avoid political involvement, such aerial reconnaissance must be conducted either from vehicles flying in friendly airspace, or—a decision on this point permitting—from vehicles whose performance is such that they can operate in Soviet airspace with greatly reduced chances of detection and interception."

The study group presented all sorts of other creative ideas for consideration, including strapping cameras to rockets that would climb 200 miles into space before tumbling back to earth. Jim Baker calculated that at that altitude, just beyond the borders of the Soviet Union, a camera with a long focal length could look out across 1,000 miles of Soviet territory, showing airfields, towns, rivers, crops, and forests. For Leghorn, however, the key section of the report dealt with his dream airplane. Chapter 11, which covered reconnaissance vehicles, talked about "a turbojet-powered, photographic, manned aircraft, in which altitude is sought at the expense of all other performance parameters." The report said such an aircraft could be operational within a few years if an existing plane were modified, pointedly noting that the Canberra might be a good candidate. Almost eight years had passed since Leghorn's epiphany about strategic reconnaissance at Bikini Atoll and his appeal at Boston University for creation of a virtually invisible and invulnerable spy plane. Now he had the endorsement of a group of respected scientists and industrialists in a report that was sure to be widely read among top officials not only in the Air Force but in the Defense Department and the White House as well.

Leghorn spent the remainder of 1952 in Washington working on his reconnaissance blueprint for Schriever. He selected specialized overhead reconnaissance as one of the top five objectives and noted the benefits of high-altitude flights: "Discovery and identification of targets, appraisal of enemy military strengths, confirmation of crucial intelligence, including atomic, radar and terrain charts." He noted the inherent advantages of aerial spying: "Timeliness, geographic coverage, accepted accuracy." To compare the different spy machines he sketched a chart showing, in ascending operational altitude, conventional aircraft, a modified Canberra, balloons, what he labeled as "all new manned light turbojet aircraft," and, at the top of the paper, a satellite. The simple drawing showed how far each could penetrate into Soviet airspace. The turbojet airplane had the dual advantages of flying above 70,000 feet and traveling 1,500 miles over Soviet territory.

Before leaving Washington in January 1953, just before Dwight Eisenhower's inauguration as president, Leghorn advised Schriever one last time to push the development of a lightweight, single-engine airplane that could be used for close-up views of specific military and industrial sites. His work for Schriever done, Leghorn once again left active duty to return to Kodak. He did not know it, but he had set in motion a sequence of events that would lead in less than two years to a crash program to build the U-2.

CHAPTER THREE

Stargazing in Santa Monica

MERT DAVIES didn't need to read about American spy planes coming under attack to be frustrated by the government's glacial progress in coming up with new methods of peering behind the Iron Curtain. His complaint had nothing to do with the failure to build Dick Leghorn's high-flying aircraft. Davies's ambition was to get America into space. He was a believer in rockets and satellites. Along with like-minded colleagues at the RAND Corporation in Santa Monica, Davies had been pushing for the development of satellites since the mid-1940s. They had made few converts in Washington—even freethinkers like Leghorn and Schriever were dubious about satellites in the near-term. But the RAND staff wouldn't give up, churning out report after report that described the feasibility of using satellites for everything from reconnaissance to weather forecasting to communications. Their dreams weren't realized until 1960, but their early work was pioneering and prescient, and without it the United States might have come much later to the day when it could look down safely at Soviet airfields and factories from more than 100 miles in space.

RAND was not a typical research operation, in attitude or geography. Like Southern California itself, it grew out of the influx of people and industry to the benign climate and open spaces of the West Coast. RAND was a creature of the aviation community that gravitated to Southern California during and after the war, drawn in part by the technological advances generated by the Guggenheim Aeronautical Lab and the Jet Propulsion Lab at Caltech and Hap Arnold's faith in the scientists working under Theodore von Karman. RAND was born in October 1945 as an Army Air Forces research and engineering shop at the Douglas Aircraft Company, the brainchild of General Arnold and other men who believed that in the postwar years the Air Forces needed to continue to tap into the thinking of civilian scientists and engineers to come up with new weapons systems. (The name was an acronym for Research ANd Development.) In the waning months of the war, Arnold told Secretary of War Henry Stimson, "During this war the Army, Army Air Forces and the Navy have made unprecedented use of scientific and industrial resources. The conclusion is inescapable that we have not yet established the balance necessary to insure the continuance of teamwork among the military, other government agencies, industry and the universities. Scientific planning must be years in advance of the actual research and development work."

Dwight Eisenhower shared the sentiment, though he was not directly involved in the creation of RAND. Appearing before the House Appropriations Committee in June 1946, when he was the army chief of staff, General Eisenhower said, "I cannot over emphasize the necessity for the maintenance of well-rounded and vigorous research and development programs. . . . In the fields of guided missiles, electronic devices and high-speed, high-performance aircraft, the possibilities are unlimited. It would be fatal to permit ourselves to be outdistanced."

From the start, RAND was an organization that encouraged unorthodox thinking on long-term issues, free from the constraints of Pentagon bureaucrats. Staff members like Davies were given great freedom and encouraged to consider novel solutions to traditional military problems, like the collection of intelligence information on enemy forces. The paperwork, turf wars, and cautious climate that stifled creativity at the Pentagon were largely absent at RAND. Its first separate home, a two-story building at the corner of Broadway and Fourth Street in Santa Monica, which the staff occupied in May 1947, was just blocks from the beach. On weekends, Davies and other employees would head for the broad swath of sand on either side of the Santa Monica Pier for sunbathing and volleyball.

Davies and his friends at RAND loved the beach. Indeed, the combination of ocean, sun, and mild temperatures had lured him to Santa

Monica in 1940 after the Army ended his flying career on the grounds that he was too tall to fit into an enclosed cockpit. The air service hadn't blinked when the 6-foot-7-inch flier volunteered for duty, but after he graduated from open to closed cockpits and started to leave his parachute behind in the hangar so he could squeeze into the cramped pilot's seat, he was washed out of the military.

Davies had honed his flying skills as a teenager. He was born in St. Paul, Minnesota, in 1917, but moved with his parents to California two years later. They settled in Palo Alto. Davies was soon spending his free time at the town's small airport by the bay and earned his pilot's license before graduating from high school and enrolling at Stanford. His uncle had been a pilot in World War I, and Davies, whose interests were already turning toward the heavens, was captivated by the idea of soaring into the sky and doing daredevil stunts. After graduating from Stanford in 1938 with a degree in mathematics, Davies moved to Reno to teach at the University of Nevada campus. He spent much of his free time flying out of the local airfield in Truckee Meadows, the high valley below the Sierra Nevada mountains, doing aerial maneuvers to test his skills and his nerve. "I enjoyed things like power stalls," he recalled. "You know, you go up and try to keep control of the plane as it stalls. It's kid's play." He laughed heartily at the memory.

While at Stanford, Davies had stumbled onto a book about space that stirred his imagination. *Rockets Through Space* by P. E. Cleator, a British scientist, described the solar system and talked about the idea of interplanetary exploration and man-made satellites circling the earth. "I still have that book at home," Davies said in 1998. "It was one of the first things that really made me think about space." Davies soon joined the American Rocket Society, which was founded in 1930, and the British Interplanetary Society, another early hotbed of ideas about exploring distant galaxies. He collected articles and books about space, including *Rockets in Planetary Space* by Hermann Oberth, the father of German rocket science. Oberth's 1923 book—rejected as outlandish by Heidelberg University a year earlier when he submitted it as his Ph.D. dissertation—described a liquid-propellant rocket that could fly fast enough to escape the earth's gravity. Oberth also endorsed the concept of an artificial satellite that could be placed in orbit around the earth. His theories and experimental work provided the foundation for later Nazi efforts to develop rocket weapons, including the V-2. Oberth himself worked on the project at Peenemünde during the war under Wernher von Braun, who had previously been his assistant. After the war, von Braun moved to the United States, where he became one of America's top rocket scientists.

Davies also studied the work of Robert H. Goddard, America's foremost rocket scientist at the time. Goddard, who grew up in Worcester, Massachusetts, read *War of the Worlds*, the H. G. Wells science fiction thriller, in 1898, when it was serialized in the newspapers, and was inspired to try to build a working spacecraft. Goddard's experimental breakthroughs—among them the first rocket motor that used liquid fuels and the first flight of a liquid-propelled rocket in March 1926 at his aunt's Massachusetts farm—essentially launched America toward space. While at Stanford, Davies read Goddard's groundbreaking 1919 Smithsonian monograph, *A Method of Reaching Extreme Altitudes*. "The possibility of getting to the planets caught my attention," he said. "There were worlds out there, and we knew so little about them."

Davies was a good deal more enthusiastic about Goddard's work than the *New York Times*. The paper's editorial page briefly noted on January 18, 1920, that Goddard's idea of sending a missile into space seemed practical and promising, but it patronizingly dismissed the thought that men might eventually travel to the moon.

Despite all the flying stunts, Reno, Nevada, bored Davies, and he returned to Stanford after a year to begin graduate studies in math. Tensions were rising in Europe. He signed up for an Army flight training program on campus, expecting he would get a chance to fly combat missions if war erupted and the United States joined the fight. When the height limitations grounded Davies, he opted for the next best thing—building planes. He had heard of Douglas and knew the company had a plant in Santa Monica, hard by the Pacific. That was enough for him. "I wanted to be near the beach," he said. He packed up his belongings in a 1941 Buick convertible and headed for Southern California. "I thought if I could work at Douglas and walk to the beach, I'd have it made." He later learned that all the other pilots in the Stanford training program were dispatched to the Pacific after Pearl Harbor and died in combat.

Davies was put to work building planes for the Navy at the Douglas plant in nearby El Segundo, where he spent the war years. He enrolled in advanced math classes that the company offered with the help of government subsidies and got to know other employees like him who were drawn to complex theoretical problems. Like Davies, many of them aspired to work for RAND after the Army Air Forces paid Douglas to create the elite research shop after the war. When Davies learned in 1946 that RAND was doing a crash study about satellites for the Army Air Forces, he requested a transfer. General LeMay, then the director of research and development for the Air Forces, had ordered up the study from RAND when he learned that the Navy had asked other companies to examine the feasibility of developing satellites. Davies moved to RAND early in 1947, not long after the completion of a second examination of satellites, this one focused on potential reconnaissance uses.

The May 1946 satellite engineering feasibility study, completed in just three weeks, looks by today's standards like something from a Buck Rogers novel. The title itself is a throwback to another age: *Preliminary Design of an Experimental World-Circling Spaceship.* The cover page shows a bullet-shaped rocket streaking into space above the earth. An illustration of the multistage rocket on the launch pad shows a rounded, streamlined vehicle that tapers to a point at the top, a sort of art deco rocket design. But by the technological yardstick of 1946, when the report was submitted to the Air Forces, it was a remarkably bold and visionary document. It said that with minimal advances in rocket engine and other technologies, which should be attainable in short order, a small satellite weighing no more than 2,000 pounds could be placed in orbit.

Though the RAND experts conceived of a satellite as a multiuse spacecraft that might even be manned someday, they saw initial systems as unmanned devices, in part because of the difficulty of sustaining life in space and returning a satellite and its human cargo safely back to earth. They clearly recognized the potential for scientific and military applications and anticipated the political implications of being the first nation to place a satellite in orbit. The RAND report said, "The achievement of a satellite craft by the United States would inflame the imagination of mankind and would probably produce repercussions in the world comparable to the explosion of the atomic bomb."

Louis N. Ridenour of the University of Pennsylvania's Nuclear Physics and Electronics Department, who was hired as a consultant by RAND to work on the report, wrote a chapter on the potential uses of a satellite. Ridenour, a radar expert, was virtually clairvoyant. He imagined that satellites could be used to guide missiles to their targets and accurately predicted that the development of intercontinental missiles and satellites would dovetail to some extent. Ridenour described how satellites could be used to monitor weather conditions and improve forecasting, and suggested how an orbiting spacecraft could instantly relay communications from continent to continent. Perhaps Ridenour's most perspicacious prediction was that satellites could serve as reconnaissance platforms. "It should also be remarked that the satellite offers an observation aircraft which cannot be brought down by an enemy who has not mastered similar techniques."

LeMay and his Air Forces staff were intrigued by the report and anxious to ensure that their service, rather than the Navy, gain control of space operations. Shortly after the RAND report was delivered, LeMay and Douglas executives agreed that the researchers should immediately begin work on the next step, which was preparation of a detailed design study for a reconnaissance satellite that could serve as the basis for contracting with companies to begin planning actual components. James E. Lipp, who headed RAND's missile division, oversaw the work, which was directed by Robert Salter. The missile group consisted of about twenty people who worked in spare quarters on the second floor of the RAND building in Santa Monica.

Early in 1947, as the cold war began to intensify in a divided Europe and American spy planes were operating along the Soviet frontier, RAND delivered a series of papers that looked more closely at some of the questions outlined in the earlier report, including rocket flight dynamics, liquid fuel systems, control of a satellite, and potential launch sites. The package was circulated by RAND on February 1. One of the papers, by Lyman Spitzer Jr., a Yale astronomer, accurately predicted that a satellite would be able to spot and track the movement of ships at sea, an important advantage in naval operations and combat. This was one of the reasons the Navy was working on its own satellite plans.

But the most provocative paper came from Lipp himself. For one thing, it hammered home the likely political consequences of failing to move ahead with the development of satellites. "Since mastery of the elements is a reliable index of material progress," Lipp predicted, "the nation that makes significant achievements in space travel will be acknowledged as the world leader in both military and scientific techniques. To visualize the impact on the world, one can imagine the consternation and admiration that would be felt here if the United States were to discover suddenly that some other nation had already put up a successful satellite."

On the hardware front, Lipp offered several important suggestions, including the first proposal that a high-powered television camera be placed aboard a satellite that could beam pictures back to earth. Lipp also looked over the horizon with two other novel ideas. One was to place a satellite in polar orbit to provide recurring reconnaissance coverage. The other was to park satellites at very high altitudes—25,000 miles into space—where their orbit would be synchronous with the rotation of the earth, allowing them to remain continuously over the same area of the world. The notion of geosynchronous orbit, which made today's network of communications satellites possible, was first suggested by Arthur C. Clarke, the science fiction writer, in 1944. Lipp ended his remarkable paper with an exhortation to move ahead immediately with the development of satellites.

The Army Air Force put off review of the RAND papers while the Pentagon was being reorganized and the Army's aviation operations were reborn as a separate armed service. A week after creation of the U.S. Air Force in September 1947, commanders instructed the Air Matériel Command to assess the RAND documents. The verdict, rendered in December, was mixed: Satellites looked feasible but impractical. The Air Force decided to ask RAND to continue planning work on satellites, looking forward to a time when construction of a system would make sense and launch vehicles would be developed, but did not make satellite development a top priority. The message from Washington was to keep studying the idea but not to expect the Air Force anytime soon to sink a lot of money into actually trying to build a satellite or get one into orbit. That decision was reaffirmed in 1948 by the Technical Evaluation Group, a Pentagon panel of civilian consultants.

Given the limitations of American rocket technology, these decisions were hard to argue with, but they left the forward-looking researchers at RAND frustrated. Davies by this time had joined Lipp's staff and had quickly learned that Washington was not as excited by satellites as the folks in Santa Monica. "So much time went into making studies and studying other people's studies," he recalled. "One of the most difficult things was to try to convince the government in Washington to put money into these things."

Over the next few years, as the demand for intelligence data about Soviet military forces increased in Washington, Davies and the rest of Lipp's staff did as much as they could with the limited mandate and funding they had been granted by the Air Force. In November 1950, RAND again urged the Air Force to authorize additional research into satellite reconnaissance missions. The Air Force intelligence staff agreed, and a few months later, Bernard Schriever gave the whole idea a boost by spelling out the Air Force requirements for a spy satellite. Schriever, who by then had been given a central role in Air Force planning, laid out three primary benchmarks at a meeting on February 16, 1951, all related to helping the Air Force learn more about the Soviet military threat and to select targets for American attack. Schriever stipulated that photographs must be of sufficient quality and magnification that potential military targets could be spotted, including airfields, harbors, and industrial plants. A satellite had to provide continuous daytime coverage of the Soviet Union and the photographs should be useful in improving aeronautical charts and maps.

RAND was anxious to show how such standards could be met. News coverage of a downed Navy spy flight off the Latvian coast in April 1950 and the outbreak of the Korean War a few months later had given added urgency to the search for new spy vehicles. In March 1951, Lipp and his colleagues conducted an elaborate exercise designed to simulate pictures of Los Angeles harbor that could be generated by a reconnaissance satellite equipped with a television camera. Air Force experts determined that the images met minimal intelligence requirements. But doubts persisted because ground features could not be seen in any detail. The classified RAND study, titled "Utility of a Satellite Vehicle for Reconnaissance," was completed in April 1951. It failed to convince the Air Force that photo coverage would be of high enough quality to warrant development of the proposed system.

The most significant contribution of the study was serendipitous. Lipp and several other members of the missile group traveled to Wright Field in Dayton later in 1951 to present their ideas to the Air Force laboratory that had been the source of so much creative thinking about aerial reconnaissance. The visit brought together for the first time the proponents of satellites and the architects of advanced camera systems. The worlds of Mert Davies and Dick Leghorn intersected, and it wasn't long before the two men themselves met and began to swap ideas. The collaboration that began in Ohio during the visit eventually led to design of the camera and film system that was used in the nation's first photoreconnaissance satellite.

Several representatives of the Boston University Optical Research Lab, which Leghorn had helped dedicate in 1946, happened to be visiting Wright Field at the same time as Jim Lipp and his RAND colleagues. In Dayton, they were reunited with Amrom Katz, the gifted physicist who had come to Wright Field from the Census Bureau in the early 1940s to help Baker design a camera system for George Goddard that would automatically adjust to pressure and temperature changes at high altitude. Katz was the chief physicist at the Dayton reconnaissance lab. All of these men were initially dubious about satellites. Katz led the skeptics. "Lipp had a nearly zero batting average," he remembered. "No one was interested."

Katz and the other men decided to demonstrate that Lipp's ideas about television pictures from space were unworkable. From such a great altitude, with the camera technology then available, the group assumed the pictures would be worthless to photo interpreters looking for

Soviet military equipment on the ground. Katz later recalled, "We were going to prove that this proposed project was ridiculous. Mind you, we didn't know or care about the incidental problems such as making the launch rocket, achieving stability in orbit and all the other important parts of the system. We were fastened on the proposed scale to be delivered to the TV sensor."

Katz at the time was struggling with telescopic lenses to get decent photographs of railroad ties from an altitude of 40,000 feet. He figured that the smaller lenses on a television camera operating 350 miles in space would show such a large area of the earth in such little detail that no useful intelligence could be gleaned from the images. With the help of Eastman Kodak, Katz managed to mount the lenses from an 8mm movie camera on a Leica camera. Photographs taken at 30,000 feet with the camera would roughly simulate the images from Lipp's satellite. Katz ordered a test flight with the Leica over Dayton. "I was confident that nothing could be seen on the enlargements."

When the photos were developed and enlarged, Katz was astonished to find that he could clearly make out the streets of downtown Dayton and the runways and buildings at Wright Field. Katz knew that television lenses, or even conventional camera lenses, would have to be improved, but the notion of collecting useful information from hundreds of miles in space no longer seemed implausible to him and his colleagues.

It certainly didn't seem improbable to the editors of *Collier's* magazine. Eager to spur public interest in the exploration of space, in March 1952 the popular magazine began publishing a series of articles on the scientific and military uses of space. The Korean War was boiling and more and more American spy planes were coming under attack as they approached Soviet airspace. Some of these incidents were making the news, heightening public sensitivity about the high dangers of the cold war. *Collier's*, like *Life* and the *Saturday Evening Post*, the other popular general-interest magazines of the era, reached millions of Americans every week and played an important role in setting the national agenda. The magazine's emphasis on space gave the idea of satellites the kind of visibility it had never had before. An equivalent jolt of publicity today might come from a series of "60 Minutes" broadcasts on a single subject over the course of a year.

The first piece was by Wernher von Braun, who had moved to the United States after the war with the assistance of the Army, which was eager to put his rocket expertise to work. Von Braun described in *Collier's* how a manned space station could be used for spying. He imagined technicians armed with powerful telescopes monitoring activities on earth and producing photographs as revealing as those made from a plane at 5,000 feet.

"Nothing will go unobserved. . . . Despite the vast territory thus covered, selected spots on the earth could receive pinpoint examination. For example, troop maneuvers, planes being readied on the flight deck of an aircraft carrier, or bombers forming in groups over an airfield will be clearly discernible. Because of the telescopic eyes and cameras of the space station, it will be almost impossible for any nation to hide warlike preparations for any length of time."

By stimulating public interest in space and satellites, *Collier's* helped bring the issue into the political arena. In 1952 the Truman administration asked Aristid V. Grosse, a Temple University physicist who had worked on the Manhattan Project, to investigate the possibility of building a satellite. Grosse met with von Braun and other scientists and engineers. He turned in his findings in 1953, after Eisenhower had succeeded Truman. The brief paper, delivered that fall to Donald Quarles, the new assistant secretary of defense for research and development, noted the potential scientific, military, and political benefits of placing a satellite in orbit. Though Grosse apparently did not have access to the RAND papers and may not even have known of their existence, he concluded that a satellite equipped with television devices could be "a valuable observation post."

The Air Force, however, advised Quarles that the report offered no new technical insights and he, in turn, took no further action on it.

RAND pressed ahead with its planning, though Davies and his colleagues were by now thoroughly disgusted with the government's handling of satellites. Davies couldn't fathom why the Beacon Hill study of Air Force reconnaissance programs had neglected the issue, and he was angry with Leghorn for not championing satellites in his dual role as an Air Force planner and Wright Field liaison officer to the Beacon Hill group. "I scolded Dick," Davies recalled. "He said he had to admit he thought satellites were too far out for Beacon Hill."

Davies finally got a chance to petition Leghorn directly in late 1952, when RAND dispatched him to Washington to work with Leghorn on his Air Force planning objectives. Leghorn was still largely unfamiliar with the RAND research on satellites. Davies's job was to fill Leghorn in on the details and to convert him into an advocate for satellites. He was pleasantly surprised by the reception he received.

"We spent the morning talking, then the afternoon. We went to dinner and then continued our discussions until after one A.M. For me, it was exciting and enjoyable to find someone so capable and interested in the studies on which we had spent so many years."

The daylong conversation did not immediately change Leghorn's mind about satellites, but it made him less resistant. Other RAND researchers and executives also pressed the Air Force. Though the service remained unwilling to commit itself to building and launching a satellite, the Air Force took a major step toward development by authorizing RAND to go ahead with its most ambitious project yet—preparation of detailed engineering specifications for a reconnaissance satellite. This time RAND would work closely with dozens of engineers at aviation and electronics companies to provide a concrete plan. The effort, led once again by Jim Lipp, was dubbed "Project Feed Back." Like earlier conceptions, it revolved around a television system. The satellite would be powered in orbit by a small nuclear reactor. That idea reflected overly optimistic expectations at the time about developing nuclear-powered rockets and other spacecraft.

Davies was assigned to work on simulated TV images and how they could be exploited by photo interpreters. He was energized by the prospect of working on a development plan, though still concerned that there seemed little immediate prospect of moving satellites from the drafting board to the launch pad. The Project Feed Back report was submitted to the Air Force on March 1, 1954, two months before Hal Austin's perilous flight over Soviet territory. The opening page boldly declared, "The over-all conclusion to be drawn from studies of simulated satellite television pictures is that reconnaissance data of considerable value can be obtained, and that complete coverage of Soviet territory with such pictures will result in a major reversal of our strategic intelligence posture with respect to the Soviets."

To quell doubts about the quality of the RAND television system, which was designed by the Radio Corporation of America, the report itemized the things that could be recognized from the projected 300-mile-high orbit. It was a list sure to catch the eye of the Air Force's top officers and anyone else interested in Soviet military power and the selection of targets should there be a war.

"1. Airfields of all sizes, and possibly indications of activities (the presence of large planes, etc.) on airfields. 2. Industrial concentrations, isolated or within cities. 3. Large plants, and possibly some indication of types of plant. 4. Harbors, and facilities such as graving docks and large ships. 5. Transportation, power and communication networks, including switching yards, bridges, canals, power lines and perhaps activities in these fields. 6. Urban areas, including the density of built-up areas. 7. Large military installations, including military camps and explosive storage. 8. Cloud pattern and structure in considerable detail."

The report contained dozens of conventional aerial photographs of American cities and military bases, representing the kind of images that RAND said could be obtained from space. Like the simulated images of the harbor area in Los Angeles used in the earlier study, these were meant to demonstrate that fairly detailed features were visible. The pictures were impressive but did not provide the kind of close-up views that were available from conventional aircraft equipped with telephoto lenses. Despite the RAND claims, it was obvious that Air Force war planners would have difficulty detecting Soviet aircraft and other specific objects that might help SAC with its targeting.

Lipp, Davies, and their associates estimated the satellite project would take seven years from inception to launch at a cost of about $165 million ($1.1 billion in today's dollars). The long time frame was acknowledgment of the technological barriers that would have to be overcome in everything from rocket design to communications with the satellite and relay of the data back to earth. Along with the rocket and satellite, the project would require construction of ground stations and sophisticated data processing systems.

Anticipating a host of novel legal issues about the use of space, including theoretical violations of national sovereignty when American satellites passed over foreign nations, the report recommended preparation of a legal and political strategy to defend American operations in space. "Use of the satellite might bring a charge of violation of Soviet sovereignty," the report said. "Probably the Soviets would do everything in their power to make the charge stick and to exploit it to their political advantage by making the United States appear as a violator of international law." As work on satellites progressed in the years ahead, these issues would loom large in Washington's preparations.

RAND executives and engineers, determined to see their ideas translated into action, traveled to Washington, Wright Field, and other Air Force locations to elaborate on the Project Feed Back study. "We were trying to talk the Air Force into funding the project," Davies recalled. They proved to be good salesmen. With a push from satellite supporters at the Air Research and Development Command, the new RAND proposal won new backers at the Pentagon.

Though still uncertain how practical the idea was, the leadership of the Air Force gave its blessing to the RAND project. The endorsement of Gen. Nathan F. Twining, the chief of staff; General LeMay, who was by this time the SAC commander; and James Doolittle, a World War II combat hero who was chairman of the Air Force Scientific Advisory Board, gave the plan the kind of heavyweight support satellite proposals had long lacked. In August, the Pentagon authorized the Air Force to begin work on building a reconnaissance satellite. Later in the year, the job was assigned to the Western Development Division of the Air Research and Development Command. The division's primary responsibility was to perfect and build a fleet of intercontinental ballistic missiles. It was a fortuitous decision, for the division, based in Southern California, was run by Bernard Schriever, now a brigadier general.

The years of brainstorming and planning were finally ending and construction of the real thing was beginning, using the RAND design scheme as the starting point. But the project in many ways remained a stepchild of the Pentagon, an alluring but distant objective that promised to produce useful pictures of the Soviet landscape but not highly detailed photos that the SAC staff could put to immediate use. At a time when television was still in its infancy and most American households were just acquiring their first black-and-white sets, the technology just wasn't good enough to make RAND's blueprint the definitive answer to Washington's intelligence gap. Secretary of Defense Charles E. Wilson captured the prevailing attitude when he responded to a prediction in 1954 that the Soviet Union would get a satellite into space before the United States. "I wouldn't care if they did," he said. RAND itself had estimated a seven-year gestation period for its system, meaning it would be 1960 before Washington could expect to put a camera system into orbit. At a time when cold war tensions were growing and the threat of a Soviet surprise attack seemed possible, the delay and questionable picture quality were considered crippling flaws.

As the Eisenhower administration in 1954 began in earnest to examine how to reduce the threat of surprise attack, it found a temporary reconnaissance fix in Dick Leghorn's ideas for an exotic spy plane. In an ironic quirk of history, Washington seized on his plan long after he had left the Air Force, and he did not even know about the construction of the plane until it was nearly ready to fly.

CHAPTER FOUR

Seeing Air

KELLY JOHNSON, America's most inventive airplane designer at mid-century, turned Dick Leghorn's aviation alchemy into a strange and remarkable flying machine. Clarence L. Johnson, nicknamed Kelly by schoolmates in second grade, was a virtuoso airplane maker, one of the most brilliant and prolific in the annals of aviation. He coupled a wonderfully intuitive feel for aerodynamic design with a brusque but highly effective management style. Under his inspired direction, the Advanced Development Projects division at Lockheed, better known as the Skunk Works, turned out many of America's most advanced military aircraft in the twentieth century, beginning in 1943 with the development of the P-80, later redesignated the F-80, the country's first tactical jet fighter, dubbed the "Shooting Star" by Lockheed. In a career that ran from 1933 to 1975, he designed more than forty airplanes. One of the first was the P-38 Lightning, a propeller-driven fighter that played a starring role in World War II. Johnson's custom plane shop in Burbank, in the San Fernando Valley just over the Hollywood hills from Los Angeles, worked under tight secrecy and daunting deadlines. It produced the U-2 and then later the ultra-high-performance A-12 Oxcart, better known as the SR-71 Blackbird, the name of the Air Force model. After Johnson's retirement, the Skunk Works developed the F-117 stealth fighter.

The Air Force didn't ask Johnson to design Dick Leghorn's spy plane. In fact, it deliberately excluded Lockheed in 1952 when it began thinking more seriously about building a new high-flying reconnaissance plane in the wake of the Beacon Hill report. But with help from some well-placed friends in Washington and a pivotal assist in 1954 from Trevor Gardner, James Killian, and Edwin Land, Johnson crashed the Air Force party. His design was so simple and yet so audacious that it trumped rival plans by other aircraft companies and won the support of President Eisenhower in October 1954. As Johnson promised, the first U-2 was in the air, under budget, nine months later, an uncommon achievement in an industry that routinely missed deadlines and exceeded planned expenditures, especially in the production of radically new airplanes.

Kelly Johnson was ideally suited for the assignment, so much so it's hard to understand why the Air Force didn't turn to him in the first place. Born on February 27, 1910, in the northern Michigan mining hamlet of Ishpeming, not far from Marquette, he was the seventh of nine children born to his Swedish immigrant parents—his father was a bricklayer, his mother a homemaker. Once he discovered the Carnegie library in town, he visited it every day and practically inhaled the collection of Tom Swift books, including *Tom Swift and his Aeroplane*. Johnson was captivated by the aviation and engineering details. "I read other books on aircraft—the Rover Boys, Collins's book on model airplanes—and decided by the time I was 12 years old that I would be an aircraft designer."

The family moved downstate to Flint in 1923. There was a building boom in the industrial city, and Johnson's father, Peter, opened a construction business, which prospered. Johnson worked at lathing houses in the summers, developing the Popeye forearms that made him virtually unbeatable in the arm wrestling competitions that later became a custom at the Skunk Works when the staff got together to celebrate the first successful flight of a new plane. After finishing high school, he enrolled at Flint Junior College, where he studied physics, mathematics, and calculus and got his first taste of engineering. Johnson was eager to learn to fly, and for $5, a princely sum at the time, he got his first ride in the air in a four-passenger biplane. He enjoyed the bumpy, noisy three-minute flight and not long afterward showed up at Bishop Airport in Flint with his life savings of $300 to sign up for ten flying lessons. Once the instructor learned that Johnson wanted to be an airplane designer, he urged him to keep the money for a college education. Johnson reluctantly decided it was good advice, and transferred to the University of Michigan in Ann Arbor in 1929. He was soon spending long hours studying aerodynamics in the university's wind tunnel as an assistant to Professor Edward A. Stalker, the chairman of the aeronautical engineering department.

Johnson was a natural. He loved the wind tunnel work and got permission from Stalker to rent the lab for private jobs, including tests on a new streamlined car that Studebaker was planning to build. Johnson found that the large headlamps slowed the car at high speeds by creating considerable wind resistance. The company redesigned the front end to fit the headlights into the fender. It was a preview of things to come for Johnson.

When he graduated in 1932, jobs were scarce because of the Depression. Sikorsky, Martin, and Curtiss, the main East Coast aircraft companies, told him not to even bother to visit. Johnson applied to the Army's air service, expecting to become an aviation cadet, but was rejected because of an old eye injury. Johnson and a friend decided to head for California in hopes of finding work at one of the airplane manufacturers that were starting to congregate in the region. They borrowed a professor's Chevrolet to make the trip. To save money on gas, Johnson tinkered with the engine, picking up three or four miles per gallon during the cross-country drive. Lockheed, which had made a name for itself as a builder of plywood aircraft and then fallen into bankruptcy during the Depression, had just been bought from receivers for $40,000 by Robert and Courtlandt Gross and some other flying enthusiasts. Richard von Hake, the chief engineer, told Johnson to return in a year when the company was likely to be hiring.

Johnson did a year of graduate work at Michigan, picking up a master's degree, and once again using the wind tunnel for a variety of tests. By chance, the university had contracted with Lockheed to check the design of the Electra, a new all-metal airplane the reorganized company was hoping to introduce as its first product. Stalker tested models in the wind tunnel. Despite some misgivings about stability and directional control, he determined the problems were no worse than other aircraft. Johnson was dubious and didn't hesitate to tell Lockheed's top executives when he returned to Burbank for a job interview in 1933. Hall L. Hibbard, the new chief engineer, and Cyril Chappellet, assistant to the president and personnel officer, were stunned when Johnson cheekily announced that the plane was unstable and that Stalker's wind-tunnel reports were invalid.

The two men were put off by Johnson's arrogance, but decided to give him a chance to prove his point. After a few months of training in California, Johnson was sent back to the Michigan wind tunnel with the Electra model in the backseat of his car. He put the model through dozens of tests before isolating the problem and figuring how to fix it. Johnson recommended redesigning the horizontal tail section to get more directional stability and added vertical tails to supplement the single vertical tail and rudder in the original design. He then found the original vertical tail in the center was unnecessary and removed it. The result was a novel twin vertical tail configuration that became the hallmark design feature of the plane. The triple tail design employed in the Lockheed Constellation airliner flown by many commercial carriers in the 1940s and 1950s came from the same wind-tunnel tests.

Once Johnson was hired, his talent and hard work quickly made him a Lockheed favorite, though his brashness and explosive temper created frictions. As he settled into his engineering work, he made good on his promise to become a pilot, which allowed him to act as the primary flight test engineer for the Electra. The airtime, and near crashes that came with test flying, convinced Johnson that airplane designers needed to see their projects from a pilot's perspective. He continued to fly for years, even after becoming a senior executive. "I figured I needed to have the hell scared out of me once a year in order to keep a proper balance and viewpoint on designing new aircraft."

With his knack for innovation, Johnson yearned to set up a small experimental department at Lockheed where airplane designers and builders could work together free from the bureaucratic conventions of a large industrial corporation. He figured that by getting everyone involved with the creation of a new plane under the same roof, he could encourage ingenuity and slash the time between design and fabrication.

If the plane designers worked next to the production floor, it would be easier to solve problems that developed as a plane was being assembled. He got his wish in 1943 when he won the Army Air Forces' contract to produce a prototype jet fighter. Johnson and Lockheed were chosen because he had designed the twin-engine P-38 Lightning, the most agile propeller-driven fighter produced during the war. Lockheed was already overextended turning out other planes for the Pentagon, but executives told Johnson, who was by then the company's chief research engineer, to go ahead with the experimental project, provided he could come up with the engineers and production staff and find some unused space at the Burbank plant.

Johnson seized the opportunity, employing a gift for improvisation. He quickly recruited two dozen of the best designers and a similar number of mechanics, then created a makeshift office in an open area near the Lockheed wind tunnel. To get the tools to build the plane, he arranged to buy out a local machine shop. For walls, he took the wood from dismantled crates that had been used to ship engines for the Hudson bomber, a modified version of the Electra that Johnson had designed for the British Royal Air Force. To cover the new work area, Johnson rented a circus tent. The Skunk Works was up and running. The plane was ready for its maiden flight 143 days after Johnson started work, well ahead of the Army deadline.

Johnson's reputation soon grew to epic proportions within Lockheed. Ben Rich, who joined Lockheed in 1954 as a thermodynamics specialist, described Johnson as an awe-inspiring figure to young engineers, though not necessarily in appearance. "All of us had seen him rushing around in his untucked shirt, a paunchy, middle-aged guy with a comical duck's waddle, slicked-down white hair and a belligerent jaw. He had a thick, round nose and reminded me a lot of W. C. Fields but without the humor."

After watching Johnson redesign the Electra as the Hudson bomber in three intense days of drafting, Hall Hibbard, one of the men who had hired Johnson, said, "That damned Swede can actually see air." New employees like Rich soon encountered Johnson's uncanny instincts themselves. One day as Rich was working on the design of an inlet for a jet engine, Johnson stopped by his desk, holding a drawing of the part. "It will be way too draggy," he told Rich. "It's about 20 percent too big. Refigure it." Rich spent the rest of the day recalculating the design and found the inlet was 18 percent too large.

James Plummer, who later modeled Lockheed's secret satellite development office on the Skunk Works, studied Johnson's management techniques before setting up the satellite operation in Palo Alto. "They were working on the U-2," Plummer recalled. "One day Kelly stopped to talk with an engineer who's working some problem about the exit nozzle on the engine. This guy is working like crazy and he's got a freshly made clay model of the nozzle sitting in front of him. Kelly took one look at it and announced, 'Not that way.' He grabbed the model, took his big old thumb and squished the clay into a different shape. This poor guy is just sitting there, figuring his work is shot. But the old man was right. It was amazing the way he ran that program."

Johnson's no-nonsense style carried over to corporate meetings. "All the divisions of Lockheed would get together periodically and their managers would report on their work," Plummer said. "Most of them would make a big presentation. Kelly would just walk up to the blackboard and write down a sales number and a profit number. He'd say, 'That's how much I sold, and that's how much I made. Now I've got to get back to work.'"

Bud Wheelon got to know Johnson well after taking over the CIA's aircraft operations in 1963. "He had enormous self-assurance," Wheelon said. "He was a towering personality. He knew all of aeronautical engineering and he drove his people hard, he expected a lot of them. He cursed like a sailor. He intimidated them, but he also led them and they loved him. He was an absolute patriot, he loved this country. He was headstrong, he was brilliant."

The Air Force was well aware of Johnson's skills as its interest in building a new reconnaissance aircraft began to grow in mid-1952, following the June delivery of the Beacon Hill study and its recommendation to develop a high-altitude spy plane. The Air Force's first move was to ask the Martin Aircraft Company to examine the possibility of adapting the B-57 bomber to enable it to fly at 64,000 feet. This plan was the

Pentagon's belated response to Dick Leghorn's previously rebuffed suggestion to reconfigure the British Canberra bomber by extending the wings, adding more powerful engines, and stripping the plane of armor plating and other combat gear. Martin was already making the B-57, an American version of the Canberra that it was producing under license with the English manufacturer.

The Wright Air Development Command in Dayton had its own ideas. Maj. John Seaberg, an aeronautical engineer recalled to active duty at Wright Field as the Korean War wore on, investigated a number of options for high-altitude flight with two German experts who had moved to the United States after the war. The three men produced a rough proposal in March 1953, the same month that Stalin died, describing a subsonic aircraft that would fly at 70,000 feet or higher with a round-trip range of about 3,500 miles and could carry up to 700 pounds of reconnaissance equipment. In July, the development command in Dayton gave contracts for initial study of the proposed plane to Bell Aircraft Corporation of Buffalo, New York, and the Fairchild Engine and Airplane Corporation of Hagerstown, Maryland. Despite Kelly Johnson's formidable reputation, the Air Force bypassed Lockheed in the mistaken belief that the California company—and other high-volume airplane makers—would not give the project sufficient attention.

As the Air Force revved up efforts to design a spy plane, it also appointed a new panel of outside advisers on intelligence matters. The advisory board, called the Intelligence Systems Panel, was formed in July 1953 largely to help guide the Air Force in development of the kind of plane Dick Leghorn championed and the Beacon Hill report had endorsed. The high-powered group included several of the most inventive and visionary members of the Beacon Hill committee. Jim Baker, the Harvard lens designer, served as chairman. Edwin Land of Polaroid was a member, as was Allen F. Donovan, head of the Aeromechanics Department at the Cornell Aeronautical Laboratory.

Sometime in November 1953—the precise date is uncertain—Lockheed first heard about the Air Force initiatives. John H. Carter, who had recently retired from the Air Force to go to work at Lockheed, learned about the plans from Eugene Kiefer during a visit to the Pentagon. As soon as he returned to Burbank, Carter urged company executives to get into the competition. His memo speculated about the useful lifetime of the airplane. "If extreme altitude performance can be realized in a practical aircraft at speeds in the vicinity of Mach 0.8, it should be capable of avoiding virtually all Russian defenses until about 1960.

Carter advised that development of the plane would "require very strenuous efforts and extraordinary procedures, as well as non-standard design philosophy." This might include elimination of conventional landing gear and the rejection of the usual military specifications, including armor, defensive weapons, and even a cabin pressurization system. The challenge sounded perfect for Johnson and his team. Once Lockheed's top executives approved the idea, in December 1953, Johnson set to work designing a plane that would meet Carter's—and by extension, Leghorn's—expectations. Lockheed called the aircraft the CL-282. Johnson noted in his log, "We started an investigation of wing area modifications and stripping procedures to modify the F-104 airplane to get the maximum possible altitude for reconnaissance purposes."

Carter had not overstated the need for unorthodox thinking. Ultrahigh altitude flight was a novelty in 1954. Some experimental aircraft had soared briefly to the rarified regions designated for the new spy plane, which was roughly 13 miles above sea level. In August 1953, a rocket-powered D-558-2, a swept-wing plane made for the Navy by the Douglas Aircraft Company, set a new altitude record of 83,000 feet.

But no jet-powered plane had soared that high and no manned aircraft of any kind could fly for sustained periods anywhere near that height—or the cruising level of 65,000 feet anticipated for the CL-282. The thin air posed numerous obstacles to man and machine. It meant reduced lift from the passage of air over the wings, the basic physical force that keeps planes aloft. The performance of jet engines would be diminished because there was less oxygen for the compression and burning. A jet engine operating at 70,000 feet would produce just 6 percent of the thrust it generated at sea level. The weight of the aircraft, among other things, had to be adjusted accordingly, for lightness was an essential requirement for long-distance flight at high altitude. Fuel was another potential problem. Conventional JP-4 kerosene fuel would boil off and evaporate because of the low air pressure at 70,000 feet. A new blend of jet fuel would have to be created.

Sustaining life in the stratosphere was no less challenging. Fluids in the human body, including blood, vaporize above 65,000 feet. Reduced air pressure would sharply increase the stress on the cardiovascular system. While a pressurized cockpit would reduce these dangers, it would not eliminate them entirely. A special pressurized flight suit would be needed to maintain constant pressure over most of a pilot's body if cabin pressure was lost or the pilot was forced to bail out at 70,000 feet and descend by parachute. In such an emergency descent, a pilot would get the bends from a buildup of nitrogen in the blood, the same potentially deadly affliction divers encounter if they rise too rapidly to the ocean surface from great depths. That danger also had to be addressed.

Johnson's solution to the aerodynamic problems was radical but elegant. He designed what can best be described as a subsonic jet-powered glider or sailplane. The plane's distinguishing feature was its elongated, narrow wings, which gave the aircraft a wingspan of 70 feet, 8 inches. The extra length meant more wing surface area, which gave the aircraft added lift. The large wings also provided space for four fuel tanks that could hold a total of 1,350 gallons of fuel, enough to fly ten hours and to cover about 4,000 nautical miles, the range required to traverse large areas of the Soviet Union. To save weight, Johnson proposed the use of separate, detachable wing panels that would be bolted to the fuselage rather than a single wing section supported by a spar that passed through the fuselage. A continuous spar—the norm in aircraft construction—was sturdier but much heavier. The wing design also opened up space in the body of the plane for photographic equipment. By using lightweight materials, Johnson managed to reduce the weight of the wings by two thirds compared to those of conventional aircraft.

In another weight-saving step that borrowed from gliders, Johnson designed a tail assembly that would be attached to the fuselage with just three five-eighths-inch high-tensile steel bolts. He also decided to do without a pressurized cockpit and to dispense with normal landing gear, two decisions he would later have to reverse to win government support. His alternative to landing gear was to fit the bottom of the plane with two skis and to reinforce the belly. Instead of setting down on wheels, the plane would do a belly landing and skid to a stop on the skis. For takeoff, Johnson planned a wheeled dolly that would be discarded as the plane became airborne. This, too, was typical of a glider. The fuselage would be constructed with unusually thin aluminum. To power the plane, Johnson selected the General Electric J73/GE3 turbojet engine, which produced 9,300 pounds of thrust. Unlike Bell Aircraft, which was designing a twin-engine plane for John Seaberg at Wright Field, Johnson preferred a single-engine airplane, in part to reduce weight and fuel consumption. Lockheed had used the General Electric engine in the F-104 jet fighter, another Johnson aircraft.

The CL-282, with its long wings and lack of landing gear, would look unlike any jet airplane that had ever been built. It would also be far more fragile. The airframe was designed to withstand a stress of 2.5 g's, less than half that required for military aircraft. Johnson's plane would carry no armaments to defend itself, counting on its high-altitude capability to provide protection from Soviet fighters and antiaircraft missiles, which could not operate effectively above 50,000 feet. The combination of plane design and the thin air where it would fly left a very small margin for error by pilots. Once they had reached maximum altitude, pilots would have to maintain a constant speed of between 388 and 394 knots per hour. If they went slower, the plane would stall and begin falling at a rate that would break loose the wings and tail section. If they exceeded the top speed, violent buffeting would tear the wings off. The elite group of pilots who were later chosen to handle the plane mordantly called this cramped safety range the "coffin corner."

A little more than a week after getting the design assignment from Lockheed, Johnson presented his bosses with a twenty-three-page memo describing the main features of the CL-282. About this time, Seaberg and his colleagues in Dayton were reviewing the plans submitted by Bell and Fairchild for a new reconnaissance plane and Martin's proposal to modify the B-57. They rejected Fairchild's proposal to build a single-engine plane with a maximum altitude of 67,200 feet. Seaberg recommended approval of Bell's plan, which called for a twin-engine aircraft that could fly at 69,500 feet. He also urged the Air Force to move ahead with modification of the B-57 as a temporary measure that would allow spy flights at 64,000 feet while Bell was building its higher-flying plane. The Air Force soon approved the Martin proposal and seemed inclined to endorse the Bell aircraft. Lockheed had to act quickly if it was to get into the competition.

In early March 1954, Johnson flew back to Washington to lay out his plan to General Schriever's Office of Development Planning. Leghorn had departed a year earlier, but two of his closest aides, Gene Kiefer and Bud Wienberg, were still present. They were intrigued by Johnson's ideas and urged Schriever to take the next step of asking Lockheed to submit a detailed proposal. He did so, and Johnson returned to the Pentagon in April for a meeting with senior civilian and military leaders of the Air Force, including Trevor Gardner and Lt. Gen. Donald L. Putt, the deputy chief of staff for development. Johnson sought approval to build thirty planes. He noted in his logs after the meeting that Gardner and the other civilians seemed more interested in his design than the Air Force officers.

He was right, though he did not realize that his appearance coincided with the Eisenhower administration's heightened interest in advances in Soviet armaments, including Moscow's missile development program and the introduction of the Bison bomber, which had first been spotted at Ramenskoye airfield outside Moscow a year earlier. Between Johnson's two visits to Washington, Eisenhower had met with Lee DuBridge's Science Advisory Committee to discuss the threat of surprise attack, the culmination of Gardner's aggressive lobbying campaign. After the meeting, DuBridge asked James Killian to consider what additional steps might be taken to study and respond to the threat. Unbeknownst to Johnson, Washington was mobilizing to deal with precisely the kind of dangers that his airplane was designed to detect, and people like Gardner and Schriever were eager to find more effective, less vulnerable ways of collecting intelligence on Soviet forces.

The intervention of Gardner and others was fortuitous. The Air Force high command thought the CL-282 design was a dud. When

Kiefer, Wienberg, and Burton Klein, a RAND economist who worked in the Office of Development Planning, took the Lockheed plan to General LeMay in early April, the SAC commander walked out of the meeting, telling Kiefer and Wienberg they were wasting his time with a plane that had no guns or landing gear. He said he could put cameras aboard his B-36 bombers if he needed high-altitude photographs.

Not long after that, as Kiefer, Wienberg, and Klein were headed down K Street in Washington to go bowling at a duck pin alley, Klein suggested that they pitch the CL-282 to Richard Bissell, a friend and fellow economist who had recently joined the CIA. They got Schriever to invite Bissell over to the Pentagon for a briefing about the Lockheed proposal and its potential benefits. "Bissell was immediately impressed and showed great interest in this airplane," Klein recalled. But the visit produced no official sign of interest from the Agency. Bissell himself seemed to forget his first brush with the plane and did not mention it years later when recounting how he learned about the Lockheed aircraft.

On June 7, Johnson was officially notified that the Air Force had decided to reject his proposal. The letter to Lockheed said the Air Force was already committed to building the modified Martin B-57. The service had also decided to proceed with construction of Bell's proposed twin-engine spy plane, called the X-16.

After reading the rejection, Johnson noted in his log, "Received a letter which turned down our proposal on the basis that it was too unusual, that it was a single-engine aircraft and that they were already committed to the Martin program." But the ground was shifting in Washington— in Kelly Johnson's and Mert Davies's favor.

CHAPTER FIVE

"I Think I Have the Plane
You Are After"

B EFORE THE YEAR WAS OUT, the Air Force verdict was overturned.
Ironically, the reversal was largely the work of just the kind of outside scientists and experts that Hap Arnold had embraced when he ran
the Army Air Corps. Though some of the formal consulting mechanisms that he nurtured had atrophied after his retirement in 1946, the
spirit of innovation and ingenuity that he had instilled endured in quiet
corners of the Pentagon like Bernard Schriever's office. Then, encouraged by Dwight Eisenhower's own faith in technology and his openness
to new ideas, the Arnold approach to weapons development flourished
anew in the mid-1950s. The partnership among the government, science, and private industry during the Eisenhower years contributed in
no small measure to the preservation of American security during the
cold war and Washington's eventual victory in the long struggle with
the Soviet Union. The first beneficiary was the CL-282.

The pivotal benefactors were Jim Killian and Edwin Land, with an
important assist from Allen Donovan, the Cornell aeronautical expert.
Donovan quickly saw the advantages of Kelly Johnson's simple design
when he got a firsthand look at the Lockheed drawings during a visit to
Burbank in early August of 1954. As a teenager in upstate New York,
Donovan had learned how to fly sailplanes, known more familiarly as
gliders. He immediately realized that Johnson had come up with a jet-
powered glider that could realistically cruise above 70,000 feet. He liked

the use of a single engine, the extended wings, and the overall weight of the plane, which was much less than the usual military jet aircraft.

Donovan, who had traveled to Burbank as a member of Jim Baker's Air Force advisory panel, returned east on August 8 and immediately told Baker of his enthusiasm for the CL-282. Within days of Donovan's call to Baker, two other panel members, Land and Philip Strong of the CIA, met in Washington to discuss the Lockheed proposal. Strong showed Kelly Johnson's conceptual drawing of the aircraft to Land and informed him that the Air Force had rejected the plane. Land quickly phoned Baker, who was also in Washington. "Jim, I think I have the plane you are after."

Baker's Intelligence Systems Panel, a creature of the Air Force, was powerless to rescue the Lockheed proposal because the service had already made the decision to move ahead with the Martin B-57 and the Bell X-16. But Land and Baker could save the CL-282. As members of a separate, White House study of intelligence matters that was just gearing up as part of Jim Killian's high-powered review of the threat of surprise attack, Baker and Land had a direct line into the Oval Office through Killian, and Land was not shy about using it to circumvent the Air Force and the CIA.

The Killian study team, known officially as the Technological Capabilities Panel and informally as the surprise attack panel, was formed by Eisenhower in 1954 to examine the state of American military and intelligence technology in light of the growing threat of a Soviet surprise attack. The idea for the secret study grew out of the rising concern in Washington about the Soviet military threat. Thanks in part to Trevor Gardner's evangelical efforts, the study was initiated by Eisenhower at the March 27, 1954, meeting the president had held with Lee DuBridge's Science Advisory Committee. After the meeting, DuBridge asked Killian, a member of the advisory committee, to come up with a plan. Killian recommended the creation, in his words, "of a technical task force to study ways of avoiding surprise attack by a searching review of weapons and intelligence technology." On July 26, Eisenhower formally invited Killian to direct the study. Killian, in turn, recruited James

B. Fisk, later to become head of Bells Labs, as associate director, and the two men soon named a small steering committee that included DuBridge, James Doolittle, the retired Air Force general, and Edwin Land.

The steering group selected three primary issues for study—continental defense, striking power, and intelligence—and established a separate subcommittee for each. Land was put in charge of the intelligence panel. Killian and Fisk assembled a professional staff of some forty scientists and engineers to work with the steering committee and subcommittees. The work began in earnest in September and continued for five months. The study's findings were presented to Eisenhower at a National Security Council meeting on February 14, 1955.

The Killian panel played a pivotal role in preparing the U.S. military and intelligence agencies to wage the cold war. Unlike most presidential commissions, which produce anodyne, quickly forgotten reports on national problems, the Killian group looked unblinkingly at the anemic state of American defenses against nuclear attack and delivered dozens of recommendations that were soon put into effect at the insistence of President Eisenhower. The study's great importance was in emphasizing the critical role that advanced technologies could play in strengthening the nation's security, and specifically in stressing the need to accelerate the development of many of the advanced weapons and intelligence systems that Washington would come to rely on in the ensuing decades of the cold war. These systems included intercontinental and intermediate range ballistic missiles, early-warning radar networks, the submarine-launched Polaris missile, and the U-2 spy plane and spy satellites.

The panel's formation came during a period of estrangement between science and the government that was provoked by the McCarthy witch hunts, especially the Atomic Energy Commission's removal in 1953 of the security clearances of J. Robert Oppenheimer, the physicist who had directed the Manhattan Project. Oppenheimer had served as chairman of the Commission's General Advisory Committee. Land and many of the other men recruited by Killian were outraged by the Oppenheimer case, but they set aside their animosity toward Washington to serve on the panel. A desire to exercise power and to play a more central role in the nation's affairs may have been a motivation for some. But Killian believed the scientists "felt an obligation to their country that overrode their dismay about a single administration."

Killian himself, though an MIT graduate, was not a scientist. But he was a man of great intellectual range and a gifted administrator who commanded the respect and loyalty of scientists across the country. He had a knack for working smoothly with strong-minded scientists and bringing them to a common conclusion. One of his successors as president of MIT, Paul E. Gray, said of Killian, "At times of contention he was peerless in the easing of tensions, the resolving of differences, and the achievement of consensus, which makes advance possible."

A native of Blacksburg, South Carolina, where he was born in 1904, Killian initially enrolled at Trinity College in his home state (the school later became Duke University), then transferred to MIT, where he read widely in the humanities while fulfilling the university's core requirements in math and engineering. His intention was to follow his father into the textile industry, and upon graduation Killian considered job offers from the textile division of the Goodrich Tire and Rubber Company and from Goodyear.

But other interests intervened. Killian was drawn to journalism, and he served as editor of the campus paper, *The Tech*, during his senior year. "I was an ardent addict of H. L. Mencken . . . and in my best imitation of Mencken's style I occasionally lambasted the Institute's administration," he recalled in a memoir. Killian's polemics brought him into contact with Harold Lobdell, a member of the dean of students' staff. The two struck up a friendship and Lobdell invited Killian to write an occasional column on undergraduate education for the MIT alumni magazine, *Technology Review*. He became the publication's editor in 1930 and from there was recruited by Karl T. Compton, the Institute's president, to be his executive assistant. After rising through a variety of administrative posts, and helping to organize MIT's extensive wartime research projects, he succeeded Compton as president in 1949.

When Killian later became the first White House science adviser, a profile in the *New York Times* said, "His somewhat cherubic countenance masks the inquisitive tough-mindedness behind it. He is as disarmingly pleasant as a successful hotel manager. Yet he can stand before an audience of scholars and get to the core of the problem of acute shortages of scientific teachers by warning that 'there has been avoidance, if not evasion, of the intellectual tax which must be paid if our intellectual budget is to be balanced.' "

Under Killian's skillful leadership, the Technological Capabilities Panel gave science a leading role in Washington. Other postwar projects and advisory boards, including the Beacon Hill group, the Air Force's Scientific Advisory Board and Intelligence Systems Panel, and the Atomic Energy Commission's General Advisory Committee, had encouraged cooperation between scientists and defense planners, with some success. One of the most effective was the Strategic Missiles Evaluation Committee, headed by John von Neumann, a brilliant mathematician at Princeton's Institute for Advanced Study who had helped design the first atomic and hydrogen bombs. It recommended a crash program to build intercontinental missiles. The von Neumann report, submitted to the Pentagon in February 1954, gave new impetus and coherence to the missile-development program. Bernard Schriever was soon put in charge of the effort, which Eisenhower made the military's top priority. The program, based in Inglewood, California, was later given the added responsibility of creating a spy satellite.

But even after the von Neumann committee completed its work, scientists largely remained on the periphery of defense policy and programs. It was not until Eisenhower turned to Killian and his associates in 1954 that science was given a decisive role in shaping the nation's cold war defenses. As his presidency progressed, Eisenhower relied increasingly on scientists for advice on military and arms control matters.

Eisenhower left the nation few greater legacies as president than his abiding faith in science as an indispensable partner with the government in preserving the nation's security. His interest in science predated his election as president. As a cadet at West Point, he studied mathematics and engineering. As Supreme Allied Commander in World War II, Eisenhower saw the lifesaving benefits produced by the scientists who broke the German codes and developed radar, and he recognized the destructive potential of the V-2 rockets that Germany fired toward London. He knew that the invention of the atomic bomb had speeded the defeat of Japan. In 1946, when serving as army chief of staff, Eisenhower stressed the importance of scientific work in a memo to top commanders and civilian officials. It captured some of the enlightened ideas about the role of science that Eisenhower later applied during his presidency to the development of new military technologies.

"Scientists and industrialists," he said in the memo, "must be given the greatest possible freedom to carry out their research. The fullest utilization by the Army of the civilian resources of the nation cannot be procured merely by prescribing the military characteristics and requirements of certain types of equipment. Scientists and industrialists are more likely to make new and unsuspected contributions to the development of the Army if detailed directions are held to a minimum. . . ."

After the war, Eisenhower served for five years as the president of Columbia University, where he formed friendships with a number of top scientists, including I. I. Rabi, winner of the 1944 Nobel Prize in physics. Rabi, who was born in Austria and joined the Columbia faculty in 1929, had worked on the development of radar and the atomic bomb and served as an adviser to the Atomic Energy Commission. Eisenhower often called on Rabi for advice during his years in the White House. "Eisenhower had a warm, personal regard for Rabi," recalled Gen. Andrew Goodpaster, who served as Eisenhower's staff secretary at the White House. "Any time I told him that Rabi was coming down to Washington to see him, the president would say, 'Oh, that's wonderful, that's wonderful.'" As Columbia's president, Eisenhower also came to know Killian, his counterpart at MIT. The two men first met in 1948 when Killian attended Eisenhower's inauguration as Columbia's president.

Eisenhower clearly relished the blunt, independent advice he got from Killian and company. He entrusted them with sensitive secrets, appreciated their discretion, and liked the fact that their judgment was not swayed by institutional loyalties and the parochial interests of the military services. As a former commander and army chief of staff, Eisenhower knew as well as anyone how narrow-minded and self-serving the services could be in making budget decisions and planning new weapons systems. After the war, he had assembled a group of young Army officers to think about the Army of the future and the role it would play in America's defense. He made clear he did not want another predictable Pentagon report. "There's only one instruction for you people," he told the officers, "and that is to take instruction from nobody."

Not long before Eisenhower died in 1969, Killian paid him a last visit at Walter Reed Hospital. "You know, Jim," Eisenhower told him, "this bunch of scientists was one of the few groups that I encountered in Washington who seemed to be there to help the country and not help themselves."

Eisenhower once told Land, "Oh, I'm so grateful to you fellows who are out of town! You can't think in Washington. You go away and think and then you tell me what you've been thinking. There's no way to think if you live here."

Reflecting on the creative partnership between Eisenhower and his science advisers, Killian noted that access to the Oval Office was a critical factor. As chairman of the surprise attack committee, and later as the White House science adviser, Killian moved freely across the top levels of government, including the West Wing. He saw Eisenhower several times a week. "My ready access to President Eisenhower made it possible for me promptly to bring to him, and to open opportunities for others to bring to him, new and important technologies, concepts and analyses that added to the strength of our nation."

The scientists and engineers whom Eisenhower turned to for advice were not specialists in military or intelligence technology. "What they did possess," Killian noted, "were imagination, creative powers, and a deep understanding of physical science and technology (and perhaps equally important, a simple love of country); and these enabled them rapidly to come to grips with weapons technology, to bring fresh points of view to bear, and to make contributions to it in a way that more routine people with less deep mastery of science and technology could not do."

The fact that Killian, Land, and other scientists served together on a number of different advisory panels fostered productive brainstorming on a wide range of issues. Killian observed that this "interdisciplinary congeniality," as he put it, "made it possible to achieve an extraordinary synthesis of minds and ideas to aid the president in achieving his goals in shaping our defense and intelligence programs and policies."

Edwin Land's route to these high-octane councils and his pivotal role in shaping revolutionary new spy technologies was anything but conventional or predictable. In many ways, he was an unlikely figure to lead the United States into a new era in spying. Land was primarily known in the 1950s as the creator of instant photography and the founder and guiding mind behind the Polaroid Corporation, the roles that still define his reputation today, more than a decade after his death. A short, intense man with dark hair and a piercing gaze, he was one of the most gifted and prolific inventors in American history, garnering more than five hundred patents over the course of his life, most in the field of optics and photography.

Long before the appearance of cyber-billionaires like Bill Gates, "Din" Land, as he was known to friends, was a fabulously wealthy scientist-cum-capitalist who captured the attention of the nation through his brilliance and enterprise. Though reclusive—he liked nothing more than to spend days at a time in his lab, shut off from the outside world—he could also be a formidable showman for his ideas and products. His spellbinding performances at Polaroid's annual stockholders meeting, when Land would unveil a new product with the flair of a Broadway star, were legendary in the corporate world and attracted extensive press coverage. Yet his greatest contribution to the country was all but unknown to most Americans during his lifetime and even now remains overshadowed by his achievements in instant photography.

For better than two decades, beginning in the early 1950s, Land served as the godfather for a series of technological breakthroughs in aerial and space-based reconnaissance that transformed the nature of spying. Through his service as an adviser to five presidents and an equal number of CIA chiefs, he inspired and guided a remarkably creative partnership between government, industry, and the academy that gave the nation new ways of looking behind the Iron Curtain. He spotted promising technologies, prodded the government to invest in them, and protected the scientists and engineers who struggled through heart-breaking failures to perfect the new machines. When there were problems with the state-of-the-art camera systems, Land would roll up his sleeves and take his place among the engineers to help solve technical problems. Killian, who brought Land into the inner circle of White House science advisers, called his Cambridge neighbor and friend "an authentic genius."

"His powers of exposition, his facility in expressing complex ideas in novel, witty, and clarifying ways, can lift a meeting or a report to a higher level of discourse," Killian said. "He pointed the way to the development of new intelligence-gathering technology, such as reconnaissance planes and satellites, that have given unique powers, benign in their operation, to American intelligence agencies, undergirding policy decisions of immense consequence and saving the nation billions of dollars."

"In meetings with presidents, his eloquence and lucid exposition incited their latent imagination and prompted them to make decisions and to undertake leadership roles that had been, until then, beyond their reach."

Richard Garwin, a physicist and government consultant who served with Land for many years on a CIA advisory board, described Land as "both a genius and a showman, and an extremely productive and forceful person."

Bud Wheelon, who came to know Land while directing the scientific and technological work at the CIA in the mid-1960s, said, "He was beguiling. . . . He had an easygoing kind of charm, but as you listened to Land you realized that he was saying a series of very profound things. He could capture one's imagination in a way that was almost spellbinding."

Later in his life, Land reflected on his contributions in a conversation with Killian. As Killian recalled, Land believed that his primary role "had been to convey to the president and other leaders something of the humanistic and aesthetic values of science. He took greater pride in this act of 'teaching' the qualities and values of science than in his immense technical contributions to the strengthening of our military, intelligence, and space technology."

Land made his first mark in optics with his invention of synthetic polarizing filters when he was nineteen years old. He first became fascinated with the properties of light as a boy growing up in Bridgeport and Norwich, Connecticut. Land's paternal grandparents, Avram and Ella, were Russian Jews who emigrated to the United States from their native Odessa in the 1880s with their two sons, Harry and Sam. Harry, who took over the family scrap metal business after his father's death, married Martha Goldfaden. Their second child, Edwin, was born in Bridgeport on May 7, 1909.

Like other boys in his neighborhood, Edwin joined the Boy Scouts and prepared studiously for his bar mitzvah. Unlike the others, he became intoxicated with the study of light, a subject that enthralled him for the rest of his life. The idea of polarized light transfixed Land, especially the notion of developing a synthetic polarizing material that could make the beneficial properties of polarized light, including the elimination of glare, widely available. A polarizing material works by absorbing the most intense rays of light while allowing less intense light waves to pass through it.

Today, polarizing filters are commonplace. They are used in sunglasses, camera lenses, pocket calculators, and digital watches to remove glare. If Land's ambitious hopes had been realized, car makers might also be using polarizing plastic to eliminate the glare from headlights. But when Land first turned to the field, the polarization of light was limited to physics labs and other esoteric uses because there was no convenient, easily manufactured polarizing material. Land set out to invent it. He was clearly motivated by a spirit of scientific inquiry as well as a healthy respect for the potential commercial applications and profits of a product that might have many uses. Throughout his life, Land worked with dazzling success at the intersection of science and business.

Harvard welcomed the putative inventor as a freshman in the fall of 1926, but he found the university confining and left before Christmas. After a short sojourn in Chicago, where he briefly and unsuccessfully concentrated on fiction writing, he moved to New York and began in earnest to study optics and light polarization. He bounced from apartment to apartment, setting up makeshift labs in basements and backrooms, all the while reading everything he could find on the subject at the New York Public Library on 42nd Street, where he would often sit all day in the majestic reading room poring over obscure books.

Previous efforts to make polarizers had relied on growing large crystals with commonly aligned molecules like those found in natural polarizing materials like calcite or tourmaline. Land experimented with this approach but found it cumbersome and unsatisfactory. He turned instead to the opposite solution: producing millions of tiny polarizing crystals and then arraying them together in low concentration in a clear sheet of glass or plastic. This sort of about-face in solving a problem, which Land called "orthogonal thinking," became a hallmark of his inventive mind.

Land returned to Harvard in September 1929 and his work on polarizers soon attracted the attention of the physics faculty. The department set him up with a small lab, an unusual privilege for an undergraduate, and he developed a productive association with George W. Wheelwright III, a physics instructor who was six years his senior. The teacher and student hit it off and Wheelwright encouraged Land to pursue his research interests. In the summer of 1932, Wheelwright suggested that Land and he set up an independent lab. They rented a room in Cambridge, then moved to an empty dairy barn in the village of Weston, in the western suburbs of Boston. The following June, Land's first patent was approved.

Over the next two decades, the Land-Wheelwright partnership grew into a creative research and industrial enterprise, as Land and the small staff of scientists that he recruited refined the technique for mass producing polarizing material. Land-Wheelwright Laboratories, the firm's initial name, called the new material Polaroid. In 1937, Land and Wheelwright folded the lab into a new company that they established and named the Polaroid Corporation. Wheelwright left the firm in 1942.

During these years of invention and growth, Land developed the instincts and affiliations that helped to make him such a valuable scientific adviser to Eisenhower and his successors. Land had a searching, open-minded intelligence that made him receptive to new ideas and inventive solutions to seemingly insurmountable problems. The network of friends that he nurtured at Harvard and MIT, including James Killian, put him in touch with some of the top scientists in the nation. His association with Kodak and other industrial companies—and the work of his own company—schooled him in the practices and creative potential of the private sector.

Polaroid's wartime projects for the government included the production of glare-reducing goggles and gun sights and the development of sophisticated range finders, periscopes, and bombsights. As the war came to a close, Land helped Vannevar Bush draft a report for Franklin Roosevelt on the postwar role science could play in American life. Bush, an electrical engineer who developed the first electronic analog computer and had taught at MIT, served as Roosevelt's main science adviser and headed the Office of Scientific Research and Development, which coordinated wartime research in the United States. The report called for the creation of an independent agency that would allocate federal money for basic research. The recommendation eventually led to the formation of the National Science Foundation in 1950.

The war left Land committed to doing whatever he could to improve the nation's military technology and introduced him to government leaders in Washington. Land's instruction in reconnaissance issues intensified with his service in the Beacon Hill group and with his appointment in 1951 to the Air Force's Scientific Advisory Board, which was headed by Theodore von Karman of Caltech, and later his membership on Jim Baker's Intelligence Systems Panel.

By the time Killian invited Land to join his landmark technological study team in 1954, Land was by training and intuition the ideal person to guide the nation into a new era of overhead reconnaissance. In a fateful accident of history, Killian's first choice for the chairmanship of the subcommittee on intelligence, Bruce S. Old of Arthur D. Little Inc., the Boston think tank, could not arrange a leave of absence. Killian, who had already named Land to the steering committee for the study, asked his friend to head the intelligence subgroup. Land accepted, making clear his intention to keep the group small enough to "fit into a taxicab." He quickly extricated himself from the project he was working on with Alfred Hitchcock to produce 3-D movies, and moved back east from Hollywood, where he had temporarily set up shop.

As Land, who was forty-five years old, packed up his belongings in Hollywood, he decided to limit the intelligence panel to six members, including himself. (Taxis in those days came with jumper seats in the back and could accommodate five passengers plus the driver.) He wanted to move briskly and decisively and knew that the larger the group got the less agile it would be. Drawing on his network of friends in science and industry, Land assembled an erudite group. The members were Jim Baker; Edward Purcell, the Harvard physicist and Nobel laureate; John W. Tukey, a Princeton mathematician; Joseph W. Kennedy, a chemist at Washington University, and Allan Latham Jr., a former colleague at Polaroid.

Land worked the panel hard, arranging frequent meetings with government officials, but also encouraged open, freewheeling discussions among the members. Land's style was to work late into the evening, a habit that shaped the schedule of many of the consulting groups he directed over the years. Richard Garwin, who got to know Land well when they served together on a science advisory panel in the 1960s and 1970s, described the long evenings. "Sometimes we would hold our meetings at a contractor's facility, and sometimes in the magnificent board room at Polaroid, where Land's cook would provide us with dinner. Once, a Land Panel meeting did not adjourn until dawn. That was unusual, but it was not unusual to work until midnight, and then to be invited to Din Land's personal laboratory for a half-hour demonstration of his latest work in color vision."

Land guided the intelligence subcommittee of the Technological Capabilities Panel with the same sense of curiosity and determination that shaped his scientific work, pushing the group to look over the horizon at new technologies that might transform the intelligence business. Sidney Drell, a Stanford physicist who later served with Land on a CIA consulting committee and played a central role in advising the government on technical intelligence projects, found Land to be a natural leader. "He exuded confidence and intelligence," Drell said. "He was a good listener and didn't talk much, but when he did say something, it was usually significant. Meetings were loose and free and he let the imagination roam."

Dick Leghorn, who came to know Land through their intersecting interest in reconnaissance technology, said that Land enjoyed working with the government's most secret intelligence projects and budgets—the black programs, as they are known in Washington. "He loved the black world," Leghorn said. "Land sensed he could get things done. He would listen, then go off and get things done."

Purcell had a similar impression. Land "knew more secrets than the rest of us did," Purcell told Land's biographer, Victor K. McElheny. Purcell found Land to be very effective "not so much for his technical advice but for his ability to convey in a personal way the relative importance of the things we were talking about. And his boldness, which, of course, was part of his business career: talking about what you really could do if you wanted to."

Land's broad vision about the nation's intelligence needs set him apart from most of the government officials and businessmen who were working on various espionage projects. They tended to focus more closely on particular issues that directly affected their companies or agencies. Land always seemed to have a bigger picture in mind. John McMahon, who served at the CIA for more than a quarter of a century and came to know Land well, thought of him as an architect. "He had the master plan of all that had to be done and how to go about it," McMahon said. "And he had the political instincts of how to play it in Washington. He understood Washington very well. His knowledge of people in the scientific world, particularly around the Washington sector, was second to none. Everybody respected him."

As part of a presidential panel, Land's group had full access to the nation's intelligence secrets and any officials the members wished to see at the Pentagon, CIA, and other agencies. The men were not impressed by what they found. "We would go in and interview generals and admirals in charge on intelligence and come away worried," Land told Don

Welzenbach, a CIA historian, in 1984. "Here we were, five or six young men, asking questions that these high-ranking officers couldn't answer." The CIA did not fare any better.

Land and his panel members knew from the beginning that the first defense against surprise attack was improved intelligence information about Soviet military forces. Their assignment was to identify weaknesses in the nation's spy operations and to recommend remedies, especially innovative technologies. They concentrated on the core question of whether the United States would be able to detect signs of an impending Soviet attack—"strategic warning," in intelligence parlance. In the case of an air attack, early indicators could include the transfer of Soviet bombers to bases along the northern periphery of the Soviet Union within striking range of the United States; the movement of nuclear bombs, aviation fuel, and air crews to these staging airfields; intensified training exercises and the mobilization of other military forces, among other signs.

The Land group also wanted to know whether the United States had a good enough picture of Soviet military forces and industrial production to make long-term assessments of Soviet power and how Washington might best marshal American resources to combat the Soviet threat while simultaneously addressing domestic needs. In its report to Eisenhower, the panel aptly summarized the critical importance of such information. "If intelligence can uncover a new military threat, we may take steps to meet it. If intelligence can reveal an opponent's specific weakness, we may prepare to exploit it. With good intelligence we can avoid wasting our resources by arming for the wrong danger or at the wrong time."

Land and Baker and some of the other members knew from past consulting work with the Pentagon that American spying was severely handicapped by the closed nature of Soviet society, the vastness of the Soviet landmass, and a lack of American intelligence-gathering systems that could overcome these obstacles. As the men examined the full range of American espionage programs and the estimates of Soviet military forces that the CIA was churning out, they realized just how little Washington really knew about current Soviet military programs and activities, let alone future ones. In a sobering statement that reverberated through the top levels of the government when the panel submitted its report in February 1955, Land and his team said, "We conclude that there is a real possibility that a surprise attack might strike us without useful, strategic early warning."

"We *must* find ways," the report said, "to increase the number of hard facts upon which our intelligence estimates are based, in order to provide better strategic warning, to minimize surprise in the kind of attack, and to reduce the danger of gross overestimation or gross underestimation of the threat." Looking ahead, the Land group suggested immediate gains were possible. "We envision as attainable in the near future a great increase in the usefulness of science in intelligence. Revolutionary new techniques will be devised to give us facts and answers instead of assumptions and estimates."

As soon as Edwin Land saw Kelly Johnson's drawing and performance expectations for the CL-282 in mid-August of 1954, he realized Lockheed had the makings of exactly that kind of revolutionary new technique. If the aircraft would fly as high as Johnson promised, and could be equipped with an equally revolutionary camera system, Washington might finally be able to get an accurate reading on Soviet military power, especially Moscow's new jet-powered Bison bombers. Using his piece of the Killian committee as both brain trust and battering ram for the CL-282, Land set to work to get the plane approved and built.

A new reconnaissance plane would only be as good as the camera it carried aloft, and no one in the country was better at fashioning new lenses than Baker. Baker agreed to start work immediately on designing a camera and lens system that would provide clear, detailed photographs from an altitude of 70,000 feet. This was no mean challenge. If Land could secure approval to produce the CL-282, Baker would have to work fast to come up with a camera system to match.

At the end of August, in a bold move to try to find an institutional sponsor for the project, Land turned to the CIA. The Agency was not an obvious choice. Although its business was collecting and analyzing intelligence information, mostly about the Soviet Union, and engaging in covert activities abroad, the CIA had little expertise in developing ad-

vanced technologies and designing or building airplanes. Its new director, Allen Dulles, appointed by Eisenhower in 1953, was the consum-
mate spy, having perfected the black arts of espionage during World
War II as the chief American agent in neutral Switzerland. His brother,
John Foster Dulles, was Eisenhower's secretary of State. Allen Dulles
had little inclination to push the CIA into a realm of technical spying
that he thought was properly the domain of the Pentagon.

Land's contact point at the CIA was Richard Bissell. Land could have
approached any number of more senior officials at the Agency, including Dulles. But Land, who was careful in choosing allies, must have
heard about Bissell from mutual friends, most likely from Killian. In
1942, Killian had helped recruit Bissell to join the MIT economics faculty.

Bissell later said he was puzzled by his conversation with Land, un-
sure just what the inventor had in mind. But he knew that when a representative of the president came calling, it was wise to show some
interest. In early September, Bissell instructed an Air Force officer on
his staff to review the nation's air reconnaissance programs. A few weeks
later he forwarded the sixteen-page study to Dulles's deputy, Lt. Gen.
Charles Pearre Cabell of the Air Force. In a cover note, Bissell urged
General Cabell to look over the section describing a specialized new aircraft proposed by Lockheed.

Land returned to Cambridge and turned his Polaroid office at 2 Os-
born Street into a nerve center for developing the Lockheed proposal.
His intelligence panel served as the focal point for the discussions,
which extended into the fall and eventually involved representatives
from Lockheed as well as Pratt & Whitney, the jet-engine manufacturer. Land also invited Richard S. Perkin, the president of the Perkin-
Elmer company, a camera manufacturer, and Henry Yutzy, a film expert
from Kodak, to meet with the panel.

Land was aiming for nothing less than a breakthrough in intelligence:
a new airplane, new camera with new lenses, and new film. He wanted to
turn the operation of the new plane over to the CIA rather than the Air
Force, a step sure to be resisted by the Air Force. He also expected the

spy agency to develop sophisticated new methods for examining the photographs that would be produced. All in all, it was an audacious plan, one that would work only if Land could gain the cooperation of all the organizations involved and deflect opposition from the Air Force, which had been warned that Kelly Johnson's proposal was being revived by the Land panel. It was not a job that seemed suited to an inventor most comfortable working in a laboratory, but Land had a steely will and a taste for bureaucratic combat that surprised his opponents. He also had the ear of the president.

As Land gathered the resources he would need to perfect his plan and sell it to Eisenhower, he first had to talk with Kelly Johnson. Land arranged a mid-September meeting with Secretary of the Air Force Harold Talbott. He was accompanied by James Fisk, the deputy director of the Killian committee. When Land told Talbott of his interest in the Lockheed aircraft and asked for permission to talk with Johnson, Talbott said he would consider the request. Land angrily responded, "All right, Mr. Secretary, I guess we'll have to tell the American people about you."

Talbott weighed the threat for a moment, then picked up the phone and called Lockheed. "I think Talbott may have had a guilty conscience," Land later recalled.

Once he was free to talk with Johnson, Land had the running room he needed to draft a comprehensive plan for a new reconnaissance system. Henry Yutzy from Kodak reported that his company was developing a Mylar-based film that was much lighter and thinner than traditional acetate-based film. The weight and thickness of conventional films had long limited the amount that could be carried aboard reconnaissance planes. That, in turn, restricted the photographic coverage the planes could provide. These were particularly sensitive issues for the CL-282 because of the need to keep the plane as light as possible so it could make extended flights at extremely high altitude. When Yutzy told the Land panel that Kodak saw little commercial potential for the new film, a signal that Kodak was not rushing to complete work on the project, Land informed him that the national interest compelled the company to proceed with the research. Kodak speeded up the project, but the new film, known as Estar, was not ready for use when the Lockheed airplane began operations.

Land felt strongly that spy flights over the Soviet Union should not be conducted by the Air Force. Flights by uniformed pilots in an armed military aircraft would be more threatening to Moscow, and more likely to draw fire, than the appearance of an unarmed aircraft commanded by a civilian pilot. Land, like Eisenhower, worried that military incursions into Soviet airspace could start a war. In Land's plan, the CL-282 would be an unmarked plane flown by a civilian working for the CIA. In fact, he planned to turn the entire project over to the Agency.

By late October, Land was ready to present his plan to the CIA and the Air Force. He and his fellow panel members met at the CIA's headquarters in Washington with Allen Dulles and Trevor Gardner. Gardner was primed to support the idea. Dulles was another matter. He was dubious about taking on a military mission, not to mention the difficult technical assignment of managing the construction of the plane. He shared none of Land's native enthusiasm for research challenges nor his vision of the CIA as a generator and user of new technologies. Dulles was noncommittal. Land was frustrated by Dulles's passivity. "We knew we could get pictures of those Russian bombers," he later told Don Welzenbach, the CIA historian.

At this point, Land and Killian quietly went to see Eisenhower to lay the groundwork for submission of a formal proposal. The Killian committee wasn't ready yet to issue its report, but the two men believed that the CL-282, equipped with a state-of-the-art camera system, could provide the country with critically needed information about the Soviet military threat. They wanted Washington to have use of the plane as soon as possible.

The visit by Killian and Land to the White House in late October was not recorded on the president's official schedule, and the precise date of the meeting is not clear, but both Killian and Land later described it to Welzenbach. Gen. Andrew Goodpaster, Eisenhower's staff secretary and his gatekeeper on these secret programs, recalled that it was not unusual for the president to meet privately with Killian and Land on matters of great sensitivity. He also said it was common for Eisenhower to give preliminary approval for an especially important plan well ahead of its formal submission to him by government agencies. This approach allowed the president to nudge the machinery of government into action without officials realizing he was involved. "He didn't want his role to be known," Goodpaster recalled. Eisenhower employed this behind-the-scenes management style in other areas as well, as Fred I. Greenstein, a Princeton political scientist, showed in his 1982 book, *The Hidden-Hand Presidency.*

In the case of the CL-282, the idea of lodging the program in the CIA rather than the Air Force was likely to cause heartburn at the Pentagon, another reason Eisenhower may have wished to disguise his early involvement. The private meeting with Killian and Land was itself a breach of the usual line of command on such an important matter, and Eisenhower could well have preferred not to let the Pentagon and CIA know he had relied so heavily on the advice of two private citizens.

Land came quickly to the point at the White House meeting. "We told the president we were confident this aircraft could and would find and photograph the Soviet Union's Bison bomber fleet."

Killian recounted the Oval Office meeting in his 1977 memoirs: "Land described the system using an unarmed plane and recommended that its development be undertaken. After listening to our proposal and asking many hard questions, Eisenhower approved the development of the system, but he stipulated that it should be handled in an unconventional way so that it would not become entangled in the bureaucracy of the Defense Department or troubled by rivalries among the services."

The CL-282 was the first tangible proposal to come from the Killian committee. Eisenhower, who had approved formation of the panel just three months earlier, was glad to learn the country might soon have use of a new, less vulnerable spy plane. "The importance of the effort at the time cannot be overemphasized," Eisenhower noted in his memoirs. "Our relative position in intelligence, compared to that of the Soviets, could scarcely have been worse."

Not long after the meeting with Killian and Land, Eisenhower got a timely reminder about the perils of lower-altitude spy flights. On Sunday, November 7, two Soviet jet fighters shot down an American B-29 photoreconnaissance plane at midday over the northern Japanese island of Hokkaido. The plane was attacked while on a mapping mission within sight of the Kurile Islands, which were occupied by the Soviet Union after World War II. The crew of eleven airmen bailed out of the crippled plane before it crashed near the town of Kenebetsu. Ten of the men survived but one was killed. Secretary of State John Foster Dulles discussed the news with the president on the phone, telling him, "Whenever the boys go over there, it's deliberate risk. We think the plane was over Japan, but the Soviets probably think it was over their territory." Eisenhower, who was scheduled to meet with a group of congressmen later that day, mused to Dulles that "we would not want to admit too much" and that he certainly did not plan to concede that Washington deliberately dispatched reconnaissance planes into Soviet airspace.

Land did not cite Eisenhower's support as he continued to try to sell the project to Dulles and the Air Force. Shortly after meeting with Eisenhower, Land turned his attention back to Dulles. On November 5, he sent the CIA director a secret, sternly worded letter making clear his expectation that Dulles would approve the project—Land was doubtless emboldened by the encounter with Eisenhower. "Here is the brief report from our panel telling why we think overflight is urgent and presently feasible. I am not sure that we have made it clear that we feel there are many reasons why this activity is appropriate for CIA, always with Air Force assistance. We told you that this seems to us the kind of action and technique that is right for the contemporary version of CIA: a modern and scientific way for an Agency that is always supposed to be looking, to do its looking. Quite strongly, we feel that you must always assert your first right to pioneer in scientific techniques for collecting intelligence—and choosing such partners to assist you as may be needed. This present opportunity for aerial photography seems to us a fine place to start."

The import of this message extended well beyond the proposed spy plane. Land was proposing a basic change in the CIA's activities. He wanted the Agency to become a leader in technological innovation.

This was not a role that the Truman administration or Congress had anticipated for the CIA when they created the organization in 1947, nor was it one that its initial directors, including Dulles, had encouraged. Land was challenging Dulles to put his organization at the cutting edge of scientific research directed at creating new intelligence-gathering systems. Until this time, the Agency had emphasized more traditional espionage work and served as a central clearinghouse for intelligence assessments. It had also moved aggressively into running covert activities abroad, including paramilitary, political, and propaganda operations. It had not invested much money or energy in science and technology.

Dulles, who was not averse to expanding the agency's reach or its budget and was certainly sensitive to presidential pressure, eventually saw the merit of Land's approach, though he never became an evangelical champion of technology. As he read Land's letter, he may not have appreciated its long-term implications, but he could not have failed to see that Kelly Johnson's jet-powered glider was headed his way. Land's forceful lobbying moved Dulles toward acceptance of the project.

But the Air Force wasn't quite ready to surrender. While Land, Killian, and Gardner were in Burbank to inspect a mockup of the CL-282 at the Skunk Works on November 9, Major Seaberg at the Wright Air Development Command was pressing the Air Force to defend the two projects he backed, the B-57 and the X-16. General Putt scheduled a meeting for November 18 to consider the different aircraft proposals. Members of the Killian steering committee were invited, including Land and Fisk. When Land learned of the meeting, he summoned several members of his intelligence panel to Washington to be sure they were in agreement about the advantages of the CL-282. He asked Allen Donovan, whose expertise on aeronautical matters was unquestioned, to come down from Cornell to discuss the CL-282 with the panel members the day before the Pentagon meeting.

Land's goal of fitting everyone into a taxi proved to be prophetic, or close to it. To keep the discussion confidential, Land arranged for everyone to assemble in a car. It was a chilly, rainy day. As Donovan approached the Old Executive Office Building on Pennsylvania Avenue, John Tukey called to him from a four-door Ford sedan that was waiting

at the curb. Tukey was driving. Donovan opened the door to discover
Land, Baker, Purcell, and Fisk sardined in the vehicle. They spent two
hours driving around Washington as Donovan patiently reviewed the
reasons why the CL-282 offered the best chance of penetrating Soviet
airspace.

On November 18, Land, Fisk, and other members of the Killian
committee met with General Putt, Major Seaberg, and a number of
other Air Force officials. Land and the scientists made it clear they preferred the Lockheed plane. Whether General Putt and his Air Force
colleagues realized by this time that Eisenhower favored the CL-282 is
not clear. But everyone in the room knew that Land and the other members of the Killian group had been appointed by Eisenhower to study
the nation's defenses. They were not to be denied.

Kelly Johnson arrived in Washington that afternoon, summoned by
Trevor Gardner, who realized a decision point was rapidly approaching.
"They wanted to be reassured that our proposal was technically feasible," Johnson noted in his diary. Gardner and his allies carefully went
over the details with Johnson, who recalled in his memoirs that "they
put me through a grilling as I had not had since college exams."

The next day Air Force Secretary Talbott hosted a lunch at the Pentagon to review the bidding about the aircraft. The guests included
Land, Johnson, Gardner, Dulles, General Cabell, the deputy director of
the CIA, and General Putt. The Air Force bowed to Land's enthusiasm
for the project though the service remained doubtful about the project,
and resentful that the CIA seemed likely to be given lead responsibility
for building and operating the plane. Cabell wrote a memo for the
record. Everyone at the lunch, he said, had agreed "that the special item
of material described by Lockheed was practical and desirable and
would be sought." The money would be drawn from secret accounts
that were not subject to normal government audits.

Johnson immediately flew back to Burbank and met that evening with
Lockheed's top executives. They approved his brash suggestion that the
Skunk Works build not just a prototype of the aircraft but the full fleet
of thirty planes. The decision transformed Johnson's small experimen-

tal design and engineering operation into an aircraft manufacturing enterprise.

Johnson set to work redesigning several features of the plane, substituting a Pratt & Whitney engine, as the Air Force had suggested, and dropping the landing skis he had originally planned in favor of a lightweight bicycle-type landing gear. He also expanded the size of the camera bay. Even so, the dimensions would be a source of contention among Johnson, Land, and Jim Baker, with Johnson trying to save space and Land and Baker pressing to expand the compartment to accommodate a larger camera.

On Monday afternoon, November 22, Dulles visited the Oval Office to review the decision with Eisenhower. Ann Whitman, the president's secretary, recorded in her diary, "Discussion of advisability of going ahead with new photographic reconnaissance plane at some considerable cost." The next day, the Intelligence Advisory Committee, an interagency group that helped set intelligence policy, approved a formal request from Dulles to build the plane. Early on November 24, the day before Thanksgiving, Dulles signed a three-page memorandum to Eisenhower seeking official permission to move ahead with the project. At 8:15 A.M., Dulles and General Cabell joined Air Force Secretary Talbott; Gen. Nathan Twining, the air force chief of staff; General Putt; Secretary of Defense Charles Wilson; and Secretary of State John Foster Dulles at the White House for a meeting with Eisenhower.

With Eisenhower due to take off that afternoon with his wife, Mamie, for a weekend of golfing at the Augusta National Golf Club in Georgia, the conversation moved briskly. John Foster Dulles, anticipating that the high-altitude spy flights might provoke problems with the Soviet Union, predicted that difficulties might arise but that "we could live through them." The meeting lasted just fifteen minutes.

Eisenhower made it clear to everyone that he expected the CIA to direct the project with assistance from the Air Force, and that he did not want the planes or pilots to be part of the U.S. military. General Twining was not pleased with the decision. Though the meeting was not the occasion to express his doubts, he believed, as he later said, that Dulles and his men were getting "too big for their britches. They did not know how to handle this kind of operation."

The idea of sending American reconnaissance planes deep into Soviet airspace was filled with risk and uncertainty, no matter how technologically advanced the aircraft might be. The ramifications were clearly on Eisenhower's mind a few hours later when he met with William Knowland, the Senate Republican leader. The California conservative was a frequent critic of Eisenhower's handling of foreign affairs, and after the Soviet attack on the American plane over Japan earlier in the month, he had called for severing diplomatic relations with Moscow.

Hoping to make clear to Knowland that his administration was not reacting passively to Soviet pressures, Eisenhower broadly hinted at the steps he was taking to track Moscow's military activities. The conversation was picked up by a tape recorder that Eisenhower activated before Knowland's arrival. Eisenhower told his visitor that "there is a very great aggressiveness on our side that you have not known about . . . in the way of reconnaissance and a great many things we are very active and there are a great many risky decisions on my part constantly . . ."

The Friday following Thanksgiving, Dulles invited Bissell to his office and informed him that Eisenhower had approved a secret project to produce a new reconnaissance aircraft. The CIA was to manage the project and operate the planes once they were built. Dulles told his startled aide that the Agency was turning the project over to him. He handed Bissell a packet of papers and told him to read them over the weekend. The next week Bissell attended a meeting in Gardner's office at the Pentagon to organize the work with the Air Force. Bissell, Gardner, General Putt, and other officials agreed that the CIA would handle security for the project, oversee the work at Lockheed, and set up a secret airfield in the western United States where the planes could be tested and pilots trained. The Air Force would play a major role as well. It would divert Pratt & Whitney J57 engines to Lockheed for use in the new planes, train the pilots, assign top officers to help Bissell manage the program, support operations overseas, and provide other technical and logistical assistance.

When the discussion turned to financing questions, specifically

which agency was going to pay Lockheed for the airplanes (not including the engines and camera systems), Bissell realized everyone around
the table was looking at him. "I got the point pretty quickly and said I
would recommend to Dulles that funding for the project be provided
from the C.I.A.'s contingency reserve." The reserve, which was used for
covert activities, was replenished periodically by Congress, and expenditures from it had to be authorized in advance by the director of the
Bureau of the Budget and approved by the president, but the account
was not subject to the same scrutiny as other Executive Branch budgets.
No written record of an expenditure, for example, was required. The
arrangements allowed for quickness and flexibility and ensured greater
secrecy, but also created opportunities for misuse that the CIA would
exploit in future years to pay for questionable programs in other areas.

The project was code-named Aquatone. On December 1, Bissell gave
Johnson verbal approval to move ahead with the project. Johnson hoped
to get the first plane into the air by summertime. One of the most audacious aircraft and intelligence projects of the century was finally under
way.

PART TWO

A New Spy Plane Takes Flight

1954–1956

CHAPTER SIX

The Role of a Lifetime

Richard M. Bissell Jr., who was forty-five years old when he took charge of what became the U-2 program, had never built an airplane before, and knew little about engineering and reconnaissance technology. But he had played a key role in managing two highly complex and important projects. During World War II, he had helped to direct the movement of American supply convoys across the Atlantic. After the war, he ran the day-to-day operations of the Marshall Plan, the American aid program in Western Europe. He was an exceptionally quick study and an effective executive who liked to move fast, delegate responsibility, and dispense with the paperwork and stratified decision-making that hobbled most federal agencies. He also didn't mind taking risks. Bissell proved to be an inspired choice to carry the CL-282 and its new camera and film system from the drawing boards to the skies over Moscow.

Bissell, who died in 1994, was a giant of the cold war, a man both admired and vilified for his work at the vortex of the conflict. Mostly, he is remembered as the eccentric mastermind of the failed 1961 Bay of Pigs invasion of Cuba, a misadventure that humiliated John F. Kennedy within months of his inauguration and swiftly led to Bissell's inglorious departure from the CIA. As chief of the Agency's covert operations from 1959 to 1962, Bissell was also the sponsor of some of the CIA's most cold-blooded—and boneheaded—overseas plots, including a series of bizarre assassination schemes against Fidel Castro, the Cuban leader.

Along with other early leaders of the spy organization, Bissell personified a blend of aristocratic idealism and arrogance that gave the CIA an enduring image as an agency where zealotry often substituted for sound judgment. Bissell's enthusiasm for clandestine activities of dubious character and purpose has understandably figured prominently in accounts of his role in the cold war. He and his compatriots tolerated a chilling disregard for democratic principles in many of the Agency's operations that cannot be excused by the exigencies of the cold war. They failed to recognize that the United States might damage itself if its intelligence services fought the cold war on Moscow's terms, using assassination, military coups, and other cutthroat techniques. They also underestimated how easily such operations could be bungled or publicly exposed—to the great embarrassment of the CIA and the United States.

Bissell wrestled with these issues years later, perhaps troubled by some of the plots he had condoned and no doubt wounded by the criticism that shadowed him into retirement. In his memoirs, completed and published two years after his death by Jonathan E. Lewis and Frances T. Pudlo, Bissell pondered whether the privileged world of elite boarding schools and Ivy League colleges that produced him and other CIA officers had somehow tainted the formative years of the Agency. "This is difficult to answer," he wrote. "Many of us who joined the CIA did not feel bound in the actions we took as staff members to observe all the ethical rules that we would have observed and regarded as valid before we joined. But in a larger sense, the patriotism, the belief in the need for the United States to play an important role in the world had some of their roots in our upbringing and education, and they certainly did affect the atmosphere in the agency."

It's a frustratingly brief and incomplete answer from a man whose private papers even now remain shielded from public examination by his family and friends.

Because of the controversies about covert operations, and the secrecy that long shrouded the full story of the development of the U-2 and the Corona spy satellite, Bissell—and the CIA—have not received the public recognition they deserve for building the overhead spy machines that helped America manage and ultimately win the cold war. The compact organizations that Bissell put together to oversee the creation of revolutionary new reconnaissance systems were models of crisp, bureaucratic-free management, unlike so many of today's cumbersome government programs. The absence of congressional oversight of the CIA in the 1950s gave him plenty of running room to handle the projects as he pleased.

Bissell, an economist by training, was drawn to the intelligence arena by a combination of social connections, the allure of serving on the front lines of the cold war, and the formidable power of his intellect. He came from an upper-class Connecticut family. His English ancestors first settled in the New World in the seventeenth century in Windsor, Connecticut, not far from Hartford, and one early family member, Sgt. Daniel Bissell, served as a spy for Gen. George Washington. Bissell's grandfather, who lived most of his life in Chicago, and Bissell's father, who brought the family back to Connecticut, enjoyed stable, prosperous careers in the insurance industry, both at the Hartford Fire Company. His father served as president of the company for twenty-five years. His mother, Marie, the daughter of a Midwest railroad executive, was a beautiful, flamboyant woman whose iconoclastic interests and zest for adventure clearly inspired her son. She favored a yellow roadster—not exactly the typical car of a Hartford society matron—enjoyed lively parties, and defied convention by producing a Gertrude Stein play.

Bissell, the youngest of three children, was born on September 18, 1909, in the Mark Twain House on Farmington Avenue in Hartford, a rambling Victorian mansion that Samuel Clemens built and used as his home while residing in the Connecticut capital. It was home to Bissell for nine years. The family summered on the Maine coast, usually in a rented house in Dark Harbor, a settlement on Isleboro, one of the islands in Penobscot Bay. During these summer sojourns, Bissell developed a passion for sailing that was to endure throughout his life. His mother was his instructor and companion as he learned to handle a small sailboat in the unforgiving waters along the Maine coast, where the tides are strong and the weather unpredictable. Marie was not averse to taking risks as she trimmed the sails and steered the boat close to the wind for maximum speed.

In later years, Bissell often turned to the sea for relief from the tensions of Washington, heading out in the *Sea Witch*, his 57-foot yawl. "I had many scrapes aboard her," he told Evan Thomas, a biographer, "but no matter how scary, they were better than the bureaucratic fights." Though he spent his workdays directing the development of state-of-the-art technology, the *Sea Witch* lacked such basic navigational instruments as radar and sonar. Bissell relished the dangers of navigating by the sound of bell buoys in the fog at night. Critics of the CIA's reckless covert operations might have found his hazardous habits at sea an apt analogy for his leadership at the Agency.

As a boy, Bissell was gangly and unathletic. He suffered from severely crossed eyes, a problem not corrected by surgery until he was eight. When he enrolled at Groton, one of New England's elite prep schools, he found himself an outcast, beset by bouts of homesickness. He retreated to the library and the world of the mind, forging lifetime friendships with other loners at the school, including Joseph Alsop, who went on to become one of Washington's most influential conservative pundits, and Louis Auchincloss, a gifted novelist and chronicler of high society. From Groton, he moved to Yale, where he majored in history.

After graduating from Yale in 1932, Bissell spent a year in Britain, studying at the London School of Economics. Impressed by the Keynesian theories taught at the school, he returned to Yale to pursue graduate studies in economics as a believer in government intervention in the economy. He also shed his inherited allegiance to the Republican Party, becoming a Democrat and supporter of Franklin Roosevelt. Bissell developed and taught the first course in Keynesian economics at Yale, a popular undergraduate class that attracted another cluster of students who would eventually hold powerful jobs in Washington, including the Bundy brothers, McGeorge and William. McGeorge Bundy served as John Kennedy's national security adviser. William Bundy was an intelligence analyst at the CIA in the early 1950s and, as an assistant secretary of state in the Johnson years, one of the architects of the Vietnam War.

Bissell collected a Ph.D. in economics from Yale in 1939, after dictating his thesis on the theory of capital at the blistering rate of twenty pages a day, and helped organize the America First Committee at the university to oppose American involvement in the intensifying European conflict. "Although I did not like the Nazi ideology, I felt it posed no invasionary threat to the United States and it did not seem to me sufficiently upsetting to justify going to war. I thought the country's most important goals should be economic." By early 1941, he was reconsidering his views and gladly accepted an offer to move to Washington in October 1941 to join the Commerce Department for a year.

The Japanese attack on Pearl Harbor on December 7, 1941, altered his plans. Within weeks he was recruited to help organize the shipment of munitions and other cargo for American military forces overseas. He was soon assigned to the War Shipping Administration, the Washington agency charged with managing the American merchant fleet. Bissell was asked to develop a forecasting system that could accurately predict when ships would be available at American and foreign ports to pick up war supplies. This was long before the age of computers. Working with a staff of four aides and card files that listed every available ship, he managed to produce forecasts three months in advance that were 95 percent accurate. It was clear that Bissell had a knack for government work and an ability to handle complex and important assignments.

The job also gave Bissell a taste of high-powered statecraft. He was a staff aide on the American delegation to the Yalta Conference in February 1945, where Roosevelt, Churchill, and Stalin discussed postwar spheres of influence in Europe. Bissell also attended the Potsdam Conference outside Berlin that summer. By then, the war in Europe was over and he came away from the uneasy talks between Truman and Stalin convinced that the wartime alliance between Washington and Moscow was disintegrating.

For the next year or so, Bissell worked at the Office of War Mobilization and Reconversion and the Office of Economic Stabilization as the Truman administration struggled to reconvert the American economy to peacetime conditions. He and his wife had settled in Georgetown, where they moved easily in a social circle that included several men who were destined to play leading roles in the CIA, including Frank Wisner, who became the Agency's first chief of covert operations, and Sherman Kent, the preeminent intelligence analyst of Soviet affairs. Bissell also developed friendships with Desmond Fitzgerald and Tracy Barnes, two other early satraps at the Agency. Still, he was eager to return to academic life. The Massachusetts Institute of Technology had held open a position for Bissell in its economics department since 1942. He and his family moved to Cambridge in September 1946.

He didn't stay for long. A call in July 1947 from Averell Harriman, Truman's secretary of commerce and the heir to the Union Pacific Railroad fortune, drew Bissell into a central role in the administration of the Marshall Plan. He described the period in his memoirs as "perhaps the most worthwhile years of my career," a statement that seemed to reflect both his genuine enthusiasm about the Marshall Plan and some ambivalence about his later work for the CIA. Bissell's job, during the fall of 1947, was to direct the preparation of a report by a committee of prominent Americans on the merits of a European aid program. The committee, headed by Harriman, who had served as ambassador to the Soviet Union during World War II, helped galvanize public and congressional support for the recovery plan, which had been proposed by Secretary of State George Marshall. Once Congress approved the Marshall Plan in April 1948, Bissell was summoned back to Washington again, this time to help run the Economic Cooperation Administration, the new government agency created by Congress to distribute the assistance and see that it was used constructively.

The post placed Bissell at the controls of what was certainly one of the most generous and enlightened programs by any country since the formation of the first nation-states. The United States, of course, was looking after its own interests by helping Europe recover from the war with an infusion of $13.3 billion over four years, the equivalent of more than $99 billion in today's dollars. The continent's economic desolation invited political unrest and provided fertile conditions for the spread of Communism. The future security and prosperity of the United States clearly depended in no small measure on the reconstruction of Europe, including the revival of free markets and the restoration of stable, democratic governments. By those standards, the Marshall Plan was a remarkably farsighted and effective act of self-interest. But on a more human scale, it was also a compassionate program that helped millions of destitute people rebuild their lives, businesses, and neighborhoods.

It's easy to see how Bissell moved easily from one method of combating Communism to another. The Marshall Plan was America's overt program to prevent the Soviet Union from extending its influence into Western Europe. The CIA ran clandestine activities with the same goal. Indeed, the degree of separation seemed so slight to Bissell that his initiation in the spy game came while he was at the Marshall Plan. In 1949, he diverted money from the Economic Cooperation Administration to support Washington's intelligence activities in Europe. The request, not surprisingly, came from Frank Wisner, who was then head of the Office of Policy Coordination, the blandly named State Department agency that was responsible for covert activities before they were transferred to the CIA. Wisner informed Bissell that Harriman had approved the transfer.

Bissell's recollection of the encounter with Wisner nicely captures the mingling of business and social connections that helped propel Bissell into the CIA a few years later. "Although I don't remember having had any previous contact with him on official business, I had met him socially and knew and trusted him because of mutual friends like Joe Alsop." The funds came from matching contributions that European countries made to the Marshall Plan in their national currency. According to Bissell, nearly all the European money—95 percent of it—was used for reconstruction. The remaining 5 percent went into a fund to help pay the administrative costs of the plan. Bissell dipped into that account for Wisner. He speculated, probably correctly, that some of the money that he gave Wisner may have found its way to the same political parties and labor unions that were already benefiting more directly from the Marshall Plan.

It wasn't long before Bissell himself migrated to the CIA. In early 1952, as the Marshall Plan wound down, Bissell accepted a job offer from the Ford Foundation, which was headed by Paul Hoffman, the former director of the Economic Cooperation Administration. Bissell's arrangement with the foundation allowed him to do consulting jobs on the side, and he soon started advising the CIA on various issues, meeting periodically at Princeton University with other Agency consultants.

Through the Marshall Plan, he had met Eleanor Dulles, who worked at the German desk at the State Department. She was the sister of Allen Dulles and John Foster Dulles, who would soon become Eisenhower's secretary of state. Eleanor Dulles, in turn, had introduced Bissell to her brothers. By late 1953, Allen Dulles was pressing Bissell to come work full time for the CIA. The Georgetown dinner circuit gave them the perfect opportunity to talk. "One evening at a fairly large dinner party hosted by Stewart Alsop," Bissell recalled, "I took Dulles's arm as he was leaving and mentioned that the special economics project I had been working on at the Ford Foundation was about to end and I was going to have to find a new position. He told me to come see him before I committed myself otherwise."

As a rising star in Washington and the academic world, Bissell could doubtless have had his choice of top government jobs, including a post at the State Department. But like other men and women considering government careers in the early 1950s, especially national security jobs, Bissell had to reckon with the specter of McCarthyism. There was nothing in his background that would attract suspicion, but he knew that the witch-hunts were terrorizing government agencies. The State Department was one of the most grievously wounded victims, in large part because John Foster Dulles had failed to stand his ground against McCarthy's attacks on the diplomatic corps, including several of Bissell's friends. Indeed, the secretary of state had hired one of McCarthy's aides to investigate subversion at the department. Allen Dulles, by contrast, refused to let himself be intimidated by McCarthy.

Bissell signed on with the CIA in February 1954 as special assistant to Dulles. It was a loosely defined job that quickly exposed him to a variety of Agency activities, including the successful coup d'état that the CIA engineered in Guatemala in the summer of 1954. The removal of Jacobo Arbenz as Guatemala's president was the high-water mark of the Agency's cold war efforts to rearrange foreign governments to suit American interests. Bissell helped to direct propaganda operations that supported the coup, including radio broadcasts and leaflet drops.

A year earlier, in August 1953, the CIA had directed a coup in Iran that replaced a left-leaning leader, Mohammed Mossadegh, with a young, pro-Western strongman, Mohammad Reza Shah Pahlavi. Confident that such covert operations were an effective way to enhance American security, the Agency, with Eisenhower's blessing, applied the same techniques in Guatemala. In both cases, the immediate objective—the installation of a leader friendly to America—was attained. But the cost for both Iran and Guatemala over the ensuing decades was severe. Guatemala was ruled by a succession of military dictators cynically supported by the United States. The Shah, though a modernizing force in Iran in some respects, relied on repression to stifle political dissent and was overthrown by Islamic fundamentalists in the 1979 revolution led by Ayatollah Ruhollah Khomeini.

Bissell came to see the downside himself, though he remained convinced that toppling foreign leaders in cases like Guatemala was a legitimate exercise of American power. "As to the question of overthrowing a foreign sovereign government, I would approve the same action today without hesitation," he noted in his memoirs. "With hindsight, however, I would be more cautious in estimating what would happen as a result of this kind of intervention and whether it was really in the best interests of the United States."

Fresh from his troubleshooting role for Dulles during the Guatemala operation, and still relatively untested in the spy business, Bissell suddenly found himself running the Agency's most important and urgent enterprise when Dulles handed him the CL-282 on November 26, 1954. For Bissell, it was the role of a lifetime. The order to build the plane came directly from the president. In Killian and Land he had powerful defenders who could ensure that he got the full cooperation of the Air Force and other agencies. Kelly Johnson was eager to make good on his promise to rewrite the laws of high-altitude flight and Jim Baker was already at work on a new camera system. Bissell's job was to synchronize all the pieces and to produce a radical new spy plane in record time—less than eight months.

Bissell's brief meeting with Dulles on the day after Thanksgiving abruptly changed his routine. Instead of fielding a variety of assignments from Dulles, most dealing with traditional espionage matters, Bissell was now running the most technologically advanced project the CIA had ever tackled. He knew almost nothing about aerodynamic engineering, aerial navigation, aviation fuels, and the risks associated with operating a manned aircraft at an altitude of 70,000 feet. Indeed, there was almost no one at the Agency who had experience in these areas because Allen Dulles and his aides had never imagined they might be ordered to build and operate their own elite air force.

"Because all the discussions had been conducted at such a high level of the executive branch," Bissell said, "nobody had really worked out how anything was to be done. Nobody knew where the money was coming from. Nobody knew how much it would cost. Nobody knew who would procure the aircraft. Nobody had even given any thought where it could develop, where flight testing could be done, where people could be trained or by whom, who would fly it or anything."

But Bissell did know how to construct and manage an efficient organization, and within hours of his conversation with Dulles he was drawing on his experience in the Marshall Plan and World War II shipping to build an agile, informal, and largely self-contained outfit. Because the program was considered so sensitive, Project Aquatone was set up as a stand-alone operation, with its own office space, staff, security, and even its own communications systems. The staff, composed of CIA aides and a contingent of skilled Air Force officers, was initially housed in an aging building on E Street, not far from the Lincoln Memorial. But the structure was so rickety that the addition of office machinery made the floor unstable. Bissell temporarily transferred the operation to sturdier quarters down the street and eventually moved to a nondescript downtown office building, across the street from the Metropolitan Club. For years, the capital's lawyers, lobbyists, and journalists went about their business on the 1700 block of H Street N.W. without any inkling that one of the most secret spy operations of the cold war was headquartered on the fifth floor of the Matomic Building at 1717 H Street N.W.

Realizing that the CIA lacked experts to oversee the highly technical work that would be done by Lockheed, as well as Kodak and the other subcontractors, Bissell relied heavily on top aides throughout the life of the spy-plane program, including a number of officers and civilians assigned to the project by the Air Force. He developed an especially close and effective partnership with Gen. Osmond Ritland of the Air Force, who served as the deputy director of the spy-plane project and a later advanced technology program that Bissell ran. The top management team included James Cunningham and John Parangosky of the CIA and Leo Geary, Stanley Beerli, and Gene Kiefer of the Air Force. Bissell also left many of the details to Kelly Johnson and his industry counterparts. "I had no technical background for this task and had to learn as I went along. The technical decisions were pretty largely left to the contractor, primarily Johnson, and, to a degree, to Pratt & Whitney."

Though unavoidable, it was still a daring strategy that removed the CIA from the kind of close supervision that federal agencies preferred, and it gave private companies wide latitude in how they spent the money Washington was providing. Duplicating the relationship today would be all but impossible, given the size of government and corporate bureaucracies and the congressional oversight requirements that grew out of a painful history of cost overruns in subsequent defense and intelligence projects and the history of CIA assassination plots uncovered by Congress in the 1970s.

The Bissell approach was unorthodox even by the more relaxed standards of the 1950s. "There weren't a heck of a lot of rules," recalled Bob King, a CIA staff member who was assigned to the project as the first planes were being flight tested in 1955 and later served as Bissell's executive officer. The free-wheeling style was vintage Bissell. One day when he was driving the wrong way down a one-way street in Washington with his secretary, he told her not to worry. "Why bother with the rule when there are no cars on the street?" he said.

This disdain for the rules carried over to the development project. John McMahon, who worked for Bissell in the late 1950s and went on to become the nation's second-ranking intelligence official, recalls that Bissell was impatient with aides who cited government rules that stood in the way of his plans. "Don't come in and tell me we can't do it," he would say. "Your job is to use the regulations and laws to permit me to do it."

Stan Beerli, who as an Air Force colonel served as one of Bissell's closest aides, saw the same spirit. "The only regulations we had were the ones we made up ourselves to get the mission done."

Bissell also used his temper as a rapier. McMahon remembers attending a budget meeting with Bissell where the finance officer fumbled with his papers and couldn't answer a question. Bissell ordered the aide out of the room and abruptly ended the meeting.

Arthur C. Lundahl, who later worked closely with Bissell as the CIA's chief photo interpreter, found Bissell's methods effective. "He knew how to get things done," Lundahl recalled. "He knew how to twist arms, how to cajole, how to influence, how to make people understand problems, how to convince people, and he was extremely well informed."

Bissell's range of interests and expertise sometimes startled colleagues. Lundahl said that late in the evening, after a full day of dealing with the spy plane, including calls to the White House, Bissell would suddenly set aside his CIA work and start dictating an economics textbook to his secretary.

Believing that Lockheed "could be trusted not to abuse the government's interest," Bissell did without the usual reporting requirements. "We kept our regular monthly progress reports to about five pages," he recalled, in contrast to the stack of paperwork that the Air Force would have demanded from Lockheed over the same period.

The high degree of secrecy surrounding the program eliminated layers of decision-making. Though Bissell reported to Dulles and his deputy, General Cabell, he made most decisions autonomously. "I worked behind a barrier of secrecy that protected my decision-making from interference," he said. Normally, copies of all CIA cable traffic about important matters were sent to the director's office. In this case, Bissell directed his staff to send Dulles only the cables that seemed to have policy implications and not to forward communications traffic about the construction and testing of the new airplane.

When Bissell was flummoxed by a technical or bureaucratic problem, he would consult with Land. The two men talked frequently, usually several times a week. They were an unlikely duo. Bissell was tall and rumpled, Land short and neat. One came from a family of affluence and social cachet, the other from an immigrant background. Bissell was a government manager, Land an independent inventor. But they were both exceedingly smart and shared a powerful desire to help their country win the cold war.

"When things were going bad, Bissell turned to Land," Bob King said. "Bissell's secretary, Doris, would often tell me when the boss was upset, 'It's going to be better, he's talking to Land, he's always better after he talks to him.'"

Bissell and Kelly Johnson were another unlikely pair. Though they were both men with combustible tempers who could not have come from more different backgrounds, they developed a cordial and informal working relationship. Bissell told Johnson his expectations were simple: "When you face a decision, I want to know about it, I want to pass judgment on it. But I've got to rely on you to tell me the potential consequences and costs of these decisions."

The two men did most of their business by phone. Johnson would sketch out the question or problem to Bissell and after a brief discussion would get a quick decision. The same curiosity that had drawn Bissell to the study of complex economic issues propelled him into an intensive series of tutorials about the technical aspects of the CL-282. He frequently quizzed Johnson, Land, and Baker as the project proceeded. Johnson found that Bissell "quickly became very knowledgeable on engineering matters." Bob King remembers Johnson and Bissell talking in detail about the tensile strength of titanium in one conversation. "Bissell loved that stuff," King said.

Bissell could also be a quirky, difficult boss. He inspired his staff more by intellectual brilliance than personal warmth. Though his manners were refined, and he could be charming, Bissell often seemed aloof and a bit awkward in his interactions with colleagues. "He was a gentleman," Bob King said. "But he wasn't much for small talk, especially at work. There, it was always business."

Bissell stood well over 6 feet tall and was famous at the Agency for walking so fast that his aides had to trot alongside to keep up. Despite the repair work on his crossed eyes when he was young, one eyeball would sometimes drift out of alignment with the other. Though he came from an affluent family, his work wardrobe consisted of two or three dark suits that were perpetually rumpled, and he drove a dilapidated car.

He was a restless figure behind his cluttered desk, constantly fidgeting with paper clips or the handkerchief he kept in his pocket. Because of a chronic sinus problem, he would periodically inhale loudly through his nose. Aides who were invited to Bissell's spacious home in Cleveland Park, a woodsy Washington neighborhood where he and his family had moved in the early 1950s, were astonished by the chaos. Betty King, Bob King's wife and herself a CIA employee, remembered coming to Sunday brunch and finding the Bissell family dog tied up to the leg of the stove and piles of laundry cascading down the staircase. Ann Bissell served steak and kidney pie, not exactly a Washington favorite.

For all his eccentricity and awkwardness, Bissell was extremely effective at motivating people. The project, of course, sold itself. The technology was new. The idea of sending an American plane over the interior of the Soviet Union was electrifying. But Bissell, brimming with self-confidence and a writ from the president to sweep away bureaucratic impediments, lent the project an air of invincibility that energized his staff.

He also sensed how to get the best work out of Kelly Johnson. Instead of giving Lockheed technical specifications for the new plane, which would have consisted of pages of detailed requirements, Bissell and his aides settled for less precise performance guidelines. That freed Johnson to follow his creative instincts. An initial letter of agreement between the Agency and the company was signed by the end of December 1954. After some negotiation between Johnson and Lawrence R. Houston, the CIA's general counsel, Lockheed and the Agency signed a formal contract on March 22, 1955. It committed the company to deliver the first of twenty planes in July. The expected cost for the fleet was $22 million. That did not include engines, which the Air Force would provide, or the camera equipment, which the CIA would pay for separately.

Even before the contract was signed, Bissell had started transferring funds to Lockheed, writing two checks for a total of $1.2 million. To maintain secrecy, and to keep the payments off the Agency's regular books, Bissell made out the checks to a fictitious company. The payments were mailed to Johnson's home in Encino, a suburb of Los Angeles. Johnson, in turn, deposited the checks in a local bank account he had established for the sham company. By early 1955, the CL-282 was taking form in the aircraft assembly area at Burbank.

CHAPTER SEVEN

"This Thing Is Made Out of Toilet Paper"

K ELLY JOHNSON had wasted no time gearing up for the project after Washington gave its approval. Even before Bissell called Johnson on December 1, 1954, to confirm that he should proceed with the project, the plane designer had started putting together an engineering team. On Friday, November 26, the day after Thanksgiving, he had summoned five of Lockheed's top engineers to his office, including Edward Baldwin and Elmer Gath, to tell them about the secret project.

Ben Rich, who had been working at Lockheed for four years as a thermodynamicist, vividly recalled the December day when he was unexpectedly invited to meet with Johnson in Building 82, the old bomber production hangar that housed the Skunk Works. Rich's specialty was dealing with the heat problems generated by high-speed flight and refining the designs for inlet and exhaust ducts on jet engines. One of Johnson's aides had told Rich he would be moving to Johnson's shop to help modify engines for a new plane that would make the kind of long-distance, high-altitude flights that no aircraft had ever flown.

Rich found Johnson in shirtsleeves seated behind a large wooden desk. "This project is so secret," Johnson told him, "that you may have a six-month to one-year hole in your résumé that can never be filled in." Johnson then described the project. "We are building a very special airplane that will fly at least fifteen thousand feet higher than any Russian fighter or missile, so it will be able to fly all across Russia, hopefully undetected, and send back beautiful picture postcards for Ike."

Johnson instructed Rich to get to work on the engine inlets and to start thinking about cabin heating and cooling as well as hydraulics and fuel control for the plane. Rich was assigned to a second-floor office occupied by six other engineers. The windows, like those throughout the hangar, were sealed and blacked-out to ensure security. Nearly everyone was a smoker, so the air in most offices was a perpetual haze. Rich expected to stay for no more than six months. He remained at the Skunk Works for thirty-six years, and took over the operation in 1975 after Johnson retired.

Rich was part of a rapidly expanding team of twenty-five engineers that Johnson assembled in the days before Christmas. They were soon working sixty-five hours a week, under strict instructions to tell no one about their work, including their families. Johnson noted in his log: "Talked to each man on the project to impress them with the necessity for speed and secrecy. It is extremely difficult to pull these engineers from other projects at this time, particularly in that I cannot tell anyone why."

The secrecy extended to all aspects of the project. Parts for the aircraft were shipped to another site in the San Fernando Valley that had no ostensible connections to Lockheed, and Skunk Works employees were ordered to use aliases when making business trips. If suppliers raised questions about unusual orders, they received a visit from CIA security officers. That happened when executives at the Kollmann Instrument Company expressed puzzlement about an order for altimeters calibrated to 80,000 feet. The normal maximum altitude was 45,000 feet. After discussions with the CIA, Kollmann executives responded to questions about the altimeters by saying they were being built for an experimental rocket plane.

In a creative departure from conventional security practices, the engineering drawings and other paperwork for the project were not marked SECRET, so they would not attract attention if they were seen by anyone who lacked a clearance to work on the plane.

The Skunk Works' crew and the subcontractors for the airplane faced monumental challenges as they struggled to translate Johnson's design plan into a working aircraft and then put it through test flights. Because of the high operating altitude set for the plane, nearly every component had to be specially engineered to perform in the thin air at the fringe of outer space. Pratt & Whitney, which made the J57 engines, modified various parts, including the alternator, oil cooler, and hydraulic pump, for high-altitude operation. Even so, the initial engines proved unreliable in the upper atmosphere when the first operational aircraft were put through a series of test flights later that year. As pilots made the last phase of their climb above 57,000 feet, the engines often flamed out with a loud bang, the aviation equivalent of a car engine stalling. The pilots called this unpredictable zone of ascent the "badlands" or the "the chimney." When they lost power, pilots were forced to glide down to around 35,000 feet to restart their engines. That was unnerving enough during test flights. If it happened over the Soviet Union it would leave the plane vulnerable to attack as it descended. Pratt & Whitney eventually substituted a more powerful and dependable engine in 1956, before the first flights over the Soviet Union.

Fuel was another obstacle. At 70,000 feet, normal jet fuel would either boil off or evaporate because of the low air pressure. Johnson had to get a new fuel formulated and manufactured. He sought help from Gen. James Doolittle, the retired Air Force commander who in 1955 served as vice president of Shell Oil Company and was a member of the Killian commission. Shell produced a low-volatility, low-vapor-pressure kerosene fuel known as LF-1A. It had a boiling point of 300 degrees at sea level and was so stable that it could not be ignited with a match. The fuel incorporated a number of petroleum by-products, including several used in a popular commercial insecticide called Flit. As Shell diverted the chemicals to the special fuel, it had to curtail production of the bug spray. Consumers across the country who wondered why there was a shortage of Flit on store shelves in 1955 had no idea that the cause was a secret spy-plane project.

The oil system on the plane presented a different problem. Because of the low atmospheric pressure at cruising altitude, oil tended to leak through the seals on the J57 engine, corrupting the cabin air-conditioning and defogging mechanisms. The leakage could deplete the entire 64-quart oil supply during a long flight. But even short of such a catastrophic outcome, the slow oozing of oil into the defogging system left the cockpit canopy covered with a film of oil. Before this problem was solved with the introduction of the new engine in 1956, Johnson equipped pilots with a diaper cloth attached to a long stick that they could use to clean the windshield. Another temporary, and unsuccessful, fix involved splicing a makeshift filter into the defogger line. The filter consisted of a small metal box stuffed with sanitary napkins.

Johnson's design called for the lightest possible airframe—the fuselage, wings, and tail section—to allow for long-distance, high-altitude flights. Every pound added to the plane's weight would sacrifice a foot in altitude. Light materials like aluminum were used wherever possible. As Johnson's crew started to assemble the aircraft, they were startled by the fragility of the airframe. Workers joked that the plane was made out of Reynolds Wrap.

The weight of the elongated wings was kept to 4 pounds per square foot, a stunningly low figure. Bob Ericson, one of the men who piloted the plane, couldn't believe how flimsy the wings seemed. He recalled, "You picked the wing up and it bent, and—holy smokes—you know, this thing is made out of toilet paper."

The long, narrow gliderlike wings, designed to give the plane added lift and to carry enough fuel for extended flights, were the plane's most distinctive feature, and the most problematic. The wingspan was roughly 70 feet, exceptionally large for an aircraft that was about 44 feet long. When Edward Baldwin plotted out the wing design on his drawing board, following Johnson's commands, he couldn't believe his boss wanted something so long and thin.

"Are you sure you want a wing that looks like this?" Baldwin asked Johnson.

"That's about right," Johnson replied.

Baldwin then informed him that his drawing board couldn't accommodate drafting paper large enough to show the full length.

"Put a little patch of paper up there to show what it looks like," Johnson said. "Then you'll have to redraw it because the blueprint machine won't handle anything wider than 42 inches."

The wings were so long they drooped toward the runway at either end, and during taxiing and takeoff had to be held up at midwing by wheeled struts that detached as the aircraft lifted off. These devices were known as "pogos" at Lockheed. If the pilot failed to trigger their release properly, or the automatic mechanism that was later added did not work, the plane was not safe to fly. In one case, the plane stalled as the pilot circled back to the airstrip to drop a hanging pogo. He was killed in the crash.

The wings housed a set of fuel tanks, allowing the plane at full load to carry 1,350 gallons of the special Shell blend. It was clear to everyone that air turbulence, especially at lower altitudes where the atmosphere was heavier, could intensify the natural swaying of the wings to the point where they might tear free of the fuselage. To reduce this danger, Johnson set the horizontal stabilizers and ailerons, the wing flaps that control the rolling and banking movements, so that the plane would fly with its nose slightly raised, making it less vulnerable to the stresses caused by wind gusts.

When Johnson had bowed to Air Force demands that he abandon his plan to land the plane on its belly rather than on conventional landing gear, he still hoped to get by with as light a landing system as possible. His solution was two lightweight wheels at the front of the aircraft and two smaller wheels beneath the tail. This design worked in tandem with the pogos to keep the plane level during takeoff, but left the plane prone to tipping to one side or the other as it slowed down after landing. He handled this problem by attaching small landing skids to the wingtips. As the aircraft came to a stop, one wing or the other would tip down until the skid made contact with the tarmac. It wasn't elegant, but it worked.

One of the most daunting challenges facing Johnson and his colleagues was creating a life-sustaining environment for the pilots. The problem was simple to articulate but difficult to solve: Human beings die almost instantly at 65,000 feet. There is not enough oxygen to sustain life. The air temperature is 70 degrees below zero Fahrenheit. And, as if that weren't enough, the fluids in the human body, including the blood, vaporize in the low air pressure. Pilots had to be provided with a life-support system that would not only allow them to operate the aircraft during long flights over Soviet territory, but would also make it possible for them to survive a sudden decompression and bailout at high altitude, if the plane malfunctioned or was disabled by Soviet air defense forces. Johnson needed a reliably pressurized cockpit and oxygen-breathing system to sustain life over a prolonged flight and a special pressure suit that would enable a pilot to live through an abrupt decompression.

These were complementary solutions to the same basic problem, namely maintaining a safe balance between the pressure inside a human body and the external pressure around it. If this balance is drastically altered, the results can be lethal. When external pressure greatly exceeds internal pressure—conditions that would typically occur deep under water—an unprotected body can be crushed. At high altitudes, as outside air pressure diminishes and pilots are forced to inhale large amounts of canned oxygen, the opposite danger develops. In extreme conditions—like those the CL-282 would routinely encounter—an unprotected body would expand or even explode.

At sea level, of course, the pressure balance is normal and no one gives the issue much thought. In modern commercial jetliners, cabin pressure is maintained at about the comfortable equivalent of 8,000 feet as the plane cruises at 35,000 to 40,000 feet. Oxygen is mixed into the air circulating in the plane, and there is no perceptible change in the pressure balance inside and outside the bodies of the passengers and crew. But the stresses involved in operating a high-performance aircraft at much higher altitudes are not as easily solved. That was especially true in the early 1950s, when jet planes were still a novelty. The CL-282 was going to stretch the boundaries of jet flight and human survival at extremely high altitudes.

It was impractical, if not impossible, at the time to design a pressurized cockpit for the CL-282 that would maintain Denver-like conditions inside the cabin while the plane was flying at 65,000 feet. Johnson settled for a cockpit that would mimic the environment at 28,000 feet, roughly the equivalent of the summit of Mount Everest. At that level, pilots would require a steady source of pure oxygen for breathing. That could be provided through a domelike helmet that enclosed the head.

For pilots to be able to inhale enough oxygen, the air pressure inside the helmet had to be elevated slightly above the norm at sea level. As long as cabin pressure was maintained at the equivalent of 28,000 feet in altitude, the additional pressure in the helmet posed no danger because a pilot's body would not expand in those conditions. But Johnson knew that if cabin pressure failed when the plane was flying above 50,000 feet, the pressure equilibrium would be shattered. The air pressure in the cockpit would plunge and the oxygen flowing into the pilot's helmet would automatically increase sharply to force the pilot to inhale the greater amount of oxygen he needed to maintain consciousness. At that critical point, the pilot's body would become dangerously distended unless it could be tightly squeezed by a special garment known as a pressure suit.

Cabin depressurization would probably happen in an instant, the result of a sudden rupture of the cockpit. This potentially deadly event is known as explosive decompression. A full-pressure suit, when activated, basically substitutes for a pressurized cabin by enclosing the pilot in a protective shell that maintains safe air-pressure levels immediately around the body while leaving enough flexibility of movement to operate the aircraft. The most elaborate full-pressure suits today are the space suits used by astronauts when they operate outside the space shuttle or space station. Less bulky full-pressure suits are commonly used by military pilots. In 1955, the best Johnson could hope for was a partial-pressure suit, an awkward garment that simply tightened mechanically around the limbs and torso of a pilot in an emergency to prevent the pilot's body from expanding. It was like wearing a jumpsuit that suddenly contracted.

To deal with these unconventional problems, Lockheed and the CIA turned to a number of adventurous men who had done groundbreaking—and in some cases life-risking—work in designing equipment to sustain life at high altitudes. Several of them went on to play important support roles in the manned space program that began in earnest in the late 1950s. Some of the work done for the CIA's first generation of spy pilots was later adapted for the space suits used by Alan Shepard, John Glenn, Wally Schirra, and the other Mercury astronauts.

The physical demands of high-altitude flight were broadly recognized but not fully understood as the prototype CL-282 started to take shape in Building 82 in Burbank. The perils of ascending into the upper levels of the atmosphere had been clear since men had first ventured aloft in balloons in the eighteenth century. Early generations of airplanes lacked pressurized cabins. As airplanes were adapted for military use during World War I, it was customary for pilots to operate at altitudes between 16,000 and 18,000 feet in open cockpits. Disorientation from lack of oxygen was common, as was hypothermia from the cold. The first oxygen systems and heated flight suits were developed for military pilots during the later stages of the war. Further advances came over the next two decades as pilots sought to fly higher and higher.

The first widely used pressurized cabin was introduced in 1937 in a modified Lockheed Model 10 Electra. It allowed crew and passengers to travel above 30,000 feet in normal clothing without oxygen equipment. These technologies had advanced far enough by 1954 to make flight at midrange altitudes fairly routine. Hal Austin and other Strategic Air Command fliers, for example, operated routinely above 40,000 feet in the pressurized cabins of their state-of-the-art bombers and reconnaissance planes.

But Kelly Johnson wanted to take the technology to an entirely new level. He needed not only to keep pilots alive while flying above 65,000 feet for eight to ten hours, but also to come up with a way to ensure their survival if they had to bail out of the plane at that altitude and descend to earth by parachute. Dr. William Randolph Lovelace II, an expert in aviation medicine, and Col. Donald D. Flickinger, a physician who studied high-altitude bailouts, advised the CIA to commission the David Clark Company of Worcester, Massachusetts, to develop a new pressure suit.

The David Clark Company in 1955 seemed an unlikely supplier for a top-secret technology project. The company, established in the 1930s, was primarily a manufacturer of girdles and brassieres. Its red, wood-frame factory at 360 Park Avenue in central Worcester was staffed mostly by seamstresses. But the company had edged into military work during the war after rubber, a key component of its lingerie products, was declared to be a strategic material restricted for military use. Without rubber, the company turned to making tents and parachutes. David Clark, the company founder, also got into the business of designing and making gravity suits, or G-suits, for pilots that would help limit the body-stretching forces generated by rapid acceleration. By the late 1940s, the company was making partial-pressure suits for the nation's top military test pilots.

It was not long after Chuck Yeager broke the sound barrier in 1947 that Joseph A. Ruseckas joined the company to help it develop more advanced pressure suits. When the CIA contracted with the Clark Company in 1955 to make new suits for the CL-282 pilots, he became the point man for the project, though he was not told at the time that he was making outfits for the intelligence agency. Indeed, Ruseckas did not know the real names of the pilots he fitted for partial-pressure suits or the kind of aircraft and mission they would be flying. It was only after he witnessed a series of pressure chamber tests at Wright-Patterson AFB that Ruseckas realized his pressure suits might be destined for use over the Soviet Union. The tip-off was the duration of the tests—pilots had to remain in the chamber more than four hours in conditions similar to those after an explosive decompression at 65,000 feet. That told Ruseckas that the pilots and pressure suits were being tested for prolonged missions over denied territory in a crippled aircraft.

Each suit produced by the David Clark Company was custom measured and tailored for a specific pilot. An exact fit was required to ensure that the suit would contract tightly when activated. The fabric was a blend of nylon and cotton—the nylon provided strength while the cotton made the outfit more comfortable against the skin. Even so, the suits were hot and quickly became soaked with sweat during flights.

The key to the model S-2 suit was a set of capstans, or inflatable tubes, that were sewn into the garment. When activated after a sudden drop in external air pressure, the capstans would expand, drawing the suit more tightly around the crewman. During Ruseckas's first years at Clark, the Navy was the main customer, as it outfitted test pilots. A new customer appeared in 1955 when Colonel Flickinger visited Worcester and placed an order on behalf of the CIA. Company executives only told Ruseckas that he could expect to see several test pilots from Lockheed who would need to be fitted with the best partial-pressure suits the company could make. Not a word was said about a new spy plane.

As Ruseckas became more aware of the extreme conditions the pilots might face, he added an expandable chest bladder to the suit at the suggestion of a colleague. It was designed to expand when pilots were exhaling to help them breath more easily if cabin pressure failed and the air pressure in the helmets increased. The chest bladder was eventually expanded so that it covered the entire torso.

Even with the improved S-4 suits, pilots still faced the danger of getting "the bends," the life-threatening condition that can develop after a rapid reduction of air pressure. It is caused by the formation of nitrogen bubbles in the blood. To avoid that danger if cabin pressure failed or they had to bail out, pilots breathed oxygen for ninety minutes before takeoff, an exercise that was called prebreathing. The preflight routine produced an incongruous scene at the remote foreign airfields where the planes were based before making flights over the Soviet Union. Before commencing some of the most dangerous aerial missions of the cold war, pilots would don an oxygen mask, settle into a comfortable armchair or lounger, and breath pure oxygen for ninety minutes.

While the various pieces of the CL-282 puzzle were being assembled, Bissell and Johnson turned to the problem of finding a suitable test site. Secrecy required that the airfield be far from public view and secure from any unauthorized access, either by land or air. But the site needed to be within reasonable flying time from the Lockheed complex in Burbank. Edwards Air Force Base, located on the western edge of the Mojave Desert, about 90 miles north of Los Angeles, had already secured a place in aviation history as the site where Yeager shattered the sound barrier in 1947 in a Bell X-1 plane. But Edwards was considered to be too close to civilian population centers. The same concern ruled out the airstrip at a Lockheed assembly plant in Palmdale, California, not far from Edwards.

Johnson assigned Lockheed's top test pilot, Tony LeVier, and Dorsey Kammerer, a logistics specialist at the Skunk Works, to find a good place. Using a Beech Bonanza, a single-engine aircraft, they surveyed possible sites in the interior deserts of California and Nevada.

On April 12, 1955, Bissell and Gen. Ritland, the senior Air Force officer assigned to the spy-plane project, joined LeVier and Johnson for an inspection flight to a dry lakebed north of Las Vegas, not far from the government's nuclear test range. Ritland was familiar with the area from earlier service with a B-29 test squadron, which had dropped nuclear weapons over the range. Ritland recalled an abandoned World War II airfield near Groom Lake. The hard lakebed appeared large enough and firm enough to handle the long landing strip that would be required for the CL-282.

Bissell recalled the discovery in his memoirs: "The area near Groom Lake, which seen from the air was approximately three to four miles in diameter and smooth as a billiard table, appeared to Johnson a promising location to accommodate the long landing requirements of the U-2. Descending for a closer look, we saw evidence of a temporary landing strip, the kind of runway that had been built in various locations throughout the United States during World War II for the benefit of pilots in training who might have to make an emergency landing. Faced with the option of landing on this strip or the lakebed, LeVier chose the lakebed. Once on the ground, we walked over to the airstrip to see if it was viable. The closer we got, the deeper we sank into soft, sagebrush-covered soil. Had we attempted to land on it, we most assuredly would have crashed."

The barren, windblown site was a two-hour flight from Burbank, all but hidden among the arid mountains and vast empty spaces of the high Southwest. It seemed ideal. Johnson playfully suggested they call the desolate site Paradise Ranch. The place acquired several other names, including Area 51 and Watertown Strip. The latter was a play on Watertown, New York, Allen Dulles's birthplace. But most people associated with the new spy plane followed Johnson's lead and simply called it The Ranch. When Bissell returned to Washington, he secured Eisenhower's approval to add the landing strip and surrounding area to the nuclear test site of the Atomic Energy Commission, a highly secure swath of Nevada territory. The airspace over the entire nuclear test site was restricted. That would keep civilian and even most military flights from spotting the secret CIA air base.

The air of mystery surrounding the nuclear test site, combined with unidentified flying objects that were occasionally seen high in the skies around the site, made the government reservation the subject of intense speculation. Over the years, Area 51, which encompassed the airfield as well as the surrounding nuclear test site, became famously associated with reports about alien spaceships. Most of the UFO sightings were stimulated by the new Lockheed plane and the subsequent test flights of ever-more-advanced aircraft that the government secretly developed during the cold war. Many of the sightings came at sunset when the lower atmosphere was already cloaked in darkness but the sun could still illuminate a plane flying in the stratosphere. In an era when no one knew the United States was building planes that could fly that high, the sight of the sunlight reflecting off an object streaking across the edge of space led to dozens of alarmed reports, many of them from commercial airline pilots mystified by the view as they flew across the Southwest.

Not long after Bissell and Johnson's inspection trip, a construction company cleared by the CIA began building a road into the site and a small air base, including a new runway, control tower, three hangars, and a mess hall. Wells were dug for water. Summertime temperatures at the lakebed often soared above 120 degrees. One of the subcontractors initially balked at the work after investigating the fictitious firm that Johnson had established as a cover for the project. A subcontractor executive told the prime contractor, "We looked them up in Dun and Bradstreet and they don't even have a credit rating." The base, which cost just $800,000 to build, was ready for use by July, though its wilderness location brought some unusual neighbors for the Lockheed crew, including a bobcat that set up house under one of the offices and a rattlesnake that turned up in the well of an airplane wheel.

Johnson rushed to keep pace with construction and his promise to turn over the first aircraft by summer. Wind-tunnel testing of a model was completed in mid-March, showing the aircraft was aerodynamically sound and capable of handling the flight conditions envisioned for it. To ensure secrecy, the main pieces of the fuselage were fabricated at night at Lockheed's main production plant and moved to the Skunk Works before regular company workers arrived in the morning. The first fuse-

lage was removed from the jig, the fixture used for holding parts together for assembly, in late May. Johnson recorded the milestone in his
log on May 21. "Number one fuselage out of jig. Having a tough time
on wing. Put almost everybody on it."

As Johnson was scrambling to complete the prototype, Soviet fighters
downed another American surveillance aircraft, this time a Navy flight
traveling at an altitude of 8,000 feet over the Bering Strait on June 22.
Three crew members were wounded, but the plane crash-landed safely
in Alaska. Uncharacteristically, Moscow expressed regret for the attack
and offered to pay for half the damages. The Soviet offer was probably
influenced by preparations for a four-power disarmament conference
scheduled in late July in Geneva that would be the first summit meeting
between Soviet and American leaders since the onset of the cold war.

The first CL-282, affectionately known around the Skunk Works as
"Kelly's Angel" but officially labeled article 351, was ready for delivery
by mid-July. "Airplane essentially completed," Johnson noted on July
15. "Terrifically long hours. Everybody almost dead." Six days later the
finished aircraft was readied for transport to Groom Lake. Johnson had
kept his promise to produce an operational aircraft within eight months
of receiving approval to proceed with the project.

The plane now needed an official name, or in military parlance an Air
Force designator. Since it was not a bomber, fighter, or transport plane,
those designations were inappropriate. To maintain secrecy, it could not
be called a reconnaissance aircraft. After some discussion, the Air Force
settled on classifying the plane as a utility aircraft. The aircraft designator handbook listed two utility planes, the U-1 and the U-3. So Kelly
Johnson's new spy plane was dubbed the U-2.

The completion of the first plane came as President Eisenhower was
making a dramatic offer to the Soviet Union that would have made it
possible to dismantle the extraordinary secrecy surrounding the U-2
and send the plane over Soviet territory with the acquiescence of the
Kremlin. The "Open Skies" proposal, which Eisenhower unexpectedly
unveiled on Thursday, July 21, at the Geneva meeting with Soviet,
British, and French leaders, called for Washington and Moscow to per-

mit one another to conduct aerial reconnaissance flights over each other's military installations. For Eisenhower, the idea was directly tied to the U-2, though he never mentioned the aircraft in his conversations with the Russians. "I'll give it one shot," the president had told aides when the plan was being drafted. "Then, if they don't accept, we'll fly the U-2."

Historians still debate Eisenhower's motivations in making an offer that seemed both idealistic and calculating. It was a grand and visionary proposal that in a single stroke could have lessened tensions between the two nations, reduced the danger of surprise attack, and provided a means for verifying arms control agreements, if such accords could be reached. The six-day Geneva gathering at the ornate Palais des Nations was ostensibly arranged so the leaders could talk about disarmament issues. The plan was fully consistent with Eisenhower's desire to put relations with Moscow on a more stable and predictable footing and to diminish the risk of a military miscalculation that could start a war. He seemed to speak from the heart as he addressed the Soviet delegation, which was led by Nikolai A. Bulganin, the prime minister, and Nikita S. Khrushchev, the leader of the Communist Party. "I have been searching my heart and mind for something that I could say here that could convince everyone of the great sincerity of the United States in approaching this problem of disarmament." As Eisenhower finished his presentation, the conference room was shaken by a loud thunderclap and the lights went out.

It is hard to imagine that Eisenhower expected the Soviet leaders to accept the proposal, or that he was unaware of the public relations advantages that would come with a Soviet rejection. Though Bulganin responded positively when his turn came to speak after the electric power had been restored, the American initiative was quickly buried by Khrushchev, who was the paramount Soviet leader. Khrushchev made his contempt clear to Eisenhower when the two men talked as the formal meeting adjourned for the day. Khrushchev, whose primacy in Moscow was not yet clear to American experts, informed Eisenhower that he did not agree with Bulganin and considered the overflight suggestion to be a transparent espionage plot. He later told his son, Sergei, that he be-lieved Washington would use the flights to refine its targeting plans for a nuclear strike against the Soviet Union.

Despite the Soviet response, Eisenhower viewed the conference as "a limited success." As he wrote in his memoirs, "The record was estab-lished: All could now see the nature of Soviet diplomatic tactics as con-trasted with those of the Free World. Peoples had been given a glowing picture of hope and, though it was badly blurred by the Soviets, at least the outlines of the picture remained."

Though the world did not know it, the Soviet rejection of the "Open Skies" proposal cleared the way for the U-2 to commence operations over the Soviet Union less than a year later.

On July 24, the day Eisenhower flew back to Washington, Kelly Johnson loaded the first U-2 aboard a transport plane for shipment to Groom Lake. Transporting the plane for its maiden test flight was no easy maneuver. Since it had to be shielded from public view, and its air worthiness had yet to be proven in flight, it could not be flown out of the Lockheed airstrip in Burbank. So, the aircraft was disassembled and the large pieces were covered in tarpaulins and loaded aboard two mo-bile ground carts. The carts were then placed aboard a C-124 transport in the middle of the night for the flight to Nevada. The recently ap-pointed commander of the new base, Dick Newton, informed Johnson that the loaded C-124 was too heavy to land on the thin, freshly paved tarmac. Johnson flew ahead to Groom Lake in a smaller plane, in-spected the landing strip, and declared that it could handle the transport plane if the air pressure in the tires was reduced. That would spread the weight across a somewhat wider area of runway when the plane landed. Johnson had to get officials in Washington to overrule Newton. The C-124 landed without incident and the two ground carts were rolled out of the plane and into one of the hangars, where the first U-2 was re-assembled and prepared for its maiden flight.

Johnson had selected Tony LeVier to put the plane through its first tests. LeVier, a fearless aviator, was born in Duluth, Minnesota, in 1913, the son of an architect who had immigrated to the United States from Norway. He first climbed into a cockpit at age fifteen and went on to become Lockheed's leading test pilot. Over the years he had piloted more than a dozen of the company's new planes into the air for the first time, including the F-94 Starfire interceptor and the XF-104 Starfighter, a supersonic fighter with unusually short wings and a needle nose that was frequently described as a "missile with a man in it." By the time he retired in 1974, LeVier had flown more than 240 types of airplanes and was a legendary figure in the aviation business.

LeVier had tested the speedy Starfighter a year earlier at Edwards AFB. When Johnson first showed him the blueprints for the U-2, with its long wings, he was amused. "First you have me flying your goddamn F-104, which has the shortest wings ever built, and now you got me flying a big goddamn sailplane with the longest wings I ever saw," he told Johnson.

On July 29, LeVier strapped himself into the cramped cockpit of the U-2 for a series of dry runs alongside the runway. The taxi tests were designed to see how the plane accelerated and to give him some sense of how the aircraft might perform in flight. At the slow ground speed set for the tests, the U-2 was not expected to take off. But on the second run, as LeVier accelerated toward 70 knots, the top speed prescribed by Johnson, the lightweight plane left the ground, thanks to the extraordinary lift provided by the sailplane design. It kept flying with the engine essentially running at idle.

Because of the absence of runway markings and the flat expanse of the lakebed, LeVier did not initially realize he was airborne. "The lakebed was so smooth I couldn't feel when the wheels were no longer touching." Once he discovered he was flying about 35 feet off the ground, he pushed the throttle forward to pick up speed, fearful that the plane would stall and crash at the lower taxi speed. The plane started to shake, a sign of the buffeting that signaled a stall was imminent. LeVier managed to get the plane back on the ground safely, though the hard landing blew out the two main tires and the plane bounced into the air and then rolled for nearly a mile across the lakebed before stopping.

Ernie L. Joiner, the chief flight test engineer for the U-2, watched the bumpy ride with Johnson from a ground vehicle that chased the plane down the runway. "The airplane disappeared in a cloud of dust and sand," he said. "We could see those long flexible wings flapping about. As we frantically chased after it, I thought Kelly was going to have a heart attack."

The overhead brakes, which seemed undersized for the aircraft, erupted in flames as the plane finally came to a stop. Johnson and Joiner roared up to the smoking U-2 and the fire was quickly put out with an extinguisher.

The scene could hardly have been more striking. One of the great airplane designers of his time, and one of the nation's top test pilots, were out in the middle of a vacant, prehistoric lakebed looking over a crippled airplane that at that moment was probably the most important and most secret piece of military hardware in the world.

"Goddamn it, LeVier, what in hell happened?" Johnson shouted.

"Kelly, the son of a bitch took off and I didn't even know it," LeVier replied.

Later that day Johnson noted dryly in his log, "No harm done. Airplane was subjected to terrific test. Pogo sticks worked real well."

The first planned flight came on August 4. Despite the thunderclouds that were forming in the area by midafternoon, LeVier pointed the plane down the runway a few minutes before 4 P.M. Moments later, after a short takeoff roll, the U-2 was airborne and it climbed almost effortlessly to 8,000 feet. "It flies like a baby buggy," LeVier radioed another Lockheed pilot, Bob Matye, who was following the U-2 in a T-33, a two-seat jet trainer that had made its first test flight six years earlier—with Tony LeVier at the controls. Johnson trailed the two planes in a C-47, a twin-propeller military transport.

Because of the threatening weather, the flight was cut short after forty-five minutes. LeVier and Johnson had argued for several days about how best to bring the plane in for a landing. Johnson wanted the plane to touch down nose first on its main landing gears at the front of the fuselage, with the tail up. LeVier figured it would be better to land on the front and rear wheels simultaneously, with the tail down. LeVier had consulted with pilots familiar with the B-47 bomber, which had a similar bicycle-type landing gear. They had advised him not to land on the nose wheel. But Johnson, who was famously obdurate, insisted on his recommendation.

"I came down and tried to put this thing on the nose wheel, like Kelly wanted, ever so gently," LeVier said. "And the moment that airplane touched the ground, it started to go into a porpoise. Well, an airplane can bounce itself to pieces, so I gunned it and straightened it out and went around and made another approach."

Nearly everyone stationed at the base had assembled by the runway to observe the test flight and landing. They watched with mounting concern as LeVier made four more attempts to land the plane according to Johnson's specifications. As LeVier descended each time, Johnson peppered him with instructions on the radio. Every time the plane made contact with the runway, it skipped and bounced back into the air.

Johnson, by this point, was getting frantic. It had started raining and he didn't care to waste any more time experimenting with landing procedures. To dispense with the debate, he ordered LeVier to retract the landing gear and make a belly landing, a flashback to his original concept for the plane.

LeVier refused. "Kelly is getting a little bit jittery, and he said, 'Put it down on the belly, put it down on the belly,'" LeVier recalled. "And I said 'I'll do it my way before I do that.' And I went around and came down just like I wanted to, and it went on perfect, and I'm down and safe." Once again, the brakes performed poorly. Within minutes a tropical downpour flooded the lakebed, rendering the runway useless for the rest of the day. Johnson and his Skunk Works crew celebrated that evening with beer and another of the arm-wrestling competitions that were common to these celebrations.

Two days later, after some quick repair work to the brakes, LeVier was back in the air. Johnson had surrendered on the landing technique, and LeVier practiced bringing the plane down his way as the Lockheed team prepared for the equivalent of a Broadway opening night—a scheduled visit on August 8 by Bissell and a handful of other government officials. Johnson, after initially dismissing LeVier's complaints about the brakes, instructed mechanics to strengthen the system.

It was a pity that Dick Leghorn would not be among the visitors, but in an odd accident of history, he at least knew by the first week in August that the airplane he had imagined for so long was finally taking form. After leaving the Air Force planning staff in frustration in January 1953, as Washington was preparing for the inauguration of Eisenhower, Leghorn had returned to Kodak and moved to London to direct the company's European operations. From there, he remained in touch with friends like Jim Baker, the lens designer, and Amrom Katz, the optics expert, and kept abreast of the Air Force's anemic efforts to develop a high-altitude reconnaissance aircraft, including the modified Canberra bomber that Leghorn had first proposed at Wright Field in 1952. But Leghorn knew nothing about the U-2.

Hoping to prod the Air Force, Leghorn submitted a paper outlining his theories to *U.S. News & World Report*. The manuscript languished there until Eisenhower unveiled his "Open Skies" proposal. Little more than a week later, just as Kelly Johnson was readying the U-2 for its first roll down the runway, the magazine went to press with a six-page story by Leghorn that appeared under the headline "U.S. Can Photograph Russia From The Air Now. Planes Available, Equipment on Hand, Techniques Set."

Drawing on his independent knowledge about the state of high-altitude flight and photography, Leghorn wrote, "Aerial spying on the Soviet Union—done covertly and without Soviet permission—can be carried out with a very, very small probability of loss and with great gains for the West."

He added, "We can easily have airplanes with the necessary characteristics to fly high and fast, for long distances."

Bissell and others involved with the U-2 project were stunned by the statements. Leghorn seemed to be exposing their secret aircraft just days before it was scheduled to make its first flight. Killian immediately telephoned Leghorn, who was back in Rochester by then, and asked him to come to Washington the next morning for a meeting. The two men had known one another since 1937 when they met at MIT through the Sigma Chi fraternity. Mystified by the summons, Leghorn flew to the capital, where he met first with Killian and Land, who seemed disgruntled by his article but did not explain why. They sent him on to see Bissell, who also complained. Then, after asking Leghorn to sign a secrecy agreement, Bissell told him about the U-2.

For Leghorn, the news was sweet vindication. "Finally, someone had seen the light and realized the importance of strategic reconnaissance," he later told Don Welzenbach, the CIA historian.

On August 8, with Bissell but not Leghorn in attendance at The Ranch, the U-2 made a flawless flight. For anyone accustomed to a normal takeoff and ascent, the sight of the long-winged spy plane lifting off the ground after rolling down the runway for a mere 200 yards or so must have been astonishing. The steep angle of ascent was equally startling. LeVier made a quick pass over the base to show off the plane, then climbed quickly to 32,000 feet.

By mid-August, LeVier had guided the plane to 52,000 feet. At the end of the month, he turned the testing over to two Lockheed colleagues and returned to Edwards AFB and Palmdale to resume test flights on the XF-104 Starfighter. In early September the U-2 reached 65,000 feet. A second and third aircraft were soon delivered to the air base, and the Skunk Works prepared to open a new production line in Oildale, a small community just north of Bakersfield in California's central valley.

Curtis LeMay and his fellow Air Force generals had watched the progress with dismay. As the plane moved from proposal to reality, their long-standing resistance to the aircraft was replaced by a sudden lust to control it. Over the summer, LeMay moved to take over the program. He met Dulles and Bissell when they were visiting Colorado Springs and gruffly told the CIA officials the Agency was unqualified to operate the planes. They refused to relinquish control. "I wanted this project very much," Bissell later noted in his memoirs. "It was a glamorous and high-priority endeavor endorsed not only by the president but by a lot of very important scientific people on the outside. It would confer a great deal of prestige on the organization that could carry it off successfully."

The dispute eventually had to be resolved by Eisenhower, who had already made clear his wish to keep the plane out of the Air Force's hands. He once again ruled in favor of the CIA. "I want this whole thing to be a civilian operation. If uniformed personnel of the armed forces of the United States fly over Russia, it is an act of war, legally, and I don't want any part of that."

Gen. Nathan Twining, the Air Force chief of staff, was furious. "They took it over lock, stock, and barrel. We had nothing to say about it. Ike approved it, too, which he shouldn't have done. . . . CIA just kind of talked him into these things."

At the beginning of December, a year after Kelly Johnson had received the go-ahead from Washington to build the plane, he didn't disguise his sense of satisfaction at the accomplishments of the Skunk Works. "We have built four flying airplanes, have the ninth airplane in the jig, and have flown over our design altitude any number of times. It's been quite a year. . . ."

With the U-2 fleet growing by the month, it would not be long before Bissell had the planes he needed to fly over the Soviet Union. Now he needed to match the aircraft with a corps of skilled pilots, a camera system that could exploit the aerial access, and an organization capable of handling and analyzing the large volume of photographs that his secret air force would produce.

CHAPTER EIGHT

Photographing the President's Cattle

Jim Baker's work on a new camera system had progressed through the winter and spring of 1955. He had a head start on Kelly Johnson because Edwin Land had told the lens designer the previous summer to come up with a new high-altitude camera, anticipating that the Lockheed project would ultimately be approved. Baker hoped to produce a new generation of aerial cameras that would be smaller, lighter, and yet more powerful than anything that existed at the time. He didn't have much choice—conventional cameras were too large and too heavy for the lightweight aircraft and they couldn't produce the kind of detailed images from 13 miles high that Land wanted.

The new plane was going to take the United States where it had not gone before during the cold war—across thousands of miles of unexamined Soviet territory, including airfields, missile sites, naval bases, and other military outposts. If Baker could produce a camera that would exploit the audacious missions planned for the plane, Washington could expect an intelligence bonanza. If he failed, President Eisenhower would have a fancy new airplane with no useful purpose.

In practical terms, Baker needed to produce a camera that would generate two very different kinds of photographs: panoramic views of broad stretches of land, and high-definition pictures of specific targets like airfields. It also had to be able to filter out haze and other atmospheric conditions that might hinder picture-taking. "Overhead reconnaissance from extreme altitude did indeed require some form of long-focal-length lenses of the highest precision," Baker recalled. "To obtain maximum results from isolated and hazardous missions, the equipment also had to be capable of photographing large tracts of land in clear sunlight or through light haze, not only directly downward but with oblique views as well."

Baker knew, as he did initial planning in October 1954, that Johnson had promised swift delivery of the first plane once he secured government approval. The realistic deadline was likely to be the following summer. Baker correctly reasoned that initially he would have to draw on proven components and engineering schemes rather than, as he put it, trying to "reach out too far technically, toward untested frontiers." But as a scientist, he aspired to be more inventive over the long term, and so set to work to produce both a stopgap solution as well as two new camera systems. His ambitious agenda called for the creation of three different camera systems. The first system would be designated the A camera, and the two newly designed systems would be the B and C cameras.

Some of the aerial cameras commonly used in the early 1950s were World War II vintage. One was the trimetrogon K-17, which consisted of three cameras taking pictures from different angles. Two faced to the side and recorded oblique exposures toward the horizon. The third, in the center, took a vertical view directly below the plane. Operating at an altitude of 33,000 feet, this system produced pictures with a resolution of 20 to 25 feet, meaning objects any smaller than 20 feet from end to end could not be seen clearly. If the K-17 camera were carried to more than twice that altitude, the pictures would not show military aircraft or other objects of interest to defense planners in Washington. With intelligence analysts seeking pictures with a resolution of less than 10 feet, the ideal camera for the CL-282 would have to be four times as powerful as the K-17.

Baker knew from his own contributions to the field that the K-17 standard had already been surpassed. The K-18 camera, which was widely used by the Air Force, made use of a 36-inch telephoto lens. For special intelligence missions, lenses with even longer focal lengths had been designed, including a monster 240-inch lens. But cameras equipped with the larger lenses were far too large and heavy for Johnson's lithe aircraft. That was true for a 48-inch panoramic lens system developed in the late 1940s that might otherwise have met Land's standard for picture quality.

After consulting with other experts in the field to see if an existing camera could be modified to meet the CIA's deadline and intelligence requirements, Baker recommended using the K-38 camera, a 24-inch aerial system that was made for the Air Force by Trevor Gardner's old firm in Pasadena, the Hycon Manufacturing Company. Richard Perkin, one of the founders of the Perkin-Elmer Corporation, an optics company, advised Baker that the K-38 could be redesigned to bring down the camera's weight. Baker himself could adjust the lenses to improve their acuity. Once the redesign was completed, the CIA contracted with Hycon to produce the modified version of the K-38, which would be called the A-1 camera. Hycon signed on Perkin-Elmer to make the improved lenses, and Perkin-Elmer, in turn, hired Baker to handle the work. At the end of January 1955, Baker set up a small company, Spica, Incorporated, to separate this work from his duties at Harvard and his consulting work for the government. By today's ethics standards, the blurring of public and corporate interests by Gardner, Perkin, and Baker would probably be unacceptable, if not illegal. In 1955, it was seen simply as a logical way to get the job done as quickly and efficiently as possible.

The A-1 system included two 24-inch cameras, one mounted vertically to look directly beneath the airplane. The other was set in a rocking assembly that would swing the camera to the left and right for oblique shots. The two large film magazines, the heaviest elements of the photographic system, unspooled the film in opposite directions to maintain a constant center of gravity in the camera bay. The A-1 also included a smaller tracking camera that supplied continuous images of the landscape the plane traveled across during its flight. This photographic record would help photo interpreters determine the location of sites captured in greater detail by the larger cameras. When a new rocking mount was developed that allowed for sufficient transverse coverage with a single lens, the second large camera was eliminated. After the mount proved to be unreliable, another configuration was tried that used three K-38 cameras, one pointed down, the other two aimed at opposite side views. The new cameras came with customized, high-definition lenses that were ground by Baker. These provided much sharper pictures than the original K-38.

The A-1 camera was ready by mid-1955, when the test flights of the U-2 began at Groom Lake. It would do the job, but Baker was determined to come up with something better. Setting aside conventional approaches, he settled on an original design that would use a single 36-inch, medium wide-angle lens to produce both horizon-to-horizon coverage and high-definition photographs of specific targets. The lens aperture—the adjustable opening that limits the amount of light passing through the lens—was fixed at f10, a relatively small diameter. This allowed him to preset the focusing at high altitudes without running the risk that too much light would stream into the lens and overexpose the film. Baker also dispensed with the large, heavy prism that normally would be placed in a capsule below the lens to direct light upward into the lens. He replaced the prism with a lightweight, swiveling mirror.

The B camera could take pictures from seven overlapping positions from horizon to horizon, producing panoramic coverage, while also recording more detailed images of objects that passed directly under the aircraft, and were therefore closer to the camera. Film was fed into the camera from two magazines on either side of the shutter and lens assembly to maintain balanced weight distribution. That was critical to a smooth flight because each spool could contain as much as 6,500 feet of film, or more than a mile of film. The two rolls of 9.5 × 18-inch film were exposed simultaneously, producing 18 × 18-inch negatives.

It was a brilliant design and became the standard camera for the U-2. By relying on one 36-inch lens instead of three 24-inch lenses, Baker did away with not only the additional lenses but also the shutter assemblies and other camera parts that came with them. That left more room for film, making it possible to take advantage of extended flights across Soviet territory. Most important, the large lens yielded startlingly clear photographs. From an altitude of 60,000 feet, or more than 11 miles high, objects as small as 2.5 feet across could clearly be seen. The earthbound equivalent would be taking a photograph of the Statue of Liberty from the George Washington Bridge that when enlarged showed a beach ball dangling from Miss Liberty's torch.

Baker's quest did not end here. His next objective was a camera with a 240-inch focal length. When Kelly Johnson refused to enlarge the camera bay to handle the oversize model, Baker scaled back his ambitions, settling for a 120-inch lens. By working with a new, light silica material developed by Pittsburgh-Corning Glass Company, he eventually extended the length to 180 inches, while keeping it within the plane's weight limits. Baker managed to design the new lens in sixteen days by using an early computer to run the complex calculations that were required. Hycon built the camera in 1956, but when it was flight tested early in 1957 it proved to be too sensitive for use in the U-2 because aircraft vibrations interfered with the acuity of the lens. A redesigned version was introduced during the Cuban missile crisis in 1962, with disappointing results.

In the early months of 1955, as Baker was working on the cameras and Johnson's team in Burbank was bolting together the first U-2, the CIA was setting up a new organization to deal with the expected deluge of photographs of the Soviet Union. The agency in 1953 had established a small office to examine photographic intelligence, recognizing that aerial reconnaissance, which had played a critical role during World War II, was likely to become more important as the cold war progressed. In a smart move, the agency had hired Arthur Lundahl away from the Navy to run the office.

Lundahl proved to be another critical figure in the intelligence revolution that unfolded during the Eisenhower administration. He was to the field of photo interpretation what Kelly Johnson was to airplane design—a brilliant innovator and motivator who advanced the frontiers of his profession in the service of his country. Lundahl, who died in 1992, is remembered in the intelligence business as one of the main architects of the modern photo-interpretation techniques and organizations that helped make aerial and space reconnaissance an invaluable source of information for presidents during and after the cold war.

Lundahl, a self-effacing man who walked with a bow-legged limp that was the result of a college football injury, was born in Chicago in 1915. He dropped out of the University of Chicago to work at a liquor distributorship, but returned to school to major in geology. In 1941–42, he participated in the Engineering, Science and Management War training program, where he became interested in analyzing photographs. He joined the Navy and after training at Dartmouth College, the Anacostia Naval Air Station in Washington, D.C., and the University of North Carolina, he was assigned to a Navy station in Adak, Alaska, in the Aleutian Islands, where he analyzed photographs of potential enemy targets in Japan.

At this remote outpost in the Bering Sea, Lundahl became expert in the arcane business of examining photographs in minute detail to determine the locations and dimensions of bombing targets. The Navy and Army Air Corps had been refining these techniques since World War I. The process of making precise measurements by means of photography is known as photogrammetry. Lundahl and his colleagues would break into teams to study different sets of targets on the aerial photographs, including harbors, airfields, fuel depots, barracks, and other military encampments, and then plot the sites on large charts. The resolution of the photographs was not great, but it was good enough to enlarge the pictures five or six times, permitting them to discern the rough dimensions and layout of various targets.

"Things like the length and width and the location and the bearing of an airstrip you could hit with 99 percent accuracy," he recalled, "but certain other problems were slippery—the nature of the surface of an airfield, whether it was crushed coral impregnated with oil or whether it was asphalt or some other material, was difficult to tell."

Lundahl enjoyed the painstaking work and quickly came to believe that photographic intelligence could be a vital resource for the United States. When the war ended, he was reassigned as a civilian to the Naval Photographic Interpretation Center in Washington. He served there from 1945 to 1953, first as chief of the photogrammetry division, then as assistant chief engineer.

Lundahl had a natural talent for explaining his arcane work in simple terms. Dino A. Brugioni, a World War II aerial reconnaissance veteran and expert on Soviet industrial enterprises who joined the CIA in 1948 and later worked closely with Lundahl, found him to be "an extremely articulate speaker" who could make "highly technical material understandable to the layman." In subsequent years, this ability made Lundahl a familiar visitor to the White House, where he was often summoned to brief presidents on the latest photographic intelligence, including the dramatic pictures of Soviet missiles in Cuba that he showed to President Kennedy on October 16, 1962, raising the curtain on the Cuban missile crisis.

Lundahl put his speaking skills to work during his stint at the Navy center in Washington, extolling the benefits of aerial reconnaissance and photo interpretation. He took every opportunity to tell military and civilian audiences that better than 80 percent of the military intelligence information during the war came from overhead photography. He often quoted Gen. Werner von Fritsch, the commander-in-chief of the German army from 1935 to 1938, as saying, "The nation with the best photographic intelligence will win the next war."

But as the years passed, Lundahl could see his crusade was not winning many converts in the Navy. "The Navy at that time didn't have the enlightened leadership, the budget, the inducements which were going to take photo interpretation anywhere," he said. The Air Force, however, was pouring resources into the field as it tried to come up with potential bombing targets in the Soviet Union. As Lundahl considered a move in 1952, the CIA called to ask if he would like to come run a new photo intelligence center it was creating. In 1953, he joined the Agency as the first chief of the Photographic Intelligence Division.

His new offices in M Building, one of the CIA's spartan quarters near the Reflecting Pool and the Lincoln Memorial, was not quite the promised land in photo interpretation. In fact, Lundahl found "very primitive conditions with minimal equipment." The Agency had no experience in the field. "I found that out for myself by looking around the place," he recalled. "I opened many doors and entered many areas, and occasionally there would be a chap sitting there with a large Sherlock Holmes

magnifying glass, looking at some kind of small formatted picture, trying to form some opinions, but that was the only sign of an instru-
mented, organized interpretation procedure."

Some Agency employees thought the new division was superfluous.
"I immediately met a certain disbelief amongst the people I was working
with, particularly from the geographic area," Lundahl said. "There
were certain people who said, 'Oh well, we know you can make some
kind of a map sketch from aerial photography, but we don't think you
can do much beyond that."

Lundahl pressed his bosses for additional resources, and by early
1954 his small staff of a dozen or so people started to make an impression with its analytical work, mostly using old photographs of Soviet
military and industrial installations. He never stopped proselytizing to
his new colleagues about the advantages of photo intelligence. "You
have no idea what photography can do for you," he would tell them.
"This old photography you're looking at, World War II vintage and
handheld pieces from the Soviet May Day parades, are nothing compared to what you can do if you get high-resolution, large-scale aerial
photography that I know is possible at the present time."

Lundahl soon got the opportunity to prove his point. On December
13, 1954, just days after Kelly Johnson had gotten the go-ahead to build
his new airplane, Lundahl, unaware of the plan, was notified that he had
been relieved of his duties and should report at once to Allen Dulles's
office. Puzzled and unnerved by the news, Lundahl rushed to the director's office, where he found both Dulles and Bissell. They told him
about the new Lockheed aircraft and the harvest of high-quality pictures it was expected to produce. They instructed Lundahl to get involved with the project immediately and to create an organization that
could make effective use of the pictures. He would report directly to
Bissell, becoming part of the self-contained operation Bissell was con-
structing to manage the reconnaissance program.

In deciding to keep the photo interpretation work under CIA control,
Dulles had rejected the advice of the Agency's chief administrative officer, Col. Lawrence "Red" White, who had suggested that the Pentagon
might be better equipped to handle the work. Dulles was not about to

let a grand opportunity to expand his intelligence empire slip away. White recalled that when he made the suggestion, Dulles lifted his wire-frame glasses to his forehead and replied, "Red, you don't think that after I've taken all those photos, I am going to let someone else tell me what they mean."

Lundahl's backwater photo shop was clearly unsuited for the volume of photographs that was expected to start arriving by mid-1956. Nor could it operate under the severe secrecy strictures that the White House had demanded. To keep the spy plane's operations as closely held as possible, even from some of the most senior military commanders and intelligence officials, the handling of the photographs and dissemination of the information extracted from them would have to be tightly controlled. Lundahl would have to build a separate, far larger operation, and do so under orders that barred him from even mentioning the project to his immediate supervisors, who were not cleared to know about the plane. They were told that Lundahl had been detached to work on a special project for the director.

Lundahl spent his first weeks on the assignment traveling around the country to meet with Edwin Land, Kelly Johnson, Jim Baker, and the other people managing various aspects of the project, advising them on the photographic standards that would best serve the photo interpreters he would be hiring. The CIA searched for a building in the Washington area that could house the equipment and large staff that would be needed to review the pictures. Even though Kodak would handle most of the film processing at another location, a monumental job in itself, Lundahl still required factory-like quarters. But they also had to be nondescript to avoid attracting attention.

There was nothing suitable among the buildings occupied by the CIA near the Reflecting Pool. The Agency examined all kinds of potential sites, including abandoned quarries and laundries. Lundahl and the CIA eventually settled on the Steuart Building, a seven-story office building at the corner of New York Avenue and 5th Street, N.W. The Steuart Motor Company, a Ford dealership, occupied the first three floors, including a showroom on the ground floor. The CIA rented the top four floors, or about 50,000 square feet of workspace.

The building was in disrepair and the location was problematic. Paint flaked off the ceilings, water leaked down the walls, there was no air-conditioning, no decent places to eat nearby, and street crime was a problem in the neighborhood, especially at night. But Lundahl had to make do with the offices, which quickly started to fill up with light tables and other technical equipment, plus a growing staff. Because the program had Eisenhower's endorsement, Lundahl was able to recruit from other agencies, including the military services, the State Department, and even the Library of Congress. Most of the staff was under thirty years of age and it included numerous women. During the war years, the military services had assigned many women to serve as photo interpreters.

The CIA needed a secret code word for Lundahl's enterprise. He suggested calling it the Automat, after the Horn and Hardart self-serve restaurants by the same name in New York, which were open twenty-four hours a day, seven days a week. "This is going to be the intelligence Automat of Washington," he advised the Agency. So the nation's newest intelligence organization was officially dubbed HTAUTOMAT. "And that was so right," Lundahl recalled after his retirement. "We never closed our doors and turned off our lights."

Before Lundahl could open the doors for the first batch of pictures, Bissell had to come up with a group of skilled pilots willing to fly the U-2 into Soviet airspace. Eisenhower had not made the job any easier by instructing Bissell to use foreign pilots. The order reflected Eisenhower's determination to distance U-2 operations from the U.S. military to make the flights less inflammatory if they were detected or intercepted by Moscow.

Finding a group of qualified foreign pilots was not easy. In June 1955, before the first test flight of the U-2, the Strategic Air Command, which had agreed to handle pilot training, came up with a number of foreign pilots. They included several Greek airmen who had flown P-51 fighters, a single-propeller World War II airplane, over Albania and Bulgaria for the CIA in the early years of the cold war. Eight of the foreigners were selected for training and sent to Craig Air Force Base in Alabama. A December 27, 1955, memo to Bissell reported that all of the pilots had "demonstrated average or above average qualifications as jet pilots." But the memo also noted that the men were not fluent in English.

The eight pilots were brought to Arizona for jet training. Four of them eventually made it to the base at Groom Lake, and several made test flights in the U-2, but they lacked the experience to handle the temperamental plane and were soon dropped from the program. "It's been decided to use only American pilots, thank God," Kelly Johnson wrote in his journal.

Eisenhower would not get his wish, but the CIA was still under orders not to use Air Force pilots on U-2 missions, at least not anyone still in the service. The creative solution was to select crack Air Force pilots, then have them resign from the service and go to work as civilians for the CIA, with a promise that they could someday resume their Air Force careers without a loss of seniority. This transmogrification was called sheep-dipping, borrowing liberally from the generic name of the liquid disinfectant that sheep are placed in before shearing to kill parasites and clean their wool.

The Air Force recommended drawing from several Strategic Fighter Wings that were soon to be disbanded at Bergstrom AFB in Texas and Turner AFB in Georgia. The pilots assigned to these wings had Korean War combat experience in F-84 jet fighters, including prolonged flights over water in the single-engine aircraft, useful preparation for marathon missions over the Soviet Union.

Martin Knutson was one of those pilots stationed at Turner AFB. One day he was unexpectedly summoned by his squadron commander, who cryptically informed Knutson that he would soon be approached by someone from another government agency. He was given no further information. The next day he received a call from a man who invited him to come to the only hotel in Albany, Georgia, the town nearest the air base. When Knutson arrived, his host flashed a government badge, then told the pilot he was under consideration for a secret government operation.

Over the next several days Knutson met with the CIA representative. "All I really knew was it was going to be a United States operation in some exotic state-of-the-art airplane on a dangerous mission for the good of the country." If Knutson passed a battery of medical and psychological tests, and cleared an exhaustive security check and polygraph examination, he would be eligible to join the clandestine program at $2,500 a month, triple his Air Force salary. Attracted by the pay and prospect of adventure, Knutson agreed. As a swaggering fighter pilot, he also imagined the new airplane would be a sleek, supersonic model that could probably travel at least twice the speed of sound. Some of the other pilots recruited at the same time figured they might be the first men to rocket into space. They were sorely disappointed when they got their first glimpse of the gawky, subsonic U-2.

Knutson, born in 1930 in St. Louis Park, a suburb of Minneapolis, started his flying career after the war as an electrical engineering student at the University of Minnesota. He was inspired by a classmate studying on the GI bill who had flown combat missions during World War II. The fellow student had lost both his legs in a crash, but nevertheless described the thrill of flying to Knutson in the hours after class when the two would repair to a nearby tavern for a few beers. Knutson joined the Air Force and as soon as he was qualified as a pilot he was ordered to Okinawa to fly combat missions during the Korean War. He had accumulated more than a thousand flying hours in single-engine jets by the time the CIA came calling at Turner AFB, enough time to meet the experience level required for the U-2.

Like the handful of other men selected at Turner and Bergstrom, Knutson was soon on his way to Washington for additional interviews. Once the Agency was satisfied that he could handle the technical and psychological pressures of long solo flights across the Soviet Union, Knutson was discharged from the Air Force, as Eisenhower had insisted. After picking up his belongings in Georgia, he began an arduous odyssey of test-taking and training that would take him to Ohio, New Mexico, and other locations as the CIA prepared to bring him to Groom Lake.

One of the first stops was the Lovelace Clinic in Albuquerque. Three years before John Glenn and his fellow Mercury astronaut candidates set foot in the same clinic for the exhaustive and sometimes torturous medical tests that Tom Wolfe would later make famous in *The Right*

Stuff, Martin Knutson arrived at the medical center for a visit that he would never forget.

The clinic captured the extemporaneous nature of the whole U-2 program. Looking back through dozens of photographs of pilots and future astronauts taking medical tests at the clinic, it is easy to see why some of the men found the place strange and forbidding. The diagnostic equipment was large and intimidating, the men always seem to have wires or tubes connected to their bodies, and the clinic staff sometimes appear eerily detached. The pictures look like scenes from a bad Hollywood science fiction movie. Despite the ostensible precision of the tests, much of the clinic's work in aviation medicine was, at the time, experimental, even improvisational, and it seems clear from the institution's history that a fair measure of opportunism was involved in its effort to attract government support and become part of the astronaut program. Still, it was a serious medical enterprise that advanced the frontiers of aviation and space medicine.

Lovelace was selected by the CIA because it was one of the few private clinics in the country that did aeromedical research, an esoteric discipline that dealt with the effects of flight on the human body. Though the Army established a School of Aviation Medicine in 1918, and later founded the Aero Medical Laboratory at Wright Field, there were still not many specialists in the field when the U-2 was ready to fly. Lovelace had the added advantage of being in Albuquerque, which at the time was a small, out-of-the-way city where the testing of pilots for a secret program was not likely to attract much attention.

The clinic, which was then a four-story adobe building on Gibson Boulevard adjacent to Kirtland AFB, was largely the creation of two uncommon men, Dr. William Randolph Lovelace and his nephew, Dr. William Randolph Lovelace II, known respectively by friends as "Uncle Doc" and Randy. The clinic grew out of the elder Lovelace's practice, which developed at the turn of the century when the newly minted St. Louis physician moved to the dry climate of the New Mexico Territory to help recover from a case of pulmonary tuberculosis. The area was advertised at the time as "nature's sanatorium for consumptives." He liked the dry, open spaces and mountains, and stayed on to practice medicine, first as a country doctor associated with the Santa Fe Railroad, then as a physician in Albuquerque. The clinic began in 1922 as a partnership between Lovelace and another Albuquerque doctor, Edgar T. Lassetter, who had also moved to New Mexico when he was tubercular.

It was Randy Lovelace—the son of Uncle Doc's older brother, Edgar—who turned it into a center for aviation and space medicine. He was a charming man with a gift for invention and a knack for self-promotion. By making important contributions to flight safety with a new oxygen mask and high-altitude bailout equipment, and forming alliances with powerful military and civilian leaders in Washington, he became a prominent figure in aviation and space circles. He supervised the medical testing of the Mercury astronauts in 1959 and was appointed NASA's director of space medicine in 1964, a year before he was killed in a plane crash in the mountains outside Aspen, Colorado.

By the time Martin Knutson got to Albuquerque in 1955, Randy Lovelace had turned the clinic into an aviation medical center that, among other things, conducted exhaustive physical and mental exams for military and civilian pilots. The CIA hired the clinic to run the U-2 pilots through an expanded testing regimen and to provide emergency medical services at Groom Lake when Tony LeVier and the other Lockheed pilots took the new plane out for its initial flight tests. Donald Kilgore, a clinic doctor who had flown eighty-one combat missions in the Pacific theater as a Navy pilot during World War II, was dispatched on short notice to the test site in the summer of 1955. On days when the spy plane was airborne, Kilgore rode along in one of the support planes that monitored the flights. "I was given a parachute and a first-aid kit," he recalled, "and told that if the U-2 crashed my job was to bail out and give medical assistance to the pilot."

When Knutson got to Albuquerque he checked into the Bird of Paradise Motel, registering under an assumed name, then reported to the clinic. The tests began after he gave the clinic a full account of his family's medical history. Every organ and bodily function was examined as the doctors tried to determine whether he could withstand the conditions he might encounter in the U-2. One of the most painful was a vertigo test, described in technical terms as "a test of labyrinthine function by the standard caloric method." In practical terms, it involved pouring ice water into Knutson's ears. Another test required Knutson to float naked in the "sensory deprivation tank," an unlit pool where he could see and hear nothing. Dr. Kilgore said most of the pilots quickly became disoriented and panicky.

Knutson and the other men could not fathom why some of the tests were done. In truth, the Lovelace clinic wasn't sure either. "It was a shotgun approach to physical evaluation," Dr. Kilgore recalled. "We were testing to determine benchmarks, but we weren't certain what would yield meaningful results. Over time we weeded out the tests that weren't important."

Knutson's preparations finally ended when he was ordered to The Ranch in January 1956. On the flight from Southern California he met the other freshman U-2 pilots for the first time. One of the men came from his old squadron in Georgia. The CIA had been so intent on preserving security that it had kept the pilots separated during their weeks of testing.

As the Lockheed shuttle flight from Burbank set down at Groom Lake, Knutson and the other men got their first look at the mystery plane they were going to fly. More than forty years later, Knutson could still remember his reaction when he saw the oddly shaped aircraft, which was most certainly not the futuristic supersonic plane he had pictured. "I took one look at it and said I don't want anything to do with this goddamned thing."

Knutson's attitude changed quickly once he started flying the plane. "I found out this was no kids' toy," he said. "It was going to take a lot of skill to handle this machine." As Tony LeVier and the other Lockheed test pilots had discovered, the U-2 was a demanding airplane that rewarded highly disciplined piloting with breathtaking performance, including the opportunity to travel at the edge of space. But there was little margin for error. Knutson said, "It was the highest-workload plane I've ever flown. You had to mind the store intently or the airplane would get out of control."

Because the aircraft lacked room for a second pilot, there was no chance for Knutson to take the U-2 aloft with an instructor at the controls. Each pilot had to learn for himself, with the aid of preflight training and advice radioed from an instructor who tailed the U-2 in another plane. (A second seat was added in later training models.) The acceleration and angle of ascent on takeoff, as LeVier knew, were tremendous. "Almost as soon as you put it at full throttle it was ready to come off the ground," Knutson said. "Keep in mind this aircraft will come apart if it goes over 240 knots at lower elevations. To keep the airspeed down after takeoff, you had to bring up her nose. Almost instantly you get into a 60-degree climb or pull back on the power. Nobody liked to pull the power back; they liked to experience that eye-watering takeoff."

Once the plane reached its cruising altitude above 60,000 feet, the pilots had to worry about the "coffin corner," the narrow band of airspeed they had to maintain to avoid a low-speed stall or a high-speed buffeting, either of which could rip off the wings or tail section. Knutson learned to fly within this 6-knot zone by constantly checking his airspeed indicator. But the pilots also had to monitor engine performance closely because the power plant lost so much thrust in the thin air. One of the design issues that had challenged Johnson and his crew looked even scarier in reality: At cruising altitude, the powerful jet engine operated at less than 10 percent of its capacity, producing barely enough thrust to keep the plane in the air. Knutson found, "You had to run it right at its design limits and temperatures. You had a readout of the exhaust gas temperature and you ran the engine within one degree of its limit."

"I got cross-eyed after a while," he said, "because you had to keep one eye fixed on the airspeed indicator because that was a life-or-death matter, and you used the other to keep track of everything else in the cockpit."

Because of space and weight limitations, Johnson had installed a minimal amount of navigational instruments. The plane came with a radio-compass and a downward-looking periscope designed by Jim Baker that allowed pilots to see points below the aircraft when there was no cloud cover. For navigation when the ground was not visible, Johnson provided a sextant that was built into the viewfinder in the cockpit. The most advanced spy plane in the world relied on an updated version of the navigational tool invented in the eighteenth century.

The U-2's flight range was phenomenal. Pilots ventured across North America on flights that lasted as long as nine hours and covered thousands of miles. The gliding ability of the plane was proven on April 14, 1956, when the engine flamed out on a U-2 as it was flying west over the Mississippi River at the Tennessee border. Jake Kratt, the pilot, managed to restart the engine, but another flameout occurred roughly 600 miles later. From there, the plane glided for 300 miles until it landed at Kirtland AFB outside Albuquerque. The CIA and Air Force had planned for just such an event by sending sealed orders to every Air Force base in the country instructing commanders on what to do if the U-2 came in for an emergency landing. The answer was to get the plane out of sight as quickly as possible. That was done at Kirtland, but not before military police got a glimpse of the aircraft and Kratt, who was wearing one of Joe Ruseckas's strange-looking pressure suits. One of the policemen said the pilot looked like he had come from Mars.

The long flights exposed some shortcomings in cockpit amenities. The David Clark Company had not anticipated that pilots might need to urinate while they were in the air. The initial fix for this oversight was to stick a catheter into the pilot's penis before he put on the suit so that urine could be collected during the flight. This solution proved to be highly uncomfortable and, by the fall of 1955, an external bladder was added that allowed the men to urinate normally during flight.

The pilots also needed to drink and eat during prolonged flights. A self-sealing hole was placed in the face mask so pilots could sip sweetened water through a tube to prevent dehydration at high altitudes. In a preview of things to come in the manned space program, pureed food was stored in soft containers. The food could be squeezed through a tube when a pilot was hungry. Even with these measures, pilots could lose as much as six pounds during an eight-hour flight.

The view from 65,000 feet made up for much of the discomfort and danger. Pilots could see 200 miles in any direction. Cloud formations drifted by far below and the curvature of the earth was plainly visible.

Overhead, stars and planets twinkled in the darkness of space. "From that height," Knutson said, "you realized that man had actually made very little impact on the earth, at least compared to what nature had done."

Once flights began over the Soviet Union, of course, there wouldn't be much time for sightseeing and spiritual contemplation. And by the spring of 1956, that time was fast approaching. The first group of pilots was nearing the end of their training period, and Kelly Johnson had produced nine planes, enough to send a detachment overseas. Pratt & Whitney was shipping the improved J57 engine that was less prone to flameouts, Jim Baker's A camera was in hand and the B camera was nearing completion, and Arthur Lundahl's photo automat was up and running.

Congress, which had been paying for the program through the CIA's budget for more than a year without knowing about it, had finally been informed on February 24 by Allen Dulles. He told the two ranking members of the Senate Armed Services Committee, Republican Leverett Saltonstall of Massachusetts and Democrat Richard B. Russell of Georgia. They, in turn, suggested that Dulles also notify the House, which he did by meeting with Republican John Taber and Democrat Clarence Cannon of the Appropriations Committee. It seems inconceivable by today's standards that the executive branch could launch and finance a secret aircraft program without first informing Congress and getting its consent. But in the 1950s, before the disclosure of CIA abuses and the establishment of congressional committees to oversee the CIA and other spy agencies, the delay in informing Congress about the U-2 was not unusual. Nor was the decision to limit the briefing to just four lawmakers. For the next four years, until Francis Gary Powers was shot down over the Soviet Union on May 1, 1960, they were the only members of Congress who were officially informed that the U-2 was flying over the Soviet Union.

The parsimonious treatment of Congress reflected the general attitude about intelligence matters that prevailed in Washington at the time. Put simply, spying was considered to be pretty much an exclusive domain of the executive branch, a business that both the White House and Congress believed was too secret and too specialized to be closely monitored on Capitol Hill. A handful of congressional leaders were kept informed about CIA activities. They, in turn, assured that adequate funding was provided for the Agency through secret accounts that were hidden in Defense Department appropriations bills.

The operating assumptions at both ends of Pennsylvania Avenue presumed that the executive branch could be trusted to handle espionage matters without tight congressional oversight and that sensitive security information was likely to be compromised if widely circulated among members of Congress. In reality, this system distorted the constitutional balance of powers by putting Congress on the sidelines and leaving the White House and CIA virtually unaccountable for intelligence activities. The unequal apportionment of power worked well enough in the case of the U-2 and other technological projects, where the CIA had the freedom to move creatively and quickly, but it proved unwise in other areas, especially covert operations, where greater congressional involvement might have kept the White House and the Agency from overreaching. The dangers were not fully appreciated until the nation learned in the 1970s about CIA assassination plots and other dubious activities.

By the end of March, the U-2 had flown at an altitude of 73,800 feet. To ensure that Eisenhower fully appreciated the dazzling hardware at his disposal, Bissell sent the U-2 over Eisenhower's farm in Gettysburg, Pennsylvania. Photographs taken from 60,000 feet showed not only some of the president's cattle but also their feeding troughs.

Andrew Goodpaster was with the president when he was shown the pictures. "Eisenhower said, 'This is close to incredible.' The idea that from 60,000 feet or more you could see that kind of detail, you could achieve that kind of resolution was really awesome."

Before the first detachment of planes could be packed up and shipped overseas, a public cover story was needed to deal with questions that were bound to come up. It was certain that the U-2, with its elongated wings, pogos, and other unconventional components, would attract attention as it took off and landed at foreign military bases, no matter how much effort was made to conceal the plane while it was on the ground.

Bissell and his staff came up with the idea that the plane's ostensible mission would be high-altitude weather research, and that its official operators would be the National Advisory Committee on Aeronautics, NACA, which was later reconstituted and renamed the National Aeronautics and Space Administration, NASA. If a U-2 was ever lost over hostile territory—a prospect that was considered unlikely in 1956—the world would be told the plane had been on a weather research mission. When Killian and Land later learned of the emergency deception plan just days before the first flight over the Soviet Union, they were alarmed. If a plane was downed, they said, Washington should take full responsibility and declare that the flights were necessary to guard against surprise attack.

On April 29, the first set of planes and support staff—Detachment A, an Air Force–led unit that worked for Bissell—was ready to make the move to Britain. On May 1, four dismantled U-2s stored aboard a C-124 transport arrived at Lakenheath air base in East Anglia, where they were reassembled. On May 7, the director of NACA, Hugh Dryden, issued a statement in Washington announcing that a new aircraft developed by Lockheed and flown by the Air Force Air Weather Service would be studying natural forces present at high altitude, including the jet stream, the ozone layer, clear air turbulence, and cosmic rays. For public consumption, Detachment A was named the 1st Weather Reconnaissance Squadron, Provisional. This designation was true to the spirit of the enterprise. Provisional Air Force units did not have to report to higher headquarters. Additional press releases described weather monitoring equipment that would be used aboard the plane and informed the public that the program would involve operations in Britain and "other parts of the world." That was a nice euphemism for the Soviet Union.

CHAPTER NINE

Big Game Hunting

DWIGHT EISENHOWER had not hesitated in October 1954 when James Killian and Edwin Land advised him to build an untested new spy plane to plumb the mysteries of Soviet military power. Now, seventeen months later, he had to decide whether to put the plane to use. This time he hesitated, for good reason.

Relations with Moscow were warming ever so slightly in 1956, and Eisenhower did not want to undermine the chances for further improvement by brazenly invading Soviet airspace, especially if there was a risk that the U-2 would be detected and shot down. Yet the White House needed concrete information about Soviet military forces now more than ever, both to gauge Moscow's strength and to dampen a growing political furor over the adequacy of American defenses. The charge that Moscow was gaining military superiority loomed as a potentially potent issue for the Democrats in the 1956 presidential and congressional elections.

The conflicting pressures bearing down on Eisenhower were intense, and he was not in the best of health. He had suffered a heart attack in late September 1955 while vacationing in Colorado, and was hospitalized there for six weeks before returning to Washington. Eisenhower had recuperated sufficiently by the end of February 1956 to announce his intention to run for reelection. Then, on the night of June 7, the president experienced intense abdominal pains, leading his wife, Mamie, to fear he was having another heart attack. He was rushed from the White House to Walter Reed Army Hospital, where physicians determined he had a blocked intestine and ordered emergency surgery. As he was recovering, Eisenhower had to decide whether to launch the U-2 into Soviet airspace the first week in July.

The demand for definitive intelligence information on Soviet bombers and missiles had only increased since Trevor Gardner had helped sound the alarm in 1953 that the United States was in danger of falling behind the Soviet Union in new weapons technology. Reports that Moscow was fielding a larger fleet of long-range bombers than Washington had become a volatile political issue in the capital as Democratic congressional leaders such as Senator Stuart Symington of Missouri and Senator Henry Jackson of Washington warned the nation about a growing "bomber gap." There was also the first stirring of public concern about Soviet missile tests and the prospect that a corresponding "Missile Gap" would someday give the Russians a decisive military advantage. Newspapers and newsmagazines carried alarming stories about the growing Soviet threat.

The political clamor about rising Soviet airpower had intensified after the first public reports about the new Bison bomber in 1954, when the aircraft made its debut by flying over Red Square during the annual May Day festivities. This was nine months after the first sighting of the plane at Ramenskoye airfield outside Moscow. Harrison Salisbury, the *New York Times* correspondent in Moscow, reported on the front page the next day, "The Soviet Union unveiled at a May Day celebration today its new four-jet, inter-continental bomber. It is big enough and has enough range to deliver the latest nuclear weapons to far distant points." Salisbury also noted that the air exhibition on the sunny spring day included a squadron of nine new medium-range bombers equipped with twin jet engines. "The new Soviet aircraft presented an exciting and formidable sight as they approached Red Square," Salisbury said. The CIA soon secretly figured the Kremlin would produce enough of the Bison bombers to start fielding operational units by the end of 1956, and estimated the Russians would have 50 aircraft by mid-1957 and 250 by mid-1959.

The prototype of America's newest intercontinental jet bomber, the eight-engine B-52, had made its maiden test flight in 1952. By May 1954, B-52s were beginning to roll off the production line at the Boeing plant in Seattle, and a second assembly site was soon opened in Wichita,

Kansas. The long-distance bombers, which could be refueled in flight, would reduce Washington's dependence on overseas bases, which were more vulnerable to attack than those in the United States.

A little more than two weeks after the sighting of Bison bombers over Red Square, Gen. Nathan Twining, the Air Force chief of staff, declared that the Bison bomber had been developed for the sole purpose of reaching "important targets in the United States." Speaking in Amarillo, Texas, on Armed Forces Day, General Twining said the Soviet air force "is by far the biggest air force in the world," and that it included "thousands more combat planes than the United States Air Force, Navy, Marines and Army combined."

When the nation's top military planners assembled at the Marine Corps base in Quantico, Virginia, on June 19, 1954, for a weekend review of American defenses, a senior Pentagon official told them that Moscow was narrowing the American lead in weapons technology. Donald A. Quarles, assistant secretary of defense for research and development, said, "We must conclude that on balance our technical position vis-à-vis the Soviets is less favorable than it was a year ago. Our margin of advantage has been narrowed and we must face the sober inferences to be drawn from these facts." The next day, Secretary of Defense Charles E. Wilson offered a somewhat more positive assessment, informing the group that American military technology was still two to three years ahead of the Soviet Union.

Though Eisenhower by this time had given Lee DuBridge and James Killian approval to start organizing a study about the threat of surprise attack, he gave no public indication of his concern while attending the Quantico conference. He arrived at the base in the Virginia countryside in an open-top limousine with a new golden-headed putter in his hands. The club had been given to him by a Republican delegation from Long Island before he departed the White House. Not long after reaching Quantico, the president teed off in a foursome that included General Twining. When his first drive carried straight and far down the fairway, reporters and photographers playfully suggested he try again. Eisenhower grinned and told his fellow golfers, "They're determined to prove it was an accident."

The contrast between Eisenhower's closed-door deliberations about the Soviet threat and his public posture was characteristic of his presidency. Even as he made far-reaching decisions in private to augment the collection of intelligence and strengthen American defenses, he publicly dismissed assertions that Washington was falling dangerously behind the Soviet Union in military power and technology and even belittled Soviet advances. This dichotomy clearly reflected a deliberate, politically expedient effort to use the presidential soapbox to reassure the nation about its defenses and prevent a needless surge in military spending. Eisenhower's inarticulateness may also have contributed to his flaccid and sometimes opaque statements.

Whatever the cause, such statements were legion. In early 1956, for example, as concern mounted in Washington about Soviet missiles, Eisenhower publicly discounted the potential value of the weapons, saying they were not as accurate as bombs dropped from planes and would therefore have to be armed with exceptionally powerful nuclear warheads and used in great numbers that would inevitably cause vast destruction. All this was true at the time—more precise guidance systems were not developed until the end of his presidency—and his views amounted to an early preview of the doctrine of nuclear deterrence, which presumes that the likelihood of mutual annihilation would discourage the United States and the Soviet Union from engaging in a nuclear war. Eisenhower also said during the same appearance that he had made the missile program the Pentagon's highest research priority. But his comments nevertheless left the impression that he was not greatly alarmed by the Soviet drive to produce long-range missiles.

The administration's effort to hold down defense spending also invited criticism that Eisenhower was neglecting security issues. This was ironic, given Eisenhower's long, distinguished service as an Army officer. But his commitment to keeping government spending down allowed his critics to argue that he was neglecting defense. The reality was a good deal more complicated. Though the administration initially did fail to make adequate investments in the American missile program and moved slowly to get the nation into space, Eisenhower was hardly indif-

ferent to national security threats. Indeed, his administration transformed American military power by developing a host of new weapons
and intelligence systems. These technological breakthroughs laid the
basis for American military might through the remainder of the twentieth century. No modern president other than Franklin Roosevelt, who
authorized the development of atomic weapons, so dramatically altered
the nature of military power.

The country, of course, could not see the full extent of Eisenhower's
initiatives as they unfolded. Programs such as the U-2 were hidden altogether from public view. And Moscow's strength was unquestionably
growing, as was its capability to launch a surprise attack. Every sign that
the Soviet strategic arsenal was expanding fueled fears about America's
vulnerability and gave both Democrats and conservative Republicans an
opportunity to raise hell.

Just such an occasion appeared on May 1, 1955, even as Kelly Johnson was racing in secret to complete the first U-2. That day the skies
over Moscow seemed to be filled with hulking Bison bombers. Western
military attachés counted more than thirty planes during the May Day
celebration, suggesting a robust rate of production. The diplomats
didn't realize the show was a clever illusion created by just ten planes
that circled around Moscow out of view before making repeated passes
over Red Square. As word spread over the next few days about the Soviet show of strength, the Pentagon issued a terse statement that
Moscow had begun running formation flights of its new intercontinental bomber, a way of saying that the new planes were coming off the production line at a fast rate and that the Russians were rapidly putting
them into service.

Senator Symington, who had served as Air Force secretary in the
Truman administration, soon demanded that the Senate examine the
unsettling developments. "It is now clear that the United States, along
with the rest of the free world, may have lost control of the air, except
for the possibility that we still have advantages in base location and
training," he said in mid-May. "But it is now also clear that in quality as
well as quantity of planes the Communists are at least in the process of

surpassing the United States, and I am confident that they are well ahead with the production of the possible ultimate weapon—the intercontinental ballistic missile."

Richard Russell, the chairman of the Senate Armed Services Committee and the Democrats' leading authority on military issues, announced on May 17 that the committee would investigate the state of American airpower. He turned the job over to a subcommittee headed by Lyndon Johnson, the Democratic floor leader. Eisenhower quickly rejected Symington's charges, assuring the nation the next day that it was "just not true" to suggest that the technical or numerical superiority of the Air Force had been "lost in a twinkling." But, in truth, neither Eisenhower nor anyone else in Washington really knew how many Bison bombers the Russians had built or how far advanced the Soviet missile program was.

In late June of 1955 a presidential commission headed by former president Herbert Hoover said as much. A commission task force, directed by one of the nation's most respected retired military figures, Gen. Mark Clark, pronounced itself "deeply concerned over the lack of adequate intelligence data from behind the Iron Curtain." The panel, which was probably unaware of the U-2 program, called on the government to "exert every conceivable and practicable effort" to acquire reliable intelligence information, including the "full use of technological capabilities."

Trevor Gardner, increasingly impatient with the fitful pace of the Pentagon's missile program, issued a warning in September about the Soviet missile threat. "The most complex and baffling technological mystery today is not the Russian capability in aircraft and nuclear weapons, but rather what the Soviet progress has been in the field of guided missiles." Throughout the fall and early winter, Gardner pressed the administration and Congress to pump an additional $200 million into General Schriever's missile program and other Air Force technology projects, roughly a 30 percent increase in the service's research and development budget. His proposal was rebuffed by the civilian leadership of the Air Force and Defense Secretary Wilson, but on February 1, 1956, Wilson said he would accelerate the missile effort and would soon appoint a civilian "czar" to manage the nation's missile programs and ensure that they received sufficient money and manpower. The Air Force and Army had competing programs at the time to develop intermediate-range ballistic missiles.

Wilson's announcement was a transparent effort to blunt Gardner's complaints and to respond to escalating criticism from the Senate about the Pentagon's missile work. Only hours before Wilson spoke, Senator Jackson had blasted the administration for underestimating Soviet military capabilities and neglecting its own missile projects. In a somber speech that drew national coverage, Jackson predicted that the Russians would test a missile with a range of 1,500 miles before the year was out. That, he said, would overturn Western military strategy and possibly disrupt the NATO alliance. As Jackson saw it, a Soviet Union armed with such missiles could use "ballistic blackmail" to pressure Western European nations to deny the United States access to air bases on their soil, forcing Washington to pull its bombers back to American territory. He called for appointment of a missile boss with the authority to run the programs with the same intensity that characterized the Manhattan Project. "Soviet victory in this race for discovery would be shattering to the morale of our allies and to our own self-confidence," he told the Senate. "For the first time, Moscow would have beaten us in a crucial scientific-industrial race."

Unimpressed by Wilson's promises—and no doubt disappointed that he was not likely to be named missile czar because of his stormy demeanor—Gardner resigned on February 8, 1956, after a final, futile round of meetings with Wilson in Miami and the Bahamas, where the defense secretary was vacationing. At a press conference earlier in the day, Eisenhower was asked to comment on the views of Jackson and Symington. "Well," he said dryly, "I am always astonished at the amount of information that others get that I don't. . . . I think, overall, we have no reason to believe that we are not doing everything that human science and brains and resources can do to keep our position in a proper posture."

In early February 1956, the Russians tested a missile with a range of 900 miles, lending credence to a *Time* magazine cover story published just a few weeks earlier. The article, which ran under the headline "Missiles Away," opened with an imaginary 1962 scenario in which the United States and its allies find themselves militarily overmatched and politically intimidated by Soviet missiles. Or as *Time* vividly put it, "Russia has the whip hand at last." The magazine called the fictional humiliation "the nightmare of the missilemen."

Nikita Khrushchev seemed to sense he had the Americans spooked. On April 23, as the first detachment of U-2 spy planes was preparing to move out to Britain, the Soviet leader boldly declared, "I am quite sure that we will have very soon a guided missile with a hydrogen-bomb warhead which could hit any point in the world."

Khrushchev might have been bluffing about his missiles, but the underlying threat of a Soviet surprise attack was reinforced at the White House a few weeks later by a sobering letter from Killian, who had reconvened the Technological Capabilities Panel to update its assessment of American vulnerability. Based on the latest intelligence estimates about Soviet long-range bombers and nuclear weapons, Killian reported in a Top Secret letter to Arthur Flemming, the director of the Office of Defense Mobilization, that his commission was moving up the date when it believed Moscow would have the means to launch a devastating nuclear strike against the United States. Killian warned in the May 14 letter that the threat was "imminent" rather than likely to materialize in 1958, as the panel had predicted in its original report in early 1955. He wrote, "The period is rapidly approaching when the Soviets could have the means to carry out a decisive surprise attack against the United States."

Despite the political pressure, Eisenhower held back on a decision to use the U-2 when Allen Dulles came to the White House on May 28 to discuss the spy plane with the president and seek his approval in principle to commence operations. Eisenhower was not ready. He worried about the consequences of sending an American spy plane, even one that was not armed and not operated by the Air Force, deep into Soviet airspace. He repeatedly told aides, "Such a decision is one of the most soul-searching questions to come before a President. We've got to think about what our reaction would be if they were to do this to us." Goodpaster knew the answer was that the United States would try to shoot down the plane.

Eisenhower realized the airplane and camera system marked a breakthrough in reconnaissance technology. If he harbored any doubts after seeing the photographs of his Gettysburg farm, they were eliminated when the CIA presented him with pictures of San Diego and several other American cities taken from 70,000 feet. "On these we could easily count the automobiles on the streets and even the lines marking the parking areas for individual cars," he recalled in his memoirs. "There was no doubt about the quality of the information to be obtained."

But he also wanted reassurances that the plane would not be tracked easily by Soviet radar or shot down by Soviet fighter jets. Test flights over the United States had demonstrated that American radar could not consistently track the aircraft and many centers couldn't even spot it. The CIA had repeatedly assured Eisenhower that Moscow's radar network, built with equipment the allies had provided during World War II, would not pick up the plane. But that assessment was unexpectedly revised during the spring of 1956. A new study, prepared by the Agency's Office of Scientific Intelligence, said detection was probable. The secret report was completed and published on May 28, the same day that Dulles met with Eisenhower. But Eisenhower does not appear to have been informed about it. The CIA's own history of the U-2 simply notes that "this study seems to have had little impact on the thinking of top project officials." Citing a 1988 interview with Bissell, it goes on to say, "They continued to believe that the Soviets would not be able to track the U-2 and might even fail to detect it, except for vague indications."

Given Eisenhower's concerns, the Agency should have made him aware of its revised assessment. It is possible that he would have held off longer before ordering the first flight, or even aborted the program, had he believed the plane would be easily detected. In his memoirs, Eisenhower reported that, based on the information he was given about Soviet air defenses, he was confident that "in the then-existing state of radar efficiency and the inability of fighter planes to operate at altitudes above some fifty thousand feet, U-2 reconnaissance could be undertaken with reasonable safety."

The CIA also told Eisenhower that in the unlikely event that one of the planes was disabled by Soviet air defenses, there was little chance that the pilot would survive and give Moscow irrefutable evidence that the spy flight was an American operation. Dulles and Bissell assured Eisenhower that a successful attack on the plane would kill the pilot and destroy the aircraft beyond recognition. Goodpaster recalled, "We were told—and it was part of our understanding of the situation—that it was almost certain that the plane would disintegrate and that we could take it as a certainty that no pilot would survive . . . and that although they would know where the plane came from, it would be difficult to prove it in any convincing way."

Eisenhower was persuaded that the plane and its pilot would be doomed if hit by a Russian missile or antiaircraft fire. "This was a cruel assumption," he recalled in his memoirs, "but I was assured that the young pilots undertaking these missions were doing so with their eyes wide open and motivated by a high degree of patriotism, a swashbuckling bravado and certain material inducements."

Just in case the dire predictions of destruction proved incorrect, the CIA had decided to equip the pilots with suicide pills. Bissell asked Dr. Alex Batlin of the Agency's Technical Services Division to come up with an effective potion. Batlin proposed a glass ampoule of liquid potassium cyanide, the same poison that Hermann Goering, the Nazi leader, had used to kill himself in prison after the war. Once the glass was broken in the mouth of a pilot, he would quickly expire. Bissell initially ordered six ampoules, which were dubbed L-pills. Pilots would be given the option of carrying one of the pills during flights over the Soviet bloc and would not be ordered to use the poison.

The instructions for use were chillingly simple.

"When the ampoule is required to be used it should be put in the mouth and held tightly between the teeth, with the lips tightly shut. The ampoule should then be crushed between the teeth. The user should then inhale through the mouth, shut the mouth again, and hold the breath as long as possible. Unconsciousness will follow in a short time, probably in about 30 seconds. It is expected that there will be no pain but there may be a feeling of constriction about the chest. Death will follow without consciousness being regained."

The risk of accidental use didn't become clear until late in 1956, after the first flights over the Soviet Union had been completed, when Carmine Vito flew a U-2 over Bulgaria. While Vito was prebreathing oxygen before the flight, one of the Air Force aides assigned to the U-2 detachment placed an L-pill in the right-hand knee pocket of Vito's pressure suit, apparently unaware that the pilot liked to stuff Lemon Drops into the same pocket to use to moisten his throat during the long flights. Pilots could open their helmets very briefly during flight. Hours later, while flying over Bulgaria, Vito unwittingly plucked the pill from among the hard candies, opened the faceplate on his helmet, and dropped it into his mouth. Fortunately, he did not bite down on the pill when it failed to produce the lemon taste he expected. He spit it into his hand. After learning of the incident, one of Bissell's aides ordered that the pills should be kept in small boxes.

The Agency was also slow to realize that the L-pill could kill a pilot if it accidentally broke open in the airplane and filled the cockpit with lethal gas. The pills were eventually replaced with an equally efficient but less volatile killer, a small needle laced with algal, a shellfish toxin. These deadly devices were precursors of the chemical and biological weapons concocted by the Agency in the unsuccessful efforts to kill off such unfriendly foreign leaders as Patrice Lumumba of the Congo and Fidel Castro.

As Eisenhower in late May was mulling over whether to use the U-2, he was well aware that capture of the plane and pilot by the Russians would be a propaganda triumph for the Kremlin. Moscow had had a field day earlier in the year when it recovered dozens of balloons equipped with cameras that the Air Force had launched into the jet stream in hopes it would carry them over Soviet territory. The reconnaissance operation, called Project Genetrix, was designed to produce the same sort of high-altitude photography as the U-2, in a safer if less controlled way. Eisenhower approved the plan on December 27, 1955. Over the next two months the Air Force sent 516 balloons into the skies over Western Europe, figuring that they would sail over Eastern Europe, the Soviet Union, and China. In theory, once the balloons crossed into international airspace over the Western Pacific, the film canisters would be recovered.

Only forty-six balloon payloads were recovered. The rest either vanished or were picked up by the Soviet Union and other Communist countries. The Russians gleefully complained about the spy equipment, which they called "espionage balloons," and exhibited a collection of gasbags, cameras, and transmitters in Moscow. The Eisenhower administration, previewing the cover story prepared for the U-2, lamely claimed that the balloons were monitoring high-altitude weather conditions. Most of the world, including the Washington press corps, doubted the explanation. Hanson Baldwin, the *New York Times* military correspondent, suggested to readers on February 19 that the administration's account had seriously undermined the credibility of the government. Baldwin wondered whether the potential military gains of the balloon flights outweighed the political damage created by their discovery.

Eisenhower concluded that they did not. He terminated the project, saying that "the balloons gave more legitimate grounds for irritation than could be matched by the good obtained from them."

Surprisingly, General Twining had proposed another balloon program in mid-March, one that would involve higher-altitude flight paths. Clearly irritated by the Air Force's persistence, Eisenhower responded that he was "not interested in any more balloons."

On May 31, Dulles and Twining sent Eisenhower a formal proposal for activating the U-2. The heavily classified paper was entitled "Aquatone Operational Plans." It called for making some preliminary flights over Eastern Europe and then moving within a matter of weeks to an initial series of missions over the Soviet Union. Eisenhower's review of the proposal was suspended after his intestinal attack on June 7.

While the president was recovering from emergency surgery, the U-2 detachment in Britain moved to an air base in Wiesbaden, West Germany. The change of scene was required because of an earlier espionage incident in Portsmouth harbor, outside London. During an April visit to Britain by Khrushchev, a frogman for the British Admiralty, sent to inspect the screws on a visiting Soviet cruiser, the *Ordzhonikidze*, was intercepted and killed by the crew of the Russian ship. The headless body of the frogman, Cmdr. Lionel Crabbe, floated ashore several days later. When the botched spy mission was exposed, Prime Minister Anthony Eden dismissed the head of the British secret service. Fearing further embarrassment, he subsequently asked Washington not to use Britain as a base for U-2 flights into Soviet airspace. John Foster Dulles, Allen Dulles, and Bissell decided to ask Konrad Adenauer, the West German chancellor, for permission to base the U-2 detachment in his country. Adenauer approved the idea after Bissell flew to Bonn to brief the chancellor and show him some of the test photographs of American cities. The move to West Germany commenced on June 11.

By this time, Bissell was impatient to start operational flights. Taking advantage of existing presidential authority for Air Force flights over Eastern Europe, he ordered the first U-2 mission over denied territory—East Germany, Czechoslovakia, and Poland—on Wednesday, June 20. The operational plan presented to Eisenhower on May 31 mentioned such preliminary flights, but Bissell did not explicitly seek the president's approval for them. Before sunrise on June 20, one of the U-2 pilots, Carl Overstreet, took off from Wiesbaden and pointed his plane toward the lightening skies in the east. He flew over the three Soviet bloc nations without incident, and two days later the photographs from his flight were delivered to Washington for analysis. Arthur Lundahl and his colleagues found the pictures to be of high quality.

The day after Overstreet's flight, Killian and Land accompanied Bissell to the White House for a crucial meeting with Goodpaster, who was representing the ailing president. The trio showed him some additional U-2 pictures and outlined Bissell's plan to begin flights into Soviet airspace as soon as the weather was suitable. Goodpaster informed his visitors that Eisenhower had approved the operational plan of May 31, but that he wanted the first series of flights to be "designed to cover all that is vital quickly." Goodpaster explained that this meant dispensing with flights just inside the Soviet border and moving swiftly to deeper operations. To avoid any misunderstanding about the degree of presidential control, Goodpaster told Bissell that Eisenhower "must be contacted before deep operations are initiated." The president also wanted regular updates once the flights began. Goodpaster summarized the conversation in a carefully worded memo that referred obliquely to the "reconnaissance project" without identifying its purpose or the existence of the U-2.

The four men also talked about possible problems, including the capture or crash of the airplane. It was during this discussion that Killian and Land questioned Bissell's plan to invoke the cover story about weather research and to deny American responsibility for spying if the U-2 was exposed. It was one of the few pieces of advice offered by Killian and Land that was ignored.

At last, Bissell had the hunting license he needed and was now just days away from giving Eisenhower a date for the first flight over Soviet territory. Bissell still had to inform Adenauer that such flights would soon begin, and he had to wait until General Twining completed a visit to Moscow, where he had been invited by Khrushchev to attend the Moscow Air Show that opened on June 23. Twining requested that no overflights be conducted before his delegation exited the Soviet Union at the end of the month.

On July 2, Bissell authorized two more flights over Eastern Europe, covering Czechoslovakia, Hungary, Romania, East Germany, Poland, and Bulgaria. That afternoon he and General Cabell, Dulles's deputy, briefed Eisenhower. They described Carl Overstreet's June 20 flight. Among other things, Eisenhower wanted to know whether Eastern European radar had tracked the U-2. Bissell reported there had been some detection but that radar operators had mistakenly believed the plane was flying at 42,000 feet, nearly 4 miles lower than its actual altitude. Eisenhower, still concerned about detection, asked for additional information about the other missions over Eastern Europe. Bissell told Goodpaster the weather over the European portion of the Soviet Union was expected to clear and he wanted to start flying immediately.

Goodpaster raised the request with Eisenhower on July 3 at Gettysburg, where the president was recuperating. The president approved a ten-day period for operations, beginning the next day. Goodpaster called Bissell at 2 P.M. to tell him he had until July 14 to complete the first series of overflights. Bissell, hoping to extend the window, asked if he could interpret Eisenhower's decision to mean ten days of good weather. "Absolutely not," Goodpaster replied. "It's ten calendar days, period. You'll have to take your chances with the weather." Goodpaster noted in another elliptical memorandum for the record that Bissell agreed to provide interim reports about tracking and any attempted interception.

Bissell was not surprised by the limitations. "I believe Eisenhower arranged things this way to keep our activities on a short leash. His idea was that we should try to get two or three flights off in the next ten days and then pause to assess the results. This proved to be sensible, as the overflights were indeed an exceedingly sensitive act so far as the Soviets were concerned."

The flight plans for the first missions were devised by Bissell and his aides in consultation with an interagency group that had been established in December 1955 at the suggestion of Land. The panel, known as the Ad Hoc Requirements Committee, included representatives from the Army, Navy, Air Force, and CIA and was chaired by James Q. Reber, an experienced intelligence officer who had run the Agency's Office of Intelligence Coordination for four years. The committee prepared a list of collection requirements, including target lists that were considered most likely to yield information about Moscow's long-range bombers and missiles and its nuclear weapons program.

The plans for the first two missions were audacious, to say the least. As Bissell later told Michael Beschloss, his team had told him, "Let's go for the big game the first time. We're safer the first time than we'll ever be again." Mission 2013 called for entering Soviet airspace over Belorussia, then swinging north to Leningrad to photograph several military airfields and the naval shipyards where Soviet submarines were built. The second flight, Mission 2014, would head straight to Moscow, where the U-2 would pass over the factory where the Bison bombers were being built, as well as the bomber test-flight center at Ramenskoye, where the big plane had first been sighted in 1953. The U-2 would also collect pictures of a missile plant and a rocket-engine center.

Shortly before midnight in Washington, after weather forecasters told Bissell the skies over the western Soviet Union were clear, he gave final approval for Mission 2013. The decision was transmitted to Wiesbaden on a secure transatlantic line. It was already light there on the morning of Wednesday, July 4. Hervey Stockman completed prebreathing and boarded one of Kelly Johnson's planes, which was innocuously marked as NACA 187, consistent with the numbering system for planes operated by the civilian aeronautical agency that was supposedly conducting the weather research flights. Bissell headed home to get some sleep.

Not long after Stockman entered Soviet airspace, he could tell his plane had been spotted and was being tracked. He could see through the downward-looking U-2 periscope that MiG fighters were swarming at lower altitudes, then ascending toward his plane until they reached their maximum altitude of 50,000 feet, when they would flip over and fall back toward earth. "They were trying to snap up and tap me," Stockman later said. The Soviet pilots couldn't get close enough to Stockman to get off a threatening shot, but it was abundantly clear that the U-2 was anything but invisible.

By coincidence, Killian was among the first people to learn that the Russians knew their airspace had been violated. He was in West Germany over the July 4 period, visiting an American eavesdropping station operated by the National Security Agency. "I found there this group of people who were listening in on what was happening in the Soviet Union, baffled and astonished at what they were hearing." The radio chatter they heard came from Soviet air defense forces trying to track the U-2. The American technicians were puzzled because the Russians seemed to be talking about a plane that was flying at an abnormally high altitude. "I didn't tell them what it was," Killian said.

The timing of the flight seemed designed to humiliate Khrushchev, who had decided to make a goodwill visit to the U.S. ambassador's residence on America's Independence Day. Khrushchev was greeted at Spaso House by Ambassador Charles Bohlen. The Soviet leader, unaware that the U-2 was at that very moment flying over Leningrad, toasted the health of President Eisenhower and wished the Americans a happy holiday. Bohlen knew about the U-2 program, but had not been told the maiden flight would take place that day. There is no indication that Bissell knew about the Khrushchev visit to Spaso House when he picked July 4 for the first flight.

Khrushchev was furious when he learned about the intrusion, but knew that for the moment he was powerless to shoot down the new American aircraft because his military forces lacked planes or missiles that could threaten the aircraft. Khrushchev's son, Sergei, later recalled, "My father could not understand why the Americans did it on the Fourth of July, because it was the second time in our postwar history when all the Soviet leadership went to the American embassy" on Independence Day. Khrushchev told his son that he imagined that the State Department and White House were "laughing" because the Russians could do nothing to stop the plane.

He was particularly piqued because he had just welcomed General Twining to the Soviet Union. "We welcomed him as a guest and entertained him," Khrushchev later said. "He left our country by air and next day sent a plane flying at great altitude into our country. . . . Only an animal like Twining would do its dirty business in the same place it eats."

The next morning, Carmine Vito took off from Wiesbaden. He, too, was pursued by Soviet defenders as he flew across Belorussia and headed for Moscow. The capital was largely obscured by clouds. Like Stockman, Vito returned unscathed to Wiesbaden.

Bissell briefed Dulles about the flights when the CIA director returned to work after the holiday on July 5. When Bissell told him the first missions had traveled over Leningrad and Moscow, Dulles was stunned. "Oh, my Lord," he said, "do you think that was wise the first time?"

"Allen," Bissell replied, "the first is the safest."

Eisenhower was anxious to know whether the U-2 had been detected. Before the initial flights, he had instructed Goodpaster to advise Dulles that the operation should be suspended "if we obtain any information or warning that any of the flights has been discovered or tracked." On July 5, he repeated his concerns to Goodpaster and asked him to advise Dulles "that if we obtain any information or warning that any of the flights has been discovered or tracked, the operation should be suspended." When Goodpaster checked with Dulles and Bissell that day, they told him that reports about tracking and interception would not be available for another thirty-six hours. When the two men met with Goodpaster still later that day, they requested permission to make additional flights. Goodpaster agreed further missions could be conducted, based on his understanding that Eisenhower had authorized operations "at the maximum rate until the first evidence of tracking was received."

It is hard to believe that Bissell, at least, was unaware of the attempted interception of the Stockman flight when he and Dulles talked with Goodpaster by phone and in person on July 5. He may genuinely have believed that more definitive information about the Soviet response was needed before he informed the White House. But it seems more likely that he wanted to squeeze in a few more flights before facing a presidential order to suspend operations. If so, the failure to inform Goodpaster and Eisenhower was virtually an act of insubordination.

On July 6, the CIA reported that an analysis of Soviet radar coverage revealed that the Russians had detected the U-2s and made several unsuccessful efforts to intercept them. But the data also showed that the Soviet radar had not been able to track the planes over the entire course of their flight and the Russians were unaware the planes had flown directly over Leningrad and Moscow.

Just when Eisenhower was told about this report is unclear. He should have been informed immediately, but the record suggests he was not. Because Soviet tracking had been intermittent, Bissell may have figured he had yet to hit the red line that Eisenhower had established. At any rate, he ordered three additional flights after July 6. There were two missions on July 9, covering Eastern Europe, Belorussia, and the Ukraine. The next day, another flight collected pictures of the Crimean Peninsula, the site of a large Soviet naval base.

Bissell's luck ran out on July 10. Early that day, Goodpaster and Eisenhower still seemed to be operating under the impression that the U-2s had yet to be tracked by the Russians. Goodpaster noted in a memorandum for the record that the president still wished to go ahead with U-2 operations "until the first reporting of tracking was actually received." The same memo indicates that in a subsequent discussion, after learning that there was some evidence of tracking, Eisenhower began to entertain serious doubts about extending the flights through the full ten-day period he had approved.

After returning to Washington from Gettysburg that afternoon, Goodpaster notified Dulles that Eisenhower was close to discontinuing operations. Goodpaster reminded the CIA chief that the president was mindful of how he would react "if they were to do this to us." Goodpaster relayed the same information to Bissell.

Eisenhower's fears were soon confirmed. That same day, the Kremlin ended its diplomatic silence about the flights by sending a stiff protest note to the American embassy in Moscow. It complained about over-flights made by a "twin-engine medium bomber of the United States Air Force." The diplomatic note described the route of the Stockman and Vito flights, though not their passage over Leningrad and Moscow, which Russian radar had failed to detect. Though the Soviet Union didn't realize initially that a radically new kind of spy plane had breached its airspace, the Kremlin protest was enough for Eisenhower. As soon as the diplomatic note reached the White House that evening, Goodpaster called Bissell and instructed him to halt U-2 operations until further notice. If there were to be any future missions, Eisenhower wanted much tighter White House control over the program.

As Eisenhower was suspending the program, the first photographs were beginning to reach Arthur Lundahl and his crew at the Steuart Building. They were stunning. As soon as Lundahl's photo interpreters examined film from the opening series of five flights over the Soviet Union, it was clear there was no "bomber gap." The July flights covered the nine major long-range bomber bases in the western portion of the Soviet Union. Only a handful of Bison bombers were spotted at the bases. Production of the plane was far more limited than Washington had suspected. The Air Force estimate that Moscow already owned nearly a hundred Bisons was simply wrong.

Dick Leghorn's vision was vindicated. In just a handful of flights, a high-altitude spy plane equipped with a high-powered camera system had erased the fear that the Soviet Union was racing ahead of the United States in the development of heavy bombers. Just as James Killian and Edwin Land had promised, advanced technologies had made it possible to see through the Iron Curtain. Based on the new information, Eisenhower could quietly but confidently hold down military spending in some areas, especially in the production rate of America's new long-range bomber, the B-52.

Virtually overnight, Kelly Johnson's ungainly airplane and Jim Baker's remarkable cameras had made the cold war less combustible and had inaugurated a new era in espionage at the edge of space. These were signal achievements. Looking back on the U-2 after his retirement, Eisenhower said the program "produced intelligence of critical importance to the United States."

"Perhaps as important as the positive information—what the Soviets did have—was the negative information it produced—what the Soviets did not have," the former president wrote. "U-2 information deprived Khrushchev of the most powerful weapon of the Communist conspiracy—international blackmail—usable only as long as the Soviets could exploit the ignorance and resulting fears of the Free World."

But in July 1956, as Eisenhower marveled at the first wave of photographs from the U-2, he was already moving to limit future flights over the Soviet Union. On July 19, Allen Dulles presented the president with startlingly clear and detailed pictures of various Russian sites, including the Winter Palace in Leningrad. To Bissell, the images showed that "we can take pictures of Moscow and Leningrad and they can't lay a mitt on us." To Eisenhower, however, they were also a symbol of a delicate diplomatic problem. The United States was flouting international law and deliberately violating Soviet airspace. Had the plane, as promised, eluded detection, there might have been few potential complications. But that was no longer the case.

Eisenhower complained to Dulles that the Agency had assured him that "not over a very minor percentage of these [flights] would be picked up," and bluntly told the CIA director he had "lost enthusiasm" for the U-2 program. If Moscow were to run similar flights over the United States, he said, "the reaction would be drastic." He was also concerned about adverse public reaction in the United States if Americans discovered their government was so openly violating international law. "Soviet protests were one thing; any loss of confidence by our own people would be quite another."

Eisenhower told Dulles, "We'd better stand down more or less indefinitely. Don't start again until you get permission." In the future, the president said, he would no longer grant approval for an unlimited number of flights over a certain period, but would instead insist that every flight plan be submitted to him for review. Bissell's secret air force was not going to get much work over its primary target. In fact, from Hervey Stockman's flight on July 4, 1956, to Francis Gary Powers's flight on May 1, 1960, the U-2 was used only twenty-four times for flights over the interior of the Soviet Union.

The fact that it was used at all after the July 1956 flights reflected the still urgent need for additional intelligence about Soviet forces, particularly Moscow's missile projects. Almost as soon as he realized Eisenhower was disillusioned with the plane, Bissell asked Land if it would be possible to make the aircraft less susceptible to detection. Edward Purcell, the Harvard physicist who had worked with Land on the Killian committee, came up with some novel ideas about how to evade radar, and Bissell soon funded a classified project in the Boston area. It was, in effect, one of the first efforts to produce a stealth airplane. The techniques proposed by Purcell to deflect or absorb radar pulses proved either ineffective or impractical—some of Purcell's ideas were tried out on the U-2 but made the plane harder to fly. Kelly Johnson was not happy with the outside meddling and made his disgust clear by calling modified versions of the U-2 "dirty birds."

The paradoxical nature of the U-2 was not lost on Johnson, Land, or the other men involved in its development. The intelligence benefits produced by the plane were invaluable, but the risks of using the aircraft over Soviet territory were great. To take full advantage of the advances in aerial reconnaissance, the United States needed to fly higher and faster. The U-2 was a transitional aircraft. Kelly Johnson would have to build something better. He was already working on it. But the ultimate answer, as Land knew, was to take America's reconnaissance operations into space.

PART THREE

Vaulting into Space
1956–1976

CHAPTER TEN

Earthbound

OUTER SPACE BECKONED, but as the U-2 went into service in July of 1956, the United States wasn't anywhere close to putting a spy satellite into orbit. In fact, the government was still struggling to develop reliable rockets and missiles, and the prospect of actually lofting any sort of object into orbit, even an empty tin can, seemed dismayingly distant. Had the Eisenhower administration taken a comprehensive look at the state of satellite development programs in mid-1956, it might have realized that it was stumbling rather than racing to place a reconnaissance system in space. That realization, unfortunately, did not come until more than a year later.

Washington did not lack for satellite proposals or even active programs. As Hervey Stockman sailed over Leningrad on July 4, 1956, the Air Force was secretly working on an ambitious satellite project that was the direct descendant of RAND's 1954 "Project Feed Back" report. The Navy, in conjunction with the National Academy of Sciences, was openly preparing to build a research satellite that would be sent aloft by the Navy's Vanguard rocket. Though the public did not know it, the scientific satellite was intended in part to clear the way for the military satellite by establishing the principle of freedom of space, the as-yet-untested doctrine that terrestrial laws, including traditional claims of sovereign airspace, did not extend into space. The Eisenhower administration knew this novel legal issue was pivotal. If the Soviet Union or other nations asserted that their restricted national airspace extended above the atmosphere, the operation of any kind of satellites, whether civilian or military, would be impeded and years of diplomatic wrangling could be expected before the legal issues were resolved.

But for the moment these potential problems remained purely theoretical because the satellite programs were hobbled by a lack of coordination, resources, and proven technologies. The Air Force had yet to come up with a photographic system that could capture detailed images from space and transmit them back to earth. The fault, ironically, rested in part with RAND, which had worked so hard to get the government to take satellites seriously. In their devotion to the concept, RAND researchers such as Bob Salter, Jim Lipp, and Mert Davies had pointed the Air Force toward electronic technologies that the nation had not yet mastered. With the trickle of money coming from the Pentagon, the Air Force and its main contractor, Lockheed, weren't likely to overcome the technical challenges anytime soon. Meantime, the Kremlin had mobilized Russian scientists and engineers to beat the United States into space, correctly sensing that such a spectacular achievement would burnish the Soviet Union's image as a progressive, scientifically advanced nation and create the impression that it had eclipsed America in science and technology.

Without rockets, of course, there could be no satellites, and the American rocket program in 1956 was just beginning to pick up momentum. For nearly a decade after World War II, it had suffered from military turf battles that dated back to the war years, when the United States set out to produce its own rockets and missiles, inspired by the example of Nazi Germany's V-2 rockets. Though the German weapons were inaccurate, the rocket attacks on Britain that commenced in late 1944 signaled the advent of a new era in warfare. Edward R. Murrow, the intrepid CBS correspondent, told the world about the rockets in a broadcast from London on November 12, 1944. "The significance of this demonstration of German skill and ingenuity lies in the fact that it makes complete nonsense out of strategic frontiers, mountain and river barriers. And, in the opinion of many able scientists, it means that within a few years present methods of aerial bombardment will be as obsolete as the Gatling gun. It serves to make more appalling the prospect or the possibility of another war."

Before the V-2 made its terrifying debut, the U.S. Army had been exploring rocket technologies, working with scientists at Caltech and engineers at the General Electric Company. Sadly, the pioneering work of Robert Goddard provided little basis for this wartime research, not because Goddard's experiments were disappointing—quite the contrary—but because his later achievements were little known. After his early, well-chronicled success with liquid-fuel rockets near his Massachusetts home in the 1920s, Goddard had moved his operations to an isolated ranch outside Roswell, New Mexico. There he found the privacy and secrecy he prized, but he all but disappeared from sight. Though Goddard conducted forty-eight test flights during fifteen years at the ranch, from 1930 to 1945, his obsession with secrecy prevented wide circulation of his ideas.

As the war in Europe wound down in early 1945, the Army realized the quickest way to energize its rocket program was to ship home a boatload of V-2 rockets and the men who had built them. Col. Gervais Trichel, who headed the Ordance Department's Rocket Development Branch, dispatched an aide to Europe with orders to assemble a list of top German rocket scientists. This mission soon grew into a concerted, clandestine effort to transfer German engineers and rocket equipment to the United States after the war, a pragmatic but morally repugnant program that eventually brought dozens of former Nazi supporters to America. The bargain behind Project Overcast and Project Paperclip, as the migration was successively code named, was simple enough. If the Germans put their expertise to work building American rockets and missiles, their association with the Nazi regime would be forgiven. Wernher von Braun, the technical director of the Nazi ballistic missile program, was the most prominent, and came to play a high-profile role in the American space program. The Soviet Union conducted a parallel effort after the war, bringing dozens of other German rocket scientists to Moscow.

By October 1945, the first group of Germans was based at the White Sands Proving Ground in New Mexico, a desolate area north of El Paso, Texas, that was already the Army's primary missile test site. Von Braun himself was settled at Fort Bliss in El Paso. At White Sands, the Germans helped assemble dozens of V-2 rockets from more than 360 metric tons of components that the United States had secretly spirited out of Germany just days after the war ended. By May 1946, German rockets, which had been designed to terrorize Londoners, were thundering into the sky over the San Andres and Sacramento Mountains in southeast New Mexico. The cold-blooded decision to make use of the Nazi rocket engineers was a fitting model for the kind of cold war calculations that often put Washington in league with foreign tyrants and brutal security forces. Unlike many of those cases, the use of the Germans ultimately enhanced American security.

Von Braun and his colleagues were not the only source of missile technology. The Army Air Forces commissioned more than two dozen missile projects involving six aircraft companies. One of the programs—Convair's Project MX-774—involved preliminary work on a ballistic missile with a range of 5,000 miles.

Worried that guided missiles would become the exclusive domain of the Army, the Navy initiated its own rocket program in 1945 and quickly added an element that had not occurred to the Army: development of a satellite. The Navy's Committee for Evaluating the Possibility of Space Rocketry concluded that a "satellite rocket" could be placed in orbit around the earth once adequate propulsion systems were devised. But when the Navy proposed in March 1946 that the Army Air Forces join in a cooperative effort to produce such a satellite, the offer was turned down. The architect of the rejection, Maj. Gen. Curtis LeMay, who had recently become deputy chief of research and development for the Air Staff, moved quickly to initiate a separate satellite plan. He hired the Douglas Aircraft Company in El Segundo to study the possibilities, and in so doing started the sequence of events that led to the creation by Douglas and the Air Forces of Project RAND and the preparation of its first report in May 1946, "Preliminary Design of an Experimental World-Circling Spaceship."

Unfortunately, the postwar boom in rocket and missile research was short-lived. Concerned about inflation and undisciplined federal spending, the Truman administration soon started cutting the Pentagon

budget, and the missile and satellite projects were among the first casu-
alties. Project MX-774 was canceled, as were ten other missile programs. LeMay asked RAND to prepare a more detailed design study on
satellites, anticipating that the next step would be assigning development work to an aircraft company. It was delivered on February 1, 1947.
But the scarcity of funds and the air service's preference for airplanes
prevented further action, despite Lipp's fervent appeal to move ahead at
once with a satellite.

The missilemen also faced doubts about the technology itself, especially the idea of long-range missiles that could span continents and
oceans. Vannevar Bush, Franklin Roosevelt's leading science adviser,
had caught the mood accurately in late 1945 when he said of intercontinental ballistic missiles, "I say technically I don't think anybody in the
world knows how to do such a thing and I feel confident it will not be
done for a long period of time to come." As of 1948, the Pentagon had
set aside all research and development work on satellites and the newly
created independent Air Force, which wanted more bombers, was funding just four missile projects.

This attitude lingered in Washington until the development of the
hydrogen bomb in 1952 and the arrival of Trevor Gardner, Donald
Quarles, and other technologically minded men at the Pentagon. The
Strategic Missile Evaluation Committee, headed by John von Neumann, reported in February 1954 that thermonuclear warheads could
be designed to be small and light enough to fit aboard a long-range missile. The group strongly urged the government to accelerate its missile
development programs.

The impact of the report could soon be seen in the performance specifications set for long-range missiles. In 1951, in a halfhearted effort to
get back in the missile business, the Air Force had initiated a new missile
program, providing just $500,000 to contractors to begin work on what
was to be called the Atlas missile. The missile was to carry a 10,000-
pound payload and strike a target 5,000 miles away with a very high degree of accuracy. Once the committee confirmed the possibility of a
smaller warhead, engineers scaled back the payload weight for intercon-

tinental missiles to 3,000 pounds and widened the margin for accuracy because of the greater explosive power of hydrogen warheads as compared to atomic warheads.

The Air Force intensified work on the Atlas in 1954 and created a separate administrative unit within the Air Research and Development Command to manage the Atlas program. The new organization, the Western Development Division, was headquartered in a former schoolhouse in Inglewood, on the western edge of Los Angeles not far from the city's main airport. The missile test site was located at Point Arguello, a vacant, windswept stretch of the California coast north of Santa Barbara. When the initial commander, Maj. Gen. James McCormack, retired, the Air Force gave the job to General Schriever. He assumed command in June 1954, determined to arm the nation as quickly as possible with advanced missiles that could strike anywhere in the world.

Like Richard Bissell, who five months later would be given responsibility for building the U-2, Schriever believed in crisp decision-making and minimal bureaucracy. He soon transformed the Inglewood operation into a creative, effective management organization that dispensed with the Air Force's cumbersome contracting procedures and paperwork. One of his first and most unconventional decisions was to ask two civilian experts, Simon Ramo and Dean E. Wooldridge, to coordinate the technical work, a move that essentially trumped the usual Air Force chain of command on research and development projects. Ramo and Wooldridge, who had met as doctoral students at Caltech, were already well known in the nascent aerospace world as the designers of sophisticated electronic systems for Hughes Aircraft Company and the founders in 1953 of the eponymous Ramo-Wooldridge Corporation, which would merge with Thompson Products, a Cleveland auto-parts company, to become TRW. The two men had served as members of von Neumann's committee. Working with Schriever, Ramo-Wooldridge provided the technical direction for the American missile program. TRW later became a prime contractor for building satellites that monitored Soviet radio communications.

Schriever also got his bosses in Washington to make it clear that missiles were the service's number one development project. That message was strongly reinforced by the White House after the Killian committee recommended in February 1955 that the Air Force proceed briskly with its missile effort, though the group wrongly predicted that the United States would not likely assemble a full arsenal of the weapons before 1965. "The development of such a missile requires the solution of a set of truly awesome technical problems," the panel found. "Its size alone is a problem; the atmosphere re-entry is a totally new problem; the firing of each test missile will probably represent an operation of great magnitude. A number of test firings will be required in the development of the missile." The committee recommended that "the development of an intercontinental ballistic missile (with about 5,500 nautical miles' range and megaton warhead) continue to receive the very substantial support necessary to complete it at the earliest possible date." Once Schriever got the missile program running at full speed, with an industrial base to match, he would guide one program after another from conception to operation, including the Atlas, Titan I and II, and the solid-fuel Minuteman ICBM's. Because of Schriever's energetic leadership, the country overcame its feeble initial efforts to produce an array of long-range missiles by the early 1960s.

Sixteen months after taking over the Western Development Division, Schriever inherited the Air Force's sole satellite project, an orphan officially known as Weapon System-117L, or WS-117L in Air Force shorthand. The program was the offshoot of RAND's Project Feed Back. The project called for incorporating a reconnaissance satellite into the second stage of a two-stage rocket, using the Atlas missile as the first-stage booster. The satellite itself was to contain a Kodak camera system that would produce photographs on which large objects like airplanes would be visible. The exposed film would be automatically processed aboard the satellite, the resulting pictures would be scanned electronically, and the video signal would be radioed to earth much like a television broadcast. The stream of electronic data would then be transformed back into a photographic image.

The design was inventive, but the ambitious technical goals were actually crippling. The number of images that could be transmitted to earth were limited by the radio bandwidth and data transmission rate, as well as the short time that the orbiting satellite would be in radio range of ground stations as it rotated around the earth. To compensate for the meager number of pictures that could be relayed daily, the satellite would need to remain in orbit for a year or more. That required a high orbit of 300 miles to reduce the atmospheric drag that would erode the orbit of a lower-flying satellite. But the orbit altitude would make it harder to produce detailed pictures, and the extended lifetime of the satellite would require equipping it with a heavy load of film.

The project had grown slowly from the March 1, 1954, RAND report to an Air Force research program to the full-fledged development program run out of Wright Field that was authorized on March 16, 1955, in a document blandly entitled "System Requirement (No. 5) for an Advanced Reconnaissance System." A secret 1962 Air Force history summarized the expectations for the early satellite system. "In many respects, as might have been anticipated, it paralleled the earlier RAND studies. It defined as the Air Force objective a means of providing continuous surveillance of 'preselected areas of the earth' in order 'to determine the status of a potential enemy's warmaking capability.' Intended for launch from fixed bases, the reconnaissance satellite was to provide daylight visual coverage in sufficient detail to permit identification of airfield runways and intercontinental missile launch stations."

The transfer of authority from Wright Field to Inglewood in October 1955 was logical. For one thing, the heavy reconnaissance satellite needed a powerful booster to lift it into orbit, and the Atlas was the most promising candidate. For another, Schriever had long been a supporter of the satellite project and had used his influence at the Pentagon to press for its development. More than any other general officer in the Air Force, Schriever appreciated the potential uses of space. With his connections to Leghorn and Land, his openness to new ideas, and his faith in science and technology, Schriever was the ideal steward for the WS-117L. Over time, the WS-117L project would encompass several different intelligence-gathering systems, including infrared sensors designed to detect Soviet missile launches.

But even Schriever was stymied by technical and funding problems.

Electronic technology for transmitting high-resolution images back to earth in a data stream was not yet perfected—and would not be for two more decades. The drawbacks were compounded by a shortage of money. Though the Air Force had formally endorsed the project, it provided minimal funding. After studying design proposals submitted by four companies—Lockheed Missile Systems Division, Bell Telephone Laboratories, Glenn L. Martin Company, and RCA—Schriever and his team designated Lockheed as the prime contractor on October 29, 1956, almost four months after President Eisenhower was informed that the Russians could track the U-2. The choice of Lockheed was poetically just—the two prime authors of the Project Feed Back report, Jim Lipp and Bob Salter, had moved to Lockheed along with several other top RAND officials. But because of budget restrictions, Lockheed had to cut the pace of work down to just one-tenth of the level it had planned. At that rate, the first working satellite would not be in operation until well after the already distant target date of March 1960.

In truth, the Pentagon was barely keeping the program alive. Gardner was gone, and Schriever was on the West Coast, where it was more difficult for him to lobby for satellite funds. Air Force leaders in Washington remained doubtful that the satellite pictures would be of much use in pinpointing Soviet military targets. With the White House and Congress leaning on the Air Force to produce missiles, and the White House trying to hold down defense spending, the Air Force was content to devote most of its space budget to missiles.

The idea of a reconnaissance satellite was also overshadowed by the administration's highly publicized goal of putting a civilian scientific research satellite in orbit no later than 1958. This project proved doubly damaging. It deflected attention and support away from the reconnaissance project, which was all but frozen for several years. More important, the ill-conceived project, specifically its reliance on a questionable Navy rocket, gave the Russians the opening they needed to beat the United States into space. The whole scheme was one of the greatest miscalculations of the cold war.

The research satellite plan grew out of a discussion among a group of American and British scientists in 1950 at the Silver Spring, Maryland, home of physicist James Van Allen. Eager to encourage high-altitude research work around the world, the men came up with the idea of staging an international scientific exercise in 1957–58, a time that would coincide with unusually high solar activity and come twenty-five years after the last such global effort, the 1932 International Polar Year. The meeting at Van Allen's home eventually led the International Council of Scientific Unions to obtain the approval of sixty-seven nations to designate 1957–58 as the occasion for a new round of cooperative research that was called the International Geophysical Year (IGY). Some of the same space scientists who had gathered at the Van Allen home recommended in 1952 that the launching of a research satellite be identified as one of the main goals of the IGY. The International Council approved the objective at a meeting in Rome in October 1954, with the assent of both Russian and American scientists.

Subsequently, the National Academy of Sciences, a society of the nation's top scientists, and the National Science Foundation, an independent government agency established in 1950 to promote and fund scientific research, worked together in 1954 and 1955 to gain White House approval for an American civilian satellite project. The administration welcomed the proposal, but not for the high-minded reasons cited by the scientists. To the White House and Pentagon, the research satellite looked like a fine way to achieve several national security objectives, namely beating the Russians into space and demonstrating that use of the heavens would be governed by the freedom-of-space principle.

The Killian panel had unambiguously outlined the overlapping interests in its February 1955 report. In part five of the classified report, the section dealing with intelligence issues, Edwin Land's task force assessed the potential uses of satellites. "We are convinced that small, inexpensive satellites can have several important uses related to intelligence. First, careful observations of the motions of the satellites would give, directly, much information about friction in the extreme upper air, and about fine details of the shape and gravitational field of the earth. This information is wanted for the design and guidance of long-range ballistic missiles and would be useful for the design of large satellites for intelligence purposes. Second, even a lightweight satellite might be constructed to open into an extended structure (resembling a bedspring) which could be an effective reflector for very-high-frequency radio and radar signals. Conceivably, this could have applications in communication and in intelligence. Third, the new prestige that the world will accord to the nation first to launch an artificial earth satellite would better go to the U.S. than to the USSR. And although it is clear that a very small satellite cannot serve as a useful carrier for reconnaissance apparatus, cameras, etc., it can serve ideally to explore or establish the principle that space, outside our atmosphere, is open to all."

Part five ended with a set of twelve recommendations, including: "Intelligence applications warrant an immediate program leading to very small artificial satellites in orbits around the earth. Construction of large surveillance satellites must be deferred until adequate solutions are found to some extraordinary technical problems in the information-gathering and -reporting system and its power supply; and should wait upon development of the ICBM rocket-propulsion system. The ultimate objective of research and development on the large satellite should be continuous surveillance that is both extensive and selective and that can give fine-scale detail sufficient for the identification of objects (airplanes, trains, buildings) on the ground."

With these conclusions still fresh in their minds, administration officials threw their support behind the civilian satellite proposal while carefully masking their ulterior interests from the public. The decisive moment came on Thursday, May 26, 1955, when Eisenhower presided over a meeting of the National Security Council. The participants included Vice President Richard Nixon, Secretary of State John Foster Dulles, Secretary of Defense Charles Wilson, Allen Dulles from the CIA, and a slew of top military officials. The scientific satellite plan was the central item on the agenda, spelled out in a draft policy statement labeled NSC 5520. Eisenhower was headed to Geneva in less than a month for the four-power disarmament summit where he would make his "Open Skies" proposal. The notion of launching a research satellite ostensibly for the benefit of mankind must have meshed well with

Eisenhower's growing interest in trying to seize the moral high ground in Geneva.

The secret policy paper listed more than half a dozen reasons to approve the satellite project, including the Pentagon's expectation that a 5- to 10-pound satellite could be launched into orbit by 1957–1958 by adapting existing rocket components. The document recalled the Killian committee recommendations and noted that top Soviet scientists were believed to be working on a satellite program. It also stressed the potential "prestige and psychological benefits" that would likely flow to the first nation in space. "The inference of such a demonstration of advanced technology and its unmistakable relationship to intercontinental ballistic missile technology might have important repercussions on the political determination of free world countries to resist Communist threats, especially if the USSR were to be the first to establish a satellite."

Nelson Rockefeller, a presidential assistant who dealt with psychological warfare issues, bluntly underscored that point in a letter that accompanied NSC 5520 and was distributed to the members of the council. Rockefeller wrote, "The stake of prestige that is involved makes this a race that we cannot afford to lose."

The policy paper plainly described the potential military and intelligence benefits of the non-military satellite. "From a military standpoint, the Joint Chiefs of Staff have stated their belief that intelligence applications strongly warrant the construction of a large surveillance satellite. While a small scientific satellite cannot carry surveillance equipment and therefore will have no direct intelligence potential, it does represent a technological step toward the achievement of the large surveillance satellite, and will be helpful to this end so long as the small scientific satellite program does not impede development of the large surveillance satellite."

Donald Quarles, the assistant secretary of defense for research and development, described the satellite program to Eisenhower and the council members. The president observed at one point that the satellite was a minor affair, but that the nation would be getting into "the big stuff" if it eventually put up a reconnaissance model.

President Dwight D. Eisenhower (with Nikita S. Khrushchev, the Soviet leader, during a visit to Camp David in 1959) secretly ordered the CIA to build new spy planes and satellites that could gauge Soviet military strength and warn Washington if the Kremlin was preparing a surprise nuclear attack. The technologically advanced projects changed the nature of espionage by creating powerful new machines that could collect more intelligence in a day than an army of spies could gather on the ground in a year. Eisenhower's faith in science was a hallmark of his presidency.

James R. Killian Jr., the president of MIT, urged Eisenhower to develop radical new military technologies to reduce the threat of surprise attack.

Edwin H. Land, the inventor of instant photography, spotted promising new spy systems such as the U-2 at an early stage and guided their development.

Trevor Gardner, a combative Air Force official, prodded the Eisenhower administration to build missiles and other modern weapons systems.

Richard S. Leghorn, a World War II reconnaissance pilot, anticipated the need for the U-2, the supersonic A-12 spy plane, and the first reconnaissance satellites.

7

8

James G. Baker *(left)*, a Harvard astronomer, designed the camera used in the U-2 to photograph Soviet military sites. A number of Bison bombers are visible at an airfield near Moscow *(below)*, photographed by the U-2 in 1956.

Clarence L. "Kelly" Johnson *(above)*, Lockheed's virtuoso airplane maker, with the U-2, the high-flying spy plane he produced ahead of schedule and under budget.

9

10

11

12

Eisenhower's audacious technological goals were achieved with critical help from three government officials.

Richard M. Bissell Jr. *(top left)*, better known for his direction of CIA covert operations, nimbly managed the spy plane and satellite projects for the Agency even though he had no aviation or aerospace background.

Gen. Bernard A. Schriever *(top right)*, who led the Air Force into space, gave critical institutional and technical support to the intelligence projects.

Arthur C. Lundahl *(bottom)* created the CIA photography interpretation center that gleaned vital information from the flood of photographs produced by the new reconnaissance systems.

The launch, orbiting, and recovery of the first reconnaissance satellites required an exquisitely precise sequence of events, beginning with the countdown at the Corona launch pad at Vandenberg AFB on the California coast *(right)*. The camera system, film, and recovery capsule, which was designed to withstand the withering heat of reentry as it plunged through the atmosphere with a load of exposed film, were housed in an Agena rocket that also served as a second-stage booster. (The recovery sequence is depicted below.) The Agena sat atop a Thor missile, which powered the spacecraft off the launch pad.

13

14

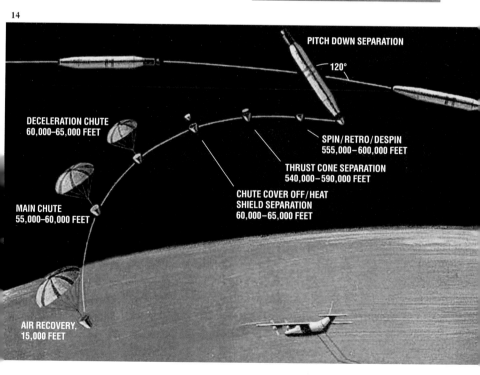

PITCH DOWN SEPARATION

120°

DECELERATION CHUTE
60,000–65,000 FEET

SPIN/RETRO/DESPIN
555,000–600,000 FEET

THRUST CONE SEPARATION
540,000–590,000 FEET

CHUTE COVER OFF/HEAT
SHIELD SEPARATION
60,000–65,000 FEET

MAIN CHUTE
55,000–60,000 FEET

AIR RECOVERY,
15,000 FEET

15

President Eisenhower marks the arrival at the White House of the first film capsule recovered from space on August 11, 1960. Because the flight was primarily
diagnostic, no film was sent aloft. Instead an American flag was placed in the capsule. Eisenhower is flanked in the Oval Office ceremony by *(left to right)* Air Force
Secretary Dudley C. Sharp, Secretary of Defense Thomas Gates, Air Force Chief
of Staff Thomas D. White, and Lt. Col. Charles "Moose" Mathison.

An April 1963 photo taken by a Corona satellite shows a Soviet nuclear-weapons
production plant near Sverdlovsk.

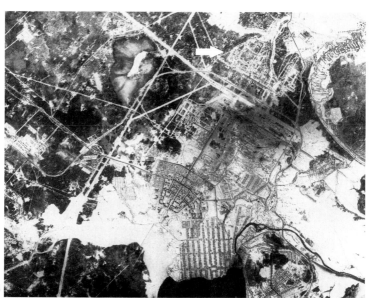

16

17

18

James W. Plummer *(left)* managed the Corona satellite project for Lockheed. Albert D. "Bud" Wheelon *(right)* created a new CIA directorate of science and technology in 1963 and initiated work on a new generation of advanced spy satellites. He also worked with Clarence L. "Kelly" Johnson to overcome technical problems with the A-12 supersonic spy plane. The Air Force model *(below)* was known as the SR-71 Blackbird.

19

The most advanced photo reconnaissance satellites in operation today, orbiting several hundred miles above the earth, can show objects on the ground as small as a football. This image shows the damage inflicted at the Al Sahra Airfield in Iraq by American warplanes in December 1998. Holes in the roof of the hangar are visible, as are several aircraft and a number of people. For security reasons, the degraded image, made public by the Defense Department, does not show the full magnification power of the satellite.

Henry Cabot Lodge, the chief American representative to the U.N., warned that the administration would have to be careful in handling its announcement about the project, evidently concerned that world opinion might turn against Washington if the government appeared to be trying to militarize space. Quarles reassured Lodge that the auspices of the International Geophysical Year would shield the United States from criticism.

As the discussion wound down, Eisenhower invited his aides to register any objections to the plan. There were none. After Allen Dulles emphasized the importance of the project, no one present could have misunderstood its potential implications for intelligence gathering. The National Security Council endorsed the paper and the next day the president officially approved the plan. It would ultimately call for launching six satellites, plus the construction of ground stations to track their movement around the earth.

As Lodge had suggested, presentation of the project to the public would be a sensitive matter. Rockefeller proposed at the NSC meeting that the announcement be made at the United Nations. That was in keeping with the policy paper's recommendation that "the United States should emphasize the peaceful purposes" of the project. In the end, the White House itself was selected as the appropriate venue. On Friday, July 29, 1955, the administration unveiled its plan at a White House news conference attended by a battery of prominent scientists. James Hagerty, the White House press secretary, told reporters, "On behalf of the president, I am now announcing that the president has approved plans by this country for going ahead with the launching of small unmanned earth-circling satellites as part of the United States participation in the International Geophysical Year. . . . This program will, for the first time in history, enable scientists throughout the world to make sustained observations in the regions beyond the earth's atmosphere. The president expressed personal gratification that the American program will provide scientists of all nations this important and unique opportunity for the advancement of science."

When Hagerty was asked if the project was linked to any satellite plans the Pentagon might have, he replied, "The only connection the

Department of Defense will have with this project is actually getting these satellites up in the air."

The splashy announcement grabbed the nation's attention. "U.S. To Launch Earth Satellite 200–300 Miles Into Outer Space; World Will Get Scientific Data," the *New York Times* proclaimed in a large front-page headline on July 30. Another front-page story, this one by Anthony Leviero, about the scientific purposes of the satellite noted two functions that it would not be able to perform:

"It will have no utility for gaining terrestrial data that might be used as part of President Eisenhower's Geneva plan for inspecting the military establishment of the United States and Russia.

"It will not be able to drop nuclear weapons, or anything else for that matter, for use against a hostile country."

With American prestige now tied emphatically to the space race, the administration had to come up with a rocket that could put the American satellite in orbit. Inexplicably, it had no clear plan. To make matters worse, the White House emphasis on the peaceful purposes of the satellite, and the Pentagon's desire not to divert money from its missile programs, drove the administration away from one of the most obvious launch vehicles, the Atlas. A review of rocket options led by Homer Stewart of the Jet Propulsion Lab produced a grievously flawed plan that doomed America's chances of getting a satellite into orbit before the Russians.

The Stewart committee had three choices. The Air Force reluctantly proposed use of the Atlas, but made clear that might distract engineers from their main goal of building a missile rather than a booster for a satellite. The two functions were not entirely complementary. It required less power but better guidance systems to fire a missile into space and direct it to a target halfway around the world than to lift a satellite into orbit. The Atlas or any other missile would need to be joined with a second- and possibly even a third-stage rocket engine to achieve the velocity necessary to carry a payload into orbit. In the summer of 1955, the Air Force also couldn't guarantee that the Atlas would be fully tested and ready for use by the end of 1958.

That left the Army and Navy, both of which still had their own missile programs, carryovers from the projects they had initiated after World War II. The Army offered use of the Redstone rocket, which von Braun and his team had developed in the early 1950s after they ran out of V-2 rockets and moved from El Paso and White Sands to the Army's Guided Missile Center at Redstone Arsenal in Huntsville, Alabama. The Redstone was a liquid-fuel rocket about 30 percent more powerful than the V-2 and considerably lighter. It was the first in a series of increasingly powerful boosters that later included the Saturn rockets that would carry Americans to the moon. With the use of two or three solid-fuel Sergeant rockets as upper stages, the Redstone, in theory, could propel a small satellite into orbit. In fact, the Office of Naval Research and Redstone Arsenal had proposed a joint satellite project in 1954 based on a similar plan. The project was called Orbiter.

The Navy, for its part, urged the Stewart committee to select its Viking rocket, the product of a program the service had inaugurated toward the end of 1946 when the Naval Research Lab contracted with the Glenn L. Martin Company to build a research rocket to carry scientific payloads into space. The first Viking was launched on May 3, 1949, climbing to an altitude of 50 miles. Like the Redstone, it would need supplemental stages to achieve orbital velocity.

On August 3, the Stewart committee by a divided vote selected the Viking. The Army team in Huntsville hotly protested the decision. Maj. Gen. Leslie Simon, the Army's assistant chief of ordnance for research and development, complained in a memo on August 15 that the Viking plan was laced with errors and based on an unrealistically rosy set of expectations about development of the rocket system. With some simple, inexpensive modifications, he said, the Redstone would be ready for the first orbital flight in January 1957 if the Pentagon immediately approved the Army proposal.

The Huntsville appeal was unsuccessful. Walter A. McDougall, a University of Pennsylvania professor and chronicler of the space race, suggested in his 1985 book, . . . *The Heavens and the Earth*, that von Braun's rocket was slighted to avoid the taint of Nazi science. He surmised that the administration did not want to give the Russians any additional excuse to challenge the free passage of an American satellite in space. McDougall reported that Washington was so concerned about von Braun's involvement that Army inspectors traveled to Cape Canaveral when the Jupiter-C, a variant of the Redstone, was later unveiled to be sure that the Germans were not trying to outflank the Navy. The Jupiter-C was used to test newly invented missile nose cones that were designed to survive reentry through the atmosphere. The Army high command feared that if von Braun equipped the rocket with additional stages rather than mock-ups, it could put a nose cone in orbit.

The sensitivity about the Germans may have made for good diplomacy, but the rejection of the Redstone ignored the clear technical advantages of the Army rocket. While the Navy program, which was named Project Vanguard, floundered, the Redstone rapidly progressed to the point where launch of a satellite seemed within reach. In September 1956, a Jupiter-C soared far into space, reaching a record altitude of 682 miles. With the addition of a live upper stage, it would likely have reached orbital speed. The Vanguard, by contrast, was beset with problems, including unexpectedly high costs, which quickly eroded Pentagon support for the project. With a long shopping list of new missiles, bombers, and missile-carrying nuclear submarines, the Defense Department was unenthusiastic about subsidizing a civilian satellite project, even one that had important military implications. The lack of support for the Vanguard program was evident when the Glenn L. Martin Company, the prime contractor for Vanguard, moved many of its top rocket engineers from Baltimore to Denver in late 1955 to work on the more profitable Titan missile program.

As evidence accumulated in 1956 that Vanguard was falling far behind schedule, and the CIA reported that the Soviet space program was advancing rapidly toward launch of a satellite, the administration stubbornly stuck by the Navy rocket. Looking back through the documentary record, it seems clear that despite all the earnest discussion about the potential propaganda benefits of being first in space, many officials failed to appreciate how traumatic a Soviet victory would be for the United States. Much of the administration, in effect, seemed to buy the illusion it had sold to the world, namely that the United States was engaged in a noble scientific experiment, not a rank race with the Russians.

There were exceptions. In late April 1956, William Y. Elliott, an aide at the White House Office of Defense Mobilization, forwarded a report to one of Eisenhower's senior aides pointing out that "it might be in the national interest" to piggyback a satellite on a Redstone during tests expected to take place in January 1957. The report had been prepared by David Z. Beckler, the executive secretary of the Office of Defense Mobilization's Science Advisory Committee. In his memo to William H. Jackson, a special assistant to the president, Elliott noted that Beckler had recently returned from a visit to the Vanguard test site "with a feeling that the Navy may fall so far behind the schedule that we will suffer a serious psychological setback."

Citing State Department anxieties about a Russian victory in the space race, Elliott told Jackson, "I think you are aware of the high psychological importance attached by State to getting this into the air on time, at least, particularly because of its obvious connection to our capabilities for an intermediate range ballistic missile, vis-à-vis the capability of the Soviet system."

But for the most part, common sense was a casualty of myopic thinking. On June 22, 1956, Homer Stewart advised Donald Quarles of some developing problems in the Vanguard program, including a shortage of qualified technical experts at the Naval Research Lab who could set specifications and coordinate the work of subcontractors. But Stewart discounted the "minor delays" and reiterated his view that Vanguard could make the 1958 IGY deadline. Once again, he rejected the idea of switching to the Redstone, even though he noted that by January 1957 it might well be ready to put a 17-pound satellite into orbit.

In a politically obtuse observation, he warned Quarles that the successful launch of a satellite in the opening weeks of 1957 would actually be a grave mistake. "Such a flight would not fulfill the nation's commitment for the International Geophysical Year because it would have to be made before the beginning of that period," Stewart wrote. "Adequate tracking and observation equipment for the scientific utilization of results would not be available at this time. Moreover, any announcement of such a flight (or worse, any leakage of information if no prior announcement were made) would seriously compromise the strong moral position internationally which the United States presently holds in the IGY due to its frank and open acts and announcements as respects Vanguard."

A few weeks later, E. V. Murphree, a top Pentagon missile adviser, made the same argument to the deputy secretary of defense, Reuben B. Robertson Jr. "While it is true that the Vanguard group does not expect to make its first satellite attempt before August 1957, whereas a satellite attempt could be made by the Army Ballistic Missile Agency as early as January 1957, little would be gained by making such an early satellite attempt as an isolated action with no follow-up program."

Some of the scientists working on the Vanguard project acknowledged the delays in an appearance before a House subcommittee in the spring of 1957. When their testimony was published by the subcommittee on May 19, John W. Finney of the *New York Times* reported that the planned launch date was being put off from September until sometime the following spring. His front-page story added, however, that the satellite program was "beset by so many uncertainties that the scientists still do not have any definite idea when the small sphere will be shot on its earth-circling trip through space."

The Russians were happy to report a few weeks later that their satellite plans were advancing briskly. The president of the Soviet Academy of Sciences, Aleksandr Nesmeyanov, announced at the end of May that Russian scientists "have created the rockets and all the instruments and equipment necessary to solve the problems of the artificial earth satellite." On June 10, Nesmeyanov predicted that Moscow would launch a satellite "within the next few months." In case anyone in Washington had missed the Soviet statements, a group of Russian scientists outlined the launch schedule again late in June at an international meeting in Brussels.

On August 26, the Kremlin startled Washington by announcing that it had successfully tested an intercontinental ballistic missile. In his dispatch from Moscow, Max Frankel of the *New York Times* reported, "The announcement said the missile, flying at an 'unprecedented' altitude, had 'covered a huge distance in a brief time' and had 'landed in the target area.' It added that the results showed a missile could be directed 'into any part of the world.' "

Frankel continued, "If the report is true, the Communist world has won what has been considered a crucial race for the perfection of a pilotless rocket capable of traversing the earth."

While the Eisenhower administration was still pondering the consequences of the Soviet missile test—Secretary of State Dulles publicly insisted it did not change the military balance of power between East and West—the Russians delivered a mighty blow to American prestige. On Friday, October 4, the Soviet Union won the first phase of the space race by placing a 184-pound satellite named Sputnik into orbit 550 miles above the earth. Moscow had not only beaten the United States, with its vaunted technology, into space, but it had done so with a satellite that was fifty times heavier than the satellite Washington was still struggling to get off the ground.

The news ricocheted around the world faster than the Soviet satellite. The huge banner headline stripped across the top of the *New York Times* said: "Soviet Fires Earth Satellite Into Space; It Is Circling The Globe at 18,000 M.P.H.; Sphere Tracked In 4 Crossings Over U.S."

The Russian breakthrough upended assumptions about American superiority in science and technology and seemed in an instant to reshape the cold war in Moscow's favor. But it also jolted the Eisenhower administration into action on a variety of space programs, and brought Killian and Land back to the White House. Working with ideas proposed by Mert Davies from RAND and Richard Leghorn, who was still proselytizing for strategic reconnaissance, and assisted by General Schriever, they soon gave new impetus to the development of a reconnaissance satellite, this time under the direction of Richard Bissell and the CIA.

CHAPTER ELEVEN

Creating Corona

SPUTNIK WAS A HUMILIATING DEFEAT for the United States—perhaps the darkest hour of the cold war—but it was also a transforming event in American life. It gave new urgency and energy to the nation's space programs and stirred new interest—and federal support—in the fields of science and education that rippled through American society for the rest of the century. In the cloistered world of secret military research projects, Sputnik was a galvanizing development that soon brought an infusion of new dollars and high-level interest. Just three days after learning of the Soviet satellite, President Eisenhower pressed the Pentagon about its efforts to develop a spy satellite.

From the vantage point of the twenty-first century, and the knowledge that the United States prevailed in the cold war, landed men on the moon, and surged far ahead of the Soviet Union in science and technology, it is difficult to appreciate the apprehension that Sputnik generated. In a single stroke, the Soviet Union seemed to have overtaken the United States not only in science but also in military technology, particularly in the new and potentially decisive arena of space. The impression of inferiority was compounded later in the fall of 1957 when the first American effort to put a satellite in orbit ended disastrously on the launch pad at Cape Canaveral, Florida, as the rocket exploded in a giant fireball two seconds after firing.

"As it beeped in the sky," James Killian later recalled, "Sputnik I created a crisis of confidence that swept the country like a windblown forest fire. Overnight there developed a widespread fear that the country lay at the mercy of the Russian military machine and that our own government and its military men had abruptly lost the power to defend the homeland itself, much less to maintain U.S. prestige and leadership in the international arena. Confidence in American science, technology, and education suddenly evaporated."

The impact was no less dramatic abroad. The United States Information Agency plainly described it shortly after Sputnik began its space odyssey. The agency's office of research and intelligence reported that American prestige had "sustained a severe blow." It said: "Soviet claims of scientific and technological superiority over the West and especially the U.S. have won greatly widened acceptance. Public opinion in friendly countries shows decided concern over the possibility that the balance of military power has shifted or may soon shift in favor of the USSR." The head of the agency, George V. Allen, would later report to Congress that Americans themselves "seemed confused, dismayed and shaken by the developments."

The Senate's two most outspoken Democratic critics of Eisenhower administration defense policies, Henry Jackson and Stuart Symington, immediately bludgeoned the White House for the setback. Jackson called the Soviet satellite "a devastating blow to the prestige of the United States as the leader in the scientific and technical world." Symington said Sputnik "is but more proof of growing Communist superiority in the all-important missile field." He added, "If this now known superiority over the United States develops into supremacy, the position of the free world will be critical."

Though Symington probably didn't realize it, his grim analysis was shared by a panel of distinguished scientists that was nearing completion of a review of Soviet missile programs for Allen Dulles. After reviewing intelligence data about the performance of Soviet intermediate-range missiles, weapons that could easily reach American and NATO bases in Western Europe, the scientists concluded that "the country is in a period of grave national emergency." Their report, which was delivered to Dulles later in October, found that the Russian missile tests showed "an unusually high reliability in launchings" and "an extremely high proficiency in guidance components." The panel in-formed Dulles that "U.S. experience in ballistic missiles does not match that of the USSR and in our opinion is lagging by two to three years."

The sense of alarm was not limited to Democrats or scientists, nor was it restricted exclusively to matters of rocket technology. Sputnik left many Americans concerned that the country had become flabby and complacent. Senator Styles Bridges, a New Hampshire Republican, caught the mood the day after the Kremlin announcement when he said, "The time has clearly come to be less concerned with the pile on the new broadloom rug or the height of the tail fin on the new car and to be more prepared to shed blood, sweat and tears if this country and the free world are to survive."

Eisenhower and his aides, badly misreading the public reaction, ini-tially tried to brush off the Soviet feat as a scientific curiosity. The pres-ident, who was informed about Sputnik on Saturday morning at his Gettysburg farm, left the administration's first response to James Hagerty, the White House press secretary. After consulting on the phone with John Foster Dulles, Hagerty minimized the significance of the Soviet achievement, lamely telling reporters that the launch was nothing to worry about. "We never thought of our program as one which was in a race with the Soviets." He insisted that the Russian satel-lite would have no effect on the American program.

Over the next few days, top officials continued to disparage the launch. At his farewell news conference, outgoing Secretary of Defense Charles Wilson called Sputnik "a nice scientific trick." Sherman Adams, the White House chief of staff, said Washington did not intend to com-pete in "an outer space basketball game." Another White House aide, Maxwell Rabb, declared that the satellite was "without military signifi-cance." Killian later dryly described these comments as "flip and inade-quate in the face of the crisis."

The military implications of Sputnik were actually extremely serious, as Eisenhower and many of his top advisers well knew. He conceded as much in his memoirs. "The Soviet scientific achievement was impres-sive," he recalled. "The size of the thrust required to propel a satellite of this weight came as a distinct surprise to us. There was no point in trying to minimize the accomplishment or the warning it gave that we must take added efforts to ensure maximum progress in missile and other scientific programs."

Killian put it more bluntly. "The capacity to lift a satellite ninety or a hundred miles above the surface of the earth, and place it into orbit, ominously suggested a capacity to lift a nuclear bomb into the upper atmosphere and send it hurtling down upon its target of choice." Though he knew that the American missile program was advancing, and that a Jupiter-C rocket, a more powerful version of the Army's Redstone, had blasted into space in August with a new nose cone that survived the fiery descent back to earth, Killian realized that the Russians had broken ahead in the critical area of long-range weapons. "Whatever the respective strengths of the two economies, theirs for the moment apparently led the world in its capacity to produce intercontinental ballistic missiles, however crude they might be."

The Pentagon's first technical assessment of Sputnik, written by Donald Quarles and sent to the president on October 7, found that "the satellite success does indicate competence in long-range ballistic missiles and does tend to corroborate their ICBM claim of August 27." That was putting it mildly. Quarles clearly felt defensive about the Vanguard program, which looked incompetent in light of the Russian accomplishment. He reminded Eisenhower that the administration had deliberately set the Navy satellite program on an independent course to avoid interference with other missile programs and that the administration had hoped that "scientific satellites, which would be non-military and clearly inoffensive, might help to establish the principle that outer space is international space."

"The military participation in rocketry," he told Eisenhower, "was de-emphasized as being incidental to the scientific program. All subsequent public releases have followed the same line."

Quarles urged Eisenhower to downplay the Soviet missile advantage in any public statements, as Hagerty had already done over the weekend in his comments to reporters. Quarles attached a draft White House statement with his secret report to the president. It said, in part, "As to the implication that the Soviet satellite launching indicates that their military rocketry is more advanced than our own, it should be noted that the rocketry being employed by our Naval Research Laboratory for launching the Vanguard satellite is separate and distinct from our ICBM and IRBM ballistic missile rocketry." While technically correct, this dodged the essential point that American missiles could not match the thrust or reliability of Russian models.

Quarles also proposed that the White House take the offensive on freedom of space by citing Sputnik as a precedent. His draft statement noted "that none of the many nations that have been overflown by the Soviet satellite appears to have raised objection on the ground that its territorial rights have been infringed. This seems to establish the validity of the concept that outer space is international in character." That was true, and the flight of Sputnik effectively settled the issue of space law in favor of open heavens, though debate about the matter went on for years in various international forums, including the United Nations.

Although government officials had long been pondering the legal issues associated with space vehicles, the subject was a novelty for many Americans. The level of unawareness was evident in the questions posed at the beginning of a *New York Times* story by Walter Sullivan that appeared on the front page on Sunday, October 13. "Is the Soviet earth satellite trespassing on the air space of all nations? If the sky is the limit of national sovereignty, how high is it? Who pays if a United States satellite falls on Westminster Abbey?"

Sullivan reported that "specialists in international law have differing ideas on the proper answers to some of these questions."

Eisenhower met with Quarles and an assortment of other officials early on Tuesday morning, October 8, to discuss the Russian satellite. In what must have been an uncomfortable encounter for Quarles, Eisenhower opened the meeting by pointedly asking whether it was true, as he had heard, that the Redstone could have placed a satellite in orbit months earlier. Quarles said the report was correct, but recalled that the administration had decided upon the advice of outside scientists not to make the United States scientific satellite program a military project. If Eisenhower wished to change that approach and order the Army to get a satellite into orbit as quickly as possible, Quarles said, the Redstone would be ready to launch in four months—still a month ahead of the Navy's target date. The president impatiently replied that Congress was certain to ask why Redstone had not been selected long ago. Though Eisenhower had endorsed the Vanguard plan in 1955, he suspected that competition between the military services had impeded the American satellite program and the Pentagon's efforts to develop intermediate and long-range missiles. He did not air this concern in the meeting with Quarles but brought it up repeatedly in subsequent discussions with Pentagon officials.

In the Tuesday morning meeting, Eisenhower turned to the future, asking the group to look ahead five years. He specifically inquired about the possibility of developing a reconnaissance satellite. Quarles described the Air Force's development project, WS-117L. Andrew Goodpaster's minutes of the meeting do not indicate whether Quarles told the president that the project lacked adequate funding and was struggling with technologies that would be hard to perfect.

Later that same day Eisenhower reviewed military budget issues for the last time with Charles Wilson, who would soon be replaced as defense secretary by Neil H. McElroy, the president of Procter & Gamble, the consumer products company. The meeting dwelled on missile programs, and the president approved Wilson's recommendation to remove overtime restrictions that the Pentagon had imposed on contractors to hold down costs. Even in the wake of the Soviet launch, Eisenhower told Wilson to make sure the elimination of the overtime cap was handled carefully so that expenses would not snowball. The men also agreed that the Pentagon should consider the Redstone as a possible alternative to the Vanguard if the Navy satellite project continued to falter.

Eisenhower did his best to mask the administration's concern about the momentous military issues raised by the Russian satellite when he faced the press on Wednesday, October 9. The president was almost as dismissive of Sputnik as Wilson, Adams, and Rabb had been, essentially offering a variation of the theme that the military and scientific implications were relatively unimportant. Speaking at a packed news conference that was unusually combative by the mild-mannered journalistic standards of the day, Eisenhower said that for all its efforts, the Soviet Union had succeeded only in putting "one small ball in the air." While he said he was concerned that the United States was not "further ahead" in the production of intercontinental ballistic missiles, and acknowledged that the Russians had developed powerful rocket engines, he showed no inclination to accelerate the American missile or satellite programs. The president's theme, mapped out with his advisers along the lines of Quarles's memo of the previous day, was that Washington's scientific satellite project needed no tweaking, let alone rethinking, and that the delay in launching the satellite did not reflect weaknesses in the nation's missile programs. Under persistent questioning about the military implications of the Russian launch, he offered the memorable observation that Sputnik did not raise his concern about the nation's security "by one iota."

The president so thoroughly belittled the issues that he left the impression he did not fully comprehend the political or military significance of the Soviet breakthrough in space. Eisenhower's shaky performance was emblematic of the administration's wobbly response to the Russian triumph. For the first time in his presidency, Eisenhower seemed in danger of losing the public's faith in his leadership on national security matters. As Killian observed, "He was startled that the American people were so psychologically vulnerable. The president had enjoyed the respect and confidence of the people to a degree that has not been common in this century, and he had come to expect that his own statements would be received by that public with some degree of confidence. But now, it seemed, he was confronted with the possibility that this confidence would be eroded."

The New York Times editorialized the next day that the administration's handling of missile and satellite programs revealed "an unexpected naivete" about the political and propaganda benefits of winning the space race. The paper exhorted Washington and the nation to "wake up to the necessities of the new age of space that has dawned upon us."

Lyndon Johnson, the Senate majority leader, saw the administration's conduct as a failure of historic dimensions. "The Roman Empire controlled the world because it could build roads. Later, when moved to sea, the British Empire was dominant because it had ships. In the air age, we were powerful because we had airplanes. Now, the Communists have established a foothold in outer space. It is not very reassuring to be told that next year we will put a better satellite into the air. Perhaps it will even have chrome trim and automatic windshield wipers." Johnson worried that by gaining control of the "high ground" of space, the Soviet Union would ultimately control the world.

Eisenhower took up the subject of spy satellites again on Thursday at a full-dress meeting of the National Security Council that had been called to review the technological and military implications of Sputnik. "The outer space implications of the launching of this satellite," Quarles told the group, "were of very great significance, especially in relation to the development of reconnaissance satellites." Eisenhower wanted to know if newspapers were correct in reporting that some American intelligence officials believed Sputnik was taking pictures of the United States. Quarles said he doubted the small satellite was equipped with a camera system, but could not be certain. Eisenhower's question was an indication of how little he knew at this point about the technological hurdles associated with trying to develop a sophisticated photoreconnaissance system that was compact and sturdy enough to fit into a satellite. Sputnik was far too small to accommodate intelligence-gathering equipment.

When the discussion turned to the state of the nation's missile programs, Eisenhower reiterated his long-standing concerns about turf battles among the military services. While agreeing that the Air Force and Army should continue working on their primary missile projects, the president said it might eventually be necessary to consolidate these and other rocket operations under a single development organization similar to the wartime Manhattan Project that produced the atomic bomb. Eisenhower cautioned Pentagon officials that they must constantly be alert to the dangers of interservice rivalries.

With the administration under mounting pressure to demonstrate that it appreciated the military potential of space, *Aviation Week* disclosed on Sunday, October 13, that the Air Force was working on a multimillion-dollar program to develop a reconnaissance satellite. The story, picked up by other news organizations, accurately described the WS-117L project and outlined the technical obstacles, including the need to devise a workable system to transmit the pictures back to earth. The *New York Times* front-page story on Monday, October 14, was headlined "U.S. Working on Satellite That Could Film the Earth— Program Is Reported Under Way Since Early 1956—First Unmanned 'Moon' Would Use TV or Regular Cameras."

The news coverage meant that after more than ten years of study by RAND and several years of preliminary developmental work by the Air Force, the concept of a photoreconnaissance satellite was receiving national attention for the first time. Ironically, the burst of publicity undermined the project by bringing it into the open just at a moment when Washington was not eager to broadcast its plans to use space for military purposes.

As doubts about the quality of American science swirled about the capital, Eisenhower welcomed Killian, Land, and other members of the Science Advisory Committee of the Office of Defense Mobilization to the White House on October 15. The late-morning meeting, which turned into a two-part session with an unexpected excursion to the Pentagon, proved to be one of the most important of the Eisenhower presidency. It elevated science to an unparalleled level of importance in Washington and led to the appointment of Killian to a newly created post of White House science adviser. From that perch, Killian, with Land's help, could cut through the Pentagon's bewildering array of technology projects to single out the most promising, urgently needed intelligence programs like spy satellites and ensure that they received adequate support.

Accounts of the meeting by some of the participants, including Eisenhower and Killian, as well as the handwritten notes made during the gathering by Robert Cutler, the president's national security adviser, describe the broad scope of the discussion, and the eloquence of some of the speakers, especially Land. The meeting, in effect, gave science a seat at the highest policy-making levels of the government.

Eisenhower welcomed the committee members by saying that he was surprised by the feverish public reaction to Sputnik. "I can't understand why the American people have got so worked up over this thing," he quipped. "It's certainly not going to drop on their heads." The president then asked the group if it thought "American science was being outdistanced."

I. I. Rabi, the committee chairman and Columbia University physicist whom Eisenhower had befriended while running the university, noted that the United States enjoyed advantages in some areas but warned that the Russians had "picked up tremendous momentum." He said that unless the United States took vigorous action, "they could pass us swiftly just as in a period of twenty to thirty years we caught up with Europe and left Western Europe far behind."

Rabi then invited Land to speak, perhaps an indication that the two men had agreed before the meeting that Land would make some observations about the place of science in American life. Land, one of the youngest members of the advisory committee but also the only one who ran a large industrial company, spoke with assurance and authority as he cast the challenge in the broadest terms. "The country recognizes it needs much from science and science needs the president," Land said. Under the Soviet system, he told Eisenhower, Russians were "learning to live the life of science and its application. They are pioneering as we did years ago. Science is becoming to them a way of life."

Land suggested that Americans had paused to enjoy the benefits of science. Now the country needed to "begin a rebirth of building, using the mind, enjoying the scientific adventure. Otherwise Russian scientific culture will leave us behind as a decadent race. The country no longer feels the thrill of the scientific life."

The president, Land said, was uniquely positioned to inspire the country to renew its enthusiasm for science by "setting our youth on a variety of scientific adventures." He concluded that the United States "must be made into a scientific country if it will survive."

Killian described Eisenhower's response: "The president was not sure that the Russians were seeking to educate their people so completely in science as Land had implied, but it was clear that he was impressed by Land's plea that he could, as an act of intellectual leadership, create a more widespread understanding of science." Goodpaster noted for the record, "The president said he would like to encourage an attitude toward science similar to the enthusiasm that was inspired by athletic endeavors in his youth."

Rabi then urged Eisenhower to appoint a full-time White House science adviser and a board of science consultants. The president expressed interest in the idea and instructed Goodpaster and other aides to pursue the suggestion. As the meeting progressed, Eisenhower decided he wanted his new defense secretary to hear from the scientists. Without breaking for lunch, the members of the advisory committee reconvened at the Pentagon in the early afternoon to meet with McElroy and his top aides.

On Saturday, November 2, as the White House was pulling together plans for the appointment of a science adviser, the Soviet Union stunned Washington again by launching into orbit a second, much heavier satellite that carried a small, shaggy dog named Laika. Weighing more than 1,100 pounds, six times heavier than the first, the second satellite demonstrated even greater Soviet superiority in the development of powerful rockets. It set off speculation among top scientists that the Russians might have achieved a breakthrough in propulsion technology. British scientists suggested that Moscow had produced a new chemical fuel or perhaps even a nuclear engine. If so, they said, it would not be long before the Soviet Union launched a rocket to the moon. The New York Times even reported in a front-page story that numerous foreign scientists thought a Russian rocket might already be headed for the moon, carrying a hydrogen bomb timed to detonate while the moon was darkened briefly in eclipse, creating a flash that would be brighter than the light of a full moon.

It was little wonder that Washington was reeling. Though Moscow had announced its intention to put up another satellite, the size of the spacecraft added to anxieties and stoked the political battle over Eisenhower's handling of the American missile programs. Lyndon Johnson and other Senate Democrats immediately renewed their call for a congressional investigation of missile and satellite projects to determine why the United States was lagging behind the Soviet Union. Senator Richard Russell, the chairman of the Armed Services Committee, described Sputnik II as "a very dramatic demonstration of Soviet achievements" and said it was "time for us to end our complacency."

The level of public interest in the Soviet space feats was worrying to officials in Washington. The day after Laika started her journey into space, a long line formed outside the Hayden Planetarium at the Museum of Natural History in New York, waiting to see a show that included information about satellites and featured a recording of the electronic beeps produced by the new Soviet satellite as it circled the earth. With the Pentagon's satellite plans still limping along, the best the administration could say to reassure Americans was that Washington's first satellite might be launched in December. Anyone familiar with the Vanguard program knew that that was an optimistic expectation. With Eisenhower's blessing, McElroy quietly gave the Army approval to act on its long-standing ambition to vault a satellite into orbit aboard the Jupiter-C rocket. McElroy said the Army program would "supplement" the Navy effort, but the real expectation in the administration was that von Braun and his team would beat the Navy into space.

To help allay public fears, Eisenhower addressed the nation from the Oval Office on Thursday, November 7. With the Army's new heat-defeating missile nose cone placed theatrically next to his desk, the president announced the appointment of Killian to the newly created post of special assistant to the president for science and technology and said he had ordered administrative changes at the Pentagon to speed the development of missiles.

He then assessed the nation's military strength. "It is my conviction, supported by trusted scientific and military advisers, that, although the Soviets are quite likely ahead in some missile and special areas and are obviously ahead of us in satellite development, as of today the over-all military strength of the free world is distinctly greater than that of the Communist countries. We must see to it that whatever advantages they have are temporary only."

"Killian's appointment marked a major step forward for American science," Robert A. Divine, a historian at the University of Texas, noted in his book about Eisenhower's response to Sputnik. "For the first time, a man who spoke for the nation's leading scientists was given a position of unquestioned national authority." With Eisenhower's approval, Killian, in turn, elevated the status of the Office of Defense Mobilization's Science Advisory Committee by adding prominent new members and renaming it the President's Science Advisory Committee. Land agreed to continue serving on the board.

The enduring impact of Eisenhower's October 15 discussion with the scientists was evident in other ways. He tried to rally the country from its shock over Sputnik with a series of nationally televised speeches on science and defense, urged Congress to increase funding for scientific research and education, and pushed the Pentagon and private industry to press ahead with their work on missiles and satellites. The negotiations with Congress led to enactment of the National Defense Education Act, a landmark bill that provided money for college scholarships, foreign-language instruction, and the training of math and science teachers.

Unexpectedly, one of the first opportunities to advance America's space programs came from the Air Force's reconnaissance satellite project. The missile nose cone that survived reentry through the atmosphere in August held the potential for a critical design change in the satellite system. Eisenhower had emphasized the importance of the nose cone during his November 7 Oval Office address to the nation. "One difficult obstacle on the way to producing a useful long-range weapon is that of bringing a missile back from outer space without its burning up like a meteor because of friction with the earth's atmosphere," he told the American people. Pointing to the nose cone by his desk, Eisenhower said, "Our scientists and engineers have solved that problem. This object here in my office is an experimental missile—a nose cone. It has been hundreds of miles to outer space and back. Here it is, completely intact."

The implications of the new technology for a photoreconnaissance satellite were striking, though they went unmentioned by Eisenhower. Instead of trying to beam images back to the ground with unproven electronic technologies, engineers could build a simpler satellite that sent a recoverable capsule packed with exposed film down to earth. Though still technically daunting, the idea looked far more practical than the television-based system at the core of the WS-117L project, which was languishing for lack of Air Force financial support. Once Land and Killian recognized the possibilities, they intervened, using their extraordinary influence to transform the spy satellite project from a backwater program into one of Washington's top priorities.

The concept of a recoverable satellite—actually only one component of the satellite, a small capsule containing exposed film, would be recovered—was not entirely new. Richard C. Raymond, a RAND physicist, had explored the idea in 1956, working with his own prior calculations about the potential advantages of a film-return system and the latest research on reentry technologies. Raymond figured that a film recovery satellite would yield twice as much data as an electro-optical satellite, which would be hobbled by the primitive state of transmission techniques and the lower resolution of the camera planned for the Air Force satellite. Based on Raymond's analysis, RAND submitted a secret report to the Air Force in March 1956 proposing development of a recoverable reconnaissance satellite.

The plan was intriguing but premature. The main obstacle was the scorching passage back through the atmosphere. As Eisenhower would say in his 1957 speech, any object that began its descent through the atmosphere at speeds in excess of 16,000 mph would generate tremendous friction and burn up like a meteor. Scientists had started to tackle the problem in the mid-1950s as rocket technology advanced and demand grew for a heat shield that would protect nuclear warheads as they plunged toward their targets in the final phase of flight through space. One counterintuitive solution was to design a blunt rather than streamlined warhead that would compress the air ahead of it as it descended, forming an insulating cushion to ward off the heat. Another approach relied on thick walls of copper to soak up the heat, but the metal casing would be prohibitively heavy. Eventually, General Electric researchers came up with a clever idea: a heat shield that would melt away during reentry, dissipating the heat. The process is called ablation cooling.

Because the reentry technology was not yet perfected in early 1956, the RAND proposal for a recoverable satellite initially dropped from sight. Still believing that the WS-117L's video transmission system was feasible, Air Force officials also questioned the time lag between taking the pictures in space, returning the film to earth, and delivering developed photographs to Washington. But Mert Davies, Amrom Katz, and other RAND researchers persisted, betting that improvements in rocketry and reentry technology would make a film-return satellite not only workable but more attractive than the video-relay WS-117L program that they had done so much to initiate a few years earlier.

The simplicity of design appealed to the RAND group. Just as Kelly Johnson had used an uncomplicated concept, the glider, as the basis for the U-2, Davies, Katz, and their colleagues in Santa Monica came to realize that designing a reconnaissance satellite around well-established photographic principles—cameras and film—would be easier and quicker than wrestling with the temperamental technology of transmitting video signals. Relaying images from space to earth as electronic data was a brilliant and daring idea, but in the mid-1950s, the technology was out of reach. When an effective heat shield was in hand, it made sense to take conventional photographs in space and send the film back to earth.

This approach was not without its own formidable technical challenges, including development of a camera that would produce useful pictures of Soviet military installations while orbiting more than 100 miles above the earth at better than 17,000 mph. New cameras and film would be needed that could withstand the wrenching physical forces of launch and the extreme temperature fluctuations of space flight. Along with rockets that could loft a satellite into orbit, a film-return system required precise deorbiting techniques that would bring a capsule back to earth at a preselected location where it could be recovered. But the timing of Davies and the other RAND scientists couldn't have been better. With Eisenhower wary of using the U-2, and the Russians moving into space, any shortcut to producing a working reconnaissance satellite was bound to be enticing.

Davies enhanced the appeal by simplifying the design for the camera system. Fairchild Camera and Instrument Corporation had developed a rotary panoramic camera for fighter aircraft. The camera and film rotated inside a drum, recording images each time it revolved past a slit in the side of the drum. Davies disliked the system because it had too many moving parts. "What a terrible design to be moving all that mass within a drum," he said. But it got him thinking about how the design might be modified for use in a satellite. His "hot idea," as he called it, was to attach a panoramic camera to a satellite and spin the entire assembly. The spinning motion would help stabilize the satellite while also bringing the camera around for a new photograph with each revolution of the satellite. The camera lenses would point through windows in the side of the satellite capsule and the images would be imprinted crosswise on the film.

With the addition of the spinning panoramic camera, RAND was eager to pitch its proposal for a recoverable satellite to the government. Davies and Katz proved to be tireless salesmen. Starting in late spring of 1957, they arranged briefings in Santa Monica for many of the people who were responsible for guiding the nation's advanced technology and space programs, including the two officers managing the WS-117L project under Schriever, Air Force Col. Frederic C. E. "Fritz" Oder and Navy Commander Robert Truax. Davies and Katz also explained their plan to members of the Air Force Scientific Advisory Board and the Science Advisory Committee of the Office of Defense Mobilization. (This was before Killian was named science adviser and the committee was moved over to the White House and renamed.) As a result of the briefings, Killian and Land were well aware of the RAND proposal by mid-1957, and it changed their thinking about the likelihood of developing an effective spy satellite before the end of the decade.

Although the two men well understood the potential benefits of a photoreconnaissance satellite, and had discussed the idea in the surprise attack report two years earlier, they had assumed that technological problems, including the development of reliable rockets, would delay the debut of a working system until the early 1960s, at best. As a result, they had pushed the Eisenhower administration to move ahead with advanced aircraft projects, starting with the U-2 and then adding a supersonic spy plane once it became clear that the U-2 could be tracked by Soviet radar. They had recognized that the WS-117L program was technically complex and probably impractical for the time being. The

RAND plan, by contrast, looked feasible. If adequately funded and effectively managed, it might produce a working satellite within a year or two. Before the summer was over, Oder convinced Schriever and his top deputy, Brig. Gen. Osmond Ritland, formerly Bissell's deputy on the U-2 project, that the RAND plan could produce a reconnaissance satellite long before the WS-117L program. They, in turn, consulted with Dick Leghorn, who was back in the picture as a member of the Aerial Inspection Subcommittee of the President's Arms Control and Disarmament Group.

Leghorn's involvement was fortuitous. During his years at Kodak, he had remained engaged with policymakers in Washington about aerial reconnaissance and disarmament issues. As the idea of a recoverable satellite began to gain momentum, no one in the country had a better appreciation for its potential benefits than Leghorn. A friend of Killian and Land, a former associate of Schriever, and a longtime acquaintance of Davies and Katz, he also understood the technological and bureaucratic barriers that would have to be overcome.

Leghorn's thinking about satellites had evolved from his work on the Beacon Hill study and his service as an aide to Schriever in the early 1950s, a period when he thought that specialized aircraft and high-altitude balloons offered the best hope of monitoring Soviet military forces. By the mid-1950s, Leghorn had warmed to the idea of spy satellites. With his customary knack for looking over the horizon, he suggested that they might also make it easier to strike arms control agreements with Moscow because satellites could help verify that the Russians were carrying out their commitments to limit or reduce their armaments. Leghorn knew that without the means to check Russian compliance, arms control deals would be unenforceable and impractical. Since there seemed little chance that the Soviet Union would permit on-site inspection of its nuclear forces, the only way to keep track of their weapons would be from the air or from space. Satellites could, in effect, substitute for the Open Skies plan that Nikita Khrushchev had dismissed at Geneva.

In October 1955, just a few months after the Geneva summit meeting, Leghorn circulated a paper to friends in the government, outlining his ideas about using satellites to support arms control accords. In July 1956, he revised the paper and sent a copy to Schriever. Then in May 1957 he lobbied the White House directly in a memorandum that urged a greatly expanded effort to produce a photoreconnaissance satellite. Leghorn wanted the project to be treated as "a priority national effort." Specifically, he said, "To collect warning and arms information for intelligence and disarmament purposes, the military invulnerability of the satellite is a unique characteristic, compared with covert intelligence, unauthorized aerial over-flight, and mutual ground and aerial inspection."

Leghorn's discussions with Oder and Schriever in 1957 coincided with his desire to start his own business. Leghorn resigned from Kodak in the summer of 1957. Before long, he and Duncan MacDonald, who had worked with Leghorn during the Bikini nuclear tests and had later run the Boston University Optical Research Laboratory, founded the Itek Corporation. Its main asset was the Boston University lab, which they bought from the university for the bargain price of $100,000— with the help of a loan from Laurence Rockefeller—after the Pentagon decided it could no longer afford to support the lab and its one-hundred-member staff. Leghorn and MacDonald hoped to turn the lab into a profit-making enterprise. They soon got a big assist from the CIA and Leghorn's friend, Richard Bissell.

Leghorn and MacDonald closed their deal with Harold Case, the president of the university, just before Bissell offered to buy the lab from the school, hoping to turn it into a CIA proprietary company. Like other proprietary firms that the Agency had established, it would appear to be privately controlled but would actually be owned and operated by the CIA to handle secret projects. Once Bissell learned that Leghorn had bought the lab, he invited him to Washington. Before long, Leghorn was assisting the CIA on several aerial reconnaissance projects, including satellites and the development of a new supersonic spy plane.

During the summer of 1957, Oder, Schriever, and Leghorn concluded that the best way to get the recoverable satellite built would be to follow the project management model used for the U-2. That would require presidential approval, separation of the program from the

WS-117L operation, and creation of another secret project office at the CIA to manage the satellite work. Oder, who had worked at the CIA before moving back to the Air Force to take over day-to-day management of the WS-117L project, suggested several additional steps that would help disguise the government effort to build a recoverable spy satellite. Because the WS-117L project had attracted news coverage, Oder proposed publicly canceling the Air Force program as the CIA geared up to handle the recoverable satellite project. In its place, the Air Force would announce that it was initiating its own biomedical scientific satellite project to supplement the Vanguard program. This partial fiction—or "second story," as Oder called it—would provide a convenient cover for the launching of the CIA's satellites from the Air Force site at Point Arguello, which would later become Vandenberg Air Force Base.

As the summer progressed, Schriever and Leghorn sold the approach to powerful allies, including Killian, Land, and Bissell. At the end of August, Schriever outlined the plan to Goodpaster. Ritland and Oder discussed it further with Bissell. But at this point, it was still an idea in search of presidential approval and action.

Their cause was indirectly helped along by the U-2. Under intense pressure from the CIA and Pentagon to resume spy flights over the Soviet interior, Eisenhower in May had reluctantly approved a series of U-2 missions over the summer to collect intelligence about Soviet missile and nuclear weapons programs. The seven flights, code-named Operation Soft Touch, originated at a secret CIA base in Lahore, Pakistan, and were concentrated over the Central Asian areas of the Soviet Union, in particular Kazakhstan. Conducted over a three-week period in August, they produced another batch of invaluable photographs, showing the rocket and missile launch center at Tyuratam, east of the Aral Sea, the nuclear testing ground at Semipalatinsk, and a previously unknown missile site in Sary Shagan, just west of Lake Balkhash.

The photographs reinforced the need for overhead reconnaissance operations, and reaffirmed the value of the U-2. But the flights once again underscored the danger of sending manned aircraft into Soviet airspace. Even though the CIA had worked on making the planes less visible to Soviet radar after the initial missions a year earlier, the new flights had been tracked by the Russians. Bissell and other officials visited the White House on August 23 to show Eisenhower some of the latest photographs. Apparently hoping that the remarkably detailed pictures would overcome Eisenhower's hesitation about using the plane, Bissell sought permission to make another flight. Eisenhower turned down the request, and most of the others that followed in the months to come. "Operation Soft Touch proved to be the high water mark of U-2 operations against the Soviet Union," the CIA reported in its history of the aircraft. If anything, Operation Soft Touch left Eisenhower more eager than ever to come up with a less vulnerable way of spying on the Soviet Union.

The launch of the two Sputniks made the RAND plan for a recoverable satellite all but irresistible. As Katz put it, "Now, by the fall of 1957, not only were the kinds of previously operating constraints removed, but Sputniks I and II were added. This permitted the entry of 'space flight' and 'satellites' in the list of Okay ideas for the military. A sense of urgency developed in the satellite business, and a corresponding sense of increased urgency in the reconnaissance business. Hence recce [reconnaissance] satellites were doubly Okay."

The turning point came during a few short weeks in October and November 1957. On October 24, the same day that Eisenhower offered Killian the science adviser's post over breakfast at the White House, the President's Board of Consultants on Foreign Intelligence Activities submitted its semiannual report. The panel's job was to give the White House independent advice about the operations and research projects of the CIA and other intelligence agencies. Killian was the chairman of this group and Land was a member. The board, among other things, had been studying proposals for advanced aerial reconnaissance systems that might replace the U-2. One involved development of a supersonic aircraft that, unlike the U-2, could actually travel undetected through Soviet airspace. The other project was the WS-117L satellite program. The board told Eisenhower that both projects were falling behind schedule and relied on technologies so sophisticated that they seemed unattainable in the near future. The short-term answer, the board suggested, might be an interim, recoverable photoreconnaissance system like the one envisioned by RAND.

Four days later, James Lay, the executive secretary of the National Security Council, informed McElroy and Allen Dulles that Eisenhower wanted a joint report from the Pentagon and the CIA on the development of the new spy plane and the Air Force's WS-117L.

By chance, Davies and Katz published their recommendation for a film-return satellite on November 12. The report, entitled "A Family of Recoverable Reconnaissance Satellites," emphasized simplicity and speed. "This memorandum describes a reconnaissance satellite system that would provide an early and continuing photographic reconnaissance capability in augmentation of the WS-117L program. Relatively simple in operation, the system would use a camera of essentially conventional design in a comparatively unsophisticated orbiting vehicle. A launching date about one year from the date of contract is contemplated. The system will produce pictures of a scale and resolution that will yield valuable intelligence information about large areas of the Soviet Union."

Davies and Katz proposed a series of satellites, beginning with a 300-pound model that would provide coverage of millions of square miles of Soviet territory. In reconnaissance terminology, this was known as broad-area search. The initial satellite would orbit about 150 miles above the earth with its camera system in operation over the Soviet Union for one day, enough time to photograph roughly half the Soviet landmass, which stretched across 5,300 miles and eleven time zones.

The scale and resolution of photographs would be good enough, they said, to identify railroads, highways, and canals. "Urban centers, industrial areas, airfields, naval facilities, seaport areas, and the like can be seen. Very likely, defense missile sites of the sort found around the Moscow area will also be identifiable. Thus, with repeated surveillance, it will be possible to find new major installations, perhaps to learn something about patterns of use of Soviet ICBM systems, and certainly to obtain clues for the direction of other, higher-resolution systems that can provide more detailed, accurate identification."

At about this time—the exact date is uncertain—Schriever paid a visit to Cambridge to see Jerome Wiesner, an MIT electrical engineer and veteran of several government-sponsored research programs, including the wartime effort to develop microwave radar. As Schriever and Wiesner talked about the comparative advantages of a film-return and data-transmission satellite, Wiesner called Land to see if they could come over to his laboratory at Polaroid. The three men talked there for several hours. "By the end of the afternoon, we had a recoverable satellite," Wiesner later recalled.

As Neil McElroy collected information so he could respond to the White House request for an update on the WS-117L program, he received a status report on November 12 from Richard E. Horner, the assistant secretary of the Air Force for research and development, which said that an interim, film-recovery satellite could likely be developed at least a year before the more complex video signal system.

During this period, officials from Lockheed and Schriever's staff in Los Angeles opened a series of discussions about how to accelerate the WS-117L program. One proposal called for modifying the program to add a recoverable satellite and to use the Thor intermediate-range missile as a booster instead of the Atlas. Lockheed had considered the ideas earlier but shelved them because of funding limitations. At the end of November, Lockheed outlined a recoverable-satellite plan to Schriever's office and on December 5 the company presented the general with a preliminary proposal. Anxious to move ahead with the project while officials in Washington were pondering whether to cloak the program in secrecy and turn it over to the CIA to manage, Schriever made preparations to include a recoverable satellite system in the WS-117L effort. It was designated as Program IIA.

On the same day that Lockheed presented its preliminary plan, Quarles, representing McElroy and Allen Dulles, gave the White House a verbal report on the status of the WS-117L project. Though official accounts of the joint Pentagon-CIA technical evaluation are scarce, it apparently affirmed the view, already held by Killian and Land, that the recoverable satellite was a more promising and practical idea than the video system.

The interim system that now enjoyed the support of the Pentagon, the CIA, and Eisenhower's trusted science advisers was essentially the system that Davies and Katz had proposed in RAND's November 12 memorandum on recoverable satellites. The satellite itself, which would contain a Fairchild panoramic camera and Kodak film, would sit atop a two-stage rocket consisting of a liquid-fuel Thor booster and solid-fuel Aerobee 75 second stage. The Aerobee, built by Aerojet, had been designed as the second-stage booster for the Vanguard program.

With momentum for the RAND proposal gathering, the main proponents of the system—including Killian, Land, Bissell, Goodpaster, Schriever, and Ritland—held secret discussions at the White House in December 1957. After reviewing all the options, they agreed the interim plan was the best. They substituted a liquid-propellant Agena booster built by Lockheed for the Aerobee. The Agena, which had been built as part of the WS-117L project, was more powerful than the Aerobee and had the added advantage of also housing the satellite itself, alleviating the need for a third-stage vehicle. As Oder had recommended, they decided to put the new project under CIA management, publicly declare the termination of Program IIA of the WS-117L project, and have the Air Force announce that it was establishing a research satellite effort that would be called Discoverer.

The planning overlapped with final preparations for the test launch of America's first satellite in early December. Unlike the Russians, who kept their rocket operations secret until they could report a successful launch, the schedule for the Vanguard program was public. As a result, the nation and world turned their attention to Cape Canaveral on Tuesday, December 3, the launch date. Dozens of reporters from around the globe assembled on Florida's Atlantic coast to cover the launch. The motels along highway A1A, including the Sea Missile, the Starlite, and the Vanguard, were filled with people who had traveled to the area to witness the rocket firing.

The flight was postponed because of technical problems, not an uncommon occurrence with missiles and rockets, as the nation came to learn as the space age unfolded. But at the time, the country had no experience with rocket launches and knew only that the Russians had already fired two satellites into orbit. The unexpected delay was a monumental embarrassment. John Foster Dulles, concerned about the impact on America's standing abroad, vented his irritation the next day at a National Security Council meeting at the White House, angrily calling the delay "a disaster for the United States" that "had made us the laughing-stock of the whole Free World."

A new launch date was quickly set for Friday morning, December 6. At 10:45, an hour before the rocket was set to lift off, the Pentagon opened a telephone circuit directly to Eisenhower's farm in Gettysburg, where the president was still recuperating from a mild stroke he had suffered on November 25. Another line was cleared to Washington so Dr. John P. Hagen, the manager of Project Vanguard, could listen to the final countdown. Seconds before ignition of the first-stage rocket, the red-and-white gantry crane pulled away from the rocket and a cloud of vaporizing liquid oxygen formed as expected at the junction of the first and second stages.

Everything seemed normal as the engine rumbled to life and the rocket started to rise slowly from the ground. But it was no more than 4 feet off the pad when the first stage exploded in flames and dark smoke and crumpled to the ground in a heap of burning debris.

The spectacular failure capped a miserable autumn in Washington. The next day's headline in the *New York Times*—coincidentally the sixteenth anniversary of the attack on Pearl Harbor—announced the failure and its consequences succinctly: "Vanguard Rocket Burns on Beach; Failure To Launch Test Satellite Assailed as Blow to U.S. Prestige." The British press had a field day. "Oh, What A Flopnik!" said the *Daily Herald* in London. The *Daily Express* headline was "U.S. Calls It Kaputnik," and the *Daily Mirror* declared, "Oh Dear!!! U.S. Sputnik Blows Up On The Ground!!!" The coverage was so withering that Soviet newspapers, accustomed to producing their own, distorted accounts about news in the United States, in this case simply reprinted news stories and editorials from American newspapers.

Killian, in one of his first actions as presidential science adviser, appointed three top scientists to review the Vanguard program. They recommended that the Pentagon rely instead on Wernher von Braun and the Army's Jupiter-C rocket to get a satellite into orbit during the International Geophysical Year that was due to expire at the end of 1958.

It was sound advice. The next Vanguard launch, scheduled for late January 1958, was scrubbed because of severe mechanical problems—the entire second-stage engine had to be replaced. With that setback, the Pentagon instructed the Army to launch the Jupiter C as soon as possible. The preliminary countdown began almost immediately at Cape Canaveral. At 10:48 P.M. on Friday, January 31, the Jupiter-C rocket, illuminated by powerful floodlights, rose from its launch pad on a plume of fiery exhaust and roared toward space with its precious cargo, a 30-pound, bullet-shaped satellite named Explorer that contained two miniature radio transmitters and a small Geiger counter to measure the intensity of cosmic radiation. It was a midget compared to Sputnik II, but it was enough to recover some of America's lost prestige.

Eisenhower had flown down to Augusta that afternoon for a week of golf and relaxation. In a sign of the anxiety that by this time surrounded the American space effort, his press secretary, Jim Hagerty, had spent the evening relaying the latest information about launch preparations to the president from Goodpaster, who had remained behind at the White House. Goodpaster, in turn, kept a line open to Army officials. When Hagerty received confirmation that the satellite was in orbit, he phoned the president at 12:44 A.M.

"Mr. President, it's in orbit," he said. "General Goodpaster has just received the official word."

"That's wonderful, that's wonderful," a jubilant Eisenhower replied. "I sure feel a lot better now."

So did the nation. In Huntsville, Alabama, home to von Braun and the Army rocket program, thousands of residents poured into the streets minutes after the rocket launching. "It was like New Year's Eve," the Times reported. "Fire engines and police cars raced through the streets, their sirens shrieking. Motorists all over the city sounded their horns." Congress celebrated the feat with an outpouring of lofty rhetoric and praise for the Army. Lyndon Johnson declared, "Now that we have started, let us press on with all the force, imagination and boldness of which America is capable."

But even as the nation and the Eisenhower administration toasted Explorer, the White House and Pentagon knew one successful launch of a tiny American scientific satellite did not close the outerspace gap with the Russians. On Thursday, February 6, as the celebrations were subsiding, Killian and Land met with McElroy, Dulles, and Quarles to go over the plans for the Air Force's interim spy satellite, which was to be presented to Eisenhower the next day. The Pentagon officials confirmed that they would separate the film-recovery system from the Air Force's other satellite work and turn it over to the CIA, a rare turf concession in Washington. Bissell would run the new program, following the streamlined management model he had employed with the U-2. The Air Force would provide technical assistance, including the rocket boosters, and make its launch site at Point Arguello available. Lockheed, which would build the second-stage rocket that would also house the camera system and film-recovery capsule, would once again serve as the main contractor, though this time the company's Missile Systems Division in Northern California would be the lead organization rather than the Skunk Works.

The next morning, Killian and Land slipped into the Oval Office with Goodpaster for a meeting with the president. The Pentagon's secret 1988 history of the satellite project described the discussion, drawing on notes taken during the meeting by Goodpaster.

"They explained to the president that the satellite would orbit the earth three times, taking pictures as it passed over the Sino-Soviet bloc, and then would deorbit the film capsule. Killian told Eisenhower that the satellite would emit no electronic signals and, therefore, could be completely covert. At Killian's request, Land explained that this specific, small project was for bona fide intelligence purposes. It would be of utmost importance to conduct it quietly, under the cloak of other activities. Comparing the satellite optics to those in the U-2, Land told the president that whereas the U-2 could photograph objects as small as 4 feet, the satellite cameras would only be able to discern objects 50 to 100 feet on a side. This being the case, it would be very easy for the Soviets, if they learned about the project, to build dummies that could 'fool' the satellite cameras; therefore, it was of paramount importance to keep them from learning of it. The satellite pictures, Land said, could be used as a 'scouting' program to guide more precise intelligence means to selected targets."

Eisenhower approved the proposal and told Killian and Land that he wanted the CIA to handle the intelligence aspects of the project. He said that only a handful of people should know about the plan.

Killian and Land left the meeting with the impression that the president, while determined to put the CIA in charge of the spy work, expected the Air Force to direct the project. Goodpaster thought Eisenhower wanted the CIA to run the effort. He returned to the Oval Office later in the day seeking clarification. Eisenhower told him emphatically that the project was to be managed by the CIA, working with the Air Force and the Advanced Research Projects Agency, a new Pentagon organization that Killian had proposed creating to encourage and oversee advanced technology research for the military. Eisenhower "believed the project should be centered in the new Defense 'space' agency, doing what the CIA wanted them to do," Goodpaster noted in a memorandum. He informed Killian.

A day or two later Land appeared unexpectedly at Bissell's office at the CIA and informed him that, in addition to directing the U-2 program, Bissell would now be running a secret reconnaissance satellite project. Bissell knew as little about space flight as he had known about aviation when he was assigned to build the U-2. Once again, he would have to rely on outside experts.

Bissell quickly brought Ozzie Ritland back to the agency from the Air Force, where he was serving as Schriever's vice commander. Ritland had worked smoothly with Bissell as his deputy on the U-2 project. He wanted Ritland, now a brigadier general, at his side again to handle liaison with the Air Force, which would be responsible for launching the spy satellites, controlling their operation in outer space, and recovering the film capsules as they neared the end of their descent back to earth. George Kucera, a member of Bissell's staff, came up with the code name for the project, inspired by one of his favorite cigars: Corona.

The first order of business was to preserve the secrecy of the project. The plan was to pretend that the WS-117L photoreconnaissance satellite project, Program IIA, was being terminated and that a new Air Force scientific satellite project, called Discoverer, was being inaugurated. This was roughly the prestidigitation that Col. Fritz Oder, the manager of WS-117L, had suggested to shield work on an interim, recoverable satellite system. Reporters were well aware of the entire WS-117L program, including the recently added recoverable satellite project. If that element of WS-117L was shut down, the theory went, news organizations—and the Russians—would believe Washington had given up on its effort to build a recoverable photoreconnaissance satellite. Meanwhile, the Discoverer program, which ostensibly involved biomedical experiments in space, would provide an innocuous explanation for the construction of a new Air Force rocket pad near Point Arguello, the satellite launches from there, and the recovery of return capsules in the skies off Hawaii.

On the last day of February, the Advanced Research Projects Agency officially ordered the cancellation of the interim photoreconnaissance system. The rest of the WS-117L program was left intact, including the video-readout satellite project, known as Samos, and the development of a satellite with infrared detectors that could provide early warning of Soviet missile launches by spotting the fiery exhaust plume of rockets as they lifted off. This was known as the Sentry project. The sudden, unexpected action puzzled contractors and government officials who were not cleared to know that the recoverable satellite project was actually being transferred to the CIA.

Mert Davies and Amrom Katz, among those who were not cleared, were dumbfounded and infuriated by the cancellation of the WS-117L recoverable satellite. Bud Wienberg, who had worked with Schriever and Leghorn in the Air Force in the early 1950s and was involved in managing the WS-117L project, was with Davies and Katz when Lockheed announced the demise of the program. He described their reaction to Cargill Hall, the Air Force historian.

"They went ballistic, Amrom particularly. Amrom took it upon himself to try to get the effort reinstated and he began going around the country briefing anyone who would listen about the unwise decision to cancel the recoverable satellite system. I mean he had a cause! He became so well known as an agitator on this that he disqualified himself for being cleared for what was now a black program—even though he had conceived it! The folks in charge knew that if they cleared Amrom, he would immediately cease agitating and that would tip everyone else that the program was under way."

Davies soon realized that some kind of clandestine program was in progress. "Dick Leghorn and a lot of other people I knew stopped talking to me about satellites," he later said. "I knew something was going on."

Davies eventually concluded that the CIA and Air Force feared that Katz, who was very talkative, might inadvertently disclose the secret and therefore decided to keep the two RAND specialists in the dark. It wasn't until 1962 that Davies was cleared by the government to be briefed about Corona. By then, the spy satellite system had been in operation for two years. A gentle and gracious man, Davies, in the last years of his life, made light of the rebuff, but it clearly wounded him. No one had done more to champion the concept of a spy satellite. For more than a decade he had coaxed the daring idea toward reality, moving it inch by inch from the first primitive proposals put together by RAND to the film-return system that Eisenhower ordered up on February 6, 1958.

Thirty years later Davies shifted uncomfortably in his chair in his spare office at RAND when asked if he thought of himself as one of the founding fathers of a technology that had helped to stabilize the cold war. He was eighty-one years old and no longer actively involved in RAND work, but he still came to the organization's offices in Santa Monica most days, energized by the same passion for space research that had brought him to RAND five decades earlier.

"I think so," he said hesitantly, "but you know, as Amrom used to say, there's enough credit to go around."

CHAPTER TWELVE

"Go Off and Build That Thing"

JAMES W. PLUMMER, a young electrical engineer at Lockheed Missile and Space Division in Palo Alto, was summoned to his boss's office in late February 1958 and handed one of the nation's most sensitive intelligence projects.

"Jim, are you willing to take on a new job?" Jack Carter, his supervisor, asked.

Plummer, a lanky, dark-haired engineer who was managing development of the satellite vehicle for the WS-117L program, liked the job he had. After joining Lockheed in 1955 and working for a spell in the company's research lab, he had met Bob Salter, one of the RAND veterans who had moved to Lockheed when development work began on the reconnaissance satellite they had designed. Impressed by Salter's enthusiasm for satellites, Plummer transferred to the WS-117L project.

He found the idea of satellites captivating. "When I read the [WS-117L] proposal, I thought, Wow! is this really possible? You know, all of a sudden you're going to take this thing and shoot it up into space and make it stay there and then you're going to stabilize it like an airplane and then you're going to control it from the ground, and it's going to go around the globe. The first time you read it, it's pretty shocking."

Now he was being invited to consider another, unspecified project. "I thought, man, I must have goofed up on something."

"We want you to go underground," Carter said. "We want you to head up a totally covert program. We want you to disappear from Lockheed and all your friends, and not tell anyone where you're going."

Carter handed Plummer a batch of rough schematic drawings that

Mert Davies and Amrom Katz had prepared while brainstorming about a recoverable satellite.

"Go off and build that thing," Carter instructed Plummer.

To Lockheed executives, Plummer seemed a natural choice, since he was already working on another satellite project. The WS-117L, like Corona, was designed to work in tandem with the company's second-stage rocket booster, called the Agena. Since Plummer was also familiar with the rocket and the technical problems of modifying it to support a large package of reconnaissance equipment in orbit after it had exhausted its fuel, he seemed ideally suited to deal with the new satellite.

Plummer wasn't so sure. When the brief meeting ended, he was dazed. "I had no place or people to work with," he said. To give himself time to collect his thoughts, he rented a motel room in Palo Alto, where he retired with the drawings.

It soon started to rain heavily. Plummer was so absorbed by the drawings that he didn't realize a small lake was forming around the motel. "I opened the door and a flood of water came rushing into my room," he recalled. Water was already up to the door of his car. Fearing that the drawings would be ruined, he rolled them up, picked up his other belongings, and drove to his home in Los Altos. He informed his wife he would be extremely busy in the months ahead. He was not permitted to tell her any more than that.

Over the next few days, Plummer recruited a few engineers he knew he could trust, and arranged to rent a vacant building along the Bayshore Freeway, the main highway between San Jose and San Francisco. The building was owned by Hiller Helicopters. Stan Hiller, who ran the company, had planned to use the building for research and development projects, including a small flying disc that could ferry individuals from place to place. When that overly ambitious project failed, Hiller had no further use for the building.

"It was perfect," Plummer recalled. "There was place for a metal working shop, an electrical shop, and the other things we would need."

The work awaiting him was formidable and the deadline improbable.

The Thor rocket, an intermediate-range missile, had been successfully tested and was already in full-scale production by the Douglas Aircraft Company. It was just about the only element of the Corona system that looked reasonably reliable at the outset. The Agena had not yet flown. In theory, the combination of the Thor and Agena would provide sufficient launch velocity to loft a camera system into orbit, but the projections had not yet been tested with an actual flight. The proposed camera system looked plausible, but no one knew for sure whether it could be wedded to the Agena and whether it would work in space. New technologies were required to control the Agena while in orbit and keep it stable enough for picture taking. Getting the film back to earth was another challenge. The film-return capsule that was part of the satellite would have to be detached in orbit and perfectly positioned so that it would drop into a small recovery area near Hawaii. Even if a heat shield kept the film from baking during reentry, the return capsule would have to be plucked from the air as it neared sea level, no easy feat.

The urgent need for the photographs, combined with the growing political pressure on the White House to overtake the Russian lead in space, produced backbreaking deadlines for the project. Design plans were to be completed in two months; a prototype satellite had to be ready two months later. Components for the first flight were supposed to be on hand within ten months and the first launch was scheduled for eleven months from the starting date.

It was not a schedule for a timid manager. The message from Plummer's bosses at Lockheed and in Washington was emphatic: "Go as fast and as hard as you can, take chances."

Plummer, who had studied Kelly Johnson's management techniques, decided he needed to create his own Northern California version of the Skunk Works. The staff would be small but highly skilled and motivated and comfortable with improvising solutions to difficult technical problems. Paperwork would be kept to a minimum. He would deal directly with Bissell and his top aides. "Kelly's operation was my model," Plummer said.

The approach meshed well with Bissell's habits. Like Johnson, Plummer found Bissell refreshingly unbureaucratic. "He trusted the contractor to do the right thing," Plummer recalled. When problems developed—and there were many as Lockheed tried to get the satellite off the ground—Bissell would ask for a technical briefing, then tell Plummer to move ahead. "There wasn't any second-guessing, there was no hiring of outside experts," Plummer said.

Though Plummer could not match Johnson's creative design talents, he was no slouch on technical issues and proved to be a deft executive. Later in his career he became general manager of the Lockheed Missiles and Space Company, then served as director of the National Reconnaissance Office and chairman of the Aerospace Corporation, a federally funded research and development corporation that oversees the Air Force's contracts with private aerospace companies.

Plummer was born in Idaho Springs, Colorado, in 1920. His father was trained as a machinist but worked as a miner. His mother, Mary, came from a family that had moved from one place to another around the world for Standard Oil. As Jim and his older brother, Roy, were growing up, Mary ran a grocery story and a service station. But during the Depression the family had to give up their home and move into a tent. Jim and Roy delivered newspapers to save enough money to go to college.

The boys looked to their uncle, Archibald, for career guidance. He was a civil engineer, and was, as Jim said, "always the model of what we wanted to do."

"We didn't want to go to the oil fields and we didn't want to go to the mines. Uncle Archibald had done all these glamorous things. He was involved in the Canadian oil pipeline and the trans-Alaska highway. He built bridges and dams."

Jim figured he, too, would become a civil engineer. But Uncle Archibald told the boys electrical engineering was more promising. "He told us it was going to be the coming thing," Plummer recalled.

With $1,500 that he had accumulated, Plummer followed Roy's example and enrolled at San Diego State and then transferred to the University of California at Berkeley, where he majored in electrical engineering. After the attack on Pearl Harbor, Plummer was eager to volunteer for the armed forces, but waited long enough to pick up his bachelor's degree from Berkeley. Like his brother, he enlisted in the Navy, which dispatched the Plummer boys to Harvard to continue their engineering studies. The brothers both wound up working on the government radar development project at MIT.

The engineering and electronic work made Plummer an ideal candidate to manage radar systems on Navy vessels, and he was soon on his way to the Pacific theater, where he participated in a number of the epic battles with Japanese forces. He also outfitted combat aircraft with the latest electronic gear, and accompanied pilots on bombing runs. He remained in the Navy after the war, working on a variety of technical assignments, then retired from the service in 1955 to work at Lockheed. He would have taken a research post at Bell Labs, which recruited him, but was so unsettled by the commotion and crowds in New York when he visited the city for a job interview that he decided he would prefer to work and live on the West Coast.

After a brief stint at Lockheed's research department, Plummer was made program director for the WS-117L project. It was a natural progression from there to the Corona program, which grew directly out of the Air Force satellite project. As he assembled a team of engineers in Palo Alto, Plummer emphasized the need for extreme secrecy. The whole effort would be undermined if the Russians learned about the satellite and took measures to disguise their military forces or filled their airfields with cardboard bombers that would appear to be real planes on the satellite photos. The workers at Hiller Helicopter were told that the company's former research center was now off-limits to them. Plummer followed the advice of security officials to take a circuitous route to work so that he could not be easily tracked.

"Only a select few were briefed on Corona," Plummer said, "and that made it a little bit difficult for us because we had to get things done without telling anyone what we were doing, and sometimes without authority. Sometimes we'd even have to go to a really smart physicist or dynamicist and say, 'Do this for me, but we won't tell you why we want it.'"

"It was a truly covert program. There were many, many steps taken by the C.I.A. and the Air Force which allowed us to stay totally submerged—such as having a separate accounting system. Our monies were all hidden in the system. And of course, the word 'Corona,' or even the letter 'C,' which scared us all to death, was never used either. We were very, very conscious of that in everything we did. You would not talk to someone unless you really knew that person was part of it."

The plans called for the Agena, once in orbit, to coast through space like an airplane in flight, sustaining the same position, or attitude, as it circled the earth. Keeping the Agena in the same position would require a sophisticated attitude-control system, using cold-gas jets, gyroscopes, and infrared horizon scanners to manage the pitch, roll, and yaw of the satellite. Even the slightest malfunction might send the Agena tumbling end-over-end through space, erasing any chance to take photographs. No one had ever built such an exquisitely controlled spacecraft. The stable design would also require an environmental control system within the satellite to avoid overheating or freezing that could damage the film.

Dick Leghorn and Itek told Bissell that they had a very promising camera design that would work well with the Agena. It was a panoramic camera, based on a novel design developed earlier by the Boston University optics lab for use on high-altitude balloon flights across the Soviet Union. "We thought we could probably get 20–25-foot ground resolution from satellite altitudes," said Walter Levison, who had worked with Leghorn back in the mid-1940s on the atomic tests in the Pacific and later helped to develop satellite cameras at Itek. The camera proposed by Levison and Leghorn would produce far more detailed images than a rival camera system produced by Fairchild.

On March 18, Bissell, Killian, and Land convened a meeting of Corona officials and contractors at the Old Executive Office Building in Washington, next door to the White House. The morning papers were filled with headlines about the orbiting of a Vanguard satellite, the first successful launch by the troubled Navy program. The tiny 6.4-inch sphere, fired into space from Cape Canaveral, was the nation's second satellite.

The Corona meeting began with presentations by Itek and Fairchild, as well as General Electric, which would build the return capsule, and Eastman Kodak, which would provide the film. Bissell and Land decided to add the Itek proposal as an alternative camera option, leaving the final choice for a future day. The decision was an important victory for Itek, which was trying to overtake Fairchild's commanding lead in the camera competition.

A week later, Bissell and General Ritland, the deputy director of the project, summoned the key contractors to two days of meetings at the Flamingo Motel in San Mateo, California, not far from the San Francisco airport. Bissell informed everyone that Itek was being brought into the project as a second camera supplier. Lockheed executives introduced Plummer as the company's project manager for the satellite. Bissell said General Electric would create a capsule that would be incorporated into the Agena to bring the film safely back to earth. Cooke Air Force Base at Point Arguello, which had recently been rechristened Vandenberg Air Force Base, would be the launch site. The atmosphere at the meeting was so optimistic that the participants settled on a fast-track schedule that quickly turned out to be unrealistic. The time line called for fabrication of the many components of the project to be completed by July 1, when a countdown would begin aimed at launching the first satellite in November. The deadline was soon pushed back to January 1959.

As the meetings at the Flamingo Motel wound down, Bissell still had no idea what the project would cost and therefore had no budget to pay for it. Or as he bluntly put it to the government and industry representatives, he was "faced with the problem at present of being broke." Because the project was still so amorphous, none of the senior figures who had approved it, including Eisenhower, Allen Dulles, Land, and Killian, knew how much it might cost. Bissell told the corporate representatives that he needed estimates from them as soon as possible. The numbers added up to roughly $7 million for just the reconnaissance gear, including cameras, film, and reentry capsules. As with the U-2 program, the money would come from the CIA director's loosely monitored discretionary account, known as the Reserve for Contingencies. The much steeper cost of the Thor and Agena rockets, construction of a launch site, tracking stations and recovery operations would, in theory, be covered by the Pentagon. It's hard to imagine a similar project getting started today with such a casual approach to budgeting.

Before returning to the East Coast, Bissell convened another meeting in San Mateo on March 26, this one at the Villa Hotel with his top aides and senior industry executives. He wanted to review the discussions of the previous two days at the Flamingo. The improvisational nature of the whole project was captured by the CIA security officer who attended the session. "This meeting was held in the Pacifica A Conference Room," he noted in a report, "and although the general security of the room was far from desirable, by remaining constantly on the alert and cautioning everyone in attendance to speak in a rather low voice, it is felt that the meeting was accomplished without any security compromise." In other words, maintaining the secrecy of America's most technologically advanced spy project depended on whether a group of men in an unguarded hotel room south of San Francisco could keep their conversation to a whisper.

Once back in Washington, Bissell started preparing a formal plan to submit to Eisenhower. His initial draft, completed on April 9, kept both camera options alive. Two days later, he dropped the Fairchild system, apparently acting on the advice of Land, who was impressed with the Itek design. "Land said the Fairchild camera was no good, it wouldn't have done the job," Plummer said. The best Fairchild could promise was 60- to 100-foot resolution, meaning any object smaller than 60 feet across would be difficult if not impossible to identify. Itek said it could reduce the resolution to 15 feet with its panoramic camera and slower film. That was well within the range to show Soviet combat aircraft and missile launch pads. To ease the blow to Fairchild, it was decided that Itek would design the camera but Fairchild would build it.

Bissell later described his reasoning in rejecting the Fairchild approach: "The alternative to this system was to stabilize the capsule with jets and to use a camera that would move within the capsule, taking pictures in a way very similar to the procedure used with the cameras in the U-2 and other reconnaissance aircraft. Eventually, we decided that the latter was the way to go, and we replaced Fairchild's spin-stabilized system with a much more convenient camera from Itek."

Bissell was now ready to go to the White House with a more detailed proposal than the sketchy plan that Killian and Land had presented to

Eisenhower back in early February. On April 16, Bissell submitted a six-page project and budget outline to General Goodpaster. Eisenhower approved the plan verbally; no written authorization was made to help maintain the strict secrecy. General Cabell may have noted the decision on the back of an envelope, but the record on that point is unclear. Goodpaster confirmed the decision in a memorandum for the record.

The proposal that Eisenhower endorsed had been approved by the director of the Advanced Research Project Agency, the assistant secretary of the Air Force for research and development, the vice commander of the Air Force Ballistic Missile Division, and Jim Killian. Bissell's outline opened with a thumbnail description of the enterprise. "Project CORONA contemplates the covert development and subsequent operational use of a short-lived reconnaissance satellite from which, at the completion of its mission, a recoverable capsule containing exposed film is separated for return and pick up in a preselected ocean area."

The satellite, Bissell said, was expected to produce photographs detailed enough to reveal "such major reconnaissance targets as missile sites under construction, previously unobserved communities or other major installations" in regions like the Soviet far north that had been inaccessible to American reconnaissance. Bissell advised the president that the program would involve twelve launchings, with the first satellite to be in operation no later than June 1959 and the last to be fired into orbit in the spring of 1960. By then, it was expected, mistakenly as it turned out, that the WS-117L electronic video transmission system would be available for use and Corona would be phased out. (In fact, the Corona program continued until 1972.) Bissell noted in the memo that a spin-stabilized version of the Corona satellite, which would not require development of a sophisticated attitude control system, could be built and launched six months sooner than the system he was proposing. The picture quality, however, would be significantly inferior.

Under the Bissell plan, the project would be jointly run by three agencies—the Pentagon's new Advanced Research Projects Agency, the Air Force Ballistic Missile Division, and the CIA. The research agency would be responsible for overall technical supervision of the satellite vehicle. The Air Force would direct that work, test the satellite and booster rockets, as well as handle the launching, tracking, and recovery, with help from the Navy in the recovery operations. The CIA, for its part, would deal with development of the reconnaissance equipment and supervise security. The Air Force, Bissell said, would pay for the twelve Thor boosters and Agena vehicles, which would be diverted to the project from the WS-117L program. The CIA would contribute $7 million to pay for the cameras and reentry capsules.

Following Eisenhower's approval of the plan, Dulles on April 25 instructed the comptroller of the CIA to make $7 million available to the Corona project, which he described as "an unprogrammed requirement for which other funds are not currently available." On the same day, Bissell gave Lockheed a succinct three-page "Work Statement" outlining the company's responsibilities.

The kinks inherent in Bissell's hydra-headed organizational plan quickly became apparent, but he managed to keep the problems from escalating out of control by working closely with his Air Force deputy, General Ritland, and using his influence and ties to Land and Killian to head off disabling battles. The overlapping responsibilities and interests, however, proved to be a fateful error that set the stage for titanic battles between the Pentagon and the CIA over the control of spy satellites in the early 1960s.

The fault was not Bissell's. He was merely reaffirming the organizational structure that Eisenhower had requested back in February. Well aware that Washington turf wars could cripple an innovative technology project, and instinctively wary of the parochial attitude of the military services, Eisenhower had placed overall management of the project in the CIA's hands, hoping to replicate the speed and efficiency of the U-2 program. But he realized the Pentagon would have to play a significant role in the Corona program by providing manpower for the project, the rockets, and the launch site, as well as handling the tracking of the satellite during flight and recovery of the film capsule. In initially authorizing the project earlier in the year, Eisenhower had decreed that the Pentagon should be involved through the Advanced Research Projects Agency and the Air Force. The integrated plan seemed sensible, since the Air Force already had on hand the rockets that could carry a satellite into space and the new research agency, championed by Killian, was supposed to be agile and forward-looking. Unfortunately, over the long run, the partnership collapsed in the face of just the kind of powerful institutional rivalries Eisenhower feared.

Some of the later conflicts were foreshadowed in the first months of the project. The budget put together by Bissell in April dissolved almost immediately when the Air Force, under pressure to accelerate its missile programs, decided that the cost of the Thor and Agena rockets would have to be borne by the Corona project rather than being covered by Air Force funds. Bissell also realized that seven additional launch boosters would be needed, four during testing and three to carry biomedical experiments into orbit to support the cover story. These and other decisions exploded Bissell's budget projections and led to a series of high-level discussions over the summer involving Killian, Bissell, General Goodpaster, Maurice Stans, the director of the Bureau of the Budget, and Donald Quarles, who had by then become deputy secretary of defense.

The budget tangle got worse as the Advanced Research Projects Agency and the Air Force juggled plans for providing the rockets. By October, Bissell concluded that the Air Force was trying to charge the Corona program for costs associated with unrelated work on the WS-117L project. Complaining about "rubbery accounting systems" and "juggling costs," he told an Air Force aide that "all of us have some embarrassing explaining to do." At one point Bissell warned General Ritland that the soaring costs might force cancellation of the program. In late November, he told another Air Force general that the involvement of so many agencies in decision-making produced "considerable confusion."

A few days later, Bissell noted his irritation in an unusually scalding memorandum that he ordered placed in the Agency's files. "For the record," he said, "the undersigned will never again assume any responsibility for the success of a major program without having a reasonable degree of control over its funding either through reliance on Agency funds or by means of an ironclad agreement with the Department of Defense."

One of the most threatening maneuvers was a decision by the Advanced Research Projects Agency to slash the number of Corona launches by a third so that money could be diverted to another satellite project. In early December, Allen Dulles strenuously objected to the plan in a note to Killian and Donald Quarles. He asked the two men to meet with him to discuss the decision before the Corona cutbacks were formally approved. The plan was dropped.

When Eisenhower assented to the Corona project, Bissell had selected the Matomic Building on H Street, site of the U-2 operations center, to house the command center for the satellite program. The Ballistic Missile Division, based in Los Angeles, was designated to handle day-to-day dealings with Lockheed and the other contractors. General Ritland, vice commander and later commander of the division, supervised these relations, but placed a liaison officer, Col. Clarence L. "Lee" Battle, in Palo Alto to manage the details and to work directly with Plummer.

Battle was an extraordinarily well-organized, famously cantankerous figure, who understood the importance of a streamlined management system. The central principles, which reflected Bissell's own preference for nimble, no-nonsense operations, came to be widely known in the government and aerospace world as "Battle's Laws." Among them were these management tenets: "Keep the program office small and quick-reacting at all cost"; "Exercise extreme care in selecting people, then rely heavily on their personal abilities"; "Cut out all unnecessary paperwork"; "Hit all flight and checkout failures hard. A fault uncorrected now will come back to haunt you"; "Don't overcommunicate with higher headquarters"; "Don't look back. History never repeats itself."

Bissell and General Ritland, who was stationed in Southern California, quickly established the same easy relationship they had enjoyed during their collaboration on the U-2, though their friendship did not prevent the bureaucratic and budget strains that buffeted the operation. In recalling his collaboration with Ritland some years later, Bissell glossed over those problems. "The program was started in a marvelously informal manner," Bissell said. "Ritland and I worked out the division of labor between the two organizations as we went along. Decisions were made jointly. There were so few people involved and their relations were so close that decisions could be and were made quickly and cleanly. We did not have the problem of having to make compromises or of endless delays awaiting agreement."

The covert nature of the program produced a variety of bureaucratic snafus, as officials who were unaware of the Corona project unwittingly worked at cross purposes with Bissell and his staff. In July, for instance, Pentagon officials recommended that Jupiter rockets be used as satellite boosters so that all Thor missiles could be put in the field as offensive weapons. The Corona team realized the shift would force them to reengineer the entire project to fit the Jupiter, which was incompatible with the Agena. The resulting delay would be at least nine months. Bissell quietly intervened and the recommendation was withdrawn.

In another case, engineers who believed the cover story that biomedical experiments would be the primary purpose of the satellite launches complained that flying the Agena in a horizontal position in orbit was not well suited to handling mice and other animals that would be sent aloft. They preferred that the Agena orbit in a vertical position. They were also puzzled to learn that the interior of the Agena would not be sufficiently air-conditioned to help sustain life. Bissell and Plummer could not tell them that an air-conditioning system might permit light into the chamber, which would ruin the film.

For Bissell, the Corona project was yet another large and demanding enterprise for his relatively small staff, which was already responsible for the operations of three Air Force–directed U-2 detachments based in Germany, Turkey, and Japan and for the development of a new ultra-high-performance reconnaissance aircraft. As Corona got under way, Bissell was still special assistant to the director of central intelligence for planning and development, but in January 1959, Allen Dulles named him deputy director for plans. The title sounded innocuous, but the job was not. It put Bissell, with his moral relativism and risk-taking tendencies, in charge of the CIA's worldwide spy operations, including an array of questionable covert activities.

But as Bissell got the Corona project up and running in early 1958, he still had sufficient time to give the effort the same jolt of energy that he had brought to the U-2 program. Once again animated by the sense that he was working on the front lines of the cold war, directing the government's most audacious spy project, he pushed his aides and industry executives to maintain a punishing schedule. At least once a month, more often when the program was flagging, he and General Ritland assembled two or three representatives from each of the major private contractors to get progress reports and identify problems. Bissell and Ritland would sit side by side at one end of the table, with the businessmen and engineers arrayed around them. Most of the meetings took place in California. Communications between meetings took place over secure telephone and cable lines that were managed by the CIA.

Every organization involved recognized that its piece of the project presented perplexing technical problems. In many cases, they were inventing new science as they went along. Or as the CIA later put it, "In the beginning, no one was exactly sure how the task of reconnaissance from a satellite was to be accomplished. Since this was one of the pioneer efforts there were no 'experts' in the field."

General Schriever said that producing highly detailed photographs from space was "like trying to photograph the belfry in Boston's North Church from the Empire State Building."

Bud Wheelon, a young physicist at the time who was working on missile programs and later played a critical role in developing new spy technologies for the CIA, remembers well the barriers Corona faced. "In the current state of technical accomplishment, we tend to forget how desperately inexperienced we all were in those early days. Vanguard had been a profound embarrassment. Thor and Atlas had gone through similar problems when they began. Titan was then experiencing repeated failures. I had worked on ballistic missile programs in Los Angeles; our monthly program review meetings were properly called 'Black Saturdays.' Upper stages were a new challenge. Our group had tried and failed three times to build an upper stage for Thor which could send a payload to the moon."

Space physics was in its infancy. Fundamental matters like designing an ascent trajectory that would insert a satellite into orbit required a whole new set of calculations, different from those needed to send a missile from one continent to another. The scientists and engineers had access to none of the sophisticated tools that are available today. "There were no integrated circuits, no transistors, no hand-held computers—only vacuum tubes and electric motors with cam switches," recalled Sam Araki, who started work at Lockheed in 1958 and was soon assigned to the Corona project. "Engineers had to rely on their slide rules, Marchant calculators and Frieden calculators for computation. The instruments they built were also crude. For example, the timer that controlled the command telemetry readout in orbit was a paper-punch device driven by an electric motor. It was not unlike the roll used by a player piano."

For Plummer, who was supposed to coordinate the work of all the subcontractors, the absence of precise guidance from the government was at once exhilarating and terrifying. The terse "Work Statement" that Bissell had provided in late April was stunningly vague and open-ended. Few, if any, major technology projects ever sponsored by the U.S. government have started with such a spare, uncluttered mandate from Washington. Years later, Plummer was still amazed by the marching orders. "The entire description of the satellite was in one paragraph," he said.

It was actually a bit longer than Plummer remembered, but not much. The critical opening sentence read, "Develop and provide, except as specifically set forth below, all equipment, services and facilities necessary to complete a program of photoreconnaissance of the Soviet Union." The exceptions were the rocket boosters and other items to be provided by the Air Force.

All the details and engineering specifications were left to Plummer and his colleagues to work out. Itek, which was based near Boston, was assigned to take long-distance photography outside the earth's atmosphere, where the stresses on lenses and other camera equipment had never been tested. As the CIA's long secret history of the project said with some understatement, "Since nothing was known about the actual operation of a panoramic camera in an orbiting satellite, a great variety of technical problems had to be solved by Itek. A testing laboratory had to be designed and fabricated to simulate operational velocity and altitude in order to check their effect on camera resolution, as well as the dynamic effect of the camera's operation on the vehicle." Put another way, the operation of the camera mechanisms might be jarring enough to throw the whole satellite off course.

The conditions during launch and space flight would be exceptionally inhospitable to delicate camera equipment. The violent vibration of the spacecraft as it rocketed toward orbit was likely to knock crucial pieces of the camera out of the precise alignment required for detailed picture taking and might cause the large spools of film to ripple, fracture, or even melt from friction as strips of film rubbed against each other. The temperature differential between the surface of the satellite that faced the sun and the side that did not was expected to be as much as 150 degrees Fahrenheit. The camera itself might experience temperature variations of as much as 50 degrees Fahrenheit from one part to another. That could easily cause distortion of the lenses and of the curved metal plates, or platens, that held the film firmly in place during exposure, throwing the picture out of focus. The vacuum and gravity-free environment promised to add to the difficulties. Indeed, once test flights began in February 1959, these and a host of other problems hounded Dick Leghorn's optical experts and camera designers.

They devised inventive remedies in some cases by substituting different materials. Thermal expansion and contraction problems, for instance, were alleviated in several parts of the camera by fabricating the components with titanium, a strong, structurally stable metal, instead of magnesium, which was more prone to changing shape. Design alterations were also made to deal with the temperature problems. A single, honeycomb frame was created to hold the various parts of the camera rather than three linked frames, eliminating the need for connecting rods and shafts that were susceptible to misalignment in the temperature extremes. The metal platens that held down the film were discarded in favor of a different, less temperature-sensitive mechanism to keep the film in place during exposure. The tension on the film spools was increased to wrap the film more tightly, preventing the welding and ripping that occurred during launch.

All these modifications and innovations were expensive and time consuming. Itek, which took on the project not long after Leghorn had transformed it from a university laboratory into a private business, was not adequately equipped to handle all the design problems. It soon fell far behind delivery schedules and expenses soared. The CIA was not pleased.

Film was another critical and challenging element. The chemists and other scientists at Eastman Kodak, in Rochester, New York, were familiar with the rarified world of high-altitude photography from their work on the U-2. More recently, they had been working on a new acetate-based film for the WS-117L satellite that had the appropriate sensitivity, speed, and resolution for that system. There was, however, a crucial difference between the WS-117L and Corona. The film carried aboard the WS-117L was to be processed aboard the spacecraft, with the pictures then scanned and beamed electronically back to earth. That required a much more forgiving environment aboard the WS-117L. The satellite chamber would be pressurized and heated to maintain the proper temperature and humidity range for film processing. Acetate-based film would work just fine in those conditions.

In the unpressurized Corona, the solvents in acetate-based film would essentially vaporize, making the film so brittle it would crumble. That was a potentially disabling problem because the Corona film would have to pass through a gauntlet of stops and turns and abrupt changes in speed as it traveled through the complex Itek camera. "There was no way that the acetate films could have or would have functioned correctly, particularly in the intricate film path system of the Corona program," recalled Don H. Schoessler, who worked on the Corona film in Kodak's research and engineering department. Indeed, the acetate film that was used on the first test flights cracked and shattered as expected.

At one of Bissell's first monthly meetings, one of the participants, concerned about film durability, naively asked Schoessler, "Is it possible to coat emulsion on thin stainless steel to get the strength that we need?"

That was probably possible, the Kodak executive replied dryly, but the steel film would be worthless because light could not pass through it, making it impossible to print photographs from it. He didn't bother to mention that the sheer weight of metallic film would be disqualifying.

The solution was to perfect Estar, the Mylar-based film Kodak had tried to develop for the U-2. It would remain sturdy and flexible enough in space to survive the twists and tugs as it passed through the camera. The company developed a new fine-grain emulsion coating for the side of the film that would be exposed to provide the sensitivity, speed, and resolution needed for space photography. But Schoessler and his colleagues also had to make sure the film would move smoothly through the camera and would not curl during processing. This was accomplished by applying a thin coating to the back of the film that, among other things, contained fine glass particles. These tiny beads prevented the film, which would be stored in 6,000-foot rolls, from becoming sticky.

Pressure to pack as much film as possible aboard the satellite inspired other innovations. A new ultrasonic technique was developed to splice long sheets of Estar film together to make the large rolls stowed on the satellites. This was no easy trick because the splice points, which normally would be weak and uneven, had to be strong enough and thin enough to run smoothly through the camera and spooling system. Conventional splicing methods were unacceptable. Special production equipment was used throughout the film manufacturing process to ensure uniform thinness.

All of Itek and Kodak's work, of course, would be wasted if the film never made it back to earth. That was General Electric's nightmare. The company's Space Re-entry Program Division in Philadelphia, under subcontract to Lockheed, faced numerous engineering challenges. Its job was to design and build a self-contained pod within the Agena that could ferry the film safely to earth. This module, known as the satellite recovery vehicle, was a precursor to the Project Mercury capsules that Alan Shepard and John Glenn and their fellow astronauts rode into space a few years later. Indeed, the work that was done to develop the Corona capsules was invaluable to NASA as it put together the first manned spacecraft.

To ensure tight security for the project, General Electric bought and refurbished a large, six-story warehouse from the A&P grocery chain at 32nd and Chestnut Street near downtown Philadelphia.

Perhaps even more than the camera system and film, the satellite recovery vehicle involved radical new technologies. There was no model to work with, no existing equipment that could be modified, nothing that could be borrowed from an earlier reconnaissance program. "G.E. had never built anything like that," Plummer said. Though a handful of Soviet and American satellites had been placed in orbit, none had been brought back to earth. The reason was not just the extreme heat generated during reentry, which would reach 4,000 degrees Fahrenheit as the capsule plunged through the thickening air at 350,000 feet. There were also complex engineering and guidance problems. The bucket-shaped film capsule had to be detached from the Agena and lined up in just the right position to put it on a precise path back to earth.

There was no margin for error in the sequence of maneuvers that fell under the technical heading of orbit ejection. Mistakes could—and did—send the film capsule spinning off into a higher orbit or start it down a descent trajectory that deposited it thousands of miles from the designated recovery area. Just such a malfunction in one of the early test flights shot the capsule higher into space, where ground stations lost track of it. Several years later it was spotted, still circling the earth. Other orbit ejection mistakes sent return capsules plummeting into Arctic regions and the jungles of Venezuela.

The satellite recovery vehicle actually served four distinct roles. On launch, the vehicle, which was mounted atop the Agena, acted as a heat-resistant nose cone during the rapid acceleration through the atmosphere. During orbit, the vehicle provided thermal and light protection for the reentry capsule, where the film was stored after exposure. Once the picture taking was completed, the vehicle with its precious cargo of film was supposed to separate from the Agena and conduct a complex series of spins and turns to align itself for reentry and brake its speed to commence the descent to earth. Finally, after retrorockets and other guidance equipment was shed, the film capsule had to survive the fiery plunge through the atmosphere and deploy a series of parachutes to decelerate enough so that specially outfitted planes could pluck it from the sky.

The separation and deorbiting phases were the trickiest. General Electric engineers placed the propulsion and guidance devices that would execute these crucial steps on a conical aluminum structure called the thrust cone. It was, in effect, the power pack for the film capsule. The cone, which was bolted to the bottom of the film capsule, was designed to lift the capsule free of the Agena, spin it up, and stabilize it in the proper position for reentry and then reduce its speed by 1,300 feet per second so it would fall from orbit. All this would have to happen in a rapid series of steps.

While in orbit, the whole spacecraft would fly backward in a horizontal position, with the Agena's rocket exhaust nozzle leading the way. Just before separation, the spacecraft would rotate into a vertical position, with the rocket nozzle on top and the tip of the satellite, including the recovery vehicle, at the bottom, facing the earth. At that point, explosive bolts would fire, separating the thrust cone and film capsule from the rest of the satellite, which by this late stage in the mission had no further function. The camera, for instance, was too heavy and big to try to bring back to earth. After separation, small gas jets would be activated to maneuver the vehicle into the correct position for ignition of the retro-rockets, which would fire for ten seconds. The thrust cone itself would then be jettisoned, and the capsule would soon begin the free-fall back to earth.

General Electric's engineers knew the sudden braking of the capsule as it hit the atmosphere would generate not just extreme heat but also powerful g-forces, possibly as high as 10gs, subjecting the craft to tremendous strains. The peak would come as the capsule streaked through an altitude of about 140,000 feet. Fortunately, by this point, it would contain few components vulnerable to breakage. It was basically just a sealed, reinforced bucket covered by a heat shield and equipped with two parachutes and a simple navigational beacon. The first and smaller of the parachutes—only 7 feet wide—was designed to deploy at 60,000 feet. Its job was to reduce the rate of descent enough so that the main parachute could be safely activated. The appearance of the smaller, deceleration parachute also triggered separation of the heat shield, which was no longer needed, from the capsule. A few seconds later, the main parachute would unfurl, at first in compressed, or reefed, form to reduce the strain on it, then in a fully opened position that brought its 30-foot span into play. By this point, in theory, the capsule would be descending slowly enough that aircraft operating between 10,000 and 20,000 feet could close in to hook the parachute lines and winch the capsule into the cargo bay.

This was easier said than done. Intercepting an object falling through the air, even one slowed by a parachute, requires great piloting skill and a specially equipped airplane. The plan devised for Corona was based on techniques developed to recover the camera-carrying Genetrix spy balloons that the Air Force had tried to float eastward across the Soviet Union from Western Europe in 1956 to take photographs of military bases. Some of the balloons that the jet stream carried all the way to the Pacific were caught in midair by C-119 airplanes trailing a trapeze from their cargo bays. The stubby, twin-propeller plane, known as the Flying Boxcar, had a cruising speed of 200 mph. In theory, if a pilot maneuvered his plane so that it passed just above the descending parachute, the trapeze dangling from the rear of the plane would catch the parachute and its rigging, which would then be winched into the aircraft along with the film capsule.

As the satellite was taking shape in the summer of 1958, the Air Force assembled a group of pilots, most of whom had worked in the balloon recovery program, to prepare for the new recovery operations off Hawaii. The 6593rd Test Squadron (Special) was formed and sent to Edwards Air Force Base in California for initial training. Crews were told they would be recovering missile nose cones. Most crew members doubted the plan would work.

Harry Conway was not one of the doubters. During World War II he had dreamed up an improbable system for rescuing American pilots downed in enemy territory. Conway's idea was to outfit pilots with a harness and a rope that could be strung between two trees or poles. A rescue plane outfitted with a tailhook would sweep in low over the ground, catch the rope, and jerk the pilot off the ground to safety. To convince skeptical colleagues, Conway demonstrated the device himself a dozen times. He survived the sudden acceleration from zero to 140 mph as he was violently lifted off the ground. Conway was assigned to the 6593rd Test Squadron.

Early rehearsals at Edwards were not encouraging. The sink rate of the main parachute—33 feet per second—was too fast. At that speed, pilots couldn't line up their planes to intercept the training capsules dropped from balloons and high-altitude airplanes. If they missed on the first pass, there was not time to make a second run before the capsule landed. The parachute was redesigned to reduce the sink rate and the crews began to have better luck. At the end of 1958, the squadron began to move to Hickam Air Force Base in Hawaii, where it would be based.

Jim Plummer's job in Palo Alto was not only to coordinate the work of the geographically dispersed subcontractors such as Kodak, G.E., and Itek, but also to fit all the hardware together into a functioning satellite. In today's world of precision space engineering, men and women working in white plastic suits in carefully sanitized rooms assemble highly sophisticated satellites according to painstakingly plotted plans. In Plummer's day, the engineers often made it up as they went along, using hammers and wrenches to make adjustments on the fly. Every pound shaved from the satellite meant another pound of film could be added. "In the very early days there were times when filing, chipping and sawing away the excess were the only solutions," the CIA noted in its history of the project.

In aerospace terminology, Plummer was responsible for assembling the payload—in this case the package of reconnaissance gear and recovery equipment that would ride into space atop the rocket. Weight and space were tightly limited. In effect, everything had to fit snugly into a compact metal tube that would be mated to the Agena rocket at the launch base. Plummer thought of it as a big football that had to be fitted with equipment and mounted on the Agena. If the satellite was too heavy, the two-stage rocket wouldn't be able to lift it into orbit. Yet it had to be roomy enough to contain the camera system, a large roll of film, and propulsion, guidance, and communications systems, as well as the recovery vehicle.

Plummer was pretty much starting from scratch, since no one had built anything quite like this before. Even before the first components were delivered to Palo Alto, the Lockheed engineers were working on how best to configure the various pieces inside the satellite and how to protect the delicate machinery throughout the turbulent flight. Fabrication of the satellite shell and internal structures, and testing of various components, was done whenever possible at the building in Palo Alto, where access was restricted to employees who had been cleared to work on the project. Some fabrication and testing, however, had to be done at Lockheed's main Northern California manufacturing plant in Sunnyvale, where the Agena rockets were built. The plant housed large thermal and altitude test chambers that were needed to expose various pieces of the satellite to the kind of punishing conditions they would face during the launch, orbit, and descent phases of flight. To maintain secrecy, Plummer arranged for the work to be done by a hand-picked crew in the middle of the night.

While work on the satellite was slowly progressing, preparation of a launch site was advancing on the seacoast near Lompoc, just south of Point Arguello, 150 miles northwest of Los Angeles. The continent comes to an end along this secluded section of the central California coast in a desolate yet arresting terrain of sandy hills, empty beaches, and scrub brush stunted by powerful Pacific winds. In the fog, which often cloaks the area in a chilly mist, the landscape is ghostly and forbidding. Until 1941, the area was occupied mostly by large ranches that dated back to Mexican land grants early in the nineteenth century. After the German Blitzkrieg in Europe in the opening months of World War II demonstrated the brutal efficiency of tank warfare, the U.S. Army needed a large, remote tract of undeveloped land to train armored and infantry units. The area around Lompoc seemed perfect, and the Army acquired control of 86,000 acres by March 1941. It named the base Camp Cooke, in honor of Maj. Gen. Philip St. George Cooke, a nineteenth-century Army cavalry officer who fought in the Mexican War, the Indian Wars, and the Civil War, and opened the first wagon trail to California in 1847. In 1957, the Army turned the sprawling reservation over to the Air Force for use as a missile base and training center. It was renamed Vandenberg Air Force Base, after Gen. Hoyt S. Vandenberg, the Air Force chief of staff from 1948 to 1953.

The site suited the Air Force because its remoteness would enhance security and its location would permit launches over the ocean, eliminating the possibility that malfunctioning or misdirected rockets might strike populated areas. The first landmass that an errant missile could hit on a southwestward course over the Pacific was Antarctica. Equally important, southerly launches from Vandenberg would put a satellite into polar orbit, bringing it over the polar regions each time it circled the earth. This was the ideal path for monitoring the Soviet Union. Because of the earth's easterly rotation, a new swath of the planet would revolve into view with each pass of the satellite overhead. In the case of the polar orbit planned for the Corona satellites, eight revolutions around the earth would give the cameras a look at most of the Soviet Union and Eastern Europe, starting in the Soviet far east and moving west. A polar orbit offered the added advantage of crossing over the recovery zone off Hawaii. If the reentry sequence was activated as the Agena flew over Alaska on a southward course, the film capsule, in theory, would come down just north of Hawaii.

The main drawback to Vandenberg was a heavily used Southern Pacific rail line that cut across the base. The tracks carried a crowded schedule of freight and passenger trains. For safety and security reasons, rocket and missile launches were banned whenever a train was on base. At some hours of the day, the time available for a launch was no more than a few minutes.

By the time the Corona project was initiated, the Air Force had built five Thor launch pads at Vandenberg, operated by the 672nd Strategic Missile Squadron. Two pads, located in an area of the base known as Space Launch Complex 1 West, were chosen for the secret satellite. The complex sits on a windswept bluff covered with saw grass and sagebrush just a few hundred yards from the beach. A visitor to the site today finds only the decaying relics of a place that once commanded the urgent attention of the nation's top officials. Rattlesnakes nest among the cracked concrete foundations and large rusting metal plates that mark the site of the launch pad itself. The remains of the original launch shelter still stand nearby. A Quonset-style building housed the Thor-Agena two-stage rockets in a horizontal position before they were lifted upright a day or two before launch. Barn owls now occupy the gutted shelter. Pieces of two block houses stand on either side of the launch pad. Protected by thick blast walls, the buildings contained the instruments and other equipment that controlled the launch sequence.

Back in the late 1950s, the launch site swarmed with technicians from Lockheed and Douglas Aircraft, the maker of the Thor booster, and an assortment of Air Force officers. They were divided into two classes: a small number of men who knew about the real purpose of the Corona project, and the rest of the workers, who did not. Keeping the secret at a work site where people without special security clearances mingled freely with more privileged technicians was no easy trick.

Since the presence of a payload atop the rockets was impossible to miss, the CIA and Air Force made no effort to hide that fact. Indeed, the Air Force advertised it, peddling the cover story that the satellites were part of a biomedical experiment to test the effects of space flight on mice and other animals in preparation for sending human beings into space.

There was, however, at least one feature on the Agena that hinted at other purposes. The side of the satellite contained a camera port that would open in orbit to permit picture taking. Fearful that the port would give away the nature of the satellite, Plummer and his colleagues in Palo Alto came up with a Rube Goldberg solution made out of paper, piano strings, and Ping-Pong balls. The idea was to cover the port with the paper while the rocket was sitting on the launch pad. Piano strings with Ping-Pong balls attached at either end would be fitted under the paper. One of Plummer's engineers figured that the air turbulence created around the rocket as it lifted off would exert enough force on the Ping-Pong balls to pull them and the paper free of the satellite.

To test the plan, the engineer mounted the paper contraption on the windshield of his German sports car late one night and headed out to the Bayshore Freeway. As he approached 90 mph, he was pulled over by the California Highway Patrol and ticketed for speeding. Corona records do not indicate what explanation he gave for the paper and Ping-Pong balls. The cover was used on one early test flight, without success. As the rocket roared out of sight, the paper was still stuck to the satellite. Fortunately, no picture taking was planned on the flight.

To deflect speculation about the project at Vandenberg and among the companies involved, the government and private contractors engaged in a number of diversionary activities. Lockheed technicians cleared to work on Corona, for instance, were instructed to shower colleagues who were not cleared with questions about all kinds of scientific issues. The inquiries were supposed to create the impression that matters like magnetic fields and spacecraft maneuverability were the focus of the flights. Anyone at Vandenberg who spotted the camera ports was told the satellite did carry a camera but that it was to be used for astronomical observation. "There were hundreds of people who worked for the program who didn't have a clue that there was a camera on board," recalled Frank Buzard, one of the senior managers of the Corona project.

Though the satellite could be created in secret, and the launch pads prepared out of public sight, there was no way to keep the launches themselves secret. The thunderous noise from the rocket engines would extend far beyond the boundaries of Vandenberg, and the fiery exhaust produced as the Thor boosters climbed through the sky would be visible up and down the central California coast. As the first launch date approached at the end of 1958, the Pentagon needed a plausible public explanation. To shield Corona, a largely fictitious program of space exploration was fashioned along the lines of the "second story" subterfuge that Col. Fritz Oder had originally proposed in the summer of 1957. Part of the Oder plan called for having the Air Force announce its own scientific satellite project sometime after it publicly canceled part of the WS-117L program. Now, in December 1958, the second act unfolded with the formal unveiling of Project Discoverer, ostensibly a new Air Force program that would study the effects of space travel on mice and monkeys as well as refine the techniques required to bring a spacecraft back to earth. All the Corona launches were publicly identified by the Pentagon as Discoverer flights. To maintain the fiction for anyone who was following the launches, including the Soviet Union, some early missions actually carried mice or mechanical creatures that were supposed to mimic the behavior of mice.

The Advanced Research Projects Agency held a news conference in Washington on December 3, 1958, to inform reporters about Project Discoverer. The carefully orchestrated disinformation strategy prepared for the briefing was spelled out in top secret papers. One put it this way: "The objective of this information plan is to insure that the various launchings in Project Discoverer receive news treatment related to their actual missions. Public releases on the project will be strictly controlled to insure such treatment. In particular, these flights must be disassociated with any U.S. reconnaissance program for which they have no capability."

The inaugural public statement said: "The initial launchings primarily will be to test the vehicle itself, especially its propulsion and guidance. Later, the satellites will contain biomedical specimens to seek data on environmental conditions which will be useful to the man-in-space program being carried out jointly by the Advanced Research Projects Agency and the National Aeronautics and Space Administration. As part of this program, live animals also will be carried aloft and their recovery attempted in order to develop the techniques involved."

To give briefers precise answers for a variety of questions that might come up, the Pentagon prepared a script for them to follow.

"Question: Is the Discoverer a reconnaissance satellite?"

"Answer: No."

"Question: Why is Discoverer being placed in polar orbit?"

"Answer: Polar orbit is the only one from Vandenberg AFB with hardware presently available. Eastward launch from Vandenberg is prevented by safety considerations. Launch to the West would entail an unacceptable speed penalty."

Long before the Pentagon unveiled the Discoverer program at its news conference, word had filtered through Washington about government efforts to perfect reconnaissance satellites. The WS-117L project was an open secret. Early in 1958, General Schriever in secret testimony had told Lyndon Johnson's preparedness subcommittee that the Air Force was working on a reconnaissance satellite with a recoverable capsule. He was referring to Program IIA, the variant of the WS-117L that had been belatedly initiated in late 1957 as problems mounted with the original video transmission system. A few days after his appearance, a sanitized transcript was circulated to reporters. The *New York Times* described Schriever's testimony in a front-page story on January 15, 1958.

By the end of the year, John W. Finney, a tenacious reporter who tracked military space programs for the *New York Times*, was familiar enough with the satellite scene from technical journals and congressional sources to add some knowledgeable perspective to the Pentagon's bland announcement about Discoverer. Finney later recalled, "I didn't know about Corona—I never heard of Corona at the time—but I viewed Discoverer as an incremental step toward the development of a military reconnaissance satellite."

His story about the Pentagon news conference on December 3 opened with a straightforward account of the announcement. "The Defense Department announced today a long-range satellite program aimed at placing mice, monkeys, then man in space.

"The first satellite in the program, known as Project Discoverer, is scheduled to be launched within the next month from the Vandenberg Air Force base."

A few paragraphs later, Finney gave readers a hint of what else might be going on. "The Defense Department will be seeking basic information for use in future practical satellites, such as reconnaissance and early warning satellites, navigational, communications and weather satellites, and recoverable space capsules."

The spy pedigree of the program was clear to anyone who had been following the WS-117L project. As *Aviation Week* noted in its account of the December 3 announcement, "The Discoverer program has been completely separated from the WS-117L Sentry program. Originally, Sentry satellites were scheduled to carry photographic, infrared, radar and other types of reconnaissance instrumentation as well as that needed for the general research work that comes under the Discoverer."

Aviation Week reported that one of the program's initial goals was to return a satellite to a predetermined landing area of about 200 square miles.

Finney and his counterparts at *Aviation Week* were digging close to Corona, but they didn't spot it. As 1958 came to a close, Bissell was ready to move ahead with the first launch, confident that the secret would hold. He expected the first working satellite to be in operation by spring. He was off by more than a year.

CHAPTER THIRTEEN

Heartbreak

As 1959 BEGAN, Eisenhower was hamstrung by charges that the Soviet Union, with its advances in rocket technology, had opened a "missile gap" with the United States. Criticism of the administration was mounting, the Corona project was limping ahead, and pressure was growing by the day to resume U-2 flights over Soviet territory. For a man who fervently did not want to risk use of the U-2 for fear of increasing tensions with Moscow or even igniting a war, it was not a happy confluence of events. Several times during the spring and summer, Eisenhower found himself alone in his opposition to renewed use of the U-2, rejecting the advice of almost all his top military and intelligence advisers, including the secretary of defense, the chairman of the Joint Chiefs of Staff, and the director of central intelligence. It was a powerful, if short-lived, example of adamantly independent presidential decision-making.

"Dad used to say that he did better when he followed his hunches than when he listened to his advisers," his son and aide, John Eisenhower, said of the president's wary attitude about the U-2. "We knew we were going to run out of luck sometime. It was like a bomber pilot bombing Germany: How many missions is that rabbit's foot going to last?"

Eisenhower himself later publicly advertised his qualms about the U-2. In his White House memoirs, he offered a correct if somewhat self-congratulatory account: "Of those concerned, I was the only principal who consistently expressed a conviction that if ever one of the planes fell in Soviet territory a wave of excitement mounting almost to panic would sweep the world, inspired by the standard Soviet claim of injustice, unfairness, aggression and ruthlessness."

The first attempt to get the Corona project into the air could hardly have been less auspicious. In fact, the initial attempt to launch the two-stage Thor-Agena rocket on January 21, 1959, was so disappointing that it was not even officially counted as the first launch. Informally, it was known as Discoverer Zero. Sixty minutes before blast-off, the countdown was proceeding smoothly when technicians initiated a planned test of the hydraulic mechanisms on the Agena engine. As electric power was applied to the system, the Agena, still very much anchored to the earth, suddenly began acting as if it was already well on its way into space. A set of small, auxiliary rocket engines, known as ullage rockets, fired. Their purpose was to give the Agena a jolt forward after it separated from the Thor to force the liquid fuel for the main engines to the bottom of the fuel tanks so it could flow at the proper pressure level into the engines. At the same time, the explosive bolts that were designed to separate the Agena from the Thor detonated. These events were programmed to take place in the sky once the Thor had completed its burn. Luckily, the Agena did not topple off the Thor and there was no explosion, but the ullage rocket firing damaged the guidance system of the Thor. The mishap, attributed to a problem in the electrical circuits of the Agena, forced Bissell and Plummer to revise the launch schedule. The government's secret history of the project reports that "Eisenhower upbraided Bissell personally" after the failed launch.

The second effort a month later was also unsuccessful—this time the rocket got off the pad, but the engineers were never sure whether the payload reached orbit. "I signed the report that said it went into orbit, but I'm really convinced that it went into the South Pacific," said Frank Buzard, one of the top Corona managers. Eisenhower began pressing Allen Dulles about the problems, according to CIA records. The second launch, which was given the official designation of Discoverer I, carried no camera or return capsule.

If Eisenhower was testy and impatient—some aides dispute the CIA account and there is certainly abundant evidence that he stood by the program during its bleakest days—it would have been understandable.

Washington was awash with missile gap anxiety as Bissell and his crew were staggering toward space. There could be no more dangerous threat to American security than a significant Soviet advantage in long-range missiles. If true, it would bring the Eisenhower presidency to an end precisely where it had begun, with the ominous prospect of a devastating surprise attack.

The charge was equally explosive as a political issue. Presidential elections were coming in 1960, and the Republican Party, absent Eisenhower, would be facing the electorate without a popular incumbent president and war hero on the national ticket. The last thing the Republican nominee would want to confront was a credible Democratic accusation that the Eisenhower administration had let the Russians achieve military superiority. As Eisenhower's vice president, Richard Nixon, the likely Republican candidate, would be particularly vulnerable on that score. Senators John F. Kennedy, Lyndon B. Johnson, and Stuart Symington, along with other aspiring Democrats, were well aware that the "missile gap" could be one of the decisive issues of the campaign.

Eisenhower himself doubted the claim. The intelligence information he saw, including reports based on the U-2's admittedly incomplete coverage of Soviet territory, offered no hard evidence that the Russians were amassing large numbers of long-range missiles or were about to gain a critical military edge over the United States. In January 1958, when Washington was still reeling from the Sputnik launches and Moscow's first successful test of an intercontinental missile, he had told the nation in his State of the Union address: "At this moment, the consensus of opinion is that we are probably somewhat behind the Soviets in some areas of long-range ballistic missile development. But it is my conviction, based on close study of all relevant intelligence, with the best information that scientists can bring to me, that if we make the necessary effort, we will have the missiles in the needed quantity and in time to sustain and strengthen the deterrent power of our increasingly efficient bombers."

Even if the Russians were producing a modest missile fleet, Eisenhower believed that Moscow would not risk starting a war unless it was confident it could quickly eliminate the possibility of a retaliatory attack. He did not think the Soviet Union could reach that threshold. In early 1958, Eisenhower had assured a scientific advisory panel, "Until an enemy has enough operational capability to destroy most of our bases simultaneously and thus prevent retaliation by us, our deterrent remains effective."

The "missile gap" clamor had been building for years. In the broadest terms, fear of Soviet superiority in long-range missiles dated back to the opening years of the Eisenhower administration. The CIA had raised the issue in one of its first examinations of Soviet missiles in late 1954. That highly classified report said, "We believe that the USSR, looking forward to a period, possibly in the next few years, when long-range bombers may no longer be a feasible means of attacking heavily defended US targets, will make a concerted effort to produce an Intercontinental Ballistic Missile. In this event it probably could have ready for series production in about 1963 (or at the earliest possible date in 1960) an IBM with a high yield nuclear warhead. . . . Advent of the IBM would create an entirely new type of threat to the US. Attacks upon the launching sites are the only countermeasures now known or in prospect. If the USSR should develop such a missile and produce it in considerable numbers before the US developed adequate counterweapons or countermeasures, the USSR would acquire such a military advantage as to constitute an extremely grave threat to US security."

Concern about long-range Soviet missiles grew steadily through the mid-1950s, but fears hardened in 1957 after the Russians announced in August of that year that they had successfully tested an intercontinental missile, the liquid-fueled SS-6. That test was followed quickly by the orbiting of Sputnik I and II in the fall, proving that Soviet rockets were far more advanced than American models. At the end of November, CIA analysts secretly predicted that the Russians could field a prototype intercontinental missile by mid-1958 and increase the number to ten by the end of that year. The same intelligence paper said that the Kremlin could marshal sufficient industrial resources to install fifty long-range missiles at launch bases by October 1959, push the total to one hundred by January 1960, and reach a level of five hundred missiles by the end of 1960.

The issue got a fresh splash of publicity in the closing days of 1957, not long after the launch of the heavier, dog-ferrying Sputnik II, when Chalmers Roberts of the *Washington Post* disclosed the secret findings of the Gaither report, the work of a presidential commission on civil defense that was initially headed by H. Rowan Gaither Jr., the chairman of the Ford Foundation. The *Post* reported that the commission found the United States was "in the gravest danger in its history. . . . It shows an America exposed to an almost immediate threat from the missile-bristling Soviet Union." Among many ominous observations, the report warned that by late 1959, Moscow would likely be able to launch a knockout attack against the United States with one hundred intercontinental missiles carrying nuclear warheads. The Gaither panel, like the Killian committee and other groups that had examined the state of American military strength, recommended accelerating the missile programs. It also urged a variety of steps to reduce the nation's vulnerability to nuclear attack, including the dispersal of Strategic Air Command bases and a crash program to build fallout shelters. Though Eisenhower thought the Gaither report was overdrawn, and refused to make it public, he followed its advice on missiles and bomber bases. He rejected the plan for fallout shelters.

After the Gaither report bombshell, the missile gap quickly built into an irresistible issue for the Democrats as they prepared for congressional elections in 1958 and the presidential contest two years later. At the end of January 1958, Senator Lyndon Johnson's military preparedness subcommittee concluded a series of high-profile hearings with a blistering report that said the United States had fallen far behind the Soviet Union in missile power.

Conservative Republicans, long concerned that the Eisenhower administration had underestimated Moscow's military prowess and shortchanged the Pentagon, raised their own alarms. Joseph Alsop, the syndicated columnist and Bissell's Groton school chum, suggested in July 1958 that the missile gap would soon grow to frightening dimensions. By 1962, he predicted in a widely read column, Moscow would have 1,500 intercontinental missiles, Washington just 130. Because Alsop and his brother and fellow columnist Stewart Alsop were known to be wired into the CIA through long-standing friendships with men like Bissell and Allen Dulles, the missile numbers they cited were accepted as gospel in many quarters in Washington.

In fact, the Alsop numbers mirrored those in the most recent top secret estimate of future Soviet missile forces, which was completed in June. Eisenhower, Allen Dulles, and others, however, weren't sure the Russians could move that fast. They recognized that official estimates projecting the size of the Kremlin arsenal in the years ahead were essentially educated guesses based on estimates of Soviet industrial capacity and intent. As of mid-1958, Washington could not confirm the existence of even a single operational intercontinental missile base in the Soviet Union. If that was correct—the CIA and other intelligence agencies had no way of knowing for sure—it was reasonable to believe that the Russians would be lucky to get twenty or thirty long-range missiles ready for use before the end of the decade. But it wasn't easy to introduce a more nuanced analysis as the alarm grew, or to indicate that some analysts believed the Russians were actually moving very slowly. Whenever someone tried, it usually backfired, reinforcing the impression of confusion and indecision within the administration.

The hubbub was amplified by a bitter debate between the CIA and the Air Force that seemed to break into the open whenever administration officials were summoned to Capitol Hill to testify about Soviet missiles. The CIA, relying largely on a close examination of images produced by the U-2, did not see evidence of a large buildup of intercontinental missiles. The Air Force, which also had access to some U-2 photographs as well as some of its own independent sources of information, said it was convinced the Russians were building missiles at a rapid rate. How much the Air Force numbers were influenced by the service's desire to increase its budget is impossible to know. But there is little doubt that the generals wielded the higher figures both to impress Congress with the importance of funding Air Force missile programs and to prod the country into reckoning with a threat many officers thought the White House was neglecting. As a former secretary of the Air Force, Senator Symington was a willing megaphone for the service's concerns.

This kind of massaging of intelligence information to serve bureaucratic, ideological, or other interests was not new, and it continues to this day. Every administration prefers to receive intelligence information that justifies and supports its foreign and military policies. Some, like the administration of Ronald Reagan, have pushed the CIA and its fellow spy agencies to bend intelligence reports to conform with policy. Others, like the Eisenhower administration, were more content to let the estimates fall where they might. The manipulation goes on within departments as well, especially at the Pentagon, where the Army, Navy, Marine Corps, and Air Force compete for dollars. As the newest of the armed services in the 1950s, and the one charged most directly with responding to a Soviet nuclear attack, the Air Force was especially aggressive in making the case for budget increases.

The Russians, who could follow the missile debate in the American press, did their best to stoke it. Just two months before the first Corona misfire in January 1959, a Russian diplomat announced in Geneva that mass production of Soviet intercontinental missiles had begun. A few days later, Khrushchev declared that he had a missile that could deliver a 5-megaton warhead to a target 8,000 miles away. On January 27, 1959, less than a week after the ullage rocket malfunction at Vandenberg, the Soviet leader opened a Soviet Communist Party congress by boasting that Moscow's rockets had shifted the balance of power in favor of the Kremlin. Echoing the words of the Russian diplomat in Geneva, he claimed "serial production of intercontinental ballistic rockets has been organized."

American officials had no way of knowing at the time that the Russians were bluffing. The SS-6 boosters, a version of the same rocket that was used to launch the Sputnik satellites, though plenty powerful, were ill-suited for warfare because the fuels that powered them—kerosene and liquid oxygen—were difficult to handle and couldn't be stored for long in rocket fuel tanks. This meant that the missiles would have to be fueled shortly before launching, a cumbersome, time-consuming process that was impractical if nuclear war was breaking out. American boosters like the Thor and Atlas suffered from the same problem. Realizing that solid-fueled missiles would be much more dependable and efficient, and could be fired from underground silos that would be difficult to disable with air strikes, both nations were rushing to develop such rockets by the late 1950s. What Washington did not realize at the time was that the Kremlin was simply not building many SS-6s, preferring to await the arrival of the solid-fuel models. All the talk about the mass production of missiles was mostly bluster. But in the absence of hard intelligence, Washington was powerless to determine what was fact and what was fiction. Given the Soviet feats in space and the missile tests at Tyuratam, the missile test center in the Soviet republic of Kazakhstan, there was reason to fear that Moscow was intent on building intercontinental missiles as fast as it could.

The Eisenhower administration didn't help matters by providing inconsistent and sometimes disquieting information itself. Allen Dulles informed members of the Senate Armed Services Committee in secret testimony on January 16, 1959, that the Soviet Union was likely to field ten or so prototype intercontinental missiles before the end of the year. He predicted that Moscow could produce an arsenal of five hundred long-range missiles by 1962 and might even reach that total a year earlier. Neil McElroy, the secretary of defense, told a news conference on January 22 that American intelligence estimates contradicted Soviet claims. A week later, he startled Washington by saying that the United States was voluntarily dropping out of the competition to match the Soviet Union in the number of long-range, land-based missiles. Instead of relying primarily on intercontinental missiles, he said, Washington would develop a diversified arsenal that also included bombers and missiles launched from submarines. General Schriever, appearing at the same Senate hearing as McElroy, took exception to the announcement. "In view of the very great danger, we should be building larger ICBM forces. We have the capacity to build more."

It wasn't every day that a top general openly quarreled with the secretary of defense. The disagreement seemed to underscore the confusion within the administration about the state of Soviet missile programs and how the United States should respond to them. While McElroy was technically correct in suggesting that a blend of bombers and land- and sea-based missiles—often called the triad of nuclear forces—was Washington's best answer to the Soviet threat, the declaration that the United

States was not going to match Moscow's quantity of missiles was politically unwise, to say the least. It merely fanned concern about the missile gap, and like the administration's feeble first response to Sputnik in October 1957, left the unfair public impression that Eisenhower and his aides were sleepwalking through the cold war. The front-page headline in the next day's *New York Times* captured the muddy message: "McElroy Says U.S. Won't Race Soviet In Making ICBM's; Air General Disagrees."

Senator Johnson and his Democratic colleagues, always on the lookout for an opening to criticize the White House, pounced on the conflicting statements. Senator Stuart Symington said he was astonished by McElroy's comments. Senator Johnson, who was presiding over the Senate hearings, summoned top intelligence officials to Capitol Hill later in the week for a closed meeting of the preparedness subcommittee to explain why the CIA had just lowered its estimates of the number of long-range Soviet missiles. The Democrats on the panel suspected that the administration was soft-pedaling the Soviet threat to justify limitations on defense spending, or as Symington would say a year later to make the same point, "The intelligence books have been juggled so that the budget books can be balanced." Eisenhower, as he had throughout his presidency, was trying to hold down military costs. Senator Symington charged that the CIA's numbers had been radically and artificially reduced over recent months.

The complaints irritated Eisenhower. He sounded off during a meeting with Killian, Land, and Edward Purcell, the Harvard physicist, on February 10. It wasn't just the unauthorized disclosure of classified information, he said, or the presentation of a distorted picture of American defenses that bothered him. There was another issue, one that increasingly worried the president and would later serve as the theme of his farewell address to the nation: the growing power of the military-industrial complex. "The munitions makers are making tremendous efforts toward getting more contracts and in fact seem to be exerting undue influence over the Senators," Eisenhower told his guests. He singled out Symington, noting that the Missouri senator often seemed to be accompanied about Washington by a vice president of Convair, the manufacturer of the Atlas missile.

At first glance, Eisenhower's concerns might seem odd coming from a man so steeped in the military culture himself. Building more arms and expanding America's industrial base hardly seem like issues that would alarm a former wartime commander. For Eisenhower, however, the prospect of ever-increasing defense expenditures, spurred by the lobbying of arms makers and the desire of members of Congress to generate jobs in their districts, pointed to the creation of just the kind of garrison state he devoutly hoped to avoid and had alluded to so eloquently in his "Chance for Peace" speech to newspaper editors in early 1953. He did not want to see America's resources devoted so heavily to defense that the rest of society withered. It was a prescient—and courageous—position for a president to take. It was also one of the reasons he put such great emphasis on improving intelligence-gathering systems. The more the country knew about the threats it faced, the more efficiently, and economically, it could plan for its defense.

Killian, Land, and Purcell came to the White House that day to brief Eisenhower about the latest spy technologies. Purcell briefly described a new balloon-mounted acoustical system that could detect the sound of Soviet missile launches. Land then briefed the president on the Corona project, reporting that progress was being made on the camera system but other aspects were not going as well, including the rockets and the recovery capsule. Land said he expected photographs would show objects on earth 20 to 50 feet in diameter. He assured Eisenhower that the purpose of the project remained secret despite "uninformed" speculation in the press about reconnaissance satellites. Killian wound up the meeting with a status report on exploratory design work for a new high-performance spy plane that could someday replace the U-2. With supersonic speed and streamlined shape, the plane, in theory, would be virtually invisible to radar.

Not surprisingly, the most promising proposal for the new airplane came from Kelly Johnson, who sometimes referred to the prospective aircraft as the U-3. Even before the U-2 had taken to the skies over the

Soviet Union in the summer of 1956, Johnson had settled on the formula for his next spy plane. "We knew we needed more altitude and, especially, more speed," he later recalled. How much more was hard to believe. Johnson wanted to build a plane that would travel for thousands of miles at more than three times the speed of sound—that is, faster than a high-velocity rifle bullet—at an altitude in excess of 85,000 feet. Or to put it another way, he was dreaming of an airplane that could outrace a missile.

Even by today's technological standards, that would be a tall order. By the aviation yardsticks of the 1950s, it seemed utterly outlandish. As Ben Rich, one of Johnson's colleagues, recalled, "Experimental rocket airplanes had flown at blinding Mach 3 speed using powerful thrusters for two or three minutes at a time until fuel ran out. But Kelly was proposing an airplane to *cruise* at more than three times the speed of sound, that could fly coast to coast in less than an hour on one tank of gas." The U-2, by comparison, was child's play. "He was proposing to build an airplane that would fly not only four times faster than the U-2 but five miles higher—and the U-2 was then the current high-altitude champion of the skies," Rich said.

Land, in his role as the chairman of a panel that advised the CIA on technology matters, had encouraged Johnson to pursue his ideas. Johnson made the first entry in his log for the project, which he called Archangel, on April 21, 1958. "I drew up the first Archangel proposal for a Mach 3 cruise airplane having a 4,000 nautical mile range at 90,000 to 95,000 feet."

Ben Rich described it this way: "It was designated A-1, and showed a striking single-seat, two-engine airplane—a long, sleek bullet-shaped fuselage with rounded inlets on big engines mounted on the tip of small delta wings that were two thirds of the way back on the fuselage. One look and even a schoolboy would realize this bird was designed for blazing speed."

In November 1958, Land and his panel members had met with Eisenhower to review competing preliminary designs produced by Lockheed and Convair. Land reported that it appeared possible to build an airplane that would be difficult for the Russians to track and that would be traveling so fast it would be all but impossible to intercept. Eisenhower approved Land's recommendation to proceed with further exploratory work and authorized Bissell to withdraw $6.5 million from the CIA reserve fund to pay for the planning effort.

None of this, of course, solved the immediate problem of determining how many missiles the Kremlin had ready to fire at the United States. Even at the lower range Symington had acidly cited, the CIA calculated that in the next few years the Kremlin would have a three-to-one advantage in intercontinental missiles. If so, there would be a dangerous imbalance in Soviet and American power.

Eager to get as accurate a reading as possible, McElroy, his deputy, Donald Quarles, and General Nathan Twining, who by this time was serving as chairman of the Joint Chiefs of Staff, appealed to Eisenhower on February 12, 1959, to resume U-2 flights, which had been suspended since March 1, 1958. Following a meeting of the National Security Council, the three men lingered behind at the White House to talk with the president.

Eisenhower had made it clear after the inaugural missions of the U-2 in July 1956, and the angry Soviet protest that followed, that any further flights would require his direct approval, which was granted sparingly. He wanted to review every flight plan himself. Bissell would come to the White House armed with maps and the targets that he had picked with the assistance of the Ad Hoc Requirements Committee. The Dulles brothers would usually accompany him, Allen to vouch for the intelligence purposes and John Foster to pass judgment on the diplomatic implications. They were usually joined by the chairman of the Joint Chiefs of Staff and the secretary of defense or his deputy. Eisenhower would study the plans and sometimes suggest target and route changes.

"He would always get the map on his desk and look at it," Bissell recalled, "and always ask me to come around and explain this or that feature of it, and there were occasions, more than once, when he would say, 'Well, you can go there, but I want you to leave out that leg and go straight that way. I want you to go from B to D because it looks to me like you might be getting a little exposed over here,' or something of this kind."

McElroy, Quarles, and Twining hadn't come to request a specific flight, but rather to petition Eisenhower to reconsider his blanket resistance to using the plane on flights over the Soviet interior. The only missions he had approved in the preceding twelve months were restricted to border areas. Going inland, the three officials argued, was the only way to gauge the size of the Soviet missile fleet. McElroy said the lack of reliable information was so severe that he did not know the location of a single operational Soviet missile base. That could mean either there were no launch bases, and the noisy Russian claims were hollow, or there were plenty of missile sites and Washington simply had not found them. The uncertainty was untenable.

The Soviet launch sites at Kapustin Yar in the Ukraine and at Tyuratam in Kazakhstan, which had been identified and photographed by the U-2, were used to test missiles and weren't what bothered the defense secretary. He was concerned about bases from which operational missiles would be launched against the United States, including a new base under construction at Plesetsk, near the White Sea. McElroy was also likely worried about mobile launchers that could be transported by road or rail, making them difficult to track and count. Citing assurances from the Joint Chiefs of Staff that the Russians still lacked the means to shoot down a U-2, McElroy requested permission to start planning new overflights. Twining seconded the recommendation.

Eisenhower demurred. For one thing, he was worried about picking a new fight with Khrushchev at a time when tensions were already running very high over Berlin. Khrushchev had announced in November that he would sign a peace treaty with East Germany in six months that would erase Allied rights in West Berlin. If Khrushchev carried through on the ultimatum, the world would face a new Berlin crisis. Given the sensitivity of the city and the postwar agreements that placed West Berlin under American, British, and French control, it was inconceivable that Eisenhower could let West Berlin fall into Communist hands. As Eisenhower recalled in his memoirs, "Our nation would never agree to the surrender of West Berlin either to the Soviets or to East Germany. . . ."

It was not a good time to risk an incident over the U-2. Underscoring the gravity with which he viewed use of the plane, he informed McElroy and the others that nothing would compel him to go to Congress more quickly to seek a declaration of war than similarly brazen violations of American airspace by Soviet spy planes. Of the many comments Eisenhower made about the U-2 during the four years the plane was used for flights far into Soviet airspace, this one most clearly captures his fear that the spy flights could ignite a war.

Eisenhower also hoped that despite the initial Corona launch failure, space-based reconnaissance might soon provide ample intelligence about Russian missiles. He told his visitors that U-2 flights should be "held to a minimum pending the availability of this new equipment." Quarles warned Eisenhower that it might be another two years before space photographs became available.

The argument failed to sway the president, who believed Soviet missile technology had not yet reached the point where the new weapons could be mass-produced or fielded in large numbers. Eisenhower's assessment was remarkably close to the mark, though he wouldn't know that until the first Corona pictures appeared eighteen months later. As of early 1959, his view was more of a gut feeling than a reasoned analysis backed up by hard data. He said he based it on corresponding construction capability within the United States and the sense that the government generally overestimated Soviet industrial and military might. He reminded his visitors that the purported Soviet advantage in long-range bombers had proven to be a mirage.

Eisenhower's analysis may also have been based in part on knowledge that the Russians had not launched any intercontinental missiles from the base at Tyuratam since May 29, 1958. To CIA analysts, the long interval suggested problems in missile development, but Eisenhower could not be sure about the cause of the delay or what it signified. Indeed, the Air Force argued that the inactivity meant the earlier test flights had gone so well the Russians felt no need to continue them and were already busy mass-producing missiles.

On February 17, only five days after the discussion with McElroy, Quarles, and Twining, launch activity resumed at Tyuratam. It was not long before the Pentagon and CIA were back at the White House with a new request to use the U-2. This time it was harder for Eisenhower to resist.

The resumption of Soviet missile tests eliminated the possibility that the Kremlin program had hit a dead end. While testing probably meant the Russians were still trying to perfect their missiles, it was clear work was continuing, with the prospect that missiles would be deployed. On April 6, upon hearing the case for additional spy flights, the president reluctantly approved two missions that would venture deep into Soviet airspace. But after sleeping on the decision, he invited McElroy and Bissell to the Oval Office the next day to tell them he had changed his mind. Andrew Goodpaster's notes about the conversation provide a revealing snapshot of Eisenhower's thinking—and agonizing.

Eisenhower opened the discussion by summarizing his concerns. "First, we now have the power to destroy the Soviets without need for detailed targeting. Second, as the world is going now, there seems no hope for the future unless we can make some progress in negotiations (it is already four years since the Geneva meeting). Third, we cannot in the present circumstances afford the revulsion of world opinion against the United States that might occur—the U.S. being the only nation that could conduct this activity. Fourth, we are putting several hundred million dollars into programs for more advanced capabilities."

In summary, Goodpaster noted, "the President said he did not agree that this project would be worth the political costs."

Eisenhower told McElroy and Bissell he was well aware of the need for hard information. He said, "This need is highlighted by the distortions several senators are making of our military position relative to that of the Soviets, and they are helped in their 'demagoguery' by our uncertainties as to Soviet programs." But Eisenhower remained fearful of "the terrible propaganda impact that would be occasioned if a reconnaissance plane were to fail."

He was unwilling to give up all hope of negotiating a reduction in tensions with Khrushchev, who seemed interested in scheduling a new summit meeting. The President felt that "there is need to make some kind of progress at the summit, even though we cannot be sure this is possible." Eisenhower wound up his comments by advising the aides to raise the matter with him again if circumstances changed.

Goodpaster, circumspect about offering his own opinions in the many memorandums he prepared for the president about sensitive issues, appended his own thoughts at the end of this memo. He, too, favored new flights. "Earlier, the President had discussed this matter at length with me. In response to his request for my advice, I analyzed the proposal as to the importance of possible costs and possible gains, and indicated I would be disposed to favor the two particular actions proposed. I added that, while I had confidence in my analysis of the costs and gains, I felt less sure of the evaluation of their relative importance and would readily defer to the President's own assessment in this respect."

Eisenhower must have wondered how long he could hold the line against U-2 flights when just seven days later the next Corona flight inconveniently deposited a return capsule on the Soviet Union's doorstep. Discoverer II, the third launch attempt, proceeded perfectly at first. After a brief launch delay because of fog at Vandenberg, the two-stage rocket blasted off at 1:18 P.M. on April 13. The Thor and Agena engines burned as planned, carrying the satellite into an elliptical polar orbit that extended from 156 miles above the earth at its closest point to 243 miles at the most distant.

The launch itself was a spectacular sight. "From their observation site 10,000 feet away," an Associated Press correspondent reported, "newsmen saw the seventy-eight-foot projectile balancing gracefully on its tail for fleeting seconds as the engine of the first-stage Thor missile, with a thrust of 150,000 pounds, ignited in a cloud of white smoke.

"Then with the roar of a dozen locomotives the rocket leaped upward, trailing a yellow plume of fire a hundred feet long. In less than three minutes, it was out of sight, its path marked by a single white vapor trail reaching miles into the blue sky."

John Finney, covering the story for the *Times* from Washington, informed readers in a page-one story the next day that the United States had placed a military satellite in orbit and hoped to recover it within a day or two. "On the basis of preliminary tracking information from radio stations in Hawaii and Alaska, the Air Force calculated that Discoverer II had gone into a near north-south orbit, as planned. With this polar orbit, the satellite will pass over virtually all of the earth's surface."

Though Finney did not know that the Discoverer program was actually a spy satellite project, he came within an inch of the truth. His account said, "In the rapidly growing technology of space, Discoverer II represents an important first attempt to stabilize a satellite in space and bring it back to earth. If successful, Discoverer II will be an important advance in the development of military reconnaissance and scientific satellites that can carry out their mission in space and then return with their information."

He also described the expected recovery operation. "The tentative recovery plans call for returning a 160-pound cone-shaped capsule of instruments from space over the Pacific Ocean. The capsule, dangling from a parachute, would be caught in mid-air by Air Force cargo planes equipped with hooks to snag the parachute."

The plan didn't work. Because of an error in resetting the timer that initiated the recovery sequence, the return capsule separated from the Agena prematurely during the satellite's seventeenth orbit. Instead of descending over the Pacific and coming into view not far from Hawaii, the capsule came down somewhere near Norway. "It was a bad night," recalled Frank Buzard. "We knew we couldn't get ahold of it but we tried to see if any other tracking stations could get to it. They couldn't. We figured it was going to Spitzbergen."

Spitzbergen Island is located in the Arctic Ocean, above the northern tip of Norway. Residents of Longyearbyen, a mining community on the island, reported seeing a "starburst" and a descending parachute.

The Pentagon, not eager to draw attention to the embarrassing mistake, blandly announced that it was abandoning the recovery effort, informing Finney and other reporters that it did not know if the separation of the capsule from the satellite had taken place. Finney reported the possibility that if the timing of the separation was off, the capsule might land somewhere in the Arctic region.

Though the return capsule contained no photographic equipment—the contents included several mechanical mice—the CIA and Pentagon feared the Russians, who operated several coal mines on Spitzbergen, would find it and deduce from the equipment that Washington was working on a project to take pictures from space and send the film back to earth. An American team was quickly dispatched to Norway to try to find the capsule in Spitzbergen's snow-covered countryside. Word of the search made it into the news on April 17.

The group was led by Lt. Col. Charles Mathison of the Air Force, a large, amiable man with a booming voice who was known among his colleagues as "Moose." He was vice commander of the 6594th Test Wing, which operated the ground control installations for Air Force satellite programs. He was not cleared to know about Corona, so he flew off to Norway unaware that his quarry was actually the capsule for a spy satellite. With the help of the Norwegian military, Mathison conducted an air and ground search, hoping to spot the gold capsule or the orange and silver parachute that had brought it down to earth. The search ended without success on April 22, but Mathison and his colleagues suspected that tracks they had seen around the likely landing site were evidence that the Russians had recovered the capsule. "There were reports from the local people that they had seen this gold ball hanging on the end of this particularly colored parachute that we had, and they noticed that there had been an ice breaker going into Spitzbergen," Plummer recalled. "Most of us were pretty convinced that the Russians got it."

General Twining informed Quarles about Mathison's investigation in a memo on April 25. "From concentric circular tracks found in the snow at the suspected impact point and leading to one of the Soviet mining concessions on the island, we strongly suspect that the Soviets are in possession of the capsule." It's little wonder that the mystery inspired Alistair MacLean to write *Ice Station Zebra*, a popular technothriller that involves an American submarine racing the Russians to a remote British weather outpost near the polar ice cap to recover top secret satellite photography. The book was published in 1963 and made into a movie in 1968.

The next two launches, on June 3 and June 25, were even more discouraging because the satellites did not reach orbit. In both cases, the Agena engine shut off before powering the payload to orbital velocity.

The June 3 flight, Discoverer III, carried four mice, selected from a sturdy breed maintained at the Air Force Aero Medical Field Laboratory at Holloman Air Force Base in New Mexico. In a sign of how little scientists knew about space travel at this point, they selected black mice to test whether cosmic rays would bleach their hair. As astronauts later discovered, cosmic rays did not produce a change in hair color.

The furry passengers were "seven to ten weeks old and weighed slightly over one ounce each," according to CIA records. "A three-day food supply was provided which consisted of a special formula containing peanuts, oatmeal, gelatin, orange juice and water. Each mouse was placed in a small individual cage about twice its size, and each had a minuscule radio strapped to its back to monitor the effects of the space trip on heart action, respiration and muscular activity."

Because the flight was genuinely a biomedical test, the Air Force was more than happy to tell the world about the mice. That was fine until the rocket dived into the ocean, killing the creatures. Animal rights groups, already exercised over the death of a monkey that had flown into space aboard one of Wernher von Braun's Jupiter rockets in late May, complained about the cavalier treatment of the animals. The British Society Against Cruel Sports filed a formal protest with the American ambassador in London, demanding that the United States send no more monkeys or mice into space until it was confident they would survive and be recovered. The furor forced the Corona managers to drop their plans to send a second batch of mice aloft on the next flight.

That opened the way to try the first launch of the Corona camera system in Discoverer IV on June 25. Like the previous flight, the Agena rocket and satellite failed to achieve orbit and fell into the sea. After five attempts, counting the ullage rocket misfiring in January, Bissell and Plummer could point to just one launch that had achieved orbit, and that mission had ended in disappointment at Spitzbergen. All in all, it was not a promising start. It looked as if the objectives might simply be unattainable with the available technology.

The setbacks were especially disheartening to Bissell, who had been spoiled by the swift development of the U-2. "Malfunctions in an experimental satellite system," he recalled, "are exceptionally frustrating to the designers and operators because there is never any human observer to see and evaluate what went wrong. If something failed on a U-2 test flight, unless it was a fatal crash, the pilot could come back and relate what happened. This was not the case with satellites. They spun out of control, burned up in the atmosphere, crashed, hopelessly lost, in the ocean, or exploded. Because the whole system was destroyed on reentry, it was often impossible to retrieve it and do an assessment. One relied on telemetry while the satellite was still in flight—sometimes it was possible to infer from the telemetry what went wrong; quite often it was difficult. You would simply have to try again and hope for the best. As failures continued to mount, I found the experience increasingly heartbreaking and frustrating. We were all aware that every one of these flights was hideously expensive. It took a certain amount of fortitude to keep going and going, hoping it would finally work."

It's doubtful that such a troubled program would survive for long in Washington today. The tolerance for failure is much lower on expensive technological projects these days, in part because they can become the victim of partisan politics as one party condemns the other for wasting money or blindly pursuing unworkable ideas. Repeated failures, chronicled by the media, can quickly undermine public and congressional support. It is also much harder now to maintain the secrecy of an ambitious military or intelligence enterprise like Corona. After just a few months of miscues, there would be tremendous pressure to cancel a project that seemed as futile as Corona did in 1959 and the first half of 1960.

Bissell, backed by Eisenhower, was determined not to give up. "The crying need to understand what was happening in the Soviet Union drove this program and gave tolerance to the risk," recalled John McMahon, who worked as a senior aid to Bissell.

Whatever irritation Eisenhower may have felt about the delays, he remained faithful to the concept, according to Goodpaster. "Eisenhower always said, 'Let's not worry about it. Let's stay with it. It's so important, and we need it. We need to just keeping going with it.' " The willingness to proceed with high-risk concepts in the face of adversity was typical of Eisenhower, Goodpaster said. "This is the man who decided in the bad weather to go ahead with the invasion of Europe."

Plummer, Lockheed's program manager for Corona, was impressed by Bissell's persistence and his refusal to panic in the face of repeated disappointments. After each failure, Bissell and General Ritland, Bissell's deputy, would listen to the reports from Plummer and his colleagues and then calmly instruct them to try again. "I suspect he learned that from working with Kelly Johnson," Plummer said. "We would present a technical problem—we might have just lost a missile—and we would tell him why we thought we could do better the next time. . . . If they were satisfied, they'd say okay, let's go, let's proceed to the next launch."

Bissell's recollection of the delays was not quite as benign. "There would be a long stand-down after each attempt to enable some modification in the equipment to be made. This would be followed by the wretched business of another flight that still didn't work. Once we cured a particular malfunction, a new malfunction would occur and the whole guessing game would begin again: what went wrong and what can be done to fix it."

Eisenhower gave Bissell the money and time he needed to sustain a busy launch schedule at Vandenberg. But at the same time, hedging his bet on Corona and once again following the advice of Killian and Land, he continued to support plans to build a sleek new spy plane to succeed the U-2. Lastly, and with the greatest reluctance, he gave the go-ahead in July for another U-2 flight.

The Russians left him little choice. The resumption of Soviet missile launches at Tyuratam in February had marked the beginning of an extensive new phase of test flights. As spring gave way to summer in 1959, with Corona showing no signs of coming on line anytime soon, just about all of Eisenhower's top national security advisers leaned on him to authorize another U-2 flight over the Soviet heartland.

Allen Dulles and Bissell visited the White House on the morning of July 7 to go over plans. They urged the president to let them proceed with a flight over Tyuratam that would originate in Pakistan and end at an abandoned World War II airfield in a remote area of Iran that two of Bissell's top aides, Col. Stanley Beerli and John Parangosky, had spotted while hunting for new landing sites in the region. The shah of Iran, Mohammad Reza Pahlavi, who had been installed with the help of the CIA in 1953, was more than happy to cooperate. The only problem with the landing strip was that the countryside around it was controlled by bandits.

Eisenhower wanted to hear from Christian Herter, who had become secretary of state in April after John Foster Dulles resigned in ill health. On July 8, Herter, Bissell, Goodpaster, and Allen Dulles assembled in the Oval Office. Eisenhower, according to Goodpaster's account of the meeting, reiterated his concerns about using the U-2, telling his aides he worried about "the possibility of getting involved in something costly and harmful."

Herter, whose recommendation was likely to be decisive, advised Eisenhower to approve the flight. He said the intelligence objective was paramount and that the chances of losing the plane seemed remote. Bissell was not quite as confident. He said the newest Russian fighter jets could probably come close to the altitude of the U-2. The risk, however, was still considered relatively limited because the Soviet planes could not fly at that height for long or maneuver effectively in the thin air. If the Russians spotted and protested the flight, the men agreed, Washington could defend itself "with an absolute disavowal and denial on the matter."

Eisenhower seemed torn. He was well aware that Khrushchev hoped to travel to the United States at the end of the summer, the first visit to America by a Soviet leader. Whether the trip might help reduce tensions wasn't clear, but there was little doubt that another U-2 flight could be disruptive.

"The President said that Khrushchev seems almost to be looking for excuses to be belligerent," Goodpaster noted. "By doing nothing he can put us in a terrible hole in Berlin. Holding the cards he does, he could very readily say that such an event as this marks the end of serious negotiations. There remains in the President's mind the question whether we are getting to the point where we must decide if we are trying to prepare to fight a war, or to prevent one."

Goodpaster didn't record which of these options he thought Eisenhower was choosing, but it seems probable that in approving the flight, the president was hoping to help prevent a war. Goodpaster simply noted, "After all the discussion, the President indicated that in view of the unanimous recommendation of the officials having the operational authority, he would assent to the operation being conducted."

On July 9, 1959, more than sixteen months after the last flight deep into Soviet airspace, a U-2 took off from the secret U-2 base at Peshawar in northwest Pakistan on a mission code-named Operation Touchdown. The CIA had secretly arranged with the Pakistani government to make use of an airfield there to take advantage of limited Soviet radar coverage along the Central Asian frontier north of the Himalayan Mountains. Bissell wanted whatever element of surprise he could still get, knowing that interception was less likely if the plane could slip into Soviet airspace undetected.

Col. Beerli, the commander of Detachment B, which was stationed at Incirlik, an American air base near Adana, Turkey, had developed a rapid deployment system to move U-2s in and out of Pakistan as quickly and surreptitiously as possible. Under the cover of darkness, all the supplies and gear needed to launch a mission, including 50-gallon barrels of the special U-2 fuel, would be loaded aboard two C-130 transport planes and flown from Incirlik to Peshawar. A few hours later, one of the Agency's U-2 pilots would bring one of the spy planes in from Turkey. After the aircraft was refueled, a fresh pilot who had flown in with the supplies and done the necessary prebreathing of oxygen, would take off before dawn for the Soviet Union.

In this case, Mission 4125, Martin Knutson was the operational pilot. After crossing into Soviet territory, he guided the plane over a number of military sites, including the nuclear test site at Semipalatinsk and the missile base at Tyuratam. He then headed east, toward the Ural Mountains and on to the airstrip in Zahedan, Iran. To secure the landing strip, the CIA had dispatched armed agents to await Knutson's arrival. "If I made it across the border and saw a cloud of black smoke, it meant that the field was being attacked by the bandits. If that happened, I was supposed to eject and bail out. I crossed the Russian border with only 100 gallons of fuel remaining. Really getting hairy. I didn't see any smoke, so I came in and landed with less than 20 gallons left in the tank."

The skies over the targets were clear, and the photographs were superb. They showed that the base at Tyuratam was being expanded with the addition of a second launch pad.

As good as the photos were, they didn't resolve whether or not there was a missile gap. With Khrushchev's visit approaching, Eisenhower was unwilling to entertain proposals for further flights during the summer. He later extended the ban through the end of the year, believing that his talks with the Soviet leader in Washington and at Camp David in mid-September had eased tensions somewhat. During the discussions, Khrushchev backed off of his threat to sign a peace treaty with East Germany and Eisenhower accepted an invitation to visit the Soviet Union the following spring. The two leaders also agreed to convene a four-power summit meeting with their British and French counterparts. Khrushchev surprised Eisenhower during their talks by never mentioning the U-2 flights, perhaps because he was embarrassed that Soviet military forces could not prevent the flagrant violations of Russian airspace. As Khrushchev barnstormed around the United States, visiting a movie studio in Los Angeles, touring a family farm in Iowa, and sightseeing in New York, the cold war momentarily seemed less threatening.

That didn't stop Khrushchev from continuing to boast about his rockets. In November he told a group of Soviet journalists, "Now we have such a stock of rockets, such an amount of atomic and hydrogen weapons, that if they attack us, we could wipe our potential enemies off the face of the earth. . . ." He added, "By the way, I shall reveal—and let the people know about it; I am making no secret of this—that in one year, 250 hydrogen warheads came off the assembly line in the factory we visited." By the end of the year, the Russians had also succeeded in sending two spacecraft to the moon, Luna I and II, both lifted into space by the same SS-6 rockets that could deliver nuclear warheads to targets in the United States. Washington was still struggling to get its rockets into orbit.

With Bissell's secret air force grounded for the time being, Eisenhower looked to Corona for answers about the missile gap. He got none.

The project was still beset with problems. Summer and fall had brought more disappointments. An August launch, Discoverer V, yielded no photographs after the camera broke down during the first orbit, apparently because of the cold, and the recovery capsule was fired farther out into space rather than back toward earth when its spin stabilization rockets misfired. Later that month, Discoverer VI made it into orbit, but the camera failed on the second orbit and the retrorocket did not work properly. Two November missions, Discoverer VII and VIII, were no more successful.

Walter Levison, who was directing work on the camera at Itek, was so discouraged that he drove up to Edwin Land's country home in Peterborough, New Hampshire, the weekend before Thanksgiving to say he didn't think a camera system could be perfected. Victor K. McElheny, Land's biographer, described the encounter: "For Levison, it was the bleakest moment of his life. He told Land, the head of the small outside committee superintending Corona, that he should carry word of Corona's failure to President Eisenhower. The project would have to 'stand down.' Levison felt frustrated and humiliated. Land, however, took another tack, calling for redoubled effort over three months to rescue the project."

As a CIA history of Corona bluntly noted, "It had become plain by the end of November 1959 that many things had to be done to correct the multiple failures that were plaguing the Corona system. Eight Thor-Agena combinations and five cameras had been expended with nothing to show for the effort except accumulated knowledge of the system's weaknesses. The project technicians knew what was going wrong but not always why."

The technicians were hampered by the weight limit of the satellite, which prevented the installation of diagnostic equipment to monitor what was going wrong with the propulsion and guidance systems and the reconnaissance package. "This meant that the engineers usually did not have enough diagnostic data to correct the problems with confidence," Bud Wheelon said. "What is remarkable is that Bissell and Ritland pressed on despite these failures, and that Eisenhower continued to support them."

The list of failures grew so long that serious consideration was given to scrapping the whole enterprise. The fact that Eisenhower stayed with the project through twelve failed launches over twenty months is evidence of both his perseverance and his desperation to replace the U-2.

Nearly every Corona component contributed to the dismal record at one time or another. The Thor and Agena engines would burn too long, flinging the satellite too far into space to be of any use. At other times, the rocket engines would cut out prematurely, leaving the satellite short of orbit and on a trajectory to crash into the sea. When the Agena vehicle was placed in the correct orbit, the stabilization system would fail, making picture taking impossible as the satellite tumbled through space. There were all sorts of electrical and mechanical problems. On the rare occasions when all the rocket and guidance equipment worked perfectly, the camera malfunctioned or the return capsule went off course during separation and sailed off toward the stars instead of falling back to earth. Before Kodak solved the acetate problem, the film simply crumbled into dust in the vacuum of space.

Bissell and General Ritland periodically suspended launch operations to give Plummer and his subcontractors a chance to evaluate and fix the problems. More preflight testing was instituted in hopes of catching design and engineering mistakes before they crippled another flight. All this cost time and money. Bissell seemed acutely aware of the unusual circumstances in January 1960 when he appealed to General Cabell, Allen Dulles's deputy, for additional funds. "Although such a sequence is regrettable," Bissell said, "there has been considerable confusion in this program as to what the amount of the overruns would be, and this has made it difficult to obtain approvals in an orderly fashion in advance."

Even the launch moratoriums failed to assure success. One of the most dramatic, and disheartening, failures occurred on February 19, 1960, just two weeks after the end of a three-month break. The mission was Discoverer X. Moments after liftoff, the Thor booster began to fishtail and wheeled northeast toward the towns of Santa Maria and San Luis Obispo. A technician sent a signal to the Thor to self-destruct. Fifty-two seconds into flight, the rocket blew up over Vandenberg. As pieces of the satellite, including the camera system, fell to the ground, security officers rushed to the crash site to shield the reconnaissance equipment. This was not exactly the way engineers had imagined the film would be recovered from the satellite.

While Bissell and Plummer wrestled with the uncooperative satellite, the administration was fueling the missile gap debate with a new set of numbers. In Senate appearances in January 1960, Allen Dulles, Thomas S. Gates, the new secretary of defense, and General Twining each produced different estimates for the number of Soviet missiles. The discrepancy—the CIA was at the low end, the Joint Chiefs at the high end—ignited a new round of catcalls from Johnson, Symington, Henry M. "Scoop" Jackson, and other Democrats. After Dulles was summoned to the Capitol again to dispel the confusion, Symington gravely announced that the CIA chief had "completely verified the fact that there had been no elimination of the ballistic missile gap or reduction in the three-to-one ratio against the United States."

Dulles was angered by the conflict. As far as he could tell from the evidence collected by the CIA, including the U-2 flights that Eisenhower had permitted, the Kremlin appeared to have fielded very few intercontinental missiles. In September the Agency had reported in a major study of Soviet missiles that "we believe it is now well established that the USSR is not engaged in a 'crash' program for ICBM development." The assessment, echoing the figures that Dulles had given to the Armed Services Committee in January 1959, estimated that just a handful of intercontinental missiles—around ten—might already be operational or nearly so. By that standard, the Air Force estimate of one hundred Russian missiles seemed wildly overblown, and inspired primarily by a desire to stampede Congress into fattening the Air Force budget. But because the U-2 flights were so secret, Dulles couldn't cite the photographic evidence in his Senate testimony.

Maintaining the secrecy of the U-2 was increasingly difficult by this time. With photographs from the overflights circulating at the Pentagon, White House, CIA, and other agencies, word had long since seeped through the capital that the government was conducting spy flights over Soviet territory. A number of journalists had learned about the plane. Hanson Baldwin, the military correspondent of the *New York Times*, had seen a U-2 at a German airfield and discovered its true purpose. When he informed the CIA in the summer of 1958 that he was preparing a story, Allen Dulles appealed to the publisher of the *Times*, Arthur Hays Sulzberger, to hold off publication. He agreed. Other publications, including the *Washington Post* and the *Cleveland Plain Dealer*, also knew about the plane but did not run stories.

As long as U-2 operations remained officially secret, Dulles knew he could not overtly use the photographs to shape the public debate about the missile gap, but with additional flights he could at least hope to still the intense arguments within the government. "As a result of these [January 1960] Senate hearings," the CIA history of the U-2 program reported, "Dulles was determined to obtain permission for more overflights in order to settle the missile-gap question once and for all and end the debate within the intelligence community."

With the support of the President's Board of Consultants on Foreign Intelligence Activities, including Gen. James Doolittle, the legendary World War II aviator, Dulles pressed Eisenhower to expand the use of the U-2. The board gathered at the White House on February 2 and urged Eisenhower to make use of the spy plane "to the maximum degree possible." When General John E. Hull reminded the president that Washington remained blind to Soviet military preparations, Eisenhower's thoughts turned once again to the possibility of another summit meeting and his standing in the free world. It looked increasingly likely that his next meeting with Khrushchev would come in Paris in May.

"The President said that he has one tremendous asset in a summit meeting," Goodpaster noted. "That is his reputation for honesty. If one of these aircraft were lost when we are engaged in apparently sincere deliberation, it could be put on display in Moscow and ruin the President's effectiveness."

How right he was.

CHAPTER FOURTEEN

"Capsule Recovered Undamaged"

From the time Kelly Johnson started designing the U-2 in late 1953, everyone involved knew the Russians would sooner or later figure out how to shoot it down. Jack Carter, the Lockheed executive who first encouraged Johnson to produce a high-altitude spy plane, had estimated in 1953 that the plane would elude Russian air defenses until 1960. But in early 1960, as the Pentagon and CIA determined there was a clear and present danger to the aircraft, the Eisenhower administration failed to heed the new warnings.

Richard Bissell knew the U-2 was becoming increasingly vulnerable. On March 14, 1960, the Air Technical Intelligence Center (ATIC), an Air Force agency, put Bissell on notice that the latest Soviet surface-to-air missile (SAM), the SA-2 Guideline, could intercept the U-2. The center reported: "The greatest threat to the U-2 is the Soviet SAM. Although the ATIC analysis concedes a remote possibility that the SAM may be less effective than estimated, their present evaluation is the SAM (Guideline) has a high probability of successful intercept at 70,000 feet providing that detection is made in sufficient time to alert the site."

These bell-ringing findings should have ended the overflights on the spot. They were presented to Bissell by one of his top aides, Col. William Burke, the acting head of the Development Projects Division, the CIA office responsible for managing the U-2, the Corona project, and the development of a supersonic spy plane. The office had asked the Air Force to conduct the study of Soviet air defenses, so it wasn't as if the

298

report arrived unexpectedly or was filed away without reaching the attention of senior officials.

At the end of March, the CIA produced a National Intelligence Estimate on the range and accuracy of Soviet surface-to-air missiles. It echoed the Air Force report. In a 1967 interview, Bissell recalled that "the intelligence estimate of the capability of the Russian surface-to-air missile conceded that the missile did have the altitude to reach the U-2."

As these reports were landing on Bissell's desk, and the administration was beginning to make plans for a May summit meeting in Paris, Bissell was already preparing for another set of U-2 flights over the Soviet Union. The decision to renew operations dated back to mid-February. After considering the appeal of Dulles, Bissell, and General Doolittle, Eisenhower had reviewed four proposed U-2 operations. Following another nudge from Dulles in early March, he approved one flight, stipulating that it be completed by the end of the month. Because it took longer than expected to get Pakistani permission to use an airfield at Peshawar to launch the flight, Bissell asked the White House to extend the deadline. On March 28, Eisenhower agreed. He pushed the time line to April 10, and at the same time approved Bissell's request to conduct a second flight, provided it could be done by April 19. Because of bad weather and other complications, that deadline would slip to May 1.

The first flight took place on April 9. It should have eliminated any lingering doubts about Soviet defenses. The mission, called Operation Square Deal, took the pilot, Bob Ericson, over three sensitive military installations—the nuclear test site at Semipalatinsk, the missile test base at Tyuratam, and the missile test range and radar complex at Sary Shagan.

Expectations that the U-2 could slip undetected into Soviet airspace from the south by flying out of Peshawar and crossing Afghanistan proved false. Electronic equipment aboard the plane showed the Russians picked up the aircraft shortly after Ericson crossed the Soviet border. He was pursued during the six-hour flight by a variety of Soviet jet fighters, some equipped with air-to-air missiles, but none was able to get within shooting range of the U-2. Aware of Soviet aeronautical advances, Kelly Johnson in 1959 had started equipping a new generation of U-2s—known as the U-2C—with a more powerful engine, the Pratt & Whitney J75-P13. Ericson was at the controls of one of these new models. The engine, though heavier than the earlier Pratt & Whitney J57 power plant, allowed the U-2 to climb more quickly, reducing the period when contrails were likely to be produced, and provided a higher cruising altitude of 74,600 feet. The extra margin of safety may have helped Ericson elude the Soviet fighters, but the far more important factor was Soviet incompetence. By the time Soviet pilots were cleared to pursue the intruder, the U-2 in most cases was already out of range as the Soviet fighter jets scrambled into the air.

Still, if the Russians could track the plane throughout the flight, and they had new missiles that could shoot it down, the obvious lesson of the Ericson mission was that it should be the last. Khrushchev didn't miss the implications. He was furious at his air defense commanders for squandering the opportunity. He knew that if they reacted faster the next time, the American plane could be shot down. Referring to the Ericson flight, Khrushchev later said, "We'd had an opportunity to shoot down a U-2, but our antiaircraft batteries were caught napping and didn't open fire soon enough."

Bissell somehow didn't get the point. In its examination of the Ericson flight, the CIA history of the U-2 noted, "Although the Soviets failed to intercept the U-2, their success at tracking it should have served as a warning against future overflights from [Peshawar] (or anywhere else, for that matter). . . . Unfortunately, neither [deleted] nor Richard Bissell took the logical step of recommending the cessation of overflights now that the risks had increased substantially."

The White House also managed to draw the wrong conclusions. The absence of a strong protest seemed to persuade Eisenhower that the Russians had decided to live with the flights. George Kistiakowsky, the Harvard chemist who had replaced James Killian as the president's science adviser in the spring of 1959, later wondered whether the Kremlin had refrained from protesting the Ericson flight in hopes of luring Washington into another mission, one that the Russians might shoot down. The silence, he noted in his diary on May 16, 1960, was "virtually inviting us to repeat the sortie."

Bissell was clearly haunted in subsequent years by his failure to appreciate the import of the April 9 flight. He reflected on the case in his memoirs: "Even though all efforts to intercept the plane failed, the incident should have served as a warning. Had we given it more attention, we might have decided to suspend future overflights. Instead, we relied on a national intelligence estimate that concluded that although a surface-to-air missile could indeed reach the U-2's flying altitude, it was optimized for 60,000 feet. Above 60,000 feet its accuracy would fall off very rapidly because there wouldn't be air dense enough for its control surfaces to bite on. The Russians could get a missile up, but they couldn't control it or bring it in for a kill, or so we believed."

His recollection conveniently fails to mention the more ominous and specific warning provided by the Air Force on March 14. As Bissell implies, though, the main problem may have been his own inattention. In March and April of 1960, he was hip-deep in Corona problems. He was also distracted by a variety of covert operations that would soon spiral into some of the CIA's most notorious mistakes, and he was overseeing development of the supersonic spy plane to succeed the U-2. Managing any one of these portfolios would have been trying enough; attempting to direct all of them was foolhardy, even for someone as smart and nimble as Bissell. All of them suffered as a result, most immediately the handling of the U-2.

As Ericson was winging his way across the Soviet Union on April 9, preparations for the next Corona launch were accelerating. The last two launch attempts, in February, had been profoundly discouraging. Despite a three-month launch moratorium and intense evaluation of all systems, Discover IX and Discover X had not even reached orbit. The problems would have been vexing enough in a civilian technology project, but the pressures bearing down on Corona were extreme because of the national security exigencies. After ten expensive failures, Bissell and his team had yet to solve some of the most basic technological challenges. They still couldn't count on the two-stage Thor-Agena rocket to reliably propel the satellite into orbit. The camera repeatedly malfunctioned. The recovery vehicle regularly veered off course.

On April 15, Bissell and Jim Plummer were ready for another Corona attempt. This time the Thor and Agena rockets powered the satellite into orbit. The mission was publicly identified as Discoverer XI. Though less than half the normal load of film was stowed on board to leave room for equipment that could monitor various mechanical systems, all the film was exposed and safely stored in the recovery capsule for the descent to earth. This alone was a triumph, since it was the first time that the film and camera system had performed as planned. The main reason was that Kodak had finally started shipping the new Mylar-based film called Estar, which could withstand the vacuum conditions in space. But the good luck ended as the recovery capsule separated from the Agena. The small rockets used to spin the vehicle into position for its return to earth once again misfired and the capsule was lost in space. It was another painful disappointment.

With both the U-2 and Corona at critical junctures that required his undivided attention in mid-April, Bissell was also quarterbacking an assortment of clandestine operations designed to destabilize or topple unfriendly foreign governments. As the CIA's deputy director for plans, the job Dulles had awarded him at the beginning of 1959, Bissell ran the Agency's worldwide spy operations. This espionage empire included spy stations abroad, dozens of covert programs, and a tidy reserve fund worth more than $100 million that he and Dulles could dispense free of the government's usual bookkeeping requirements. The Agency was surreptitiously intervening, or soon would be, in the internal affairs of a host of troublespots, including Cuba, the Dominican Republic, Tibet, Laos, and the Congo. The rules were dangerously loose, giving Bissell the freedom to cook up all manner of madcap plots, including schemes to poison foreign leaders. With the White House's encouragement, the prime target in the spring of 1960 was Fidel Castro, who had seized power in Cuba a year earlier and established a Communist dictatorship on the island.

Drawing on his familiarity with the CIA-engineered coup in Guatemala in 1954, which he helped put together, Bissell had presented a similar destabilization plan for Cuba to Eisenhower on March 17. The president approved the proposal, which was labeled "A Program of Covert Action Against the Castro Regime." This scheme would eventually mutate into the failed Bay of Pigs invasion in 1961 and a loony plot to disable or kill Castro with an exploding cigar, as well as a variety of other inane assassination ideas. Before the end of March, Bissell quietly traveled to Athens to see if James Critchfield, one of the Agency's top operatives, was willing to run the Cuba operation. Critchfield declined.

In hindsight, it seems clear Bissell was juggling too many responsibilities. At just the moment when he should have advised Eisenhower to terminate the U-2 flights, Bissell instead asked the president to extend the deadline for the second April mission to May 1. Andrew Goodpaster recorded the fateful decision in a memorandum on April 25. "After checking with the President, I informed Mr. Bissell that one additional operation may be undertaken, provided it is carried out prior to May 1. No operation is to be carried out after May 1."

Though Eisenhower was ultimately responsible for sending Francis Gary Powers into Soviet airspace at an inopportune time, he was acting on Bissell's advice and may well have lacked a full understanding of the growing Soviet threat when he told Goodpaster to extend the deadline to May 1. Eisenhower thought there was little chance that the plane and pilot would survive a successful attack, which gave him a false sense of confidence. In his White House memoirs, he recalled that the CIA and Joint Chiefs had insisted that the plane would "virtually disintegrate," meaning the Russians would be left with little definitive evidence that the United States was invading its airspace.

If that was his understanding, no one had bothered to inform him that the film was almost sure to survive almost any calamity and would certainly give away the nature and provenance of the overflight. In describing these matters in his own memoirs, Bissell left unclear just how much the president was told about all this:

"By the beginning of 1960 there were signs that the Russians had made considerable improvements in their air defense system. The possibility of losing a U-2 received serious consideration in policy circles. We told Eisenhower that it was most unlikely that a pilot would survive if shot down, by which we meant that a pilot would not survive a direct hit, because the U-2 was a very light aircraft, more like a glider, and would disintegrate on impact. We believed that if a U-2 was shot down over Soviet territory, all the Russians would have was the wreckage of an aircraft. We did not give sufficient weight to the possibility that a near miss might incapacitate the aircraft but leave the pilot uninjured and able to bail out.

"There was unanimous agreement that the big rolls of film aboard the plane would not be destroyed, even if the plane was hit. They were virtually indestructible. Their nonflammable base would prevent them from burning, and they could be dropped from a height of ten miles and survive. We always knew that in the event of a crash there was going to be a couple of rolls of film lying around, and there was not much we could do about it."

When asked in 1999 whether Eisenhower was aware of the Air Force warning and other information about the acute nature of the Soviet threat before he authorized Powers's flight, Goodpaster said, "I don't think so. Not in a specific way. We had the general view that over time the risks were going to become greater and greater, and they would finally gain the capability of shooting it down. But I think I would remember if we had had that kind of notice during the discussion in the president's office, and I don't remember such a thing. I can't positively say that it didn't happen, but I can be very close to positive."

Bissell, in his memoirs, seems to pin primary responsibility for the miscalculation on Eisenhower. After citing the Goodpaster memo of April 25 to disprove any suggestion that the CIA had dispatched the plane without presidential approval, Bissell points directly to Eisenhower. "It looks to have been a grave mistake to have given us the general authority to fly so close to the summit, but the decision was an explicit one on Eisenhower's part. All of us, including the president, had become a little too confident about the success of the U-2. I am sure that Eisenhower's decision to grant us the week's extension was greatly influenced by the fact that the Soviets had been unable to shoot our plane down earlier in the month. They had seen a lot of planes by now, he probably thought, and to send one off a week before the summit wasn't going to be any worse than two weeks before, which he'd already agreed to."

Considering how cautious Eisenhower had been about using the U-2, it is hard to believe that he would have approved the Powers mission had he been fully informed about the close tracking of the Ericson flight and the Air Force's dire assessment of the range and accuracy of the Soviet Guideline missiles. No one seems to have told him that a red line had been crossed and that the probability of a successful Soviet attack on the plane had been established and was now an immediate danger. With the summit conference in Paris rapidly approaching, Eisenhower would likely have been especially sensitive to the possibility of a diplomatic furor if one of the planes was shot down. He had warned about just such a fiasco in his February 2 meeting with Dulles and Doolittle.

The flight plan for Powers on Sunday morning, May 1, was the most audacious that target selectors had designed since the inception of the program in 1956, perhaps because they realized the safety margin for the U-2 was rapidly eroding and there might not be many more flights. Instead of a race course route that would end in the same region as the mission began, Operation Grand Slam would carry Powers clear across the midsection of the Soviet Union, from south to north. He would take off at Peshawar and nine hours and 3,300 nautical miles later land at the northern Norwegian seacoast town of Bodo. Along the way, Powers could photograph the new missile base at Plesetsk, in the northwestern corner of the Soviet Union, which CIA analysts were eager to examine more closely. He would also pass over the test base at Tyuratam, the nuclear research and bomb-making complex at Chelyabinsk, south of Sverdlovsk, and a number of other military sites. The duration of the flight would give the Russians plenty of time to track the U-2 and get their latest antiaircraft missiles into the air.

Mission 4154, code-named Operation Grand Slam, was the twenty-fourth U-2 flight deep into Soviet airspace. For Powers, who was a veteran of the U-2 program, it was the second such flight. He had also flown the spy plane over China and piloted the U-2 along Soviet border areas six times. The aircraft selected for the flight was article 360, which Lockheed had rebuilt after a crash landing in September 1959. It was equipped with one of the new Pratt & Whitney engines.

Powers took off thirty minutes behind schedule because of difficulties in relaying the final order from Washington to Peshawar. "Once airborne," the CIA recorded in its history of the plane, "Powers guided his aircraft toward Afghanistan. Following standard operating procedure, Powers clicked his radio switch when he reached penetration altitude of 66,000 feet, which signaled the operations unit at [deleted] that everything aboard the aircraft was working and the mission would proceed as planned."

Soviet radar detected the plane while it was still over Afghanistan. Burned by the failure to bring down Ericson three weeks earlier, Soviet forces were primed to respond. Because it was May Day, a major holiday in the Soviet Union, there was little military air traffic to distract defense units, and civilian air travel in the affected region was quickly banned. Powers didn't know it, but he was headed into an aerial shooting gallery ideally set up to track and attack his plane.

"This latest flight, towards Sverdlovsk, was an especially deep penetration into our territory and therefore an especially arrogant violation of our sovereignty," Khrushchev recalled. "We were sick and tired of these unpleasant surprises, sick and tired of being subjected to these indignities. They were making these flights to show up our impotence. Well, we weren't impotent any longer."

Four and a half hours into his flight, Powers neared Sverdlovsk, an important political and industrial center on the eastern flank of the Urals. In 1918, the deposed Czar Nicholas II and his family, who had been brought to the city after the revolution and kept there under house arrest, were executed in Sverdlovsk by the Bolsheviks. If CIA flight planners had realized there was a new missile battery in the area they would have set a different course. Unluckily for Powers and Eisenhower, the existence of the site was not known in Washington. The Russians fired three SA-2 missiles. One mistakenly hit a Soviet fighter that was pursuing the U-2, instantly destroying the Russian plane. A second missile flew harmlessly off course. The third detonated at 70,500 feet, just behind the U-2.

Powers felt a thud as an orange fireball lit up the sky around the aircraft. "Instinctively I grasped the throttle with my left hand, and keeping my right hand on the wheel, checked instruments. All readings normal. Engine functioning O.K. The right wing started to droop. I turned the wheel and it came back up. Fine. Now the nose, very slowly, started to go down. Proper correction for that is to pull back on the wheel to bring it up. I pulled, but it kept going down. Either the control cable had severed or the tail was gone. I knew then that I had no control of the aircraft."

Kelly Johnson's fragile aircraft, notoriously temperamental even in normal flight conditions, was breaking up and spinning toward earth. Powers struggled against the powerful centrifugal forces to deal with the emergency. Fearful that his legs would be severed if he activated the ejection seat, he pushed the cockpit canopy free so he could bail out. He later said he tried to arm the destruction device aboard the plane before he exited but was thrown partway out of the cockpit as soon as he released his seat belt. With the loss of cabin pressure, Powers's pressure suit had inflated, just as Joe Ruseckas at the David Clark Company had planned. That may have helped save his life, but it also further restricted his movements. The only thing holding Powers to the airplane was the oxygen hose attached to his suit. He could no longer reach the destruction switch, which was designed to blow up the camera but not the entire aircraft. As the plane neared the ground, the hose broke and Powers fell free of the aircraft. His parachute automatically opened. He landed on the grounds of a collective farm outside Sverdlovsk, where he was quickly captured. What was left of the plane, which was a good deal more than the experts had assured Eisenhower would survive a crash, plowed into the ground nearby.

When Powers failed to arrive in Bodo, word was relayed to Washington that the U-2 was overdue. Goodpaster was informed at home and phoned the president, who was spending the weekend at Camp David. "One of our reconnaissance planes on a scheduled flight is overdue and possibly lost," he informed Eisenhower.

Michael Beschloss recounted their brief but telling conversation in *Mayday*, his book about the downing of the U-2.

"Goodpaster recalled the president's old forecast of what could happen if a U-2 crashed in Russia and predicted that 'the winds are going to blow.'

" 'You're probably right,' came the reply."

Unbeknownst to Eisenhower and everyone else in Washington, Khrushchev not only had the wreckage of an American spy plane to show the world, he had a live American pilot. He cannily set a trap that unwittingly but perfectly capitalized on Bissell's misguided plan for dealing with a shootdown. The Kremlin would denounce the spy flight, but in hopes of luring Washington into a misleading explanation of the affair, would say nothing initially about the capture of Powers. "Our intention here was to confuse the government circles of the United States," Khrushchev later said.

Having ignored Edwin Land and Jim Killian's sound advice back in June 1956 to deal forthrightly with the loss of a plane over Soviet territory, Bissell set in motion the flimsy cover story that he and the CIA had concocted and sold to Eisenhower. Instead of taking responsibility for the flight, and informing the world that it had been employing the U-2 for years to prevent a surprise attack—the public relations strategy recommended by Land and Killian—the Eisenhower administration claimed that a NASA weather observation plane had gone astray while flying near the Turkish-Soviet border.

The plan was simple—and breathtakingly dishonest.

A secret White House summary provided an abbreviated script: "Following is cover plan to be implemented immediately: 'U-2 aircraft was on weather mission originating Adana, Turkey. Purpose was study of clear air turbulence. During flight in Southeast Turkey, pilot reported he had oxygen difficulties. The last word heard at 0700Z over emergency frequency. U-2 aircraft did not land Adana as planned and it can only be assumed is now down. A search effort is under way in Lake Van area.' "

Though journalists and historians often point to the government's lies about Vietnam and Watergate as the pivotal events that undermined the faith of Americans in the honesty and integrity of their government, the Eisenhower administration's handling of the U-2 incident struck an earlier and powerful blow to the body politic that should not be underestimated. It set a shocking new standard of deceit at the time, and left many Americans wondering whether they could trust their leaders.

Unaware that Powers had survived and been captured, the administration dispatched a NASA spokesman to present the cover story to the press. Lincoln White, a State Department spokesman, repeated the same line later in the day, confidently telling correspondents that the pilot had radioed back to base to report he was having problems with the oxygen system. White said, "It is entirely possible that having a failure in the oxygen equipment, which could result in the pilot losing consciousness, the plane continued on automatic pilot for a considerable distance and accidentally violated Soviet airspace."

Jack Raymond of the *New York Times*, citing the NASA statement, reported, "The plane was flying at an altitude close to 55,000 feet, making weather observations over the Lake Van area of Turkey as part of a world-wide research program begun in 1956." Eisenhower later told congressional leaders he had endorsed the cover story only after being assured by Bissell and his colleagues that the phony account would hold. "It would have been good to count to ten" before putting out the story, he said.

Khrushchev was ready to pounce. He later recalled, "As long as the Americans thought the pilot was dead, they would keep putting out the story that perhaps the plane had accidentally strayed off course and had been shot down in the mountains on the Soviet side of the border." On Saturday, May 7, Khrushchev gleefully announced that the Russians had captured Powers and that he had confessed the flight was a spy mission designed to photograph Soviet military installations all the way from Afghanistan to Norway.

The stunning news flashed around the world. A panicked and unprepared Eisenhower administration, after remaining publicly silent all day, responded that evening by confirming the espionage flight but insisting no one in Washington had authorized the mission.

The half-baked response, cooked up on Saturday afternoon in Washington by a group of senior officials, including Secretary of State Herter, had been cleared by Eisenhower late in the afternoon. He had chosen to spend the weekend at Gettysburg so as not to seem preoccupied by the U-2 affair. After talking with Herter on the phone about the plan, Eisenhower told Goodpaster he feared the statement "might prove to be a mistake." It was.

Lincoln White, whose credibility was pulverized by the U-2 affair, was dispatched again to feed the press the revised fiction. He offered a statement that still stands as one of the most brazen lies ever uttered by the American government. "As a result of the inquiry ordered by the President it has been established that insofar as the authorities in Washington are concerned there was no authorization for any such flight as described by Mr. Khrushchev."

Having disclaimed direct responsibility for the flight, White went on to concede that there likely had been a deliberate invasion of Soviet airspace. "It appears that in endeavoring to obtain information now concealed behind the Iron Curtain a flight over Soviet territory was probably undertaken by an unarmed civilian U-2 plane."

James Reston, the Washington bureau chief of the *New York Times*, chronicled the administration's reaction in a front-page story that aptly captured the surreal quality of the day in Washington.

"The United States admitted tonight that one of this country's planes equipped for intelligence purposes had 'probably' flown over Soviet territory.

"An official statement stressed, however, that 'there was no authorization for any such flight' from authorities in Washington.

"As to who might have authorized the flight, officials refused to comment. If this particular flight of the U-2 was not authorized here, it could only be assumed that someone in the chain of command in the Middle East or Europe had given the order."

The implication of the administration's statements was unavoidable: either it was lying or it was incompetent. The idea that an American spy plane could be sent over Soviet territory without the direct approval of top officials in Washington seemed fantastic. It reinforced the prevailing view that Eisenhower was not minding the store. The fact that he had spent Saturday afternoon golfing in Gettysburg only added to the picture of presidential detachment.

Reston, unaware that Eisenhower kept a tight leash on the U-2 program and approved each flight plan, hit the competence issue hard in a Sunday opinion piece. "The heart of the problem here is that the presidency has been parceled out, first to Sherman Adams, then to John Foster Dulles, and in this case to somebody else—probably to Allen Dulles, but we still don't know."

Walter Lippmann concurred in the *New York Herald Tribune*. "In denying that it authorized the flight, the Administration has entered a plea of incompetence," he wrote.

The mishandling of the affair seemed like a replay of the administration's feckless response to Sputnik nearly three years earlier. After watching the doubts escalate on Sunday, Reston reported: "This was a sad and perplexed capital tonight, caught in a swirl of charges of clumsy administration, bad judgment and bad faith.

"It was depressed and humiliated by the United States having been caught spying over the Soviet Union and trying to cover up its activities in a series of misleading official announcements."

Eisenhower returned to work Monday morning in a glum mood. "I would like to resign," he told Ann Whitman, his secretary. She recorded in her diary that the president "seemed very depressed in the morning, but by afternoon he had bounced back with his characteristic ability to accept the bad news, not dwell on it, and so go ahead."

Vice President Nixon and Thomas Gates, the secretary of defense, were appalled by the dodgy strategy that Herter had devised. Gates telephoned the secretary of state early Monday morning to complain, saying somebody had to take responsibility for the policy. An hour later Nixon called Herter with the same message. Nixon bluntly warned that the assertion that the president was unaware of the spy flights created the impression that a war could start without Eisenhower's knowledge.

Between the two calls, Eisenhower telephoned Herter to say that perhaps Allen Dulles should make a statement that the president had long ago made clear he wanted the government to collect intelligence information about Soviet military forces and fully realized that such spying would require unusual methods.

Later that day Herter tried to still the commotion by conceding to reporters that Washington had, in fact, been flying spy missions around and over the Soviet Union for years to protect against surprise attack. This was a critical admission, a rare acknowledgment by the United States that it was conducting peacetime espionage operations. To shield

Eisenhower, however, Herter falsely said that specific missions had not required presidential approval. Eisenhower himself wanted to maintain this posture in hopes that some separation from day-to-day management of the U-2 flights would preserve his ability to work with Khrushchev and retain his high standing in world opinion. He told the National Security Council "the impression should not be given that the President has approved specific flights, precise missions or the timing of specific flights."

Eisenhower belatedly addressed the U-2 affair himself on Wednesday, May 11, at a news conference. Though the immediate subject was the U-2, the president spoke broadly and bluntly about the need for reliable intelligence information. His remarks were the most complete statement he had ever given the nation about his administration's secret reconnaissance programs. Since he did not mention Corona or any of the other reconnaissance projects that were still in the development stage, the American people had no idea that Eisenhower was describing one of the most ambitious—and successful—initiatives of his presidency.

"No one wants another Pearl Harbor," Eisenhower said. "This means that we must have knowledge of military forces and preparations around the world, especially those capable of massive surprise attacks. . . . since the beginning of my administration I have issued directives to gather, in every feasible way, the information required to protect the United States and the free world against surprise attack and to enable them to make effective preparations for defense."

Addressing the clandestine nature of the spying activities, Eisenhower said, "These have a special and secret character. They are, so to speak, 'below the surface' activities. They are secret because they must circumvent measures designed by other countries to protect secrecy of military preparations. They are divorced from the regular visible agencies of government which stay clear of operational involvement in specific detailed activities."

"We do not use our Army, Navy or Air Force for this purpose, first to avoid any possibility of the use of force in connection with these activities, and second, because our military forces, for obvious reasons, cannot be given latitude under broad directives but must be kept under strict control in every detail."

Tensions escalated sharply over the next few days as Khrushchev threatened to attack foreign air bases used by American spy planes. Secretary of State Herter said Washington would not hesitate to continue the reconnaissance missions and Khrushchev warned that further spy flights could lead to war.

Harry Truman, no doubt sensing the U-2 affair could help the Democrats, interrupted his retirement to boast, incorrectly, that he had rejected proposals for aerial espionage flights over the Soviet Union during his administration. "Espionage is a dirty deal," he told reporters in Chicago. "I didn't want to be part of it." Either his memory of authorizing early overflights of the Soviet Union had failed or he had decided it was politically convenient to act as if Eisenhower and the Republicans had come up with the idea.

Much of the public mystery about the U-2 was eliminated on May 15 by a story by Hanson Baldwin, the military correspondent of the *Times*, who had been holding back information about the reconnaissance program for years in deference to national security considerations. Baldwin's long account, which the *Times* cautiously printed deep inside the Sunday paper rather than displaying it on the front page, was an impressively comprehensive history at a time when almost everything about the development and use of the plane was still heavily classified. Among other things, Baldwin stripped away any remaining doubt about Eisenhower's role in managing the flights. "The actual air reconnaissance program over Russia was known to, and authorized by, President Eisenhower himself and the National Security Council. The Central Intelligence Agency was the directing agency and provided the funds. The U-2 program had been known to a few key Congressmen and to others at the top in Washington for years, but the secret was closely guarded. Whether top officials in Washington knew ahead of time of the May 1 flight is unknown, but no orders from Washington, which closely controlled the overall program, were sent to halt such 'overflights' of Russia."

Eisenhower's worst fears about the diplomatic consequences of losing a U-2 over the Soviet Union were realized at the opening session of the four-power summit conference in Paris on the morning of May 16. Khrushchev angrily told Eisenhower he was no longer welcome to visit the Soviet Union in June and announced there was no point in continuing the meeting because the Americans had refused to apologize for the flight. Though Eisenhower announced he had suspended U-2 flights and would not resume them—concessions that Khrushchev had demanded—the gathering ended abruptly and acrimoniously the next day.

Instead of defrosting the cold war, which had been Eisenhower's ardent hope for the summit, the meeting left the world tenser than ever. The White House could blame Khrushchev for wrecking the summit conference, but everyone knew the U-2 flight had handed him the perfect excuse.

Eisenhower addressed the nation about the U-2 affair and the collapse of the Paris summit meeting in a televised speech on May 25. Toward the end of the broadcast, he gave the country its first glimpse of the remarkable pictures that could be produced by Kelly Johnson's aircraft and Jim Baker's powerful lenses. As a photograph of a military base appeared on the screen, Eisenhower said, "This is a photograph of the North Island Naval Station in San Diego. It was taken from an altitude of more than 70,000 feet. You may not perhaps be able to see them on your television screens, but the white lines in the parking strips around the field are clearly discernible from 13 miles up. Those lines are just 6 inches wide."

Paying tribute to the accomplishments of the U-2 program, Eisenhower told the nation, "It must be remembered that over a long period these flights had given us information of the greatest importance to the nation's security. In fact, their success has been nothing short of remarkable."

The irony of the Powers flight could not have been lost on Dick Leghorn, Edwin Land, Kelly Johnson, and the other men who had created the plane and its reconnaissance equipment. An aircraft that had done so much to stabilize the cold war ended its service over the Soviet

Union as the centerpiece of a painfully embarrassing episode for the United States.

The U-2 never flew again over the Soviet Union. Even so, the program, as George Tenet, the director of Central Intelligence, said in 1998, "constituted nothing less than a revolution in intelligence."

The CIA calculated that in four years of intermittent service, the U-2 program generated 1,285,000 feet of film, covering 1.3 million square miles of Soviet territory, or roughly 15 percent of the Soviet landmass. From that film, Arthur Lundahl and his photo interpreters determined that there was no bomber gap and correctly surmised that the Russians were not fielding hundreds of intercontinental missiles. They also monitored the development of Moscow's nuclear weapons programs, tracking the production of bomb-making materials and the testing of weapons. With the help of U-2 photographs, the Pentagon revised and refined the list of targets that American bombers and missiles would strike if war began, and pinpointed the location of the radar complexes, airfields, and other Soviet defense sites that attacking forces would have to overcome.

Looking back over the program not long after Powers was shot down, Allen Dulles said of the U-2, "in terms of reliability, of precision, of access to otherwise inaccessible installations, its contribution has been unique. And in the opinion of the military, of the scientists and of the senior officials responsible for our national security it has been, to put it simply, invaluable."

He told the Senate Foreign Relations Committee, meeting in secret session at the end of May 1960, that the U-2 project "was one of the most valuable intelligence collection operations that any country has ever mounted at any time."

It was all true, but once Eisenhower grounded the fleet, he lost the only means he had to look deep inside the Soviet Union. As Bissell was still dealing with the stinging fallout from the Powers flight, he had to turn his attention back to Corona. The moment Power's plane crashed outside Sverdlovsk, the satellite project became Washington's number one intelligence priority.

When the National Security Council convened at the White House on May 24, several cabinet members stressed the need to move ahead quickly with satellite projects, though there was apparently no specific reference to Corona by name to preserve the secrecy of the program.

"Secretary Herter said he hoped we would move ahead fast and not back down with respect to the reconnaissance satellite program," the minutes of the meeting noted. "In Paris, Khrushchev's reaction had been extraordinary when De Gaulle [President Charles De Gaulle of France] chided him about the Soviet 'space ship' which was going over Paris sixteen to eighteen times a day. Khrushchev said he did not care how many satellites flew over his territory. Secretary Herter thought it would be very useful for our allies and other friendly nations of the Free World to be reassured that if one kind of reconnaissance against surprise attack had to be suspended, another kind would soon be available. The President agreed and added that in Paris Khrushchev had said anyone might take all the pictures he wished from satellites over Soviet territory."

Despite the attraction of publicizing the secret satellite programs to reassure the nation that the loss of the U-2 would not cripple America's ability to gather intelligence on Soviet military forces, Eisenhower declined to do so. "With respect to questions that might be asked about reconnaissance satellites," the minutes of the meeting continued, "the President thought that Administration officials need not attempt to reply to every question which some idiot was able to ask. He felt it would be enough to quote Khrushchev's statement. If we went too far in describing our reconnaissance satellites, information concerning their infra-red and all their other capabilities would become public."

Eisenhower could also take heart that the Russians had registered no complaint about a NASA weather satellite, Tiros I, that had been placed in orbit on April 1 and had merrily been taking pictures of the cloud cover over the Soviet Union and electronically relaying them back to earth. The cameras aboard the satellite were nowhere near as powerful as the system built for Corona and served no useful intelligence purpose. Nor was its electronic transmission system precise enough to transmit finely detailed pictures, but it did show that images could be relayed back to earth electronically, even if in a primitive fashion.

The White House meeting ended with a decision to review the status of various satellite programs to determine if they could be accelerated. Gates said it would take an additional $40 million to speed up the work. Eisenhower asked Kistiakowsky, his science adviser, to look into the matter and report back to him.

It didn't require an advanced degree to realize that most of the satellite projects sponsored by the CIA and Pentagon were in trouble. The only program that seemed near success was an Air Force project designed to provide instant warning of missile launches around the world. The satellite system, which had been named Sentry and later renamed Midas (for Missile Defense Alarm System), employed infrared sensors to detect the heated exhaust plume produced by missiles as they climbed into the sky. By chance, the Atlas rocket carrying the first Midas into orbit was launched from Cape Canaveral the same day as the National Security Council meeting. It was placed in an equatorial orbit and did not pass over the Soviet Union as it circled the earth.

Corona, of course, could claim no such luck. By the time the U-2 went down, there had been twelve Discoverer launch attempts, including the first abortive countdown that hadn't been officially counted. The Agena spacecraft had reached orbit just seven times, and not one capsule had been recovered. The Air Force, for its part, was stumbling along with several other projects, the latest iteration of RAND's original video-transmission satellite proposal, now known as the Samos program. In this system, film would be developed aboard the satellite and the pictures would then be scanned and beamed back to earth. The Tiros I used similar technology.

Even before Eisenhower asked him to review the satellite programs, Kistiakowsky knew they were foundering. He had told Gordon Gray, the national security adviser, that "the whole intelligence business is in chaos." He thought a committee of high-powered scientists and technical experts should be appointed to examine the projects.

Two days after the National Security Council meeting, Kistiakowsky went over his idea with the president, Gray, and Goodpaster. He was just warming to the subject, ready to give Eisenhower a bill of particulars about satellite problems, when the president interrupted. He recalled, "My account of the unsatisfactory progress of the Discoverer and Samos satellite projects was cut short by the president, who didn't require more than a small fraction of the ammunition I had to decide in the firmest possible terms that a corrective action was necessary."

Congress was also eager to give satellite projects a jolt. Worried about a "reconnaissance gap" after Eisenhower terminated U-2 flights over the Soviet Union, the Senate Appropriations Committee voted on June 10 to add $84 million to the Samos program. The increase more than made up for the $50 million that the Pentagon had excised from the Samos budget in mid-April. Because Corona was secret, no money was publicly earmarked for the CIA project.

As far as most Americans knew, spy satellites remained a distant hope. In mid-June, Hanson Baldwin of the *Times* reported, "Reconnaissance satellites are still in a very early stage of development—though some prototype launchings have been conducted and some components of the system tested." After describing the Midas and Samos projects, but making no mention of Corona, Baldwin advised readers that "Midas and Samos and other reconnaissance satellites, though theoretically within the state of the art, are practically at least two to three years, perhaps more, away."

There wasn't a lot that Bissell could say to blunt the growing impatience at the White House and on Capitol Hill. After the two Corona failures in April, he had once again suspended launch operations as Plummer and his engineers frantically tried to debug the whole system. They failed. On June 29, Discoverer XII blasted off from Vandenberg, carrying a package of diagnostic instruments rather than a camera. Once again, the Agena fell short of orbit.

While the dismal record didn't give Bissell or Plummer much reason for hope, success was closer than they realized. Through the long months of reevaluation and modification, many of the problems had been remedied. The arrival of the new polyester-based film coated with a high-resolution emulsion had eliminated one of the most serious maladies, the shattering of the acetate-based strips first shipped by Kodak. Changes in the thermal painting applied to the exterior of the Agena vehicle helped to stabilize the temperature in the satellite at safe levels for operating the delicate equipment. The weight of the Agena, including the reconnaissance gear it carried, had been reduced, in some cases with the use of metal shears and files. Battery power and reliability had been improved. And in one of the most important engineering adjustments, Willis M. Hawkins, a Lockheed executive, suggested that a cold-gas propulsion system be substituted for the unreliable solid-propellant rockets that were supposed to stabilize the recovery vehicle during reentry. A number of the rockets had exploded or not fired simultaneously when activated. The replacement system was much less temperamental. The engineers had also refined the timing and accuracy of the crucial maneuvers that put the satellite recovery vehicle into a descent trajectory that would bring it down in the target area off Hawaii. The tiniest imperfections in this space choreography had several times been responsible for sending the spacecraft hopelessly off course.

Improvised repairwork was fairly common, often using whatever was handy. A case in point was the answer to the excessive heat that developed during ascent at the point where the recovery capsule—the tip of the rocket—was joined to the rest of the satellite vehicle. This seam was right above the section of the satellite where the camera and film were housed. Some kind of cooling element was needed in the area where the heat built up. "I got to thinking, well, the way you normally cool things is by evaporating a liquid," Jim Plummer recalled. "I said, why couldn't we put an epoxy seal or ring around that so we have a void we can put water in, then put pinholes in the skin and let the water evaporate and take the heat away. Well, we didn't like the idea of water near the film, so I said go down and buy a bunch of sanitary napkins. We stuck the ring full of those and inserted a measured amount of water. That's high-risk engineering."

The next launch came on August 10. Like the previous mission at the end of June, Discoverer XIII was designed primarily to monitor the performance of the various components rather than to take photographs. No camera and film were installed aboard the Agena. At the last minute,

Plummer stowed an American flag in the recovery capsule. It wasn't easy to find one the right size, and he had to race from Palo Alto to San Jose in his Porsche roadster on a Saturday morning to pick up the flag at a hardware store moments before it closed. "I didn't want an old beat up flag," he recalled.

Early on the afternoon of August 10, with Vandenberg shrouded in fog, the Thor booster lifted off the pad with a deafening roar. For a change, everything worked nearly perfectly. The Agena settled into orbit and during the seventeenth revolution around the earth, as the spacecraft passed over Alaska, the recovery vehicle was ejected and began the descent toward the Pacific Ocean, where recovery planes from Hawaii were waiting in the air. The return capsule missed the target area, making an air snatch impossible, but splashed down close enough that one of the Navy ships assigned to the mission, the U.S.S. *Haiti Victory*, reached it while the capsule was still afloat. It was the morning of August 12. Maj. R. J. Ford of the Air Force flashed an encrypted cable to Washington. "Capsule recovered undamaged." A secret history of the Corona project noted, "It was both the shortest and the most welcome of the thousands of communications over that network in the previous two years."

Back in Palo Alto, Plummer and his colleagues cheered their belated triumph. Later that day they celebrated at Rickey's, a local hotel, where Plummer, still dressed in a suit and tie, was joyfully tossed into the swimming pool. Decades later, Plummer still treasured a photograph that captured the scene. It shows him standing by the pool in his drenched outfit, holding a wet victory cigar in his right hand and sporting a broad smile.

It was the first time a man-made object had been recovered from orbit. (Ten days later, the Russians matched the feat when Sputnik V, carrying two dogs, Belka and Strelka, landed safely on Soviet territory.) The American water recovery technique, which was a fallback option for Corona, was soon adapted by NASA for the manned space program.

The recovery was front-page news. John Finney wrote about it in the *Times*. Though Finney still did not realize that the Discoverer program was actually a shell game employed to disguise a spy satellite project, he recognized that the recovery technology had important implications. "The technological feat marks an important step toward the development of reconnaissance satellites that will be able to spy from space. The same ejection and recovery techniques eventually will be used for returning photographs taken by reconnaissance satellites."

Excited by the success of Discoverer XIII, Bissell and Ritland moved quickly to the next launch, on August 18. This time the satellite would carry a camera and 20 pounds of film. Discoverer XIV blasted off from Vandenberg just before 1 P.M. The Agena reached orbit, but initially failed to stabilize itself in the proper position and threatened to start tumbling through space. Fortunately, the satellite righted itself and the camera began working. With each orbit, the satellite passed over a new swath of Soviet territory, much of it never before photographed by the United States. As ground stations silently tracked the satellite, technicians could tell that the camera was working and the film was collecting in the capsule. On the seventeenth orbit, as planned, the recovery capsule was ejected and maneuvered into position to begin the plunge back to earth. The heat shield did its job as the bucket descended, and the parachutes deployed right on time.

The date was Friday, August 19, a warm, clear summer afternoon in Hawaii. Capt. Harold E. Mitchell of Bloomington, Illinois, piloting a C-119 Flying Boxcar, snagged the capsule at 8,500 feet on his third pass and delivered it to Hickam Air Force Base outside Honolulu. "I was so nervous I could hardly handle it," Mitchell told reporters. The midair catch was one of the top news stories of the day. The next morning's edition of the *New York Times* displayed a three-column, three-line headline: "Space Capsule Is Caught in Mid-Air by U.S. Plane on Re-Entry from Orbit." The story included only a brief reference to possible espionage applications of the recovery. In an extraordinary quirk of history, the other big story of the day was the espionage conviction in Moscow of Francis Gary Powers, who was sentenced to ten years in a Soviet prison. Only a handful of Americans who were privy to the secrets of Corona realized that the conviction fell on the same day that the nation collected the first photographs of the Soviet Union taken by a spy satellite.

From Hawaii the capsule was transported to Sunnyvale, and on to the East Coast, where the film was processed in Rochester, New York, by Kodak and brought to Art Lundahl and his photo analysis crew in the Steuart Building on New York Avenue in Washington. Lundahl and his colleagues gathered in a large, secure room on the fourth floor for their first look at the pictures. After every U-2 mission, the photo interpreters had assembled when the film arrived to be briefed about the targets that had been covered during the flight. The route of the plane would be shown as a thin, circuitous line on a map of the Soviet Union. With the appearance of the Corona film, there was a stunning new map. It showed the passage of the satellite over Soviet territory in six or seven wide, bold stripes, beginning in the polar region and sweeping south across the country.

Dino A. Brugioni, one of Lundahl's top aides, recalled the scene years later. "There was elation, just a feeling of joy. For most of the areas covered, we didn't have anything. It was the first time we'd seen these places."

"When the film from Mission 9009 arrived at the Steuart Building . . . it was the start of a new era," said David Doyle, an imagery analyst.

Lundahl and Bissell were soon headed to the White House with a selection of pictures to brief Eisenhower. "I remember how gratified the president was," recalled Goodpaster, who attended the presentation. "After all those failures, we had finally succeeded. We knew it was of historic importance."

The 20 pounds of film—about 3,600 feet—covered more than 1.5 million square miles of the Soviet Union. It was, as Bissell noted in his memoirs, "more coverage than all the pictures of that country taken during the entire U-2 program."

The resolution was good—objects with a dimension of 35 feet or more could be identified. Considering that the pictures had been shot from more than 100 miles out in space, the quality was remarkable. It was better than Land had predicted when he and Jim Killian first outlined the Corona plans to Eisenhower early in 1958. However, the resolution was not as sharp as Leghorn had promised when he sold the Itek camera design to Bissell or as fine as Bissell had advertised to Eisenhower when seeking formal approval for the project in April 1958. The pictures were certainly not as detailed as those taken by the U-2, which flew at an altitude of 13 miles and had a resolution of less than 2 feet.

Still, the first batch of Corona images gave the photo interpreters plenty to examine, including sixty-four airfields and twenty-six surface-to-air missile sites that Washington had never seen before. Once the Corona satellites went into operation, the missile gap quickly disappeared—or more accurately, turned in America's favor.

On February 5, 1961, just days after taking office as John F. Kennedy's secretary of defense, Robert McNamara told reporters at a background briefing in his Pentagon office that there was no disparity in the number of American and Soviet operational strategic missiles. The next day, the *New York Times* carried a page-one story under the headline, "Kennedy Defense Study Finds No Evidence of a 'Missile Gap.'"

The coup de grâce was a National Intelligence Estimate on Soviet long-range ballistic missiles that was delivered to President Kennedy in September 1961. It said: "New information, providing a much firmer base for estimates on Soviet long-range ballistic missiles, has caused a sharp downward revision in our estimate of present Soviet ICBM strength but strongly supports our estimate of medium-range missile strength. We now estimate that the present Soviet ICBM strength is in the range of 10–25 launchers from which missiles can be fired against the US, and that this force level will not increase markedly during the months immediately ahead."

Eisenhower seems not to have left a record of his reaction upon seeing the first Corona photographs. But his role in creating new intelligence-gathering technologies was poignantly captured on February 13, 1969, eight years after he left the White House. Eisenhower was gravely ill, resting at Walter Reed Army Hospital in Washington. President Nixon ordered Richard Helms, the director of Central Intelligence, to show the former president the latest photographs taken from space.

Eisenhower lay in bed, propped up by several pillows. Because the pictures were so secret, the blinds were drawn and doctors and nurses asked to step outside. Helms, Arthur Lundahl, and Tom Logan,

Lundahl's special assistant, arrived with a package of materials specially selected for the occasion. Lundahl wanted to show Eisenhower how far they had come since the first U-2 flight in 1956.

Lundahl described the scene. "Mr. Helms sat to the left of the bed; I stood on the right, and with Tom Logan standing at the foot of the bed holding up the briefing boards, I went through the 'how it was and how it is.' "

The men showed Eisenhower clear pictures of Soviet missile silos, shipyards, and submarine bases. Objects as small as 6 feet in size could clearly be seen from 120 miles out in space. Eisenhower peered at the pictures closely, marveling at the fine resolution and telling detail. He took notes as Lundahl spoke.

He seemed pleased to see how far the technology had advanced. "The General was just absolutely flabbergasted about the improvements achieved in the systems," Lundahl recalled. Eisenhower died six weeks later.

Though Eisenhower's determination to put new technologies to work to defend the United States against surprise attack was perhaps the greatest legacy of his presidency, the spy satellites that he helped create remained so secret in his lifetime he said not a word about them in his memoirs.

CHAPTER FIFTEEN

A Stradivarius, Not a
Cracker Box

Though the Corona program was planned as a temporary measure to provide satellite photographs until the Air Force's more technologically ambitious video transmission system could be perfected, the CIA satellites were not easily dislodged. As refinements were made in the camera system, the quality of the pictures improved substantially, eventually making it possible to identify objects as small as 5 feet in size. The introduction in 1962 of a new camera system called Mural, which utilized two cameras to take pictures from different angles, provided stereoscopic photos with a three-dimensional quality. The volume of film increased as well over time, giving analysts an enormous quantity of film to review. By the time the program was nearing its end in the early 1970s, the volume of film produced from each mission had grown to 32,000 linear feet, a tenfold increase over the first successful flight in 1960. Later generations of Corona satellites carried two recovery capsules, making it possible to extend the life of the satellite for eighteen days while returning film to earth as the mission progressed.

Art Lundahl gave some idea of the scale of the photographic harvest from Corona satellites in describing a briefing with President Kennedy. "When he had trouble understanding the magnitude of the film that was involved, he said to me, 'Lundahl, give it to me in some single example I can recall.' 'Well, Mr. President,' I said, 'if you like, think of it as a single photograph which is wider than the right-hand side of the freeway, extending from Washington to Baltimore, and we photo-interpreters, all of us, are crawling along on our hands and knees between Washington and Baltimore looking for objects about the size of the things on our watch.' "

Lundahl's operation grew to keep pace with the flood of photographs. The small CIA photo analysis shop that he had set up in the early 1950s with a staff of thirteen people expanded to more than fifteen hundred staff members by 1972. A special security system was created for handling the Corona pictures and restricting access to them. The system was called Talent-Keyhole, an adaptation of the system used for U-2 photographs, which was labeled Talent. Everything involving Corona was classified and stamped Talent-Keyhole.

By the time the Corona program ended in 1972 after 145 launches—quite a run for an interim system—it had covered more than 520 million square miles of territory. By mid-1964, the satellites had photographed all twenty-five ICBM complexes in the Soviet Union. The total cost of the program was $850 million, a real bargain.

Before the return-film technology was retired, the Corona satellites kept Washington informed about Soviet military forces, including the introduction of new weapons, and created an invaluable photographic archive about nearly every aspect of Soviet military power. That included all Soviet missile launching sites as well as the critically important naval construction facilities at Severodvinsk, on the White Sea coast near Arkhangel'sk, which produced the Soviet Union's fleet of missile-carrying nuclear submarines. Hal Austin had flown over this area on his 1954 flight. The Corona program provided crucial information about the Soviet nuclear weapons program, and air and ground forces. It also made arms control agreements possible by providing the means to monitor Soviet compliance and transformed the craft of mapmaking by giving military cartographers photographs of the places they were mapping. Looking back on Corona years later, Bud Wheelon, who took over the Corona program at the CIA in 1963, called it "a triumph of American technology."

It was that, and something more. It played a critical role in preserving the peace, limiting defense spending, and reducing the threat of nuclear war.

President Lyndon Johnson summed it up nicely in 1967 during a visit to Nashville. "We've spent $35 billion or $40 billion on the space program," he said. "And if nothing else had come of it except the knowledge we've gained from space photography, it would be worth 10 times what the whole program has cost. Because tonight we know how many missiles the enemy had and, it turned out, our guesses were way off. We were doing things we didn't need to do. We were building things we didn't need to build. We were harboring fears we didn't need to harbor."

In 1985, on the twenty-fifth anniversary of the first successful Corona flight, President Ronald Reagan addressed a gathering of Corona veterans. He told them, "President Eisenhower once remarked to General George Goddard, the grand old man of this business, that without aerial reconnaissance 'you would only have your fears on which to plan your own defense arrangements and your whole military establishment. Now, if you are going to use nothing but fear . . . you are going to make us an armed camp.' This is no less true today than in President Eisenhower's time, and I reaffirm his conclusion that the knowledge which only overhead reconnaissance can provide is absolutely vital for the United States."

That knowledge was so vital that policymakers and intelligence officials wanted even more powerful spy satellites. In science and technology, landmark achievements have a way of raising expectations. That is what happened in the early 1960s as American officials pored over the torrent of photographs produced by the first series of Corona satellites. The intelligence information gleaned from the satellites was breathtaking, yet it was imperfect. The pictures, though they covered a much wider area than those produced by the U-2, lacked the clarity and detail produced by the lower-flying spy plane. The recoverable satellite system, for all the ingenuity that went into creating it, was frustratingly slow in moving photographs from space down to the desks of policymakers in Washington. If there happened to be no satellite in orbit or ready for launch when a foreign threat suddenly materialized, no satellite images were available to assist the president and his senior aides. That weakness was highlighted during the Cuban missile crisis in October 1962, when the Kennedy administration was forced to rely on the

U-2 and low-level reconnaissance flights by other aircraft over the island to monitor the installation of Soviet missile sites. Maj. Rudolph Anderson, an Air Force U-2 pilot, was killed when his plane was shot down over Cuba in late October.

The limitations were evident again during the 1967 war in the Middle East, when satellite pictures arrived too late to give Washington much help in monitoring the brief but intense six-day conflict between Israel and its Arab neighbors. In August 1968, a Corona satellite was not nimble enough to warn the White House that Soviet forces were about to invade Czechoslovakia to end the liberal reforms introduced by Alexander Dubcek, the Czech leader. One reel of film shot early in August indicated an invasion was not imminent. A second batch recorded by the same satellite later in the month showed Russian forces preparing to attack. By the time that film arrived in Washington, the invasion had begun.

Bud Wheelon, as head of the CIA's Office of Scientific Intelligence, which studied Soviet missiles and other weapons systems, worked alongside Arthur Lundahl at the Steuart Building during the tense days of the Cuban missile crisis and took part in the daily presentation of photographs and other intelligence information to President Kennedy. He was struck by the absence of satellite data as the showdown unfolded. The turnaround time for Corona wasn't fast enough. "Corona was totally useless during the Cuban missile crisis because of the long delay in getting the film back," Wheelon recalled. "We needed the data back that day, not a month from now."

Wheelon was soon in a position to do something about the problem. In June 1963, at the age of thirty-four, he was given responsibility for the CIA's science and technology activities. Richard Bissell had departed a year earlier, a victim of the failed Bay of Pigs invasion of Cuba, which he directed. Though Kennedy at the last minute withheld air support for the invasion by Cuban exiles trained by the CIA, he was nevertheless embarrassed by the clumsy attack and wanted new leadership at the CIA. Unwilling to accept a demotion, Bissell resigned in February 1962, three months after Allen Dulles was replaced by John McCone, a wealthy California businessman.

By the time he exited, Bissell had lost favor with Jim Killian and Edwin Land, who continued to exercise considerable influence over the CIA's affairs. "Bissell found himself in a major struggle with Killian and Land," the CIA noted in its secret history of the U-2. They had concluded that Bissell was not devoting sufficient attention to the overhead reconnaissance programs. They were especially disturbed by Bissell's use of the U-2 to gather intelligence for some of the Agency's covert actions in Laos, not exactly the sort of high-minded missions they had in mind when they had pressed Eisenhower to develop the plane. Killian and Land found his attitude so troubling that they advised President Kennedy in 1961 to take the reconnaissance work away from Bissell and place it in a new science directorate that they favored creating at the Agency.

Reflecting on his career at the CIA, Bissell later noted candidly that he departed "with successes and regrets and a legacy that still has not been put to rest historically and perhaps never will be." That was certainly true when Bissell died at the age of eighty-four in 1994. The *New York Times* looked first to the Bay of Pigs invasion in writing about Bissell's career. His role in directing the development of the U-2, the Corona satellites, and the A-12 supersonic spy plane, better known by the designation of the Air Force model, the SR-71, was subordinated in the obituary. The news judgment was understandable, but was a disservice to his role in revolutionizing the spy business.

For a time after Bissell's exit from the CIA, it looked as if the Agency might drop out of the satellite business, yielding the field to the Pentagon, which was pressing to gain control. Wheelon's appointment rallied the CIA. Though relatively young and largely untested in Washington's power centers, Wheelon turned out to be an inspired choice. As a precocious Stanford- and MIT-trained physicist, he brought scientific depth to the job. Several years of classified work untangling intercepted flight data from Soviet missile tests had given him an appreciation for the important role intelligence could play in managing the cold war. From his perch at the Office of Scientific Intelligence, he correctly suspected that giving the Pentagon a monopoly on satellites might serve short-term military needs but would deprive the nation of the kind of broad-gauged strategic intelligence it needed to measure and contain the Soviet threat. He proved to be tenacious in defending the interests of the CIA and the nation.

In three action-packed years that often found Wheelon in fierce bureaucratic combat with the Pentagon, he established a powerful and innovative new Directorate of Science and Technology at the CIA. With the help of James Killian and Edwin Land, Wheelon brought Kelly Johnson's supersonic spy plane into operation after years of delay and initiated work on three revolutionary new satellite systems that transformed the world of espionage in the closing decades of the twentieth century as profoundly as the U-2 and Corona did in their day.

Indeed, the dazzling capabilities of the systems that Wheelon set out to build within months of his appointment in 1963 made the Corona satellites look like Tinkertoys. Some of these systems, and the even more advanced models that followed them, continue to serve the nation today and play an important role in the war against terrorism. American officials, for instance, can almost instantaneously look at satellite images as they are recorded in space. The idea of waiting for a bucket of film to drop back to earth seems almost quaint today. The photographic detail of today's photos is so fine that someone in Washington looking at the satellite image of a crowd of people in Moscow, Beijing, or Kabul can clearly see individuals and objects the size of a football. Radar-based imaging systems see through clouds and operate equally well during the day and at night. Because the satellites can swing from side to side, ground controllers can adjust the direction at which they are looking, making it possible to aim first at one target and then switch to another. Other satellites, many placed in stationary orbit high above the earth, vacuum up worldwide electronic communications as the signals travel through space.

These satellites remain officially classified, but a good deal of information about them has seeped into the public domain over the years, primarily through the research of journalists and scholars, congressional testimony, industry briefings, and from criminal cases involving the illegal transfer of secret information about the satellites to the Soviet Union.

In 1994, looking back over Wheelon's record, William Perry, then secretary of defense, said, "The national reconnaissance systems which the United States now has, which are truly jewels in our crown, all stem, in my judgment, from the creative work that Bud Wheelon did in the sixties."

When Wheelon took over the Agency's science and technology operations, the CIA's pioneering scientific spirit was in danger of extinction. The primary cause was the creation of a new reconnaissance office at the Pentagon that tried to muscle the Agency out of the satellite business.

The new office grew out of the Air Force's ineffectual efforts to produce the Samos video-relay satellite, the original WS-117L project. Troubled by mismanagement of the Samos project, Eisenhower in June 1960 had asked his aides to review the program and the way the Pentagon went about developing and operating satellites. The inquiry was directed by George Kistiakowsky, Eisenhower's science adviser. One outcome, favorable to the CIA, was to restructure and expand Arthur Lundahl's photo interpretation organization. In one of his last acts as president, in January 1961, Eisenhower folded the Pentagon's separate photo analysis operations into Lundahl's center and renamed it the National Photographic Interpretation Center, emphasizing its role as the primary source of imagery analysis for the government.

The other major recommendation of the Kistiakowsky panel soon produced trouble for the CIA. The group suggested establishment of a new Pentagon organization to put military satellite programs more firmly under high-level civilian management. The office was run by the undersecretary of the Air Force. It posed no immediate threat to the Agency when it opened for business, but it was quickly supplanted by a more powerful entity, the National Reconnaissance Office, which was created in September 1961. In theory, the NRO, whose existence was widely known but officially classified until 1992, would coordinate satellite projects by drawing on the resources of the CIA and the Air Force. The hope was to institutionalize the high-level cooperation between the Air Force and the CIA that was often evident during the U-2 and Corona programs. In reality, the idea was an invitation to conflict, even though it was well intentioned and supported by Killian and Land, whose clout on spy matters was undiminished as the presidency changed hands in January 1961. Killian served as chairman of the White House intelligence advisory board. Land was a member of the same board and head of a separate panel that advised the CIA on technological issues.

The new interagency arrangement worked relatively well at first under the leadership of Joseph V. Charyk, the undersecretary of the Air Force. Bissell, who had hoped to run the new organization while retaining his top job at the CIA, settled for a subsidiary role after Allen Dulles advised him to steer clear of management responsibilities at the Pentagon. Charyk, among other things, mapped out the structure of the NRO, creating separate satellite programs for the Air Force, CIA, and the Navy. In June 1960, two months before the first successful Corona launch, the Naval Research Laboratory had placed in orbit a small satellite that collected Soviet radar signals. The Navy would later operate its own fleet of spy satellites to track the movement of surface ships and submarines. Charyk's basic organizational blueprint and designation of the three divisions as Program A, Program B, and Program C caught on and remained intact until 1993.

But the harmony was short-lived. With Bissell wounded by the Bay of Pigs debacle, the Pentagon moved to expand its authority over satellite programs. Dulles, whose career was also mortally injured by the Cuban fiasco, could not muster much opposition. When McCone took over at the CIA, he initially acquiesced, not recognizing the importance of overhead reconnaissance—or the money and power attendant to it. Not long after taking charge of the CIA, McCone naively asked John McMahon, an Agency official, "What are you people doing in the airplane business?" Herbert J. Scoville Jr., known to his colleagues as Pete, took over the CIA's research work when Bissell resigned and made a valiant but unsuccessful effort to resist the Pentagon power grab. He was also frustrated by a Balkanized array of science and technology offices at the CIA and McCone's indifference to scientific projects. After fifteen months as the Agency's deputy director for research, he resigned in disgust.

McCone immediately offered the post to Wheelon. After consulting with Scoville, Wheelon informed the CIA director he didn't want the job unless McCone and the Kennedy administration were prepared to roll back the erosion of CIA resources and guarantee the Agency a major role in the development of new satellites. "I said this is even more important than nuclear weapons, where two laboratories are competing successfully. We've got to get this right and get the very best systems," Wheelon recalled. "The only organization in this field that's really done anything worthwhile is the CIA, and you're ready to take them out of it. Is that really in the national interest?" If McCone was unwilling to make the commitment, Wheelon told him, he was quite prepared to quit and move back to California.

It was a brash performance for someone who had been at the CIA for only a year, but no surprise to anyone who knew Wheelon. With a Ph.D. in physics in his pocket by the time he was twenty-three, little tolerance for political knavery, and potentially unlimited job options in the academic world and the private sector, he had no desire to remain in Washington for long. When he joined the CIA in 1962, Wheelon told McCone he planned to stay no more than four years. "It's going to take me a year to understand what needs to be done, two years to get it done, and if I do it, I'm going to break enough crockery that I ought to leave in four," he said. He exited after almost exactly four years.

Wheelon was a whiz kid. Growing up in Southern California, he had developed an interest in physics and engineering from his father, Orville, an accomplished aeronautical engineer and the inventor of the Verson-Wheelon press, a machine tool that changed the way aircraft parts were made. Orville Wheelon was also the first aircraft builder to work extensively with titanium, an achievement that won him a prestigious Wright Brothers Award in 1952. His son would later come to appreciate the feat as he watched Kelly Johnson wrestle with the supersonic A-12, which was built mostly with titanium. During World War II, Bud Wheelon spent his summer vacations working at Douglas Aircraft in Los Angeles, testing the seams and rivets on airplane fuel tanks. A gifted math and science student, he enrolled at Stanford at the age of sixteen. He was soon befriended by Fred Terman, the dean of the engineering school, who encouraged Wheelon to disregard the required engineering curriculum so he could take graduate-level courses in physics and math. Terman pointed him to MIT for graduate work.

The MIT Physics Department was a mecca for some of the nation's brightest students, and the company that Wheelon kept in Cambridge until he collected his Ph.D. in 1952 was quite extraordinary. He shared an office with Murray Gell-Mann, who went on to win a Nobel Prize in physics. Sidney Drell, a postdoctoral student, became the deputy director of the Stanford Linear Accelerator Center and spent four decades advising the government on intelligence and arms control issues after Wheelon persuaded him to help solve a problem with the Corona camera system in 1963. Another MIT physics student at the time, Robert Noyce, founded Intel in 1968 with Gordon Moore.

Wheelon's work in physics led him indirectly to the CIA. Along the way, he participated in several of the most pivotal technical enterprises of the cold war and collaborated with scientists and engineers who, along with Wheelon, would soon come to play central roles in the creation of stunning new espionage technologies.

The first project was the 1953–1954 evaluation of America's nascent missile programs initiated by Trevor Gardner and directed by John von Neumann of the Institute for Advanced Study at Princeton. As one of the first employees hired by Simon Ramo and Dean Wooldridge when they founded the Ramo-Wooldridge Corporation in Southern California in 1953, Wheelon was assigned to do staff work for the von Neumann committee. Ramo and Wooldridge were members of the missile panel. Fresh out of graduate school, Wheelon found himself working with some of the nation's most illustrious scientists, including George Kistiakowsky of Harvard and Jerome Wiesner of MIT, both of whom later served as presidential science advisers.

"I was in the backroom, the little elf making shoes at night," Wheelon recalled. "They'd all come in and give me problems to work on and expect to have the answers the next morning."

One of the problems he tackled was missile guidance systems. "I was basically in the business of trying to develop guidance systems and understand what their fundamental physical limitations were," he said.

Missiles were still a novelty. Guidance systems for the Atlas, Thor, and Titan missiles initially relied on radio and radar signals to direct missiles to their targets. These ground-based systems were vulnerable to enemy attack. When Charles Stark Draper from MIT proposed a more reliable and secure system using gyroscopes and accelerometers, which measure acceleration, Ramo and Schriever assigned Wheelon to meet with him. After a day of discussion, Wheelon reported that the Draper plan was workable and recommended funding the project. Draper soon developed the self-contained inertial navigation system that was carried aboard missiles and was not dependent on ground installations. It became the primary guidance mechanism for missiles and airplanes until the introduction of the Global Positioning System satellite network in the early 1990s.

At the same time, Wheelon did his own study of the kinematics, or dynamics, of ballistic missiles in flight to determine how accurately velocity needed to be controlled to hit distant targets. His paper serves as one of the basic building blocks of missile engineering to this day.

After the Russians launched Sputnik I in October 1957, Wheelon was sent to Washington to help the CIA take a closer look at photographs of Soviet rockets and missiles collected by the U-2. General Schriever, the head of the Air Force missile development program, and Allen Dulles were behind the idea. "I heard that Allen Dulles said let's get some people from our own missile program to come in and look at these pictures to see if they can make sense out of them," Wheelon recalled. One of the other men assigned to the project was Carl Duckett, an Army missile expert who later worked closely with Wheelon at the CIA and played a central role in developing new spy satellites.

Wheelon's next job placed him squarely at the center of one of the cold war's crowning espionage achievements. The operation, which has not received the attention it deserves, tapped into the stream of performance data produced by Soviet missiles as they thundered off their launching pads and streaked downrange on test flights.

While the U-2 had intermittently been taking pictures of Soviet missile test sites, secret American listening posts in Turkey had been collecting flight data from Russian missile tests. The data, or telemetry, was transmitted by radio from the missiles to Soviet ground stations. It was potentially a gold mine of information for anyone trying to understand how quickly the Russians were advancing in missile technology. Satellite pictures could show when and where missiles were being fielded, but not how they performed. Telemetry could supply that information.

Intelligence specialists, comparing the two sources of information, like to argue, as they put it, whether "a picture is worth 1000 signals," or "a signal is worth 1000 pictures." In ideal circumstances, they can work with both, as well as information provided by informants. In the early 1960s, the CIA got that kind of help from Oleg Penkovsky, a lieutenant colonel in the Soviet military intelligence service. He gave the United States a good deal of information about Soviet missiles before he was unmasked in late 1962 and executed.

The problem in the late 1950s was that the telemetry data had been gathering dust in Washington because no one had tried to pry apart the forty-eight different channels of information and figure out what they showed. Wheelon's assignment, once again encouraged by General Schriever, was to unscramble the telemetry. If he succeeded, Washington would know almost as much about Soviet missiles as the Kremlin.

The National Security Agency had started the eavesdropping program, with the assistance of technical experts from Sylvania's Electronic Defense Laboratories, in the mid-1950s by setting up a listening post outside the coastal town of Sinop in northern Turkey. The site afforded a clear line of sight across the Black Sea to the Kapustin Yar missile test range in the Ukraine that was used to test intermediate-range missiles.

At first, the effort failed because it relied on receivers designed to pick up the FM frequencies commonly used by American missiles. Then a smart young Sylvania mathematician and systems engineer from Stanford and Penn State, recalling that the Russians had adopted German rocketry techniques, suggested building receivers tuned to the AM frequencies that the Germans had used in their rocket programs. As soon as the change was made, the Russian transmissions came in loud and clear. Another post was soon opened by the CIA high in the mountains of northeast Iran, overlooking the Tyuratam range used to test ICBMs.

A third monitoring station was later established by the Agency in western China during the Carter administration.

The Sylvania engineer was William Perry. It was the first of many significant contributions Perry would make to the nation's security as a prolific creator of new military and intelligence technologies. He and Wheelon later collaborated on several projects, including the development of an advanced satellite system that collected Soviet missile telemetry and Russian and Chinese communications traffic. As the undersecretary of defense for research and engineering in the Carter administration, Perry launched work on the F-117 stealth fighter, another Skunk Works airplane, as well as the laser-guided missiles that the United States used in the 1991 Gulf War, the 1999 air war in Kosovo, and more recently in the 2001–2002 war in Afghanistan. He served as defense secretary during Bill Clinton's first term as president. Though his role as a champion of new technologies is well known in the government, Perry's service to the national intelligence effort has not received the public recognition it merits.

The National Security Agency enlisted nongovernment scientists and engineers to study the telemetry data, including Wheelon and Perry. The group was called the Telemetry and Beacon Analysis Committee, or Tebac. "Nobody had figured out how to use this data," Wheelon recalled. It was not encrypted, or scrambled, by the Russians—that would come many years later. But it was still hard to differentiate between the signals to identify different elements of a missile's performance, like rocket thrust, motor performance, guidance system operation, engine shut-down, and warhead separation and dispersal.

It took the group eighteen months during the course of 1958 and 1959 to deconstruct the telemetry. The payoff was worth every hour. As Wheelon put it, "We'd not only figured out what all the channels were but also had the calibrations, which meant for almost two decades we could read Soviet flight data on every shot. Here was a chance to look at the other poker player's hand."

Wheelon was brought aboard the CIA in June 1962 to run the Office of Scientific Intelligence. He quickly discovered that the CIA's scientific activities, including the development of new spy technologies, were underfunded and spread out among a jumble of different offices that were often prevented by security regulations from sharing information.

As Wheelon was debating whether to stay at the agency in 1963 after Scoville's departure, Killian and Land, troubled by the patchwork arrangements and Bissell's use of the U-2 in covert operations like the Bay of Pigs invasion, were pressing President Kennedy and McCone to strengthen the CIA's commitment to science. Among other things, they didn't want high-concept technology systems like the U-2 put at the service of quixotic escapades like the Bay of Pigs attack.

Echoing language that Land had used nine years earlier in sternly urging Allen Dulles to invest in technology and support development of the U-2, Killian's White House intelligence advisory board recommended that McCone establish "an administrative arrangement in the CIA whereby the whole spectrum of modern science and technology can be brought into contact with major programs and projects of the Agency." The panel complained that "the present fragmentation and compartmentation of research and development in CIA severely inhibits this function."

Faced with the board's recommendations and Wheelon's demands, McCone reorganized the Agency to give Wheelon full control of all scientific work. The new kingdom was called the Directorate of Science and Technology. It was a troubled realm as Wheelon took charge.

One of his first headaches was Kelly Johnson's supersonic spy plane. The project had been a backbreaker for Johnson and the Skunk Works. "The idea of attaining and staying at Mach 3.2 over long flights was the toughest job the Skunk Works ever had and the most difficult of my career," Johnson later said.

Even an apprentice airplane builder could quickly calculate that an object moving at that velocity—Mach 3.2, or 2,373 mph—would produce so much friction that surface temperatures on the leading edges of the aircraft would soar above 500 degrees Fahrenheit, and top 1,000 degrees in some hot spots around the engines. That might be acceptable for a few minutes of high-speed flight, but was unsustainable for longer periods. Aluminum, the customary material used in airframe manufacturing, couldn't withstand the heat. The usual lubricants would wilt. The most advanced aviation fuel, including the special blend made for the U-2, would boil off and the cockpit would turn as hot as a home oven on Thanksgiving.

Johnson and his colleagues practically had to reinvent the business of building airplanes to overcome the challenges. He later itemized the obstacles: "Aircraft operating at those speeds and altitudes would require development of special fuels, structural materials, manufacturing tools and techniques, hydraulic fluid, fuel-tank sealant, paints, plastics, wiring and connecting plugs, as well as basic aircraft and engine design. Everything about the aircraft had to be invented. Everything."

The plane was so novel, Richard Bissell said, "it practically spawned its own industrial base."

The Skunk Works crew had gone through one model after another trying to come up with a workable design. Meeting the speed and altitude specifications, tough as they were, was not the primary design problem. The main challenge was reimagining the shape of supersonic planes to bring down the radar profile.

Most supersonic planes at the time were bullet-shaped, with tapered noses that came to a needlelike point. That was essentially the appearance of Johnson's initial A-1 design and the many that followed it. The cylindrical portion of the fuselage, however, presented a fat, reflective target for radar systems. After going through eleven different designs, Johnson had been stumped by the radar problem.

Then one of Johnson's designers had an ingenious idea—why not alter the shape of the fuselage by adding a sloping skirt, or chine, on both sides of the fuselage? This surface would extend forward from the wings in the rear all the way to the nose, giving the plane the appearance of a cobra. The addition of the chine created a tapered, streamlined shape that reduced the radar cross-section by 90 percent. The A-12 spy plane, wryly dubbed the "Oxcart" by the CIA, was born.

Once the Eisenhower administration had given Lockheed the go-ahead to build the spy plane in July 1959, Johnson had to solve the formidable manufacturing problems. "Early in the development stage," Johnson later said, "I promised $50 to anyone who could find anything easy to do. I might as well have offered $1,000 because I still have the money."

The use of titanium, which had been pioneered by Bud Wheelon's father, was a case in point. With aluminum out of the picture because of the scorching heat, Johnson could use stainless steel or titanium as the primary metal for the plane. Stainless steel was a good high-temperature material, but after visiting a Lockheed plant in Georgia that was working with the metal for the supersonic B-70 bomber, he concluded the sterile conditions needed in manufacturing wouldn't suit the Skunk Works. "The more complexity, the more potential for problems," he said.

Titanium, which seemed attractive because it was lightweight and impervious to the kind of heat the A-12 would endure, proved to be no less demanding. Just getting enough of the scarce alloy to make the metal for the A-12 was a challenge. The CIA gave Johnson an assist by covertly importing titanium alloy from the Soviet Union, which didn't realize it was ultimately headed for Johnson's airplane factory in Burbank.

Handling titanium was an airplane maker's nightmare. The metal's hardness made machining and shaping of parts exceedingly difficult. Drill bits that sliced through aluminum shattered when they hit titanium. Yet titanium was also highly sensitive to contaminants. Cadmium-plated tools, for example, couldn't be used because microscopic pieces of cadmium would interact with the titanium and weaken it. Johnson had discovered the connection when titanium bolt heads that had been tightened with cadmium wrenches broke off at high temperatures. Chlorine was another threat. Ben Rich described the problem: "We were stunned when spot welds on panels began to fail within six or seven weeks. Some intensive sleuthing revealed that the panels had been welded during July and August, when the Burbank water system was heavily chlorinated to prevent algae growth. The panels had to be washed after acid treatment, so we immediately began using only distilled water."

By the time Wheelon assumed command of the project in the summer of 1963, Johnson had conquered many of the design and fabrication

problems and test flights were under way at the agency's secret airfield
at Groom Lake in Nevada, which had been greatly expanded to accommodate the new plane and the large workforce that supported it.

However, getting the A-12 to fly safely and reliably at high speed was
another matter. "We have been at Mach 2.5 and as high as 70,000 feet,
but we are in trouble from Mach 2.0 up," Johnson reported in his log on
March 20, 1963. Wheelon found that the project was, as he recalled, "in
trouble, in fundamental trouble."

Johnson had produced the first prototype in February 1962, nearly a
year behind schedule. Like the U-2, the plane was so secret it couldn't
be flown out of Burbank for fear of being spotted. Unlike the U-2, the
A-12 was too large to crate up and stow aboard a cargo plane. So, in the
dead of night on February 26, 1962, an enormous trailer truck pulled
out of the Skunk Works complex, headed for the freeway with the disassembled plane carefully hidden in a massive box. A Lockheed history
matter-of-factly noted that an earlier survey of the route determined
that "some obstructing road signs would have to be removed and select
trees would have to be trimmed." Late-night drivers must have wondered if they were hallucinating when they encountered the bizarre caravan proceeding eastward across the California desert that night. The
driver of a Greyhound bus that accidentally grazed the trailer was
handed $3,500 in cash by CIA security officers to settle the matter and
prevent the filing of an accident report.

The A-12 took to the air for the first time two months later. The inaugural flight, like that of the U-2 seven years earlier, was terrifying for
the pilot and ground crew at Groom Lake. Lou Schalk, the test pilot,
struggled to get the plane under control after it left the ground. He then
overshot the runway, landing on the desert floor. As the plane skittered
across the bone-dry lakebed in a cloud of dust, no one in the control
tower could see if Schalk was going to be able to stop. "Everyone was
having a heart attack," he said later. "I finally made the turn and came
out of the cloud of dust, and they saw I hadn't run into the mountains on
the other side of the lake and blown up the airplane, so there was a big
sigh of relief."

As the test flights continued, and the fleet of A-12s at Groom Lake grew, Johnson discovered that the plane had a potentially fatal flaw. The flow of air into the massive Pratt & Whitney J58 engines was not adequately controlled during the upper ranges of supersonic flight. As a result, engines would stall or blow out. The sudden loss of power at such high speeds made the plane shudder violently, cracking the heads of pilots against the cockpit glass. Fearing the airplane was breaking up, several pilots bailed out at this point during test flights, and one was killed when his parachute failed to open.

The problem was traced to the retractable inlet cones mounted in front of the engines. These spikes were designed to regulate the flow of air onto the engine fan blades. The hydraulic control units selected by Johnson couldn't adjust quickly enough at high speeds to manage the supersonic air flow. The slightest change in the angle of the air stream, which was pouring into the inlets at 100,000 cubic feet per second at top speed, could deflect it from the optimum point of contact with the fan blades, extinguishing the engine. The defect crippled high-speed flight testing. As 1964 came to a close, there were eleven A-12 planes at Groom Lake. Though they had logged more than twelve hundred flights totaling nearly seventeen hundred hours of flying time, the fleet had managed to accumulate a grand total of just thirty-three minutes of flying time at Mach 3.2, the advertised cruising speed for the airplane.

For a while, Johnson stubbornly resisted Wheelon's suggestion to switch to an electronic spike control system that could adjust the air flow more quickly and precisely. "Kelly had many wonderful features, but he didn't feel comfortable with electronics," Wheelon said. "He understood that whole damned airplane. He understood the aerodynamics, the structures, the components. The only thing he didn't understand was electronics."

Johnson finally yielded in 1964 when Wheelon threatened to cancel the program unless the change was made. It took more than a year of fine-tuning by Ben Rich to come up with a system that worked. "Developing this air-inlet control system was the most exhausting, difficult, and nerve-racking work of my professional life," he said. On January 27, 1965, an A-12 took off from Groom Lake and traveled for an hour and fifteen minutes at Mach 3.1.

The A-12 was a remarkable aircraft, but its operating days were numbered. President Eisenhower's ban on spy flights over the Soviet Union after the downing of the U-2 on May 1, 1960, was not lifted by his successors, and the A-12 never flew over Soviet territory. The CIA used the plane sparingly over North Korea and during the Vietnam War to gather intelligence on North Vietnam, then retired its fleet in 1968 because of the high cost of operating the aircraft. The Air Force made frequent use of its two-seat model of the plane, the SR-71, during the Vietnam conflict and in a variety of trouble spots during the 1980s, then mothballed its fleet in 1990 for the same reason. Some of the planes are now parked at aviation museums around the country. Even in repose, the black, streamlined machines are an impressive sight and even now appear to be the creation of some future civilization. The SR-71 "Blackbird" still holds the speed record for many long-distance flights, including New York to London—one hour, fifty-four minutes, and fifty-seven seconds, which is more than one hour faster than the Concorde supersonic airliner. The Blackbird's flying time from Los Angeles to Washington was sixty-eight minutes, seventeen seconds, or about as long as many Washington commuters spend on the beltway most mornings going to work.

While Wheelon and Johnson were coaxing the A-12 into operation—at one point Wheelon infuriated McCone by recklessly going along on a test flight aboard a two-seat version of the plane used for pilot training—Wheelon was trying to look over the horizon at future satellite systems. The exercise stemmed, in part, from Corona's limits. Corona, in reconnaissance parlance, was a broad area search system, meaning it supplied photographic coverage of large bands of Soviet territory. It allowed photo analysts to identify new airfields, missile bases, shipyards, and other sizable military sites, but couldn't offer a closer look at smaller targets. A different kind of photoreconnaissance satellite, known as a spotting system, was needed to produce high-resolution pictures of Russian missiles, airplanes, ships, submarines, tanks, and other objects.

The Air Force, unable to produce useful pictures from the Samos satellites, had embarked on an effort to develop a spotting system that returned exposed film to the earth in a capsule, like Corona. The project was code-named Gambit. The first Gambit satellite was launched in July 1963. The new system nicely complemented Corona, producing detailed pictures in which analysts could see an object as small as 18 inches in size. That was comparable to the U-2 and at least three times more detailed than anything Corona could show.

Since the Air Force was using Gambit primarily to refine targeting plans in the event of war, and photo interpreters could not make out important Soviet facilities in the Corona photographs, Wheelon wanted a satellite with improved resolution that could be used to gather information about new Soviet weapons, industrial installations, nuclear test grounds, and other matters of keen interest to policymakers. In October 1963, he selected Sid Drell to direct a satellite study. The group's mandate was to determine whether Corona could be improved enough to serve as a spotting system as well as a search system or whether a new satellite was required.

Drell, by this point, had already helped Wheelon diagnose and fix a serious problem in the Corona camera system that had flummoxed technical experts from Itek, the Leghorn company that supplied the Corona cameras. Film was coming back from space blotted with white streaks. With the assistance of several other high-powered physicists, including Luis Alvarez from the University of California at Berkeley, who would win the Nobel Prize in physics in 1968, Drell's panel found that the rollers that fed the film through the camera were producing an electrical discharge that streaked the film. The problem was eventually remedied by making the rollers out of a different material.

The Drell committee, the Satellite Photography Working Group, advised Wheelon that the resolution of the Corona camera system couldn't be improved significantly. "They said the whole scheme had pretty well reached its natural limit and that if we were going to do better than Corona, we really needed to start again." Wheelon agreed, and set out to develop a new satellite, later code-named Hexagon, that would provide broad area coverage at higher resolution.

The plan generated months of skirmishing with the National Reconnaissance Office and its new director, Brockway McMillan, an MIT mathematician and former Bell Laboratories executive who wanted to take over the CIA's satellite programs.

There had been bad blood between Wheelon and McMillan before they got to Washington. As a prepublication reviewer of papers submitted to *Physical Review*, a scholarly journal for physicists, McMillan had rejected an article by Wheelon about radio waves. Wheelon felt the assessment was unfair and uninformed. He complained to the editor, who overruled McMillan and published the paper. Once ensconced in Washington, the two men were propelled into conflict by institutional rivalry, personal animosity, and the core struggle over whether the CIA should remain a major player in the rapidly expanding, and increasingly pivotal, world of spy satellites.

The bureaucratic warfare over control of satellites was unusually ferocious, even by Washington's cutthroat standards. In the early rounds, Wheelon and McMillan were the leading combatants, but as the conflict played out over the years many top officials were drawn into the fray. The fighting in the early 1960s shredded an agreement about the role of the NRO that McCone and Roswell L. Gilpatric, the deputy secretary of defense, signed on May 2, 1962, and even defied a peacemaking effort by President Kennedy in 1963. Kennedy invited Wheelon and McMillan to the White House to discuss the tensions, but failed to win their cooperation.

Decades later, McMillan still bristled when asked about Wheelon. "I didn't trust his technical judgment," he said. It was one of his milder comments—he asked that the others not be quoted. In retrospect, McMillan said, he regretted that he had let his views about Wheelon color his management of the NRO and relations with the CIA. But he defended his record as director of the NRO. "My job was to produce intelligence and plan for future systems and that's what I tried to do."

The memos that Wheelon and McMillan wrote during the mid-1960s were so heated they were still smoldering in the archives more than three decades later when they were unclassified.

The main disagreement at first centered around McMillan's effort to take over the Corona program after a series of failed missions in 1962–1963. "I feel that it is essential for me to establish a single point of authority within the NRO for the Corona program, to which I can then assign full responsibility for the successful conduct of the program," McMillan notified the directors of Program A and Program B in late 1963.

Wheelon fired back in a memo to McCone, protesting that a reassignment of Corona would not solve the technical problems. Rather than yielding control to the NRO and Air Force, Wheelon said, "More vigorous CIA participation on the technical and programmatic front is required."

A month later, after reviewing the Corona program, Wheelon advised McCone that the CIA was "at a turning point in the NRO and there is no honorable way to lose this one. If we agree to the Corona transfer, I predict we will never re-enter the satellite field in a meaningful way."

Wheelon acidly noted that the McMillan plan "would substitute orthodox Air Force procurement procedures for those of the CIA at the critical contractors. Of course, his proposal is enormously pleasing to the uniformed Air Force, as it completes their monopoly of all satellite programs."

In late June 1964, with no cease-fire in sight, McMillan declared in a memo, "It is my considered judgment that the Corona project will never operate reliably and responsibly, and will never uniformly achieve the quality of which it is known to be capable, as long as the Government's management of it is as diffuse as it now is."

The dispute over Corona seemed to be headed toward resolution in January 1965 with the drafting of a secret Memorandum of Agreement. Under the accord, Wheelon and the CIA largely retained control. McMillan, unhappy with the terms negotiated by his aides, declined to sign the agreement.

In March the conflict escalated when McMillan peremptorily canceled the planned launch of a Corona satellite from Vandenberg. The action infuriated Wheelon and his aides. They prepared a memo to Gen. Marshall Carter, the deputy director of the CIA, that opened by saying, "Dr. McMillan's willful cancellation of the Corona Mission 1018 launch on 23 March 1965 culminates a series of actions dating back to the early days of the NRO to force the Agency either out of the satellite reconnaissance business or submit its activities to the desires and control of the Air Force."

The Corona dispute was finally quieted in the summer of 1965 after McMillan was dismissed as NRO director. Thanks to the intervention of Cyrus Vance, the deputy secretary of defense, and Adm. William F. Raborn, who had succeeded McCone earlier that year, the CIA and Pentagon reached agreement on the respective responsibilities of the CIA and NRO. It awarded the CIA most of the powers it had been fighting to retain.

Frictions persisted, however, impeding development of new satellites. Hexagon, for instance, was stalled for several years. Wheelon got final approval from the Johnson administration to move ahead with the project in April 1966, five months before he left the CIA. The program was later informally dubbed "Big Bird" because of the satellite's size—40 feet long, 10 feet in diameter, and weighing 15 tons.

Hexagon realized Wheelon's ambition for a high-resolution search system, though it was not ready for service until June 1971, five years after he left the CIA. The two powerful cameras aboard the satellite could cover a far wider area of the Soviet Union with each orbit than Corona while taking pictures almost as detailed as those produced by Gambit. It also carried four return capsules, extending the operational life of the satellite to several months.

For Wheelon, the planning for Hexagon was just the beginning of the technical leap he yearned to make.

One Sunday afternoon in the fall of 1963 he had a brainstorm as he sat in his living room in northern Virginia. "I was watching an NFL game on television that was being played in San Francisco. It suddenly struck me that if I could do that, the technology was finally ready to view the earth's surface from orbit and to observe the scene as it was being received in the spacecraft."

Instant images from space—it was the Holy Grail of spy technology. Mert Davies and his RAND colleagues had first proposed the idea in Project Feed Back in 1954. The Air Force had expended millions of dollars trying to build a video-relay system—Project Samos—but had failed to produce a satellite that could match Corona in picture resolution. Now Bud Wheelon was setting his sights on the same elusive goal, known in the spy business as near real-time intelligence.

The day after watching the San Francisco 49ers game, Wheelon returned to work and called Leslie Dirks, one of the brightest scientists in the CIA research shop. Dirks had studied physics at MIT and Oxford, where he was a Rhodes Scholar. He had joined the Agency in 1961, a year before Wheelon.

Wheelon described his epiphany to Dirks, then told him, "You're detached from all other duties. I'll give you whatever money you need and let's get started on figuring how we can build a readout system that really makes sense."

Broadcasting a pro football game across the country was one thing, taking and televising high-resolution pictures from 100 miles out in space was quite another, as the Air Force had learned to its dismay. Even though television technology was advancing rapidly, the airing of the football game offered only the most rudimentary model of what Wheelon would need for a spy satellite. The television cameras used at Kezar Stadium in San Francisco that Sunday afternoon converted the optical image of the action on the field into electrical signals, which were then transmitted across the country. That was a start. But they did so with electronic equipment that could never produce the kind of high-resolution images expected from a spy satellite. If Wheelon and Dirks were to make any headway, they would need a different and far more precise way of converting light into electrons.

By chance, not far away in New Jersey, two scientists at Bell Laboratories were hard at work on a new technology that would, among other things, solve the problem. Their research would not only make it possible to create the satellite that Wheelon imagined but also play a central role in changing the way images and information were recorded and transmitted. William S. Boyle and George E. Smith, working with silicon semiconductors, were inventing charge-coupled devices, or CCDs.

The devices are basically extremely sensitive photo sensors that turn light into a stream of electronic signals that can be recorded and displayed on a computer monitor or television screen. The more familiar term for the resulting technology is digital imaging.

The work of Boyle and Smith had the potential to make film obsolete. CCDs convert light energy into tiny electric charges that can be stored, measured exactly, and converted into numbers representing shades of color that can be transmitted and used to reassemble the images. CCDs are employed today in all sorts of familiar civilian and military technologies, including video cameras, digital cameras, high-definition television, medical imaging machines, and the Hubble space telescope.

Wheelon learned about the research from William O. Baker, the head of Bell Labs and an influential adviser on scientific and intelligence matters to numerous presidents, including Eisenhower and Kennedy. Though the lab did not publicly disclose its work on CCDs until 1970, Baker informed Wheelon about Boyle and Smith's progress in 1963. "Baker said we usually don't let technology out until it's pretty well proven, but for this purpose we'll let you have it," Wheelon recalled. "So we got a handful of CCDs from Bell Labs and started the quest."

It lasted more than a decade, and turned into one of the most ambitious technological projects the government has ever attempted. "It was a huge technical challenge, like going to the moon," said Jimmie D. Hill, who worked on the program and served for many years as the deputy director of the National Reconnaissance Office. As with the Corona program in the late 1950s, the CIA and the companies it hired to work on the new satellite had to invent new technologies as they proceeded. The CIA was trying to compress the development time for major new electronic technologies that were just starting to emerge in the 1960s and 1970s.

"You're pushing it faster than industry at the time was heading," Sid Drell said.

The grand idea of matching up CCDs with a high-definition optical system to create an electro-optical satellite was compelling, but the difficulties were enormous. As Drell, an accomplished violinist, aptly put it, "It's not just a cracker box, it's a Stradivarius."

The CCDs first had to be perfected and then assembled in large arrays to ensure good contrast and picture quality. The scientists wanted to measure light rays practically one atomic particle at a time, and they had to create a system that could produce a crisp signal from just a few photons, the basic unit of light, while suppressing other ambient energy sources that could clutter the image. The electronic circuitry involved was exquisitely intricate. New telescopic lenses had to be fashioned, using a complex system of mirrors to increase the focal length, the key to obtaining highly magnified images. The optical system, in turn, had to be married to the sensors.

Getting the optical data back to earth was no small challenge. The data had to be moved out of the satellite as fast as it was recorded so it would reach Washington nearly instantaneously and also not overload the limited capacity of onboard storage devices. Transmitting it directly to ground stations, however, would not be possible while the satellite was flying over Soviet territory, far beyond the range of American receivers. The only solution was to create a fleet of relay satellites that acted like an electronic bucket brigade, conveying the data across the heavens and down to a ground station outside Washington.

Moving large volumes of digital information through the relay system and processing it in Washington required groundbreaking telecommunications research. Sophisticated new electronic machines were needed to reconstruct the images from the digitized data and make them available to analysts so they could be enlarged and examined in minute detail. The list of challenges grew to epic proportions—and expense. And everything had to be done in secret.

Wheelon got the project started, then turned it over to his successor, Carl Duckett, who in turn handed it off to his successor, Les Dirks. Over the years, dozens of American aerospace and electronics companies developed components, with Lockheed serving as the prime contractor. Westinghouse Electric Company did much of the work refining the CCDs.

Despite its importance, the project was not immune to the feuding between the CIA and NRO. If anything, its novelty made it more vulnerable to attack. The Air Force doubted the new system could be perfected and pressed hard during Richard Nixon's first term as president for its own new spy satellite project, an incremental improvement of Gambit. As the Pentagon, led by Defense Secretary Melvin Laird, marshaled resources to lobby for the Air Force plan in 1971, Edwin Land's CIA advisory panel on technology took the case for the electro-optical system directly to the White House.

Sid Drell and Richard Garwin, an eminent IBM physicist and longtime Land panel member, made an appointment to see Henry Kissinger, Nixon's national security adviser. With help from Carl Duckett, they prepared briefing materials. "Sid and I carefully drafted a top-secret code-word handwritten letter that was personally delivered to Kissinger at what seems to have been the last possible moment to obtain a favorable decision for the electro-optical system," Garwin recalled. To ensure secrecy, Garwin and Drell met with Kissinger in the secure Situation Room in the White House basement.

Land, meantime, discussed the project with Nixon directly, arguing that the novel technology offered a chance to radically improve the state of reconnaissance satellites. The White House approved the CIA plan in the spring of 1971. The underlying science, by then, seemed firmly within reach and the Agency felt it was ready to proceed with construction of the satellite and its support systems. The satellite, variously called Kennan, Crystal, and the KH-11, was launched on December 19, 1976. The first pictures were presented to Jimmy Carter on January 21, 1977, the day after his inauguration. In remarkable detail, they showed his inaugural ceremony.

Two years later, in one of the most serious security breaches of the cold war, William Kampiles, a disgruntled CIA employee, sold a copy of the top-secret technical manual for the satellite to Soviet agents for $3,000. Transfer of the manual, for which Kampiles was convicted and sentenced to a forty-year prison term, gave the Russians more than enough information about the spying powers of the satellite to take evasive action by disguising new weapons systems and trying to shield them from sight. Still, despite the compromising of the satellite system, it returned priceless intelligence about the Soviet Union for years, and today advanced models provide Washington with pictures of North Korean missile sites, Iranian nuclear reactors, Iraqi military and industrial complexes, terrorist training camps, and an infinite variety of other potential threats.

Wheelon's last big project—creation of a new kind of satellite to intercept missile telemetry and long-distance telephone communications—began with the same sort of serendipitous moment that gave rise to the electro-optical system. Wheelon, as was his custom, arrived at the CIA early one morning in July 1963. As he read the *New York Herald Tribune*, he spotted a story about a new communications satellite sponsored jointly by NASA and the Pentagon, the first of its kind. The satellite had been placed in orbit more than 22,000 miles out in space, far beyond the low, elliptical orbits favored for photoreconnaissance satellites. The orbit was so high it allowed the satellite, called Syncom II, to revolve in tandem with the earth—it was traveling around the planet at the same rate that the earth was revolving around its axis, thus staying over the same spot on earth. In that stable position, called a geosynchronous orbit, it could serve as a relay point for telephone calls and other communications traffic, eliminating the need for undersea cables. Engineers at Hughes Aircraft, which built the satellite, had solved a number of tricky problems that made it difficult to keep a satellite in stationary orbit.

Wheelon realized that the geosynchronous orbit could provide great advantages in trying to pick off telemetry and communications signals as they flashed through space. "I said, Whoa!, that's got something to do with what we're doing. If we could sit up there, stationary in space, and listen, we could probably solve a lot of problems."

In theory, a satellite in the proper geostationary orbit hovering over the equator in the vicinity of the Soviet Union and China could harvest the telemetry from Russian missiles fired from all the Soviet test sites, supplementing the information gathered by the listening posts in Turkey and Iran. A satellite would have the added advantage of being able to monitor telemetry produced during the final phase of flight over eastern Siberia. This last stage of flight included reentry through the atmosphere. The powered phase of flight as a missile lifts off and climbs through the atmosphere, and the final phase, as the warhead descends, are the most critical for telemetry gathering. American ground stations in Japan and on Shemya Island near the tip of the Aleutian archipelago collected telemetry as the warheads neared the Soviet target zone on the Kamchatka Peninsula.

A geosynchronous satellite would also be able to pick up Russian and Chinese radio and telephone communications and cable traffic, especially military communications that were not then encrypted.

Wheelon called together the members of his signals intelligence brain trust and asked them to examine the feasibility of developing such a satellite. He also asked Bill Perry to take a look. Perry by this time had founded his own research firm, Electronic Systems Laboratory in San Jose.

A satellite in high orbit would have the advantage of hovering indefinitely over an area, and picking up signals from a much wider region, but it would have to be equipped with exceedingly sophisticated signal processing equipment to extract the readable telemetry from the background noise, including TV signals that traveled far into space. It would also require a mammoth dish antenna and a large new ground station, most likely in Australia. "We were talking about signal processing far ahead of anything that was being done at the time," Perry recalled.

Nevertheless, after studying the matter, Perry advised Wheelon that the technological barriers could be overcome. Wheelon picked Lloyd K. Lauderdale, a Naval Academy graduate on his staff who had a Ph.D. in electrical engineering from Johns Hopkins, to manage the project. It was code-named Rhyolite.

It, too, became a hostage of the Washington infighting between the CIA and NRO, and the first model was not put in orbit until June 1969. It performed brilliantly, giving Washington a flood of new data about Soviet missiles and an abundant supply of intercepted communications. It was as though the CIA had implanted a giant bugging device in Moscow that could monitor many of the Soviet Union's most sensitive military communications. Unfortunately, like the electro-optical system a few years later, the satellite system was soon betrayed.

In this instance, the secrets of the spacecraft were sold to the Russians in 1975–1976 by a clerk at TRW (the expanded version of Ramo-

Wooldridge), the company that built the satellite and helped operate it. The clerk, Christopher John Boyce, worked in the "Black Vault" at TRW's headquarters outside Los Angeles. Much of the intelligence traffic from the new satellites passed through the heavily secured facility on its way to Washington from the ground station in Pine Gap, Australia, that had been specially constructed for the new satellite. With encouragement from a friend, Andrew Daulton Lee, Boyce started selling information about the satellite to Russian agents in Mexico City and Vienna. The exchanges continued for twenty-one months. The two were caught in 1977, convicted and sentenced to long prison terms. Their betrayal was the subject of *The Falcon and the Snowman*, Robert Lindsey's 1979 bestseller.

With information about Rhyolite, the Russians moved to encrypt their telemetry and switch their most sensitive military communications to land lines as rapidly as they could. Despite these efforts, Rhyolite continued to pick up a staggering volume of valuable information and relay it on to Washington.

In fact, as all these systems came into operation, and even more advanced models were added in the 1980s and 1990s, the problem in Washington was no longer collecting information but making use of it. The trickle of intelligence about the Soviet Union that frustrated Dwight Eisenhower when he moved into the White House at mid-century had turned, by the end of the century, into a tidal wave of information that threatened to engulf Washington and overwhelm the ability of analysts to identify the most urgent and important intelligence and then make sense of it. At the same time, the expense and energy that went into building and operating these fabulously ingenious technical systems drained resources from the more mundane but indispensable business of training intelligence officers and sending them abroad to recruit informants, penetrate hostile governments or terrorist networks, and gather the kind of critical information that even the most sophisticated satellites could not find. Information, for example, about Osama bin Laden's plan to attack New York and Washington on September 11, 2001.

No one understood these dangers better than Bud Wheelon, the man who set Washington on course to develop ever more powerful espionage technologies. Sitting in his meticulously organized home office outside Santa Barbara late one afternoon in August 1998, he talked about the unintended impact of spy satellites on the CIA's clandestine service, which manages thousands of spies around the world. "You're getting these wonderful pictures and intercepts, and you don't have to take as many chances, lose as many people, take as many risks," he said.

Asked what kind of information spy satellites are unable to provide about America's new enemies, such as terrorists, he replied, "Oh, everything that you want to know, like where they are headed, what they are going to do, and when they are going to pull the trigger."

Losing the Inventive Spark

T HE UNINTENDED CONSEQUENCES and limitations of an intelligence empire built around spy satellites was clearly evident long before September 11, 2001, and the realization that the United States faced a lethal new threat at home from Islamic terrorists. Weaknesses in the nation's intelligence agencies had been mounting for years, and some of the problems could be traced to policies and budgets that devoted a disproportionate share of resources to technical collection systems like satellites while neglecting more prosaic espionage methods like the use of human agents. For more than four decades, Richard Leghorn's vision of strategic reconnaissance and the overhead spy systems it spawned had served the nation brilliantly, but by the mid-1990s it was apparent that other forms of intelligence gathering needed attention. It was also increasingly evident that the remarkable spy machines of the cold war—and the institutions that had been created in Washington to process and analyze the intelligence data that they produced—were not versatile or agile enough to cope with the array of new threats the country confronted.

The Clinton administration discovered some of these realities on May 11, 1998. As Bill Clinton's top national security aides reported to work in Washington early that Monday morning, they received startling and disturbing news: India had detonated several nuclear weapons at an underground test site 350 miles southwest of New Delhi. The explosions at the Pokharan test range in Rajasthan state signaled the opening of a new, highly dangerous nuclear arms race in South Asia between India and Pakistan, bitter enemies that had fought three wars since 1947 when the two became independent states. With India openly brandishing a nuclear arsenal—it had tested an atomic bomb in 1974 but subsequently left unclear whether it was building a stockpile of weapons—Pakistan was sure to lift the restraints on its own nuclear program and test its first bomb within a matter of days. The Indian action was a devastating blow to American-led international efforts to prevent the spread of nuclear weapons. What made the test especially infuriating to officials in Washington was that they learned about it on CNN. America's intelligence services, relying on an armada of sophisticated spy satellites, provided no advance warning, eliminating any chance Washington might have had to intervene diplomatically to head off the test.

Deputy Secretary of State Strobe Talbott, the Clinton administration's point man for India and Pakistan, had just arrived at his elegantly furnished seventh-floor office at the State Department on May 11 when he heard about the test from the department's operations center. He immediately called the CIA on a secure line to get more information. He was astounded to find that the Agency wasn't even aware there had been a test. "I told them," Talbott later recalled. "They didn't know!"

The intelligence failure was stunning. Nearly forty years after launching the first successful photoreconnaissance satellite, and better than two decades after creating remarkably powerful intelligence-gathering systems that could see the license plate, though not the license number, on a car from hundreds of miles out in space and relay the images back to Washington almost instantaneously, the United States had somehow missed visual signs that the Indians were making final preparations for an explosion at Pokharan. These activities included the laying of large cables from monitoring equipment on the surface to the entrance to the shaft drilled deep into the earth where the nuclear weapons were placed. Having relied on reconnaissance satellites for many years to observe the primary Soviet testing ground near Semipalatinsk in Kazakhstan, intelligence analysts in Washington were familiar with the preparatory work that usually preceded an underground blast. The Indians followed a similar routine.

In fact, thanks to satellite pictures, the CIA had detected just such signs at the Indian site in late 1995. In hopes of preventing an explosion,

Frank Wisner Jr., the U.S. ambassador to India, had quietly met with one of Prime Minister Narasimha Rao's top aides in New Delhi in December 1995 to appeal for restraint. To make plain that Washington knew precisely what was happening at Pokharan, Wisner came to the meeting armed with a revealing photograph of the test range taken by one of Washington's most advanced spy satellites. He unveiled it briefly during the conversation. The Indians refrained from testing, though Wisner and his colleagues back in Washington could not be sure whether his intervention was the cause or whether the Rao government had hesitated for other reasons or had been bluffing all along.

Strobe Talbott had no opportunity to appeal to the Indians two and a half years later. One reason was that the Indians, learning from the 1995 episode, had gone to great lengths to conceal work at the testing complex. Because the orbital path of all military and civilian satellites must be registered with the United Nations under a 1975 agreement, the Indians could calculate when one of America's KH-11 near real-time imagery satellites would pass over the desert area at Pokharan. During those brief periods, which came two or three times a day, preparations had apparently been suspended. Other work had been camouflaged.

But Indian subterfuge was not the only explanation. As the Clinton administration investigated why it had received no warning, it found fundamental weaknesses in the government's entire intelligence-gathering apparatus, some of them linked to its reliance on spy satellites and the analytical operations established to exploit the river of information streaming in from space every day. The findings were sobering: Spy satellites produced far more raw information than the government's battalion of overworked analysts could handle. The CIA relied so heavily on satellites and other high-tech devices to gather information overseas that it had failed to cultivate informants in places like India, where human spies were essential to learning about secret military plans. Top intelligence officials, wedded to long-standing assumptions about foreign threats to American security, were slow to recognize new dangers and to redirect technical systems like spy satellites to monitor them. So much effort was going into making satellite data available to military forces to correct intelligence deficiencies found during the Gulf War in 1991 that some areas critical to policymakers were being neglected.

The organizational and operational disabilities identified in 1998 have a direct bearing on how well the nation can defend itself today against terrorist organizations and other foreign threats. Retired Adm. David E. Jeremiah, a former vice chairman of the Joint Chiefs of Staff who was brought in by the Clinton administration to determine what had gone wrong before the Indian test, reported among other things that spy technologies had outpaced the ability of the government to exploit the advanced systems.

"We have an imbalance today," he said, "between the human skills associated with reading photography, looking at reports, understanding what goes on in a nation, and the ability to technically collect that information. In everyday language, that means there is an awful lot of stuff on the cutting-room floor at the end of the day that we have not seen."

As for gathering information on the ground—old-fashioned spying by trained officers who know how to build networks of local informants—Admiral Jeremiah offered a short but withering assessment: "I think that generally across the board, without being specific to India, we could say our human intelligence capacity is seriously limited."

In reconstructing the intelligence record prior to the Indian test, Admiral Jeremiah found that despite the concealment efforts at Pokharan, there had been visual evidence that should have tipped off Washington. Unfortunately, only one analyst had been regularly assigned to review satellite imagery of the test site. That meant some initial preparations had been missed, including the arrival of several bulldozers near the test site on Friday, May 8. At 3 A.M. the following Monday in Washington, just hours before the test, the latest satellite pictures were transmitted to Washington. The lone analyst on duty that night who was responsible for checking on the Indian site noted that fences around the test area were being removed, a good indication that a test was imminent, but the photo interpreter did not raise the alarm in Washington. Four or five hours passed before more experienced intelligence officers got to work. By then the Indian government had announced that it had tested three nuclear devices. When a team of ten photo interpreters went over the entire photographic record retrospectively for Admiral Jeremiah, they identified a good deal of activity in the days before May 11 pointing toward a test.

Admiral Jeremiah also faulted intelligence officials for failing to seriously consider the possibility that the new Indian government, led by the head of a Hindu nationalist party that had openly championed the development of nuclear weapons, was more likely to conduct a test than previous governments dominated by the more moderate Congress party. After aspiring for fifty years to gain power, the Hindu nationalists, led by Prime Minister Atal Bihari Vajpayee, had made no secret of their desire to demonstrate that India was a great power militarily and politically, even if that risked frictions with the United States.

But instead of devoting additional espionage resources to the Indian nuclear program after the installation of the Vajpayee government in March 1998, intelligence officials, like the rest of the Clinton administration, accepted misleading assurances from the Indian leadership that it was not rushing to test nuclear arms. The assumption in Washington was that the Hindu nationalists, anxious to increase trade with the United States, had little interest in provoking a crisis by testing nuclear weapons. After Pakistan provocatively tested a new intermediate-range missile in early April that could reach India's largest cities, the Imagery Requirements Subcommittee, an interagency group that controls the movements of American spy satellites, directed that attention be focused on Indian missile ranges. As a result, the Pokharan test site was photographed just once every three days or so. The White House and CIA ordered no new review of India's nuclear program, and the fleet of American spy satellites in operation at the time, including two advanced KH-11 photoreconnaissance systems and two Lacrosse radar satellites, was not redirected in May to look more frequently at the Pokharan complex as test preparations proceeded.

The problems identified by Admiral Jeremiah were not unique to the Indian test. They are chronic ailments that played a role in the government's failure to detect and prevent the terror attacks in New York and Washington on September 11, 2001. They still impede American espionage operations today. Ironically, the extraordinary advances in spying technology that began nearly fifty years ago under the direction of Dwight Eisenhower contributed over time to distortions in the nation's intelligence agencies, including an overreliance on dazzling machines and a shortage of resources in more traditional fields like the recruitment and training of spies. By a cruel coincidence of history, it is these very failings that make American intelligence agencies ill prepared to track and thwart terrorist groups and have forced President George W. Bush to order the overhaul of the CIA and other agencies so they can more effectively deal with terrorist threats.

Until September 11, 2001, American spy agencies were still largely creatures of the cold war, designed to collect intelligence about static espionage targets like Soviet airfields, missile bases, shipyards, and easily identifiable military activities such as the movement of tank divisions and fuel tankers. High-flying spy planes and sophisticated spy satellites, when properly utilized, were ideal instruments for monitoring the Soviet Union and its allies, verifying compliance with arms control agreements, and warning the United States if hostile military forces were being readied for war. But the spy machinery of the cold war—and the lumbering government institutions that were built to operate and maintain it—are not well matched to the task of gathering intelligence about terrorist groups.

Terrorists are everything Soviet military forces were not: invisible, elusive, improvisational, and cunningly creative. Spy satellites can provide pictures of their training camps and intercept their communications if they are careless about the telephone systems they use, but satellites cannot supply the kind of round-the-clock surveillance that is required to detect unfolding plots, and they offer no help in recruiting sources inside terror cells. These are jobs that can only be performed by seasoned spies who have studied the languages, customs, and operational practices of groups like Al Qaeda and have cultivated allies within the intelligence services of countries like Pakistan, Egypt, Saudi Arabia, and Israel that are more knowledgeable about Islamic terrorist organizations. Such spies, known as case officers at the CIA, are in short supply in the Agency's clandestine service after years of insufficient investment in human spying. Over the years, the high cost of building spy satellites, and the tendency to see them as a magic potion that would solve most intelligence problems, led Washington to neglect other aspects of the spy game. Richard Bissell had anticipated just such a danger years earlier as he was coaxing the new technologies into operation. In a prophetic 1959 letter to a CIA colleague who had helped manage the development of the U-2, Bissell worried that "the company," as he referred to the Agency, would lose interest in the taxing discipline of developing new informants. "There is no way to start accomplishing what we want except by establishing contacts with people," he wrote. "To be sure, this is a very old way of doing business, lacking the glamour of modern technology and requiring a lot of dull hard work. Nevertheless, there is no substitute for it as an approach." The CIA, which began upgrading its antiterrorist capabilities before the 2001 attacks on the World Trade Center and the Pentagon, will be scrambling for years to assemble the army of expert field agents and covert operatives that the country must have if it is to dismantle terror networks and prevent further attacks.

In July 2002, a congressional subcommittee spotlighted some of the CIA's weaknesses in a report about the intelligence failures preceding the attacks of September 11, 2001. The Subcommittee on Terrorism and Homeland Security of the House Permanent Select Committee on Intelligence reported: "Because of the perceived reduction in the threat environment in the early to mid-1990s, and the concomitant reduction in resources for basic human intelligence collection, there were fewer operations officers, fewer stations, fewer agents, and fewer intelligence reports produced. This likely gave the CIA fewer opportunities for accessing agents useful in the counterterrorism campaign and eroded overall capabilities."

Spy satellites can make an important contribution in tracking new threats—if government leaders deal smartly with problems that undermine the effective use of the space-based collection systems. As Admiral Jeremiah discovered, there are not enough experienced photo interpreters on hand to look closely at all the images that need to be examined. There will never be enough analysts to keep up with the flood of images collected daily by spy satellites—the volume is just too great. But the government lacks a sufficient number simply to inspect top-priority images in a timely manner, including anything that might shed light on terrorist plots and the development of nuclear, biological, and chemical weapons abroad.

The same is true for translators dealing with the even greater volume of communication intercepts that are swept up by American eavesdropping satellites. Before September 11, 2001, the National Security Agency, which handles the intercepts, did not have nearly enough Arabic speakers to process message traffic from the Middle East and Central Asia. Several conversations picked up from Afghanistan on September 10, 2001, that alluded in a general way to a major terror attack the next day, were not given immediate attention and were not translated until September 12. They did not identify the time, place, or suicidal nature of the attacks, but someday there may be more informative intercepts that could save lives if translated immediately.

The number of photo interpreters employed by the government's main national imagery analysis center was slashed by 50 percent during the 1990s, eliminating hundreds of jobs as intelligence budgets were cut in the expectation that the end of the cold war would reduce foreign threats to the United States. The government's photo interpretation operations were also reorganized in 1996 in a wrenching consolidation that merged the CIA's proudly independent National Photographic Interpretation Center—the creation of Arthur Lundahl—with a variety of Pentagon analytical shops and the Defense Mapping Agency.

The new organization, the National Imagery and Mapping Agency (NIMA), was placed under Pentagon control. Many veteran CIA photo analysts, fearing that the Pentagon takeover would put a premium on producing tactical intelligence reports for the military services, retired as NIMA was being formed. The expertise vacuum created by their departure has yet to be filled, though by 2001 the recruitment and training of new photo interpreters had brought staffing back up to the level reached in 1989, before the budget reductions commenced. The agency, which has offices scattered around the Washington and St. Louis metropolitan areas, employs roughly fifteen thousand people, evenly divided between government workers and private contractors. Several thousand of them are photo analysts.

Even so, NIMA is straining to meet the ever-increasing demand for imagery intelligence from policymakers and military commanders. The two customer bases have very different needs. The president, secretary of state, and other top officials work primarily with what Washington calls national intelligence information. That is raw data and analytical reports dealing with international matters such as China's nuclear arms, North Korea's ballistic missiles, Russia's nuclear assistance to Iran, tensions between India and Pakistan, and the worldwide threat presented by terrorist groups like Al Qaeda. While the Pentagon's civilian leadership is also interested in these issues, the military services need tactical military information that can be used to plan and wage wars—or what is known in the capital as combat support intelligence. With the advent of cruise missiles, laser-guided munitions, and other sophisticated weapons systems that depend on satellite data for precise targeting and guidance, the Pentagon cannot operate effectively without a constant stream of imagery intelligence, including highly detailed maps of unfamiliar war zones like Afghanistan that are based on satellite pictures.

In recent years, combat support needs have sometimes drained attention from national intelligence requirements. That is understandable in wartime, when American forces must have access to the latest satellite images to ensure their own safety and to hit enemy targets as accurately as possible. But when it comes to fighting terrorist groups like Al Qaeda, distinctions between intelligence functions can disappear. For example, the latest information about a terrorist group can be as important to an Army special forces officer calling in air strikes in the mountains of Afghanistan as it is to White House and Pentagon officials directing the overall war against terrorism. But ever since Gen. Norman Schwarzkopf angrily complained during the Gulf War that imagery intelligence was not reaching his field commanders quickly enough to be of use on the battlefield, Washington has devoted so much attention to fixing that problem that other vital uses for satellite data have sometimes been shortchanged.

The uneven results are readily apparent. Great progress has been made in giving military forces instant access to intelligence information from airborne and space-based reconnaissance systems. This required some simple changes such as lowering the classification level of imagery so military officers without special security clearances could view it, and some difficult technical steps such as compressing the data stream so it could be more easily transmitted to mobile units in remote locations. The fusion of intelligence information with combat operations helped produce the quick victories over Taliban and Al Qaeda forces in Afghanistan in 2001 and 2002.

Meantime, NIMA, which should be brimming with state-of-the-art computers designed for examining digital imagery, limps along with outmoded equipment. As of 2002, only 15 percent of the satellite pictures transmitted to Washington were called up on computer terminals and examined by photo interpreters using the latest software for enhancing and enlarging the images. The rest of the digital images had to be transformed into conventional black-and-white photographs that were then studied with magnifying equipment using the same basic technology that was available when Bud Wheelon ordered Les Dirks to start work on an instant imaging system in 1963. Some photo interpreters prefer working with film—for one thing, they can keep it handy instead of going through a cumbersome process to get digital images transferred from a central tape bank to a computer station. Still, it was as though the government had developed a sleek, beautifully engineered racing car and then hitched it to an ox to haul it around the track. It was only after the terror attacks in 2001 that the Bush administration and Congress acted to equip NIMA with enough computer work stations to remedy the imbalance. By 2004, the agency expects that 85 percent of its photo interpretation work will be done with computers.

Even NIMA's belated modernization program may soon prove insufficient because the number of imagery satellites is expected to grow rapidly in mid-decade with the launch of a new generation of smaller, less expensive photoreconnaissance and radar-imaging systems. This program, labeled Future Imagery Architecture (FIA) by its sponsor, the National Reconnaissance Office, was devised in the 1990s to supplement and eventually supplant the KH-11 program.

The impulse was not simply to replace an aging program that had served the nation for a quarter century but also to deal with a technological paradox created by the mammoth KH-11 satellites that are equipped with both optical and infrared sensing systems. They were, in effect, too much of a good thing. The powerful satellites were so large and expensive—more than $1 billion apiece—that the government never operated more than two or three at a time, limiting coverage of the globe. And if the replacement for a retiring KH-11 was lost on launch because of a rocket failure, months might pass before another satellite was built and ready to be placed in orbit, hindering Washington's intelligence gathering.

The heavy investment in these systems also left insufficient money in the intelligence budget to produce new broad-area search systems like the KH-9, or Hexagon, that could provide a look at out-of-the-way places and large swaths of remote territory that high-resolution systems could not adequately watch, even after the newest KH-11 models, called Improved Crystal, were outfitted with some broad-search capabilities. The last Hexagon satellite stopped working in 1984. Though search satellites lack the kind of eye-popping detail produced by the KH-11's high-resolution optics, they can show terror training camps, weapons development centers, and other sites that might alert the United States to developing threats. Panoramic pictures are also essential to the Pentagon in preparing for military operations in areas like Afghanistan, where battle planners need to scan hundreds of square miles of territory at one time so they can identify enemy positions, locate airfields and potential landing zones, plot the movement of American aircraft and ground troops, and mark civilian settlements and refugee camps so they will not be accidentally attacked. Maps based on such photographs are critically important to combat pilots when operating over unfamiliar terrain.

The Future Imagery Architecture program, which at an estimated cost of more than $4 billion is the most expensive spy project in the nation's history, will give Washington a much larger fleet of reconnaissance satellites. Instead of four or five large imagery satellites in orbit at any time, there will be nearly a dozen smaller photo and radar-imaging satellites. In theory, that should provide more continuous and comprehensive coverage of the earth's surface, allowing Washington to monitor trouble spots without the prolonged blackout periods that are common now as photo interpreters wait for satellites to make another pass over a particular place. The more compact satellites, which are being built by Boeing with the assistance of dozens of subcontractors, will sacrifice some resolution in the interest of obtaining more extensive coverage. The Raytheon Systems Company is developing a new network of ground stations to handle the new satellites and the data they generate.

For now, the government's answer to the shortage of panoramic images is to buy pictures taken by privately operated systems like the Ikonos satellite put in orbit in 1999 by Space Imaging, Incorporated, a Colorado company. The company sells much of its imagery to the government, which retains the right to exercise "shutter control" over private American satellite operators during wartime by ordering them to give Washington sole access to pictures of potentially sensitive locations like Afghanistan, Pakistan, and Iraq.

When the Pentagon turned to Space Imaging for help after September 11, 2001, however, taking advantage of Washington's "shutter control" powers turned out to be a lot more complicated than the Clinton administration had anticipated in the mid-1990s, revealing another unforeseen flaw in the spy satellite empire. The company was not the problem—it was content to sell the Pentagon all its images of Afghanistan and Pakistan. But when technicians at Space Imaging's headquarters outside Denver tried to transmit the digital images to NIMA in Washington on high-speed commercial lines, they discovered the agency couldn't handle the data stream. Though NIMA's electronic systems were compatible with the government's spy satellites, they lacked the bandwidth to receive the data from Space Imaging. The company improvised by copying the images on CD-ROMs and shipping them overnight to Washington, but they then sat unused for several weeks in the imagery library at Bolling Air Force Base. Because of the delay, American pilots had to rely on Russian maps of Afghanistan and other outdated sources during the first weeks of the war.

As Washington regroups to deal with terrorist threats and abandons its historic reluctance to use military force preemptively to protect the nation from potential attack, the dream of intelligence planners is to create a constellation of space and airborne reconnaissance systems that is better designed than the present one to gather information about terror groups. In the word of one NIMA official, these new systems, working together, would provide a "God's-eye view" of the world—the ability to look anywhere, anytime. Or to put it in more technical terms, the goal is to move from periodic reconnaissance to constant surveillance.

For now, omnipresent surveillance is beyond the nation's reach, though the government has taken some strides toward that goal in recent years with the development of unmanned, remote-controlled spy planes like the Predator and Global Hawk. The Predator made its operational debut in a limited role during the air war over Kosovo in 1999, then moved to center stage in the war in Afghanistan, where it gave the CIA and military commanders a remarkably clear view of ground action as it unfolded. The Predator, which was developed for the CIA by General Atomics Aeronautical Systems, and the Global Hawk, produced for the Air Force by Northrop Grumman, can hover for many hours over one location—something reconnaissance satellites cannot do—or perform a variety of other surveillance jobs, like following a caravan of vehicles as it crosses the desert or mountains. Thanks to some creative engineering touches encouraged by the CIA, the Predator can be armed with Hellfire air-to surface missiles. On November 3, 2002, a missile fired from a Predator killed a suspected Al Qaeda leader as he was traveling by car through a remote area of Yemen.

Unhappily, advances in spy technology like the Predator and Global Hawk have been more the exception than the rule in recent years. Indeed, the nation is still working mostly with technologies that were first developed during the 1950s and refined in the 1960s and 1970s. That is a tribute to the extraordinary advances that were made then, and a testament to the absence of comparable innovation in the years since. Given the deadening weight of large governmental and business institutions and the political and financial penalties associated with projects that take time to perfect, it is an open question whether government, industry, and the academic community can rekindle the kind of creative partnerships that flourished in earlier years. In the 1990s, universities and new technology companies, often working in tandem, acted as engines of innovation in America, leaving government agencies like the CIA and NSA struggling to keep up with rapid advances in information technologies, including computing, encryption, data processing, and telecommunications.

There are plenty of people at the White House, Pentagon, CIA, NRO, NSA, and NIMA talking about the urgent need for a new burst of innovation to produce technologies tailored to collecting intelligence on terror networks and tracking the proliferation of chemical, biological, and nuclear weapons. Nearly every spy agency now has a department devoted to looking over the horizon at new ideas. After September 11, 2001, they all got an infusion of money to fund research and development projects. There may be ways, for example, to spin off new surveillance technologies from the rapid advances in semiconductors and microcircuitry produced by companies in Silicon Valley and other high-tech centers.

It won't be easy to shed the bad habits that developed in the closing years of the last century when the science and technology shop at the CIA, once the flywheel of innovation in the spy business, lost its inventive spark, the NRO was beset with management problems, and a series of presidents relegated their science advisers to back offices where they were rarely seen or heard. It is hard to imagine people like Jim Killian or Edwin Land being given license today to visit the Oval Office at any time to draw the president's attention to daring technological projects germinating in the private sector that the Pentagon and other government organizations are reluctant to pursue. There is a tendency now, as Jimmie Hill, the former deputy director of the NRO, said, "to exaggerate the capabilities and underestimate the cost" of new overhead reconnaissance systems. Robert Gates, the director of central intelligence during the presidency of George H. W. Bush, worried even before September 11, 2001, about "a bureaucratic chase for the money" that stunts the imaginative work needed to make technological advances in the intelligence business.

Not long after the attacks of September 11, 2001, the CIA quietly invited Bud Wheelon and other surviving pioneers of the cold war spy technologies to return to Washington for a few days to advise the Agency on how it might recapture the creative spirit of an earlier era and apply it to a dangerous new world. It is not an idle matter to wonder whether the United States, as it mobilizes to confront some of the gravest threats it has ever faced, will again see the likes of the inventors and risk-takers who revolutionized spying, opened the gateway to space, and helped safeguard the nation during the most perilous years of the cold war.

NOTES

Abbreviations

The following abbreviations are used throughout the notes:

AW: Aviation Week & Space Technology

CU: Columbia University Oral History Research Office

DDEL: Dwight D. Eisenhower Presidential Library

> AW: Ann Whitman Files (Eisenhower's Papers as President of the United States)
>
> WHCF: White House Central Files
>
> NSC: White House Office Files, Office of the Special Assistant for National Security Affairs, NSC Series
>
> OCB: White House Office Files, Office of the Special Assistant for National Security Affairs, OCB Series
>
> SA: White House Office Files, Office of the Special Assistant for National Security Affairs, Special Assistant Series
>
> OSS: White House Office Files, Office of the Special Assistant for National Security Affairs, Office of the Staff Secretary Series, 1952–1961

NARA: National Archives and Records Administration

NRO: National Reconnaissance Office

NYT: The New York Times

Epigraph

vii "Corona: A Triumph of Technology," address at a symposium titled "Piercing the Curtain: Corona and the Revolution in Intelligence," sponsored by the CIA Center for the Study of Intelligence, at George Washington University, Washington, D.C., May 23, 1995.

Chapter 1: "Racing Toward Catastrophe"

4 *chilling, cold war calculus:* R. Cargill Hall, "The Truth About Overflights," *Quarterly Journal of Military History*, Spring 1997, p. 32.

5 *kept a tight rein:* Andrew Goodpaster interview, Nov. 2, 1999.

5 *authority to declare war:* At a 1959 meeting of the National Security Council, Eisenhower expressed his concern about approving more U-2 flights. According to notes prepared by his son, John S. D. Eisenhower, "Nothing, he says, would make him request authority to declare war more quickly than violation of our airspace by Soviet aircraft. He stated that while one or two flights might possibly be permissible, he is against an extensive program." Memorandum for the Record, Feb. 12, 1959. DDEL, OSS, Subject Series, Alphabetical Subseries, Box 15, Intelligence Matters (8).

8 *ineffectual performance:* Hall, "The Truth About Overflights," p. 34.

9 *broke off pursuit:* The Soviet military provided MiG pilots with no more fuel than was necessary for a mission, a system designed to discourage the pilots from defecting with their planes.

10 *air battle:* Harold R. Austin, "A Cold War Overflight of the USSR," *Daedalus Flyer,* Spring 1995, p. 17.

11 *Born in the seaside city:* http://www.spacecom.af.mil/hqafspc/history/gardner .htm

12 *"bastard":* Michael R. Beschloss, *Mayday: The U-2 Affair* (New York: Harper & Row, 1986), p. 73.

12 *received a highly secret report:* Ibid., p. 73.

12 *They examined:* A. J. Wohlstetter et al., *Vulnerability of U.S. Strategic Air Power to a Surprise Enemy Attack in 1956, SM-15* (Santa Monica, Calif.: RAND Corp., 1953).

13 *Gardner was so alarmed:* Beschloss, *Mayday,* p. 73.

13 *"the true story":* Ibid., pp. 73–74.

14 *"racing toward catastrophe":* Robert H. Ferrell, ed., *The Eisenhower Diaries* (New York: W. W. Norton, 1981), p. 262.

14 *John Hersey's harrowing account:* John Hersey, "Hiroshima," *New Yorker,* Aug. 31, 1946.

15 *"I see nothing":* Dwight D. Eisenhower, *Crusade in Europe* (New York: Doubleday, 1948), pp. 459–469.

15 *"This common purpose":* Dwight D. Eisenhower, "Chance for Peace," speech before the American Society of Newspaper Editors, Apr. 16,.1953.

16 *"equating security with territory":* John Lewis Gaddis, *We Know Now: Rethinking Cold War History* (Oxford: Oxford University Press, 1997), p. 15.

16 *the speech was alarming:* David McCullough, *Truman* (New York: Simon & Schuster, 1992), p. 486.

17 *"a political force":* George Kennan, "The Long Telegram," in *Foreign Relations of the United States, 1946,* vol. 6: *Eastern Europe, The Soviet Union,* Department of State Publication 8470 (Washington, D.C.: U.S. Government Printing Office, 1969), pp. 696–709.

19 *Lilienthal flew:* McCullough, *Truman,* pp. 747–748.

19 *Truman feared:* Ibid., p. 775.

20 *Ramenskoye airfield:* Gregory W. Pedlow and Donald E. Welzenbach, *The CIA*

and the U-2 Program, 1954–1974 (Washington, D.C.: CIA Center for the Study of Intelligence, 1998), p. 20.

20 *The new aircraft:* John Prados, *The Soviet Estimate: U.S. Intelligence Analysis and Russian Military Strength* (New York: Dial Press, 1982), p. 40.

21 *"We saw a flash":* Andrei Sakharov, *Memoirs* (New York: Alfred A. Knopf, 1990), p. 174.

21 *smaller and lighter:* The reduction in weight and size without a loss of explosive power is accomplished by, in effect, supercharging the weapons. This technique, called boosting, increases the explosive yield of an initial fission reaction that, in turn, helps power the fusion reaction. A hydrogen bomb is composed of two main parts, a small fission bomb, known as the primary stage, and a fusion bomb, called the secondary stage. The primary stage explodes first. The energy release and resulting high temperature drive together the light nuclei in the secondary stage, initiating a fusion reaction. Boosting is done by injecting a mixture of tritium and deuterium gas into the plutonium in the primary assembly. In the resulting atomic stew, the splitting of the plutonium atoms heats the tritium and deuterium mixture to the point where their atoms start fusing. The fusion, in turn, amplifies the fission by bombarding the plutonium atoms with an additional stream of high-energy neutrons. It is the equivalent of throwing kerosene on a fire. The boost in energy released by the primary assembly spikes the power of the secondary assembly.

22 *Strategic Missile Evaluation Committee:* George B. Kistiakowsky, *A Scientist in the White House* (Cambridge, Mass.: Harvard University Press, 1976), p. xxxiii.

23 *Moscow's efforts:* Prados, *The Soviet Estimate*, pp. 52–53; K. E. Tsiolkovsky, "Reactive Flying Machines," in *Exploring the Unknown: Selected Documents in the History of the U.S. Civil Space Program*, ed. John M. Logsdon (Washington, D.C.: National Aeronautics and Space Administration, 1995), p. 59.

23 *German engineers:* Prados, *The Soviet Estimate*, p. 58; William E. Burrows, *Deep Black: Space Espionage and National Security* (New York: Random House, 1986), p. 66.

23 *over Kapustin Yar:* Hall, "The Truth About Overflights," p. 33; Paul Lashmar, *Spy Flights of the Cold War* (London: Sutton Publishing, 1996), p. 79.

24 *"just appalling":* *NYT*, Sept. 12, 1995, p. C-1.

24 *"extraordinary absence of knowledge":* Richard Helms interview, Nov. 2, 1999.

24 *Most were shot down:* Burrows, *Deep Black*, p. 62.

25 *Battle of the Bulge:* Dwayne A. Day, John M. Logsdon, and Brian Latell, eds., *Eye in the Sky: The Story of the Corona Spy Satellites* (Washington, D.C.: Smithsonian Institution Press, 1998), p. 173.

25 *"We have no plan":* Peter Grose, *Gentleman Spy: The Life of Allen Dulles* (New York: Houghton Mifflin, 1994), p. 352; Emmett Hughes, *Ordeal of Power* (New York: Atheneum, 1963), p. 101.

25 *"no accurate prediction":* Dwight D. Eisenhower, remarks to cabinet on Fiscal Year 1954 budget. DDEL, WHCF, Confidential File, Box 45, National Security (1).

26 *clear superiority:* See, for example, National Intelligence Estimate 11-4-54, "Soviet Capabilities and Probable Courses of Action Through Mid-1959," Aug. 28, 1954. DDEL, NSC, Subject Subseries, Box 10, NIE 11-4-54 (2).

26 *"The problem of defense":* Victor McElheny, *Insisting on the Impossible: The Life of Edwin Land* (Reading, Mass.: Perseus Books, 1998), p. 282.

27 *"haunted":* Beschloss, *Mayday*, p. 74.

27 *"Surprise attack has a capacity":* Dwight D. Eisenhower, *The White House Years, 1953–56: Mandate for Change* (New York: Doubleday, 1963), p. 516.

27 *single 10-megaton bomb:* "The Report to the President by the Technological Capabilities Panel of the Science Advisory Committee," Feb. 14, 1955, DDEL, p. 3.

28 *"a cross of iron":* Dwight D. Eisenhower, "Chance for Peace," speech before the American Society of Newspaper Editors, Apr. 16, 1953.

28 *"We must know accurately":* Albert D. Wheelon, "Corona: The First Reconnaissance Satellites," *Physics Today*, Feb. 1997, p. 24.

29 *"Eisenhower directed the discussion":* James R. Killian Jr., *Sputnik, Scientists and Eisenhower* (Cambridge, Mass.: MIT Press, 1977), p. 68.

29 *"highly unsatisfactory":* Grose, *Gentleman Spy*, p. 403.

29 *awaiting presidential action:* R. Cargill Hall, "Post War Strategic Reconnaissance and the Genesis of Project Corona," in *Corona: Between the Sun and the Earth, the First NRO Reconnaissance Eye in Space*, ed. Robert A. McDonald (Bethesda, Md.: American Society for Photogrammetry and Remote Sensing, 1997), p. 35.

30 *Closer to home: NYT, Washington Post*, May 7–9, 1954.

30 *"The new craft is believed": NYT*, May 6, 1954.

30 *fallout shelters:* Margot A. Henriksen, *Dr. Strangelove's America: Society and Culture in the Atomic Age* (Berkeley: University of California Press, 1997), p. 95.

31 *Prosperity was spreading: Historical Statistics of the United States* (Washington, D.C.: U.S. Bureau of the Census, 1975).

31 *ambivalent mood:* Henriksen, *Dr. Strangelove's America*, p. 113.

31 *the first scheme:* F. H. Clauser, "Preliminary Design of an Experimental World-Circling Spaceship," SM-11827 (Santa Monica, Calif.: RAND Corp., May 2, 1946).

32 *nearly insurmountable:* Pedlow and Welzenbach, *The CIA and the U-2*, p. 62.

32 *work with Alfred Hitchcock:* McElheny, *Insisting on the Impossible*, p. 294.

34 *"an enormous floodlight": NYT*, Sept. 12, 1995.

CHAPTER 2: THE ORIGINS OF STRATEGIC INTELLIGENCE

35 *sobering scene:* Richard S. Leghorn interview, Dec. 2, 1999.

35 *more controlled circumstances:* Leghorn interview; Donald E. Welzenbach, unpublished manuscript, 1999, with permission of the author; "Operation Crossroads Fact Sheet," U.S. Naval Historical Center, http://www.history.navy.mil/faqs/faq76-1.htm.

36 *"for the good of mankind":* Jack Niedenthal, "A Short History of the People of Bikini Atoll," http://www.bikiniatoll.com.

37 *"awesome and frightful":* R. Cargill Hall, "Post War Strategic Reconnaissance and the Genesis of Project Corona," in *Corona: Between the Sun and the Earth, the First NRO Reconnaissance Eye in Space,* ed. Robert A. McDonald (Bethesda, Md.: American Society for Photogrammetry and Remote Sensing, 1997), pp. 27–28.

38 *presented them in Boston:* Richard S. Leghorn, "Objectives for Research and Development in Military Aerial Reconnaissance," Dec. 13, 1946, in *Selected Readings in Aerial Reconnaissance: A Reissue of a Collection of Papers from 1946 and 1948,* ed. Amrom H. Katz, P-2762 (Santa Monica, Calif.: RAND Corp., 1963).

39 *Fearing the loss:* Leghorn interview, Welzenbach manuscript; Hall, "Post War Strategic Reconnaissance," p. 29.

40 *traditional spying methods:* R. Cargill Hall, "Strategic Reconnaissance in the Cold War," *Prologue,* Summer 1996, p. 107.

40 *bold ideas and a fine eye:* George W. Goddard, with DeWitt S. Copp, *Overview: A Lifelong Adventure in Aerial Photography* (New York: Doubleday, 1969); Dik Daso, "Origins of Airpower: Hap Arnold's Early Career in Aviation Technology, 1903–1935," *Airpower Journal,* Winter 1996; Daso, "Origins of Airpower: Hap Arnold's Command Years and Aviation Technology, 1936–1945," *Airpower Journal,* Fall 1997.

42 *"rough and unpleasant":* Goddard, *Overview,* p. 11.

42 *"If you could fly high enough":* Ibid., pp. 245–246.

43 *Mees told Goddard:* Ibid., p. 273; Welzenbach manuscript.

43 *from the Boston area:* Welzenbach manuscript.

44 *"didn't bat an eye":* Goddard, *Overview,* p. 275.

44 *incongruous but productive:* Ibid., p. 276.

45 *Leghorn tested:* Leghorn interview; Welzenbach manuscript.

45 *The most creative minds:* Welzenbach manuscript.

47 *no exact accounting:* Ibid.

47 *"Americans were dying":* Richard S. Leghorn interview, May 30, 2000.

48 *flummox Soviet radar:* Richard S. Leghorn, "Aerial Reconnaissance: A paper presented to the Reconnaissance Symposium [Topeka Air Force Base], Friday, Dec. 3, 1948," in Katz, *Selected Readings in Aerial Reconnaissance,* pp. 6–12.

48 *underlined the need:* Merton E. Davies and William R. Harris, *RAND's Role in the Evolution of Balloon and Satellite Observation Systems and Related U.S. Space Technology,* R-3692 (Santa Monica, Calif.: RAND Corp., 1988), pp. 35–39.

49 *"first real attempt":* Harold F. Wienberg interview, June 4, 2000.

49 *Canberra PR3:* Leghorn interview, Dec. 2, 1999; Dick Van der Aart, *Aerial Espionage: Secret Intelligence Flights by East and West* (New York: Arco/Prentice Hall Press, 1984), p. 18.

49 *customized reconnaissance model:* Gregory W. Pedlow and Donald E. Welzenbach, *The CIA and the U-2 Program, 1954–1974* (Washington, D.C.: CIA Center for the Study of Intelligence, 1998), pp. 4–7.

49 *"pioneering in aviation":* Wienberg interview, Oct. 18, 2000.

49 *conventional thinking:* Pedlow and Welzenbach, *The CIA and the U-2*, p. 6; Leghorn interview, May 30, 2000.

50 *Truman first approved:* R. Cargill Hall, "The Truth About Overflights," *Quarterly Journal of Military History*, Spring 1997, p. 28.

51 *"real visionary":* Wienberg interview.

52 *"I had the good fortune":* Bernard A. Schriever interview, Nov. 1, 1999.

52 *"I don't want ever again":* Thomas A. Sturm, *The USAF Scientific Advisory Board: Its First Twenty Years, 1944–1964* (Washington, D.C.: USAF Historical Division Liaison Office, 1967), pp. 2–5.

54 *"difficult to believe":* Memorandum for General Craigie, Colonel Schriever, Sept. 4, 1952, NARA Record Group 341, Entry 10, Box 13, 360.6 Intelligence and Reconnaissance.

54 *distinguished consultants:* R. Cargill Hall, "Strategic Reconnaissance in the Cold War," *Prologue*, Summer 1996, p. 115.

55 *"a period in history":* "Problems of Air Force Intelligence and Reconnaissance," Beacon Hill Report, Project Lincoln, Massachusetts Institute of Technology, June 15, 1952, Personal Papers of Richard Leghorn, pp. 163–164.

55 *"turbojet-powered":* Ibid., p. 167.

55 *one of the top five objectives:* Richard S. Leghorn, "Development Planning Objectives for Intelligence and Reconnaissance: An Interim Report," June 18, 1952, Personal Papers of Richard Leghorn, pp. 13–14 and 18.

CHAPTER 3: STARGAZING IN SANTA MONICA

58 *"unprecedented use": The RAND Corporation: 40th Year* (Santa Monica, Calif.: RAND Corp., 1988), p. 3.

58 *"vigorous research and development":* Rip Bulkeley, *The Sputniks Crisis and Early United States Space Policy* (Bloomington: Indiana University Press, 1991), p. 21.

58 *blocks from the beach:* Merton E. Davies interview, Aug. 24, 1998.

59 Rockets through Space: Davies interview; Jeffrey T. Richelson, *America's Secret Eyes in Space* (New York: HarperCollins Publishers, 1990), p. 1.

61 *moved to RAND:* RAND was fully detached from Douglas in 1948 and turned into an independent, nonprofit corporation that for many years served primarily as a high-powered Air Force think tank.

61 *minimal advances:* F. H. Clauser et al., *Preliminary Design of an Experimental World-Circling Spaceship*, SM-11827 (Santa Monica, Calif.: The RAND Corp., 1946).

62 *"inflame the imagination":* Ibid., p. 2.

62 *"observation aircraft":* Ibid., p. 10.

63 *"consternation and admiration":* James E. Lipp et al., *Reference Papers Relating to a Satellite Study*, RA-15032 (Santa Monica, Calif.: RAND Corp., 1947), in *RAND's Role in the Evolution of Balloon and Satellite Observation Systems and Related U.S. Space Technology*, ed. Merton E. Davies and William R. Harris, R-3692-RC (Santa Monica, Calif.: RAND Corp., 1988), pp. 16–17.

63 *geosynchronous orbit:* Arthur C. Clarke, *Voices from the Sky: Previews of the Coming Space Age* (New York: Harper & Row, 1965).

63 *feasible but impractical:* Davies and Harris, *RAND's Role,* p. 17; Richelson, *America's Secret Eyes in Space,* p. 4.

64 *three primary benchmarks:* Richelson, *America's Secret Eyes in Space,* p. 5.

66 *"ridiculous":* Davies and Harris, *RAND's Role,* p. 28.

66 *no longer seemed implausible:* Ibid., pp. 27–30.

67 *"impossible for any nation to hide":* Wernher Von Braun, "Crossing the Last Frontier," *Collier's,* Mar. 22, 1952, in *Exploring the Unknown: Selected Documents in the History of the U.S. Civil Space Program,* ed. John M. Logsdon (Washington, D.C.: NASA, 1995), p. 180.

67 *"valuable observation post":* A. V. Grosse, "Report on the Present Status of the Satellite Problem," Aug. 25, 1953. DDEL, NASA Papers, Box 1, "Present Status of Satellite Program, 1953," p. 5.

67 *took no further action:* "Satellite Programs," DDEL.

68 *"I scolded Dick":* Davies interview.

69 *"Airfields of all sizes":* James E. Lipp and R. M. Salter, eds., *Project Feed Back Summary Report,* R-262 (Santa Monica, Calif.: RAND Corp., March 1, 1954), p. 5.

70 *"Soviet sovereignty":* Ibid., p. 146.

CHAPTER 4: SEEING AIR

73 *"I read other books":* Clarence L. "Kelly" Johnson, with Maggie Smith, *Kelly: More Than My Share of It All* (Washington, D.C.: Smithsonian Institution Press, 1989), p. 7.

74 *studying aerodynamics:* Ibid., pp. 10–15.

74 *Johnson was a natural:* Ibid., p. 16.

74 *return in a year:* Ibid., pp. 19–21.

75 *Johnson cheekily announced:* Ibid., p. 21.

75 *triple tail design:* Ibid., pp. 23–24.

75 *"hell scared out of me":* Ibid., p. 28.

76 *Skunk Works:* The Skunk Works was named after the work of a character in the comic strip "Li'l Abner."

76 *143 days:* Johnson, *Kelly,* pp. 97–99.

76 *"comical duck's waddle":* Ben R. Rich and Leo Janos, *Skunk Works* (New York: Little, Brown, 1994), pp. 107–108.

76 *"That damned Swede":* Ibid., p. 114.

77 *18 percent too large:* Ibid., p. 108.

77 *"the old man was right":* James Plummer interview, Sept. 2, 1998.

77 *"walk up to the blackboard":* Ibid.

77 *"towering personality":* Albert Wheelon interview, Aug. 27, 1998.

77 *adapting the B-57:* Gregory W. Pedlow and Donald E. Welzenbach, *The CIA and the U-2 Program, 1954–1974* (Washington, D.C.: CIA Center for the Study of Intelligence, 1998, p. 8.

78 *bypassed Lockheed:* Ibid., pp. 8–9 and 21–22.

79 *"until about 1960":* Ibid., pp. 9–10; Jay Miller, *Lockheed U-2* (Austin, Tex.: Aerofax, 1983).

79 *"maximum possible altitude":* Jay Miller, *Lockheed Martin's Skunk Works* (Leicester, Eng.: Midland Publishing, 1995), p. 73.

80 *new blend of jet fuel:* Ibid., p. 72.

80 *subsonic jet-powered glider:* Pedlow and Welzenbach, *The CIA and the U-2*, p. 47; Rich, *Skunk Works*, p. 125.

81 *"coffin corner":* Pedlow and Welzenbach, *The CIA and the U-2*, p. 76.

83 *wasting his time:* Ibid., p. 12; Harold Wienberg interview, June 4, 2000.

83 *"Bissell was immediately impressed":* R. Cargill Hall, "Post War Strategic Reconnaissance and the Genesis of Project Corona," in *Corona: Between the Sun and the Earth, the First NRO Reconnaissance Eye in Space,* ed. Robert A. McDonald (Bethesda, Md.: American Society for Photogrammetry and Remote Sensing, 1997), p. 38.

83 *"turned down our proposal":* Miller, *Skunk Works*, p. 74.

Chapter 5: "I Think I Have the Plane You Are After"

84 *fly sailplanes:* Donald E. Welzenbach interview, May 2002.

85 *"I have the plane":* Gregory W. Pedlow and Donald E. Welzenbach, *The CIA and the U-2 Program, 1954–1974* (Washington, D.C.: CIA Center for the Study of Intelligence, 1998), p. 30.

85 *invited Killian:* James R. Killian Jr., *Sputnik, Scientists and Eisenhower: A Memoir of the First Special Assistant to the President for Science and Technology* (Cambridge, Mass.: MIT Press, 1977), pp. 67–68.

87 *"felt an obligation":* Ibid., p. 86.

87 *"he was peerless":* http://www.harvardsquarelibrary.org/unitarians/killian.html

87 *"addict of H. L. Mencken":* James R. Killian Jr., *The Education of a College President, A Memoir* (Cambridge, Mass.: MIT Press, 1985), p. 1.

88 *" 'intellectual tax' ":* *NYT,* Nov. 8, 1957, p. 10.

89 *"greatest possible freedom":* Killian, *Sputnik, Scientists and Eisenhower,* p. 59.

89 *" 'that's wonderful' ":* Andrew Goodpaster interview, Nov. 2, 1999.

90 *"take instruction from nobody":* Ibid.

90 *"not help themselves":* Killian, *Sputnik, Scientists and Eisenhower,* p. 241.

90 *"I'm so grateful":* Victor McElheny, *Insisting on the Impossible: The Life of Edwin Land* (Reading, Mass.: Perseus Books, 1998), p. 301.

90 *"ready access to . . . Eisenhower":* Killian, *The Education of a College President,* p. 455.

90 *"imagination, creative powers":* Killian, *Sputnik, Scientists and Eisenhower,* p. 89.

91 *"interdisciplinary congeniality":* Killian, *The Education of a College President,* p. 455.

92 *"an authentic genius":* Killian, *Sputnik, Scientists and Eisenhower,* p. 87.

92 *"of immense consequence":* Ibid.

92 *"In meetings with presidents":* Ibid.

92 *"a genius and a showman"*: Dwayne A. Day, John M. Logsdon, and Brian Latell, eds., *Eye in the Sky: The Story of the Corona Spy Satellites* (Washington, D.C.: Smithsonian Institution Press, 1998), p. 187.

92 *"spellbinding"*: Albert Wheelon interview, Aug. 27, 1998.

92 *"values of science"*: Killian, *Sputnik, Scientists and Eisenhower*, p. 88.

93 *Their second child, Edwin:* McElheny, *Insisting on the Impossible*, pp. 13–14.

93 *intersection of science and business:* Ibid., p. 19.

94 *"orthogonal thinking"*: Ibid., p. 35.

94 *Land's first patent:* Ibid., pp. 42–49.

96 *Alfred Hitchcock:* Pedlow and Welzenbach, *The CIA and the U-2*, p. 29.

96 *"personal laboratory"*: Donald E. Welzenbach, "Din Land: Patriot from Polaroid," *Optics & Photonics News*, Oct. 1994, p. 24.

97 *"exuded confidence and intelligence"*: Sidney Drell interview, Nov. 13, 1998.

97 *"loved the black world"*: Richard S. Leghorn interview, Dec. 2, 1999.

97 *"knew more secrets"*: McElheny, *Insisting on the Impossible*, p. 328.

97 *"Everybody respected him"*: John McMahon interview, Nov. 12, 1999.

98 *"avoid wasting our resources"*: Report of the Technological Capabilities Panel, vol. 1, p. 25, DDEL.

99 *"attack might strike us"*: Ibid., vol. 2, p. 136.

99 *"answers instead of assumptions"*: Ibid., vol. 1, p. 26.

100 *proposed by Lockheed:* Pedlow and Welzenbach, *The CIA and the U-2*, pp. 30–31.

100 *Henry Yutzy:* Ibid., p. 31.

101 *"a guilty conscience"*: Welzenbach, "Din Land," p. 25.

101 *national interest compelled:* Ibid.

103 *"didn't want his role"*: Andrew Goodpaster interview, Jan. 18, 2001.

103 *behind-the-scenes:* Fred I. Greenstein, *The Hidden-Hand Presidency: Eisenhower as Leader* (New York: Basic Books, 1982).

103 *"find and photograph"*: Donald E. Welzenbach, "Science and Technology: Origins of a Directorate," *Studies in Intelligence* 30 (Summer 1986):19.

103 *"an unconventional way"*: Killian, *Sputnik, Scientists and Eisenhower*, p. 82.

103 *"could scarcely have been worse"*: Dwight D. Eisenhower, *The White House Years, 1956–61: Waging Peace* (Garden City, N.Y.: Doubleday, 1965), p. 545.

103 *B-29 photoreconnaissance plane: NYT*, Nov. 8, 1954.

104 *"admit too much"*: Michael R. Beschloss, *Mayday: The U-2 Affair* (New York: Harper & Row, 1986), p. 81.

104 *"overflight is urgent"*: Pedlow and Welzenbach, *The CIA and the U-2*, p. 33.

106 *driving around Washington:* Welzenbach, "Din Land," p. 28.

106 *"technically feasible"*: Beschloss, *Mayday*, p. 82.

106 *"through a grilling"*: Clarence L. "Kelly" Johnson, with Maggie Smith, *Kelly: More Than My Share of It All* (Washington, D.C.: Smithsonian Institution Press, 1989), p. 121.

106 *secret accounts:* Pedlow and Welzenbach, *The CIA and the U-2*, p. 36.

107 *"big for their britches"*: Nathan Twining interview with John Mason, June–September 1967, CU.

109 *"contingency reserve"*: Richard M. Bissell Jr., with Jonathan E. Lewis and Frances T. Pudlo, *Reflections of a Cold Warrior: From Yalta to Bay of Pigs* (New Haven, Conn.: Yale University Press, 1996), p. 96.

CHAPTER 6: THE ROLE OF A LIFETIME

114 *"difficult to answer"*: Richard M. Bissell Jr., with Jonathan E. Lewis and Frances T. Pudlo, *Reflections of a Cold Warrior: From Yalta to Bay of Pigs* (New Haven, Conn.: Yale University Press, 1996), p. 7.

115 *iconoclastic interests:* Evan Thomas, *The Very Best Men: Four Who Dared, the Early Years of the CIA* (New York: Simon & Schuster, 1995), p. 89.

116 *the* Sea Witch: Ibid., p. 177.

117 *"most important goals"*: Bissell, *Reflections of a Cold Warrior,* p. 13.

118 *"most worthwhile years"*: Ibid., p. 29.

119 *"met him socially"*: Ibid., p. 68.

120 *"before I committed"*: Ibid., p. 77.

121 *"With hindsight"*: Ibid., pp. 90–91.

122 *"Nobody knew"*: Richard M. Bissell interview with Ed Edwin, June 5, 1967, DDEL.

123 *"no technical background"*: Richard M. Bissell interview with Ed Edwin, Nov. 9, 1976, DDEL.

123 *"a lot of rules"*: Bob King interview, Oct. 19, 1999.

123 *"Why bother"*: Ibid.

123 *"Don't come in"*: John McMahon interview, Nov. 12, 1999.

124 *"only regulations"*: Stanley Beerli interview, Sept. 23, 1999.

124 *"how to twist arms"*: Arthur Lundahl interview with Peter Jessup, June 10–Oct. 8, 1981, CU.

124 *"about five pages"*: Bissell, *Reflections of a Cold Warrior,* p. 99.

124 *"barrier of secrecy"*: Ibid., p. 100.

125 *"Bissell turned to Land"*: King interview.

125 *"potential consequences"*: Bissell, *Reflections of a Cold Warrior,* p. 100.

125 *"very knowledgeable"*: Clarence L. "Kelly" Johnson, with Maggie Smith, *Kelly: More Than My Share of It All* (Washington, D.C.: Smithsonian Institution Press, 1989), p. 122.

125 *"loved that stuff"*: King interview.

125 *"always business"*: Ibid.

126 *steak and kidney pie:* Betty King interview, Oct. 19, 1999.

CHAPTER 7: "THIS THING IS MADE OUT OF TOILET PAPER"

128 *"beautiful picture postcards"*: Ben R. Rich and Leo Janos, *Skunk Works* (New York: Little, Brown, 1994), pp. 117–118.

129 *"speed and secrecy"*: Jay Miller, *Lockheed Martin's Skunk Works* (Leicester, Eng.: Midland Publishing, 1995), p. 77.

129 *expressed puzzlement:* Gregory W. Pedlow and Donald E. Welzenbach, *The CIA and the U-2 Program, 1954–1974* (Washington, D.C.: CIA Center for the Study of Intelligence, 1998), p. 60.

129 *not marked* SECRET: Presentation by Henry G. Combs, U-2 History Symposium, National Defense University, Sept. 17, 1998.

130 *shortage of Flit:* Pedlow and Welzenbach, *The CIA and the U-2*, p. 62.

131 *stuffed with sanitary napkins:* William E. Burrows, "That New Black Magic," *Air & Space*, Dec. 1998–Jan. 1999, p. 32.

131 *"made out of toilet paper":* Transcript, "Spy in the Sky," *The American Experience*, PBS.

131 *"redraw it":* Burrows, "That New Black Magic," p. 31.

132 *less vulnerable:* Pedlow and Welzenbach, *The CIA and the U-2*, p. 47.

135 *not fully understood:* Richard P. Hallion, Air Force History and Museums Program, "Aerospace Medicine Nears the Millennium: Adaptation, Anticipation and Advancement," address before the Aerospace Medical Association, May 17, 1999.

135 *new pressure suit:* Both Lovelace and Flickinger had firsthand experience with high-altitude parachuting. Dr. Lovelace had tested oxygen equipment specially designed for bailouts by jumping from a B-17 bomber at 40,000 feet over Washington State on June 25, 1943. The daring jump—Lovelace's first and last—was chronicled by both *Life* and *Look* magazines, a public relations coup in those days. He was knocked unconscious when his parachute opened with tremendous force in the thin air and his left hand was badly frostbitten in the subzero temperature after two layers of gloves came loose. Limply swinging like a rag doll in his parachute harness, Lovelace drifted back to earth for better than ten minutes before regaining consciousness at about 8,000 feet. He landed in a daze in a wheat field. During World War II, Dr. Flickinger had jumped from planes over the border between Burma and China to give medical assistance to pilots who had been shot down ferrying cargo to China. After the war years he had worked on aircraft ejection seats that incorporated oxygen canisters that would prevent pilots from blacking out as they descended to lower altitudes.

138 *long landing strip:* Chris Pocock, *The U-2 Spyplane: Toward the Unknown* (Atglen, Pa.: Schiffer Publishing, 2000), p. 27.

138 *"the deeper we sank":* Richard M. Bissell Jr., with Jonathan E. Lewis and Frances T. Pudlo, *Reflections of a Cold Warrior: From Yalta to Bay of Pigs* (New Haven, Conn.: Yale University Press, 1996), p. 102.

139 *the edge of space:* Pedlow and Welzenbach, *The CIA and the U-2*, pp. 72–73.

139 *"don't even have a credit rating":* Clarence L. "Kelly" Johnson, with Maggie Smith, *Kelly: More Than My Share of It All* (Washington, D.C.: Smithsonian Institution Press, 1989), p. 123.

140 *"fuselage out of jig":* Jay Miller, *Lockheed U-2* (Austin, Tex.: Aerofax, 1983), p. 78.

140 *dubbed the U-2:* Pedlow and Welzenbach, *The CIA and the U-2*, p. 66.

141 *"I'll give it one shot":* Michael R. Beschloss, *Mayday: The U-2 Affair* (New York: Harper & Row, 1986), p. 105.

141 *"searching my heart and mind"*: Dwight D. Eisenhower, *The White House Years, 1953–56: Mandate for Change* (Garden City, N.Y.: Doubleday, 1963), p. 520.

142 *refine its targeting plans:* Sergei Khrushchev interview with R. Cargill Hall and Richard S. Leghorn, July 5, 1995.

142 *"a limited success"*: Eisenhower, *Mandate for Change*, p. 530.

143 *"a big goddamn sailplane"*: Rich and Janos, *Skunk Works*, p. 131.

143 *"so smooth"*: Ibid., p. 135.

144 *"wings flapping about"*: Presentation by Ernest Joiner, U-2 History Symposium, National Defense University, Sept. 17, 1998.

144 *"Pogo sticks worked real well"*: Miller, *Lockheed U-2*, p. 79.

145 *"bounce itself to pieces"*: "Spy in the Sky" transcript.

145 *"down and safe"*: Ibid.

146 *nothing about the U-2:* Donald E. Welzenbach unpublished manuscript.

146 *"great gains for the West"*: *U.S. News & World Report*, Aug. 5, 1955, pp. 70–75.

146 *"easily have airplanes"*: Ibid.

147 *Bissell told him:* Welzenbach manuscript.

147 *"seen the light"*: Ibid.

147 *"glamorous and high-priority"*: Bissell, *Reflections of a Cold Warrior*, p. 109.

148 *"civilian operation"*: Beschloss, *Mayday*, p. 106.

148 *"lock, stock, and barrel"*: Nathan Twining interview with John Mason, June–September 1967, CU.

148 *"quite a year"*: Miller, *Skunk Works*, p. 80.

CHAPTER 8: PHOTOGRAPHING THE PRESIDENT'S CATTLE

149 *"long-focal-length"*: "The U-2 Camera, Its Creation and Technical Capabilities," presentation by James G. Baker, U-2 History Symposium, National Defense University, Sept. 17, 1998.

150 *"untested frontiers"*: Ibid.

151 *logical way:* Gregory W. Pedlow and Donald E. Welzenbach, *The CIA and the U-2 Program, 1954–1974* (Washington, D.C.: CIA Center for the Study of Intelligence, 1998), pp. 48–55.

152 *sharper pictures:* Ibid.

152 *replaced the prism:* Ibid.; Baker, "The U-2 Camera"; Chris Pocock, *The U-2 Spyplane: Toward the Unknown* (Atglen, Pa.: Schiffer Publishing, 2000), pp. 25–26.

152 *exposed simultaneously:* Pocock, *The U-2 Spyplane*, pp. 25–26.

153 *disappointing results:* Pedlow and Welzenbach, *The CIA and the U-2*, p. 55.

154 *good enough to enlarge:* Arthur Lundahl interview with Peter Jessup, June 10–Oct. 8, 1981, CU.

154 *"other problems were slippery"*: Ibid.

155 *"articulate speaker"*: Dino A. Brugioni, *Eyeball to Eyeball: The Inside Story of the Cuban Missile Crisis* (New York: Random House, 1990), p. 11.

155 *"win the next war"*: Lundahl interview.

155 *"enlightened leadership"*: Ibid.

155 *"primitive conditions"*: Ibid.
155 *"Sherlock Holmes"*: Ibid.
156 *"certain disbelief"*: Ibid.
156 *"nothing compared"*: Ibid.
157 *"you don't think"*: Peter Grose, *Gentleman Spy: The Life of Allen Dulles* (New York: Houghton Mifflin, 1994), p. 404.
158 *"intelligence Automat"*: Lundahl interview.
159 *"above average qualifications"*: Memorandum for Mr. Richard Bissell, Dec. 27, 1955, NARA, Record Group 263, CIA Declassified Reference Material, Box 44, Folder 13.
159 *lacked the experience:* Pocock, *The U-2 Spyplane*, p. 35.
159 *"only American pilots"*: Ben R. Rich and Leo Janos, *Skunk Works* (New York: Little, Brown, 1994), p. 142.
159 *secret government operation:* Martin Knutson interview, Nov. 22, 1999.
159 *"exotic state-of-the-art airplane"*: Ibid.
161 *serious medical enterprise:* Photographs in private collection of Dr. Donald E. Kilgore Jr., former chief executive officer of the clinic.
161 *"nature's sanatorium"*: Jake W. Spidle Jr., *The Lovelace Medical Center: Pioneer in American Health Care* (Albuquerque: University of New Mexico Press, 1987), p. 5.
162 *clinic began in 1922:* Spidle, *The Lovelace Medical Center,* p. 36; Richard G. Elliott, "On a Comet, Always: A Biography of Dr. W. Randolph Lovelace II," *New Mexico Quarterly* 36, no. 4, 1966, pp. 356–357; Shirley Thomas, *Men of Space: Profiles of the Leaders in Space Research, Development and Exploration* (Philadelphia: Chilton, 1960), p. 42.
162 *"parachute and a first-aid kit"*: Donald Kilgore interview, Mar. 18, 2001.
163 *"shotgun approach"*: Ibid.
163 *"one look at it"*: Knutson interview.
163 *"no kids' toy"*: Ibid.
163 *"highest-workload plane"*: Ibid.
164 *"aircraft will come apart"*: Ibid.
165 *from Mars:* Pedlow and Welzenbach, *The CIA and the U-2,* pp. 78–79; Pocock, *The U-2 Spyplane*, p. 39; Richard M. Bissell Jr., with Jonathan E. Lewis and Frances T. Pudlo, *Reflections of a Cold Warrior: From Yalta to Bay of Pigs* (New Haven, Conn.: Yale University Press, 1996), p. 107.
165 *external bladder:* Pedlow and Welzenbach, *The CIA and the U-2,* p. 64.
165 *as much as six pounds:* Ibid., p. 65.
166 *members of Congress:* Ibid., p. 88.
167 *"close to incredible"*: Andrew Goodpaster interview, November 2, 1999; transcript, "Spy in the Sky," *The American Experience,* PBS.
168 *full responsibility:* Pedlow and Welzenbach, *The CIA and the U-2,* p. 89.
168 *"other parts of the world"*: Ibid., p. 94; Pocock, *The U-2 Spyplane*, p. 43.

CHAPTER 9: BIG GAME HUNTING

170 *"formidable sight"*: *NYT,* May 2, 1954, p. 1.

170 *Bison bombers:* NIE 11-4-54, "Soviet Capabilities and Probable Courses of Action Through Mid-1959," Sept. 14, 1954, in *Estimates on Soviet Military Power 1954 to 1984, A Selection,* ed. Donald P. Steury (Washington, D.C.: CIA Center for the Study of Intelligence, December 1994), p. 36.

171 *"biggest air force"*: *NYT,* May 15, 1954, p. 5.

171 *"sober inferences"*: *NYT,* June 20, 1954, p. 1.

171 *somewhat more positive: NYT,* June 21, 1954, p. 1.

172 *vast destruction: NYT,* Feb. 9, 1956, p. 1.

173 *"in the process of surpassing"*: *NYT,* May 18, 1955, p. 1.

174 *"just not true"*: *NYT,* May 19, 1955, p. 1.

174 *"deeply concerned"*: *NYT,* June 29, 1955, p. 1.

174 *"exert every . . . effort"*: *NYT,* June 29, 1955, p. 1.

174 *"technological mystery"*: *AW,* Sept. 26, 1955, p. 14.

175 *"crucial scientific-industrial race"*: *NYT,* Feb. 2, 1956, p. 10.

175 *"proper posture"*: *NYT,* Feb. 9, 1956, p. 1. Eisenhower wished Gardner "success in the years ahead," but at least in public showed little sign that he recognized the vital role the irascible Welshman had played in pushing Washington to deal with the Soviet threat by making use of new technologies. In a brief, understated farewell letter that must have incensed Gardner, Eisenhower said Wilson "has advised me of the energy you have displayed in your work during the past three years, and I commend it." Gardner soon resumed a senior management role at Hycon Manufacturing Company, the Pasadena firm where he had worked before joining the Eisenhower administration. Before his resignation from the Air Force, the Senate Permanent Subcommittee on Investigations had questioned Gardner about possible conflicts of interest involving his role in the missile program and Hycon's work as a subcontractor. Gardner denied any conflict, but the issue stirred speculation in Washington that the problem might have spurred his resignation. Gardner died in 1963 at the age of forty-eight.

176 *"nightmare of the missilemen"*: *Time,* Jan. 30, 1956, pp. 52–56.

176 *"any point in the world"*: *U.S. News & World Report,* May 4, 1956, p. 34.

176 *"decisive surprise attack"*: J. R. Killian Jr. to Arthur S. Flemming, May 14, 1956, DDEL, OSS, Subject Series, Alphabetical Subseries, Box 16, Killian report (1).

176 *"soul-searching questions"*: Michael R. Beschloss, *Mayday: The U-2 Affair* (New York: Harper & Row, 1986), p. 118.

177 *"count the automobiles"*: Dwight D. Eisenhower, *The White House Years, 1956–61: Waging Peace* (Garden City, N.Y.: Doubleday, 1965), p. 41 of photo collection.

177 *"fail to detect it"*: Gregory W. Pedlow and Donald E. Welzenbach, *The CIA and the U-2 Program, 1954–1974* (Washington, D.C.: CIA Center for the Study of Intelligence, 1998), p. 97.

177 *"reasonable safety"*: Eisenhower, *Waging Peace*, pp. 545–546.

178 *"plane would disintegrate"*: Beschloss, *Mayday*, p. 118.

178 *"swashbuckling bravado"*: Eisenhower, *Waging Peace*, p. 546.

178 *L-pills:* Pedlow and Welzenbach, *The CIA and the U-2*, pp. 65–66.

179 *"Death will follow"*: Liquid "L" Ampoules, undated memo, NARA, Record Group 263, CIA Declassified Reference Material, Box 43, Folder 8.

179 *Lemon Drops:* Pedlow and Welzenbach, *The CIA and the U-2*, p. 125.

179 *shellfish toxin:* Ibid.

179 *deadly devices:* Evan Thomas, *The Very Best Men: Four Who Dared: The Early Years of the CIA* (New York: Simon & Schuster, 1995), p. 222. In the fall of 1960, when Bissell was directing a plot to assassinate Lumumba, he was offered a choice of toxins, including rabbit fever, undulant fever, tuberculosis, anthrax, smallpox, and sleeping sickness.

180 *outweighed the political damage: NYT*, Feb. 19, 1956, p. 24.

180 *"grounds for irritation"*: Memorandum for the Record, Conference of Joint Chiefs of Staff with the President, Feb. 10, 1956, DDEL, OSS, Alphabetical Subseries.

180 *"not interested"*: Memorandum for the Record, Mar. 13, 1956, DDEL, OSS, Subject Series, Alphabetical Subseries, Box 14, Intelligence Matters (1).

181 *test photographs:* Beschloss, *Mayday*, p. 116.

182 *"deep operations"*: Memorandum for the Record, June 21, 1956, DDEL, OSS, Subject Series, Alphabetical Subseries, Box 14, Intelligence Matters (1).

183 *"ten calendar days"*: Richard M. Bissell Jr., with Jonathan E. Lewis and Frances T. Pudlo, *Reflections of a Cold Warrior: From Yalta to Bay of Pigs* (New Haven, Conn.: Yale University Press, 1996), p. 111.

183 *elliptical memorandum:* Memorandum for the Record, July 3, 1956, DDEL, OSS, Subject Series, Alphabetical Subseries, Box 14, Intelligence Matters (2).

183 *"short leash"*: Bissell, *Reflections of a Cold Warrior*, p. 111.

183 *"big game"*: Beschloss, *Mayday*, p. 121.

183 *Mission 2013:* Pedlow and Welzenbach, *The CIA and the U-2*, pp. 104–105.

184 *"snap up and tap me"*: Transcript, "Spy in the Sky," *The American Experience*, PBS.

184 *"I didn't tell them"*: Beschloss, *Mayday*, p. 123.

184 *Bohlen . . . had not been told:* Ibid., pp. 121–122.

185 *"Fourth of July"*: "Spy in the Sky" transcript.

185 *"laughing"*: Ibid.

185 *"We welcomed him"*: *AW*, May 16, 1960; *NYT*, May 10, 1950, p. 1.

185 *"the first is the safest"*: Pedlow and Welzenbach, *The CIA and the U-2*, p. 105.

185 *"discovered or tracked"*: Ibid., p. 106.

185 *"should be suspended"*: Ibid.

186 *"at the maximum rate"*: Ibid.

186 *"actually received"*: Memorandum, for the Record, July 10, 1956, DDEL, OSS, Subject Series, Alphabetical Subseries, Box 14, Intelligence Matters (2).

187 *simply wrong:* Pedlow and Welzenbach, *The CIA and the U-2*, p. 111.

188 *"deprived Khrushchev"*: Eisenhower, *Waging Peace*, p. 547fn.

188 *"can't lay a mitt on us"*: Beschloss, *Mayday*, p. 133.

188 *"minor percentage"*: Pedlow and Welzenbach, *The CIA and the U-2*, p. 110.

189 *"loss of confidence"*: Ibid.

189 *every flight plan be submitted*: Beschloss, *Mayday*, p. 133.

189 *"dirty birds"*: Pedlow and Welzenbach, *The CIA and the U-2*, pp. 128–133.

CHAPTER 10: EARTHBOUND

194 *"more appalling"*: William E. Burrows, *This New Ocean: The Story of the First Space Age* (New York: Random House, 1998), p. 102.

195 *achievements were little known*: Walter A. McDougall, ... *The Heavens and the Earth: A Political History of the Space Age* (New York: Basic Books, 1985), p. 77.

196 *dozens of V-2 rockets*: Ibid., p. 89.

196 *Project MX-774*: Ibid., p. 97.

197 *"for a long period of time"*: Ibid., p. 98.

197 *independent Air Force*: Ibid., p. 103.

197 *smaller warhead*: Ibid., p. 106.

199 *number one ... project*: Ibid., p. 107.

199 *"truly awesome technical problems"*: Report of the Technological Capabilities Panel, DDEL, p. 63.

199 *"intercontinental ballistic missile"*: Ibid., p. 64.

199 *crippling*: R. Cargill Hall, "Post War Strategic Reconnaissance and the Genesis of Project Corona," in *Corona: Between the Sun and the Earth, the First NRO Reconnaissance Eye in Space*, ed. Robert A. McDonald (Bethesda, Md.: American Society for Photogrammetry and Remote Sensing, 1997), pp. 107–108.

200 *"System Requirement (No. 5)"*: Merton E. Davies and William R. Harris, *RAND's Role in the Evolution of Balloon and Satellite Observation Systems and Related U.S. Space Technology*, R-3692-RC (Santa Monica, Calif.: 1988), p. 61.

200 *"daylight visual coverage"*: Ibid., p. 62.

201 *one-tenth of the level*: National Reconnaissance Office, "The Corona Story," 1988, p. 5.

202 *Polar Year*: The first International Polar Year was 1882 and the second fifty years later, but scientists at that time decided it should be held every twenty-five years.

202 *a research satellite*: McDougall, ... *The Heavens*, pp. 118–119.

202 *"small, inexpensive satellites"*: Report of the Technological Capabilities Panel, p. 147.

203 *"immediate program"*: Ibid., p. 152.

204 *"psychological benefits"*: NSC 5520, "Draft Statement of Policy on U.S. Scientific Satellite Program, General Considerations," DDEL, NSC, Policy Papers Subseries, Box 16, NSC 5520 (2), p. 3.

204 *"cannot afford to lose"*: NSC 5520, Annex B.

204 *"large surveillance satellite"*: NSC 5520, pp. 2–3.

205 *register any objections:* Minutes of 250th NSC meeting, DDEL, AW, NSC Series, Box 6, 250th NSC meeting.

205 *"peaceful purposes":* NSC 5520, p. 4.

205 *"I am now announcing":* NYT, July 30, 1955, p. 8.

205 *"The only connection":* Ibid.

206 *"no utility":* Ibid., p. 1.

207 *The first Viking:* Burrows, *This New Ocean,* p. 134.

207 *Redstone would be ready:* Army Satellite Chronology, Dec. 12, 1957, DDEL, Bryce Harlow Papers, Box 2, Satellites and Missiles 1958–60, p. 2.

207 *von Braun's rocket:* McDougall, . . . *The Heavens,* p. 123.

208 *Jupiter-C:* Ibid., p. 130.

208 *more profitable Titan:* Burrows, *This New Ocean,* p. 172.

209 *"psychological importance":* Memorandum for Mr. William H. Jackson, DDEL, OCB, Subject Series, Box 8, Space Satellites, Rockets etc. (1) 1956–57.

209 *"strong moral position":* Memorandum for the Assistant Secretary of Defense, June 22, 1956, DDEL, OSS, Subject Series, Department of Defense Subseries, Box 6, Missiles and Satellites, vol. I, Jan. 56–May 57 (1).

210 *"an isolated action":* Ibid.

210 *"so many uncertainties":* NYT, May 20, 1957, p. 1.

210 *"solve the problems":* NYT, June 2, 1957, p. 1.

210 *"within the next few months":* NYT, June 11, 1957, p. 2.

210 *outlined the launch schedule:* NYT, June 23, 1957, p. 12.

211 *"the Communist world has won":* NYT, Aug. 27, 1957, p. 1.

211 *"Soviet Fires Earth Satellite":* NYT, Oct. 5, 1957, p. 1.

CHAPTER 11: CREATING CORONA

212 *"crisis of confidence":* James R. Killian Jr., *Sputnik, Scientists and Eisenhower: A Memoir of the First Special Assistant to the President for Science and Technology* (Cambridge, Mass.: MIT Press, 1977), p. 7.

213 *"a severe blow":* USIA Office of Research and Intelligence, "World Opinion and the Soviet Satellite, A Preliminary Evaluation," Oct. 17, 1957, DDEL, NSC, Briefing Notes Subseries, Box 7, Earth Satellites (3).

213 *"confused, dismayed and shaken":* Statement by George V. Allen, Director, U.S. Information Agency, before House Science and Astronautics Committee, Jan. 22, 1960, DDEL, PCIAA, Box 5, Science and Technology, No. 23 (2).

213 *"a devastating blow":* NYT, Oct. 6, 1957, p. 1.

213 *"the position . . . will be critical":* NYT, Oct. 6, 1957, p. 1.

214 *"high proficiency":* Robert R. McMath, Lawrence A. Hyland, George B. Kistiakowsky, and Francis H. Clauser to Allen W. Dulles, Oct. 23, 1957, DDEL, Papers of the Special Assistant for Science and Technology, Box 1, CIA Oct. 1957–Oct. 1958.

214 *"prepared to shed blood":* McMath et al. to Dulles, Oct. 23, 1957.

214 *"never thought of our program":* NYT, Oct. 6, 1957, p. 1.

214 *"without . . . significance"*: Robert A. Divine, *The Sputnik Challenge* (New York: Oxford University Press, 1993), p. xv.

214 *"flip and inadequate"*: Killian, *Sputnik, Scientists and Eisenhower,* p. 10.

214 *"impressive"*: Dwight D. Eisenhower, *The White House Years, 1956–61: Waging Peace* (Garden City, N.Y.: Doubleday, 1965), p. 205.

215 *"ominously suggested"*: Killian, *Sputnik, Scientists and Eisenhower,* p. 3.

215 *"respective strengths"*: Ibid., p. 5.

216 *"outer space is international"*: Proposed White House Release, Oct. 7, 1957, DDEL, James Hagerty Papers, Box 9, Satellite Announcement.

216 *"limit of national sovereignty"*: *NYT,* Oct. 13, 1957, p. 1.

217 *lacked adequate funding*: Memorandum of Conference with the President, Oct. 8, 1957, DDEL, AW, DDE Diary, Box 27, Oct. 57 staff notes (2).

217 *possible alternative*: Memorandum of Conference with the President, Oct. 8, 1957.

218 *"by one iota"*: *NYT,* Oct. 10, 1957, p. 1.

218 *"He was startled"*: Killian, *Sputnik, Scientists and Eisenhower,* pp. 10–11.

218 *"an unexpected naivete"*: *NYT,* Oct. 10, 1957, p. 1.

219 *"foothold in outer space"*: Killian, *Sputnik, Scientists and Eisenhower,* p. 9.

219 *equipped with a camera*: Minutes of 339th NSC Meeting, DDEL, AW, NSC Series, Box 9, 339th NSC Meeting, Oct. 10, 1957, p. 4.

219 *interservice rivalries*: Ibid., pp. 10–12.

220 *"Satellite That Could Film the Earth"*: *NYT,* Oct. 14, 1957, p. 1.

221 *"scientific country"*: Handwritten notes by Andrew G. Goodpaster, ODM Science Advisory Committee meeting, Oct. 15, 1957, DDEL, SA, Subject Subseries, Box 7, Science Advisory Committee (2) Mar.–Oct. 1957.

221 *"intellectual leadership"*: Killian, *Sputnik, Scientists and Eisenhower,* p. 16.

222 *"attitude toward science"*: Memorandum of Conference with the President, Oct. 15, 1957, DDEL, AW, DDE Diary, Box 27, Oct. 57 staff notes (2).

222 *second, much heavier satellite*: *NYT,* Nov. 5, 1957, p. 1.

223 *"dramatic demonstration"*: *NYT,* Nov. 4, 1957, p. 10.

223 *electronic beeps*: Ibid.

223 *still limping along*: *NYT,* Nov. 9, 1957, p. 1.

223 *"distinctly greater"*: *NYT,* Nov. 8, 1957, p. 10.

224 *"unquestioned national authority"*: Divine, *The Sputnik Challenge,* p. 50.

224 *"completely intact"*: Dwight D. Eisenhower speech, "Science in National Security," Nov. 7, 1957, DDEL, AW, Speech Series, Box 23, "Science in National Security."

225 *ablation cooling*: T. A. Heppenheimer, *Countdown: A History of Space Flight* (New York: John Wiley & Sons, 1997), pp. 83–84.

227 *"terrible design"*: Merton E. Davies and William R. Harris, *RAND's Role in the Evolution of Balloon and Satellite Observation Systems and Related U.S. Space Technology,* R-3692-RC (Santa Monica, Calif.: 1988), p. 79.

227 *well aware*: R. Cargill Hall, "Post War Strategic Reconnaissance and the Genesis of Project Corona," in *Corona: Between the Sun and the Earth, the First NRO*

Reconnaissance Eye in Space, ed. Robert A. McDonald (Bethesda, Md.: American Society for Photogrammetry and Remote Sensing, 1997), pp. 110–111.

229 *copy to Schriever:* "A History of Satellite Reconnaissance, vol. 1: Corona," National Reconnaissance Office, 1988, pp. 10–11.

229 *"priority national effort":* Richard Leghorn, memo to David Beckler, May 16, 1957, DDEL.

229 *"aerial inspection":* Because secret spy satellites were so critical to the arms control process, officials had to come up with a declassified way of talking about them to reassure the public that the agreements were verifiable. The answer was one of the oddest euphemisms of the cold war. The government, arms control officials would say, could monitor Soviet compliance through "national technical means."

230 *"second story":* Hall, "Post War Strategic Reconnaissance," p. 111.

230 *end of August:* National Reconnaissance Office, "The Corona Story," p. 11.

231 *"high water mark":* Gregory W. Pedlow and Donald E. Welzenbach, *The CIA and the U-2 Program, 1954–1974* (Washington, D.C.: CIA Center for the Study of Intelligence, 1998), p. 143.

232 *"valuable intelligence":* Merton E. Davies and Amron H. Katz et al., *A Family of Recoverable Satellites*, RM-2012 (Santa Monica, Calif.: RAND Corp., 1957), p. 1.

232 *"detailed, accurate identification":* Ibid., p. 23.

233 *"By the end":* Victor McElheny, *Insisting on the Impossible: The Life of Edwin Land* (Reading, Mass.: Perseus Books, 1998), pp. 326–327.

233 *Lockheed outlined:* WS-117L Development Plan for Program Acceleration, Lockheed Aircraft Corp., Jan. 6, 1958, foreword and introduction.

235 *"laughing-stock":* Minutes of 347th NSC Meeting, Dec. 5, 1957, DDEL, AW, NSC Series, Box 9, 347th NSC Meeting.

235 *"Vanguard Rocket Burns": NYT,* Dec. 7, 1957, p. 1.

235 *Soviet newspapers: NYT,* Dec. 8, 1957, p. 1.

236 *"New Year's Eve": NYT,* Feb. 1, 1958, p. 1.

236 *"imagination and boldness": NYT,* Feb. 2, 1958, p. 42.

238 *"selected targets":* NRO, "The Corona Story," p. 20.

238 *"Defense 'space' agency":* Memorandum of Conference with the President, Feb. 7, 1958, DDEL.

238 *favorite cigars:* NRO, "The Corona Story," p. 21.

239 *"They went ballistic":* Hall, "Post War Strategic Reconnaissance," p. 114.

240 *"stopped talking to me":* Merton Davies interview, Aug. 24, 1998.

Chapter 12: "Go Off and Build That Thing"

241 *"pretty shocking":* James Plummer interview, Sept. 2, 1998.

242 *"a flood of water":* Ibid.; Dwayne A. Day, John M. Logsdon, and Brian Latell, eds., *Eye in the Sky: The Story of the Corona Spy Satellites* (Washington, D.C.: Smithsonian Institution Press, 1998), p. 191.

243 *"take chances"*: Plummer interview.

244 *"second-guessing"*: Ibid.

245 *"without telling anyone"*: Day et al., *Eye in the Sky*, p. 192.

246 *"scared us all"*: Ibid., p. 185.

246 *"25-foot ground resolution"*: Ibid., p. 195.

246 *Old Executive Office Building*: No records of this meeting have been found, and there is some discrepancy in recollections of where it was held. Although the official NRO history of Corona's development places it in Cambridge, historian R. Cargill Hall notes that some sources recall meetings were held in Cambridge, while others specifically remember making a trip to Washington. Ibid., p. 273; National Reconnaissance Office, "The Corona Story," 1988, p. 25.

247 *add the Itek proposal*: NRO, "The Corona Story," p. 25.

247 *"being broke"*: "Corona Program History, Vol. 1: Program Overview," Directorate of Science and Technology, CIA, May 19, 1976, NRO, p. 2-2.

248 *casual approach*: NRO, "The Corona Story," p. 26.

248 *"speak in a . . . low voice"*: Memorandum for Project Security Officer, Mar. 27, 1958, NRO.

249 *"more convenient camera"*: Richard M. Bissell Jr., with Jonathan E. Lewis and Frances T. Pudlo, *Reflections of a Cold Warrior: From Yalta to Bay of Pigs* (New Haven, Conn.: Yale University Press, 1996), p. 136.

249 *approved the plan verbally*: NRO, "The Corona Story," p. 28.

249 *"preselected ocean area"*: Project Corona Outline, Apr. 15, 1958, NRO.

250 *"unprogrammed requirement"*: Memorandum for the Comptroller, reprinted in *Corona: Between the Sun and the Earth—The First NRO Reconnaissance Eye in Space*, ed. Robert A. McDonald (Bethesda, Md.: American Society for Photogrammetry and Remote Sensing, 1997), p. 309.

251 *"juggling costs"*: NRO, "The Corona Story," p. 41.

251 *force cancellation*: Ibid.

251 *"considerable confusion"*: Memorandum for Maj. Gen. Jacob E. Smart, Nov. 25, 1958, NRO.

252 *"ironclad agreement"*: "Corona Program History, Vol. 2: Governmental Activities," Directorate of Science and Technology, CIA, May 19, 1976, NRO, pp. 3-2, 4-64 and 4-65.

252 *Corona cutbacks*: Memorandum for Deputy Secretary of Defense and Special Assistant to the President for Science and Technology, in CIA Office of Special Projects History, Vol. 3, Appendix A, NRO.

252 *"Battle's Laws"*: reprinted in McDonald, *Corona*, p. 308.

253 *"quickly and cleanly"*: NRO, "The Corona Story," p. 30.

253 *ruin the film*: Ibid., p. 35.

254 *"no 'experts' "*: "Corona Program History, Vol. 5: System Integration," Directorate of Science and Technology, CIA, May 19, 1976, NRO, p. 1–5.

254 *"photograph the belfry"*: War College Speech Given by Maj. Gen. Bernard Schriever, Apr. 1, 1959, NRO.

254 " *'Black Saturdays'* ": Albert D. Wheelon, "Corona: A Triumph of American Technology," in Day et al., *Eye in the Sky*, p. 37.

255 *"player piano"*: McDonald, *Corona*, p. 270.

255 *"one paragraph"*: Plummer interview.

255 *"Develop and provide"*: Work Statement: Development of a Satellite Reconnaissance and Recovery System, Apr. 25, 1958, NRO.

256 *"nothing was known"*: "Corona Program History, Vol. 2: Governmental Activities," Directorate of Science and Technology, CIA, May 19, 1976, NRO, p. 3-7.

256 *host of other problems*: "Corona Program History, Vol. 3: Corona Cameras," Directorate of Science and Technology, CIA, May 19, 1976, NRO, pp. 2-3, 2-4, 4-1, 4-2.

256 *Design alterations*: "Corona Program History, Vol. 3," pp. 4-1, 4-2.

257 *far behind*: "Corona Program History, Vol. 2," p. 3-7.

257 *"There was no way"*: Don H. Schoessler and Charles Spoelhof interview with Cargill Hall, May 16, 1997, NRO.

258 *steel film*: Ibid.

258 *fine glass particles*: Ibid.

260 *rapid series of steps*: "Corona Program History, Vol. 4: Recovery from Orbit," Directorate of Science and Technology, CIA, May 19, 1976, NRO, p. 2-12.

260 *After separation*: "Corona Program History, Vol. 4," pp. 2-12–2-15.

261 *doubted the plan*: Curtis Peebles, *The Corona Project: America's First Spy Satellites* (Annapolis, Md.: Naval Institute Press, 1997), p. 59.

262 *"filing, chipping and sawing"*: "Corona Program History, Vol. 5," p. 1-10.

266 *camera ports*: NRO, "The Corona Story," p. 44.

266 *"hundreds of people"*: "Spies Above: National Photographic Interpretation Center," video produced by NRO.

267 *"no capability"*: "Corona Program History, Vol. 2," p. 4-43.

267 *"live animals"*: Ibid., p. 4-39.

267 *"Polar orbit"*: Ibid., p. 4-42.

268 *"I didn't know"*: John Finney interview, Oct. 21, 1999.

268 *"basic information"*: *NYT*, Dec. 4, 1958, p. 1.

269 *200 square miles*: *AW*, Dec. 8, 1958, p. 31.

CHAPTER 13: HEARTBREAK

270 *"followed his hunches"*: Michael R. Beschloss, *Mayday: The U-2 Affair* (New York: Harper & Row, 1986), p. 161.

270 *"mounting almost to panic"*: Dwight D. Eisenhower, *The White House Years, 1956–61: Waging Peace* (Garden City, N.Y.: Doubleday, 1965), p. 546.

271 *The mishap*: Memorandum for the Record, Feb. 6, 1959, NRO.

271 *"Eisenhower upbraided"*: National Reconnaissance Office, "The Corona Story," 1988, p. 47.

271 *"signed the report"*: "Secret Satellite," video produced by NRO.

271 *carried no camera:* NRO, "The Corona Story," p. 47.

273 *"deterrent remains effective"*: Memorandum of Conference with the President, Feb. 4, 1958, DDEL, AW, DDE Diaries Series, Box 18, Staff Notes Feb. 1958.

273 *"new type of threat"*: National Intelligence Estimate 11-6-54, "Soviet Capabilities and Probably Programs in the Guided Missile Field," Oct. 5, 1954, in *Sherman Kent and the Board of National Estimates: Collected Essays*, ed. Donald Steury, (Washington, D.C.: CIA Center for the Study of Intelligence, 1994), p. 56.

273 *intercontinental missile:* Addendum to CIA Draft of Special National Intelligence Estimate 11-10-57, "Soviet ICBM Production and Deployment," in *CIA's Analysis of the Soviet Union 1947–1991: A Documentary Collection*, eds. Gerald K. Haines and Robert E. Leggett (Washington, D.C.: CIA Center for the Study of Intelligence, 2001), p. 9.

274 *"gravest danger": Washington Post*, Dec. 20, 1957.

274 *knockout attack:* Eisenhower, *Waging Peace*, p. 220.

274 *Joseph Alsop:* Edgar M. Bottome, *The Missile Gap: A Study of the Formulation of Military and Political Policy* (Rutherford, N.J.: Fairleigh Dickinson University Press, 1971), p. 80.

275 *top secret estimate:* Memorandum of Conference with the President, June 18, 1958, DDEL, AW, DDE Diaries Series, Box 20, Staff Notes June 1958.

276 *5-megaton warhead:* Gregory W. Pedlow and Donald E. Welzenbach, *The CIA and the U-2 Program, 1954–1974* (Washington, D.C.: CIA Center for the Study of Intelligence, 1998), pp. 159–60.

276 *balance of power: NYT*, Jan. 28, 1959, p. 1.

276 *"serial production"*: Pedlow and Welzenbach, *The CIA and the U-2*, p. 160.

277 *arsenal of five hundred:* Briefing of the Director of Central Intelligence, Senate Armed Services Committee, CIA Subcommittee, Jan. 16, 1959, NARA, Record Group 263, CIA Declassified Reference Material, Box 25, Folder 6, pp. 6 and 9.

277 *"very great danger": NYT*, Jan. 30, 1959, p. 1.

278 *"Won't Race":* Ibid.

278 *"books have been juggled"*: John Prados, *The Soviet Estimate: U.S. Intelligence Analysis and Russian Military Strength* (New York: Dial Press, 1982), p. 90.

278 *artificially reduced:* Pedlow and Welzenbach, *The CIA and the U-2*, pp. 159–161.

278 *"undue influence"*: Memorandum of a Conference with the President, Feb. 10, 1959, DDEL, OSS, Subject Series, Alphabetical Subseries, Box 15, Intelligence Matters (8).

279 *U-3:* Jay Miller, *Lockheed Martin's Skunk Works* (Leicester, Eng.: Midland Publishing, 1995), p. 114.

280 *"especially, more speed"*: Clarence L. "Kelly" Johnson, with Maggie Smith, *Kelly: More Than My Share of It All* (Washington, D.C.: Smithsonian Institution Press, 1989), p. 135.

280 *"three times the speed of sound"*: Ben R. Rich and Leo Janos, *Skunk Works* (New York: Little, Brown, 1994), p. 193.

280 *"five miles higher"*: Ibid.

280 *"Archangel"*: Miller, *Skunk Works*, p. 114.

280 *"blazing speed"*: Rich and Janos, *Skunk Works,* p. 197.

281 *"get the map"*: Richard M. Bissell Jr. interview with Ed Edwin, June 5, 1967, DDEL.

282 *Twining seconded:* Memorandum for the Record, John S. D. Eisenhower, Feb. 12, 1959, DDEL, OSS, Subject Series, Alphabetical Subseries, Box 15, Intelligence Matters (8).

282 *"surrender of West Berlin"*: Eisenhower, *Waging Peace*, p. 446.

283 *brazen violations:* Memorandum for the Record, John S. D. Eisenhower, DDEL.

283 *ample intelligence:* Pedlow and Welzenbach, *The CIA and the U-2*, pp. 147 and 161–162.

283 *warned Eisenhower:* Ibid., pp. 161–162.

283 *a mirage:* Memorandum for the Record, John S. D. Eisenhower, Feb. 12, 1959.

283 *at Tyuratam:* Pedlow and Welzenbach, *The CIA and the U-2*, p. 160.

284 *"political costs"*: Memorandum of Conference with the President, Apr. 7, 1959, DDEL, OSS, Subject Series, Alphabetical Subseries, Box 15, Intelligence Matters (10).

284 *"terrible propaganda"*: Ibid.

284 *"some kind of progress"*: Ibid.

285 *"I felt less sure"*: Ibid.

285 *"cloud of white smoke"*: *NYT,* Apr. 14, 1959, p. 1.

286 *"north-south orbit"*: Ibid.

286 *"return with their information"*: Ibid.

286 *"snag the parachute"*: Ibid.

286 *"It was a bad night"*: Frank Buzard interview, Nov. 17, 1999.

286 *"starburst"*: *NYT,* Apr. 23, 1959.

286 *embarrassing mistake: NYT,* Apr. 15, 1959, p. 1.

287 *"pretty convinced"*: James Plummer interview, Sept. 2, 1998.

287 *"circular tracks"*: Dwayne A. Day, "The Development and Improvement of the Corona Satellite," in Dwayne A. Day, John M. Logsdon, and Brian Latell, eds., *Eye in the Sky: The Story of the Corona Spy Satellites* (Washington, D.C.: Smithsonian Institution Press, 1998), p. 53.

288 *furry passengers:* "Corona Program History, Vol. 1: Program Overview," p. 5-2.

288 *Animal rights groups:* Ibid.

289 *"hideously expensive"*: Richard M. Bissell Jr., with Jonathan E. Lewis and Frances T. Pudlo, *Reflections of a Cold Warrior: From Yalta to Bay of Pigs* (New Haven, Conn.: Yale University Press, 1996), p. 137.

289 *"crying need"*: Day et al., *Eye in the Sky*, p. 182.

289 *" 'It's so important' "*: Ibid., p. 174.

290 *"bad weather"*: Andrew Goodpaster interview, Nov. 2, 1999.

290 *"let's proceed"*: Plummer interview.

290 *"guessing game"*: Bissell, *Reflections of a Cold Warrior,* p. 137.

291 *controlled by bandits:* Memorandum for the Record, Andrew Goodpaster, July 7,

1959, DDEL; Chris Pocock, *The U-2 Spyplane: Toward the Unknown* (Atglen, Pa.: Schiffer Publishing, 2000), p. 152.

291 *"costly and harmful"*: Memorandum of a Conference with the President, July 8, 1959, DDEL.

292 *"fight a war"*: Ibid.

292 *"assent to the operation"*: Ibid.

292 *take off before dawn*: Stanley Beerli interview, Sept. 23, 1999; Pocock, *The U-2 Spyplane*, pp. 152–153.

293 *"Really getting hairy"*: Rich and Janos, *Skunk Works*, p. 150.

293 *photographs were superb*: Pedlow and Welzenbach, *The CIA and the U-2*, p. 163.

293 *"stock of rockets"*: William E. Burrows, *Deep Black: Space Espionage and National Security* (New York: Random House, 1986), p. 101.

294 *beset with problems*: "Corona Program History, Vol. 1: Program Overview," pp. 5-3 and 5-4.

294 *"bleakest moment"*: Victor McElheny, *Insisting on the Impossible: The Life of Edwin Land* (Reading, Mass.: Perseus Books, 1998) p. 331.

294 *"multiple failures"*: "Corona Program History, Vol. 1: Program Overview," p. 5-4.

295 *"pressed on"*: Albert D. Wheelon, "Corona: A Triumph of American Technology," in Day et al., *Eye in the Sky*, p. 38.

295 *crumbled into dust*: National Reconnaissance Office, "The Corona Story," 1988, pp. 48–52.

295 *"considerable confusion"*: "Corona Program History, Vol. 1: Program Overview," p. 5-4.

296 *pieces of the satellite*: Ibid.

296 *"completely verified"*: *NYT*, Feb. 25, 1960, p. 1.

296 *" 'crash' program"*: National Intelligence Estimate 11-5-59, "Soviet Capabilities in Guided Missiles and Space Vehicles," Sept. 1959, in *CIA's Analysis of the Soviet Union, 1947–1991, A Documentary Collection*, eds. Gerald K. Haines and Robert E. Leggett (Washington, D.C.: CIA Center for the Study of Intelligence, 2001), pp. 126–135.

297 *true purpose*: Beschloss, *Mayday*, p. 234.

297 *"Dulles was determined"*: Pedlow and Welzenbach, *The CIA and the U-2*, p. 165.

297 *"one tremendous asset"*: Memorandum for the Record, Feb. 8, 1960, DDEL, OSS, Subject Series, Alphabetical Subseries, Box 15, Intelligence Matters (13).

CHAPTER 14: "CAPSULE RECOVERED UNDAMAGED"

298 *"high probability"*: Gregory W. Pedlow and Donald E. Welzenbach, *The CIA and the U-2 Program, 1954–1974* (Washington, D.C.: CIA Center for the Study of Intelligence, 1998), p. 168.

298 *bell-ringing findings*: Ibid.

299 *"the intelligence estimate"*: Richard M. Bissell interview with Ed Edwin, DDEL.

299 *approved one flight*: Pedlow and Welzenbach, *The CIA and the U-2*, p. 167.

299 *Operation Square Deal:* Chris Pocock, *The U-2 Spyplane: Toward the Unknown* (Atglen, Pa.: Schiffer Publishing 2000), p. 171.

300 *higher cruising altitude:* Pedlow and Welzenbach, *The CIA and the U-2*, p. 152.

300 *out of range:* Pocock, *The U-2 Spyplane*, pp. 172–173.

300 *"had an opportunity":* Nikita Khrushchev, *Khrushchev Remembers: The Last Testament* (Boston: Little, Brown, 1974), p. 443.

300 *"logical step":* Pedlow and Welzenbach, *The CIA and the U-2*, p. 170. Part of this material has been redacted by the CIA; however, it seems logical to surmise that the first blank space referred to Pakistan or Peshawar and the second is a reference to Allen Dulles.

300 *"virtually inviting us":* George Kistiakowsky, *A Scientist in the White House: A Private Diary of President Eisenhower's Special Assistant for Science and Technology* (Cambridge, Mass.: Harvard University Press, 1976), p. 328.

301 *"or so we believed":* Richard M. Bissell Jr., with Jonathan E. Lewis and Frances T. Pudlo, *Reflections of a Cold Warrior: From Yalta to Bay of Pigs* (New Haven, Conn.: Yale University Press, 1996), pp. 123–134.

302 *lost in space:* "Corona Program History, Vol. 1: Program Overview," 1988, p. 5-7, NRO.

303 *Critchfield declined:* Evan Thomas, *The Very Best Men: Four Who Dared: The Early Years of the CIA* (New York: Simon & Schuster, 1995), pp. 205–206.

303 *"one additional operation":* Memorandum for the Record, Apr. 25, 1960, DDEL, OSS, Subject Series, Alphabetical Subseries, Box 15, Intelligence Matters 3-5/60 (14).

303 *"virtually disintegrate":* Dwight D. Eisenhower, *The White House Years, 1956–61: Waging Peace* (Garden City, N.Y.: Doubleday, 1965), p. 546.

304 *"big rolls of film":* Bissell, *Reflections of a Cold Warrior,* pp. 121–122.

304 *"greater and greater":* Andrew D. Goodpaster interview.

304 *"a grave mistake":* Bissell, *Reflections of a Cold Warrior,* p. 125.

305 *veteran of the U-2 program:* Pedlow and Welzenbach, *The CIA and the U-2*, p. 174.

305 *article 360:* Ibid., p. 175.

305 *"Once airborne":* Ibid., p. 176.

306 *"sick and tired":* Khrushchev, *The Last Testament,* p. 444.

306 *orange fireball:* Francis Gary Powers, with Curt Gentry, *Operation Overflight: The U-2 Pilot Tells His Story for the First Time* (New York: Holt, Rinehart and Winston, 1970), p. 82.

307 *destruction switch:* Ibid., pp. 82–88.

307 *plowed into the ground:* Bissell and other CIA officers initially suspected that pilot error or an engine flameout had brought the U-2 down to around 50,000 before it was attacked—a view that assumed the Russians really couldn't hit the aircraft at its cruising altitude above 70,000 feet. Later evidence showed that the plane was flying at the higher altitude.

307 *" 'winds are going to blow' ":* Michael R. Beschloss, *Mayday: The U-2 Affair* (New York: Harper & Row, 1986), p. 34.

308 *"confuse the government"*: Khrushchev, *The Last Testament*, p. 446.

308 *" 'Lake Van area' "*: Untitled document, May 2, 1960, DDEL, OSS, Subject Series, Alphabetical Subseries, Box 15, Intelligence Matters (14).

309 *"weather observations"*: *NYT*, May 6, 1960, p. 1.

309 *"count to ten"*: Memorandum of Conversation, Bipartisan Leaders Breakfast with the President, May 26, 1960, DDEL, OSS, Subject Series, Alphabetical Subseries, Box 25, U-2 Incident, Vol. 1, May 1960 (8), p. 6.

309 *"pilot was dead"*: Khrushchev, *The Last Testament*, p. 446.

309 *"prove to be a mistake"*: Beschloss, *Mayday*, p. 248.

310 *"no authorization"*: Transcript, State Department press and radio news briefing, May 7, 1960, DDEL, OSS, Subject Series, Alphabetical Subseries, Box 25, U-2 Incident, Vol. 1, May 1960 (2).

310 *"United States admitted"*: *NYT*, May 8, 1960, p. 1.

310 *"presidency has been parceled out"*: Ibid.

311 *"incompetence"*: New York Herald Tribune, May 10, 1960.

311 *"depressed and humiliated"*: *NYT*, May 9, 1960, p. 1.

311 *"seemed very depressed"*: Diary entry, Ann C. Whitman, May 9, 1960, DDEL, AW, Ann Whitman Diary Series, Box 11, ACW Diary, May 1960.

311 *dodgy strategy*: Telephone Calls, May 9, 1960, 9:10 A.M., DDEL, Christian A. Herter Papers, 1957–61, Box 10, Presidential Telephone Calls 1–6/60 (1).

311 *Nixon bluntly warned*: Telephone Calls, May 9, 1960, 10:15 A.M., DDEL, Christian A. Herter Papers, 1957–61, Box 12, CAH Telephone Calls 3/28–6/30/60 (2).

311 *unusual methods*: Telephone Calls, May 9, 1960, 9:55 A.M., DDEL, Christian A. Herter Papers, 1957–61, Box 10, Presidential Telephone Calls, 1–6/60 (1).

312 *"approved specific flights"*: Minutes of National Security Council Meeting, May 24, 1960, DDEL, AW, NSC Series, Box 12, 445th NSC Meeting.

313 *"under strict control"*: White House news conference transcript, May 11, 1960, DDEL, AW, Press Conference Series, Box 10, Press and Radio Conference 5/11/60.

313 *"a dirty deal"*: *NYT*, June 7, 1960, p. 1.

313 *"known to . . . Eisenhower"*: *NYT*, May 15, 1960, p. E-4.

315 *"revolution in intelligence"*: George Tenet, speech at U-2 History Symposium, National Defense University, Sept. 17, 1998.

315 *15 percent of the Soviet landmass*: Pedlow and Welzenbach, *The CIA and the U-2*, p. 316.

315 *"invaluable"*: Ibid., p. 318.

316 *"not back down"*: Minutes of National Security Council meeting, May 24, 1960, DDEL, AW, NSC Series, Box 12, 445th NSC Meeting.

316 *"some idiot"*: Ibid.

317 *additional $40 million*: Ibid.

317 *first Midas*: *NYT*, May 25, 1960, p. 1.

317 *"in chaos"*: Kistiakowsky, *A Scientist at the White House*, p. 331.

318 *"unsatisfactory progress"*: Ibid., p. 336.

318 *"reconnaissance gap"*: *NYT*, June 11, 1960, p. 1.

318 *"very early stage"*: *NYT*, June 12, 1960, Section IV, p. 6.

319 *tiniest imperfections*: "Corona Program History, Vol. 1: Program Overview," p. 5-5.

319 *"high-risk engineering"*: James Plummer interview.

320 *stowed an American flag*: Ibid.

320 *"shortest and most welcome"*: National Reconnaissance Office, "The Corona Story," 1988, p. 52.

320 *Belka and Strelka*: Ibid.

320 *did not realize*: The recovered capsule was supposed to be transported quietly to Sunnyvale so Lockheed technicians could examine it. It was to be exchanged there for a substitute capsule, that would be delivered to Washington to mark the historic occasion. These plans were scuttled by Colonel Mathison, the impulsive Air Force officer who had led the search mission to Spitzbergen. Apparently hoping to score a publicity coup for the Air Force, Mathison unexpectedly appeared on the flight deck of the *Haiti Victory* in a helicopter shortly after the capsule was winched aboard, and flew off with his prize. He stopped briefly in Honolulu for a photo opportunity, then flew on to Sunnyvale, opening the capsule en route to the dismay of project engineers. From Sunnyvale, he proceeded on to Washington with the original capsule, where Mathison joined a delegation of top officials that presented it to Eisenhower on Aug. 15, along with the flag it had carried into space.

321 *espionage applications*: *NYT*, Aug. 20, 1960, p. 1.

321 *espionage conviction*: Ibid.

322 *Steuart Building*: NRO, "The Corona Story," p. 59; "Corona Program History, Vol. 1: Program Overview," p. 6-1.

322 *stunning new map*: Jeffrey T. Richelson, *America's Secret Eyes in Space: The U.S. Keyhole Spy Satellite Program* (New York: HarperBusiness, 1990), p. 43.

322 *"There was elation"*: Dino Brugioni interview, Mar. 11, 2002.

322 *"new era"*: Dwayne A. Day, John M. Logsdon, and Brian Latell, eds., *Eye in the Sky: The Story of the Corona Spy Satellites* (Washington, D.C.: Smithsonian Institution Press, 1998), p. 221.

322 *"historic importance"*: Andrew Goodpaster interview, Mar. 12, 2002. George Kistiakowsky, Eisenhower's science adviser, places the president's first viewing of the Corona photos the next day, August 25, before a morning meeting of the National Security Council. In his memoirs, Kistiakowsky obliquely refers to the events: "In President's office with Dulles, Killian, Land, and Gray, to show him certain intelligence information and remind him of certain projects related to SAMOS which we propose not to discuss at the following briefing but which influenced our recommendations." George Kistiakowsky, *A Scientist at the White House*, p. 387.

322 *"more coverage"*: Bissell, *Reflections of a Cold Warrior*, p. 138.

323 *plenty to examine*: Dwayne Day, "The Development and Improvement of the Corona Satellite," in *Eye in the Sky*, p. 61.

323 *"not increase markedly"*: National Intelligence Estimate 11-8/1-61, "Strength and Deployment of Soviet Long Range Ballistic Missile Force," Sept. 21, 1961, reprinted in *Corona: America's First Satellite Program*, ed. Kevin Ruffner (Washington, D.C.: CIA Center for the Study of Intelligence, 1995), p. 130.

323 *Eisenhower lay in bed*: Dino A. Brugioni, *Eyeball to Eyeball: The Inside Story of the Cuban Missile Crisis* (New York: Random House, 1990), p. 568.

324 *"absolutely flabbergasted"*: Ibid.

324 *Eisenhower died*: Richard Helms interview, Nov. 2, 1999.

CHAPTER 15: A STRADIVARIUS, NOT A CRACKER BOX

326 " *'crawling along' "*: Arthur Lundahl's Speech Transcript, Corona Museum dedication, in "Corona Program History, Vol. 2: Governmental Activities," pp. 4-31–4-33.

326 *Talent-Keyhole*: Keyhole also gave rise to the technical designation of the six generations of Corona satellites, KH-1 through KH-4B, as well as successor photoreconnaissance systems, which ran up through KH-13 as of 2002.

326 *quite a run*: "Corona Program History, Vol. 2: Governmental Activities," p. 4-31.

326 *all twenty-five ICBM complexes*: Kenneth E. Greer, "Corona," *Studies in Intelligence*, Supplement 17, Spring 1973; Kevin C. Ruffner, ed., *Corona: America's First Satellite Program* (Washington, D.C.: CIA Center for the Study of Intelligence 1995), p. 37.

326 *$850 million*: Stephen I. Schwartz noted in a letter to the editor of the *New York Times* on Sept. 20, 1995, that John McMahon disclosed this budget number during the 1995 Corona conference.

326 *"triumph of American technology"*: Albert D. Wheelon, "Corona: A Triumph of American Technology," in *Eye in the Sky: The Story of the Corona Spy Satellites*, eds. Dwayne A. Day, John M. Logsdon, and Brian Latell (Washington, D.C.: Smithsonian Institution Press, 1998), p. 47.

327 *"our guesses were way off"*: William E. Burrows, *Deep Black: Space Espionage and National Security* (New York: Random House, 1986), p. vii.

327 *"absolutely vital"*: Speech by Ronald Reagan for the 25th Anniversary of Project Corona, Aug. 1985, NRO.

328 *invasion had begun*: Jeffrey T. Richelson, *The Wizards of Langley: Inside the CIA's Directorate of Science and Technology* (Boulder, Colo.: Westview Press, 2001), pp. 169–170.

328 *"totally useless"*: Albert D. Wheelon interview. Subsequent quotations from Wheelon in this chapter come from the same series of conversations at his home outside Santa Barbara, Calif., on Aug. 27–29, 1998, as well as later discussions by telephone in the spring of 2002.

329 *"successes and regrets"*: Richard M. Bissell Jr., with Jonathan E. Lewis and Frances T. Pudlo, *Reflections of a Cold Warrior: From Yalta to Bay of Pigs* (New Haven, Conn.: Yale University Press, 1996), p. 203.

329 *a disservice: NYT,* Feb. 8, 1994, Section D, p. 23.

331 *"jewels in our crown":* James Woolsey, address at presentation of the R. V. Jones Intelligence Award to Albert D. Wheelon, Dec. 13, 1994.

332 *steer clear of management:* Jeffrey T. Richelson, *America's Secret Eyes in Space: The U.S. Keyhole Satellite Program* (New York: HarperBusiness, 1990), p. 47.

332 *"airplane business":* Richelson, *The Wizards of Langley,* p. 61.

337 *monitoring station:* William Perry interview, Nov. 16, 1999.

338 *"fragmentation":* Donald E. Welzenbach, "Science and Technology: Origins of a Directorate," *Studies in Intelligence,* Summer 1986, pp. 24–25.

338 *"the toughest job":* Clarence L. "Kelly" Johnson, with Maggie Smith, *Kelly: More Than My Share of It All* (Washington, D.C.: Smithsonian Institution Press, 1989), pp. 136–137.

339 *"Everything . . . had to be invented":* Ibid., p. 137.

339 *"its own industrial base":* Bissell, *Reflections of a Cold Warrior,* p. 133.

339 *"anything easy":* Johnson, *Kelly,* p. 137.

340 *"potential for problems":* Ibid., pp. 139–140.

340 *titanium alloy:* Ben R. Rich and Leo Janos, *Skunk Works* (New York: Little, Brown, 1994), p. 203.

340 *"distilled water":* Ibid., p. 214.

341 *"Mach 2.5":* Jay Miller, *Lockheed Martin's Skunk Works* (Leicester, Eng.: Midland Publishing, 1995), p. 121.

341 *"obstructing road signs":* Ibid., p. 119.

341 *$3,500 in cash:* Rich and Janos, *Skunk Works,* p. 218.

341 *"having a heart attack":* Miller, *Skunk Works,* p. 120.

342 *pouring into the inlets:* Rich and Janos, *Skunk Works,* p. 208.

342 *at Mach 3.2:* Miller, *Skunk Works,* p. 123.

342 *"nerve-racking work":* Rich and Janos, *Skunk Works,* p. 209.

344 *different material:* Sidney Drell interview, Nov. 13, 1998.

344 *Drell committee:* Richelson, *The Wizards of Langley,* p. 123.

345 *discuss the tensions:* Ibid., p. 112.

345 *"didn't trust":* Brockway McMillan interview, Mar. 26, 2002.

346 *"single point of authority":* Memorandum for Director, NRO Program A and NRO Program B, undated, NRO.

346 *"More vigorous":* Memorandum for Director of Central Intelligence, Nov. 18, 1963, NRO.

346 *"turning point":* Memorandum for Director of Central Intelligence, Dec. 21, 1963, NRO.

346 *"enormously pleasing":* Ibid.

346 *"never operate reliably":* Memorandum for General Carter, CIA, June 30, 1964, NRO.

346 *Wheelon and the CIA:* Memorandum of Agreement, Jan. 13, 1965, NRO.

346 *"willful cancellation":* Memorandum for Deputy Director of Central Intelligence, undated, NRO.

347 *"Big Bird"*: Richelson, *America's Secret Eyes in Space*, p. 106.

347 *"watching an NFL game"*: Albert Wheelon to Richard Helms, Jan. 13, 1999.

349 *"like going to the moon"*: Jimmie Hill interview, Oct. 20, 1999.

349 *"pushing it faster"*: Drell interview.

349 *"Stradivarius"*: Ibid.

351 *"last possible moment"*: Richard Garwin, remarks at Sidney Drell retirement ceremony, Stanford University, July 31, 1998.

351 *radically improve*: Richelson, *The Wizards of Langley*, p. 172.

351 *remarkable detail*: Ibid., p. 202.

353 *"far ahead of anything"*: William Perry interview.

EPILOGUE: LOSING THE INVENTIVE SPARK

357 *its first bomb*: Pakistan tested a nuclear weapon on May 30.

357 *"I told them"*: Strobe Talbott interview, Mar. 27, 2002.

358 *bluffing*: Frank Wisner Jr. interview, June 11, 2002.

358 *slow to recognize*: *NYT*, June 3, 1998, p. 1.

359 *"imbalance"*: Transcript, Jeremiah News Conference, June 2, 1998, CIA, http://www.cia.gov/cia/public_affairs/press_release/archives/1998/jeremiah.html.

359 *"seriously limited"*: Ibid.

360 *team of ten*: Ibid.; *NYT*, May 25, 1998, p. 1: *Time*, May 25, 1998.

360 *not redirected*: *NYT*, May 25, 1998, p. 1; interviews with NIMA officials who asked not to be identified, June 10, 2002.

362 *Richard Bissell*: Richard M. Bissell Jr. letter to Anthony D. Marshall, March 14, 1959. Provided to the author by Mr. Marshall.

362 *assemble the army*: The findings continued: "Several management decisions also likely degraded CIA's [counterterrorism] capabilities by, for example, redirecting funds earmarked for core field collection and analysis to headquarters; paying insufficient attention to CIA's unilateral [counterterrorism] capability; relying too much on liaison of [counterterrorism]; and neglecting sufficient investment of foreign-language training and exploitation. The dramatic increase in resources for intelligence since 9-11 improves the outlook for CIA's [counterterrorism] capabilities, but only if CIA management acknowledges and deals with the systemic problems outlined in this report." The committee recommended: "CIA leadership must ensure that [human intelligence] collection remains a central core competency of the agency, and should develop additional operational tools, in conjunction with other appropriate agencies (FBI, etc.), penetrate terrorist cells, disrupt terrorist operations, and capture and render terrorists to law enforcement as appropriate. More core collectors need to be put on the streets." "Counterterrorism Intelligence Capabilities and Performance Prior to 9-11: A Report to the Speaker of the House of Representatives and the Minority Leader," Subcommittee on Terrorism and Homeland Security, House Permanent Select Committee on Intelligence, July 2002, p. ii.

363 *September 12*: *NYT*, June 20, 2002.

363 *NIMA:* NIMA interviews.

365 *85 percent:* Ibid.

367 *Space Imaging:* Space Imaging was created after the Clinton administration lifted technical restrictions on American satellite companies in 1994, allowing them to build imagery systems capable of showing objects on the ground as small as a yard across. The government had previously permitted optical systems that provided less detailed—and less marketable—pictures. The White House decision was driven by the realization that foreign satellite firms, which were not bound by the American limitations, could capture the potentially large market for higher-resolution satellite pictures and possibly sell them to countries or groups hostile to the United States. Though they never put it quite so bluntly in public, Clinton administration officials acted to give American companies like Space Imaging a head start in hopes that they would dominate the field and discourage foreign competitors from building high-resolution satellites. The strategy worked for a while, but foreign companies are now springing up. The day may soon be coming when unfriendly governments or even terror groups will be able to use finely detailed satellite photos obtained from private companies to plan attacks against American targets.

367 *outdated sources: NYT,* May 11, 2002, p. A-12; interviews with Space Imaging, Dec. 9, 1999.

368 *Hellfire: NYT,* Nov. 4, 2002, A-1.

369 *"exaggerate the capabilities":* Jimmie Hill interview, Oct. 20, 1999.

369 *"bureaucratic chase":* Robert Gates interview, Sept. 30, 1999.

BIBLIOGRAPHY

INTERVIEWS AND ORAL HISTORIES

with Philip Taubman

Teuvo "Gus" Ahola, July 10, 1997, Honolulu, Hawaii, by telephone

Edwin "Pete" Aldridge, November 1, 1999, Roslyn, Virginia

Sam Araki, November 17, 1999, Sunnyvale, California

Harold R. "Hal" Austin, August 25–26, 1998, Riverside, California

Burton Barrett, September 21, 1999, Independence, Oregon

Stanley Beerli, September 22 and 23, 1999, Hillsboro, Oregon

Dino A. Brugioni, March 12, 2002, Hartwood, Virginia, by telephone

Merton E. Davies, August 24, 1998, Santa Monica, California

Sidney Drell, November 13, 1998, Stanford, California; March 15, 2000, by telephone

Robert Einhorn, April 3, 2002, Washington, D.C., by telephone

John W. Finney, October 21, 1999, Washington, D.C.

Lew Franklin, November 11, 1999, Stanford, California

John Gannon, April 4, 2002, Washington, D.C., by telephone

Richard Garwin, October 29, 1999, Yorktown, New York

Robert Gates, September 30, 1999, New York, New York

Andrew J. Goodpaster, November 2, 1999, Washington, D.C.; January 18, 2001, by telephone; March 12, 2002, by telephone

Richard Helms, November 2, 1999, Washington, D.C.

Charles Hill, November 3, 1999, Cambridge, Massachusetts, by telephone

Jimmie D. Hill, October 20, 1999, McLean, Virginia

Robb Hoover, October 7, 1999, Reno, Nevada

Bob Inman, December 4, 1999, Austin, Texas

Donald Kilgore, March 18, 2001, Albuquerque, New Mexico

Bob and Betty King, October 19, 1999, Washington, D.C.

Martin Knutson, November 22, 1999, Los Altos, California

Richard S. Leghorn, December 2 and 3, 1999, Silver City, New Mexico; May 30, 2000, by telephone

John McMahon, November 12, 1999, Los Altos Hills, California; April 1, 2002, by telephone

Brockway McMillan, March 26, 2002, Sedgwick, Maine, by telephone

Jean O'Kelley, November 13, 1999, Napa, California

William Perry, November 16, 1999, Stanford, California

James Plummer, September 2–4, 1998, Bend, Oregon

Joseph A. Ruseckas, April 7, 2001, Worcester, Massachusetts
Bernard Schriever, November 1, 1999, Washington, D.C.
George Shultz, November 15, 1999, Stanford, California
Strobe Talbott, March 27, 2002, New Haven, Connecticut, by telephone
Charles Vick, November 3, 1999, Fredericksburg, Virginia
Albert D. "Bud" Wheelon, August 27–29, 1998, Montecito, California
Harold F. "Bud" Wienberg, October 18, 2000, Folsom, California; June 4, 2000, by telephone
Frank Wisner Jr., June 10, 2002, New York, New York
James Woolsey, October 21, 1999, Washington, D.C.
at the National Imagery and Mapping Agency, June 10, 2002, Bethesda, Maryland: David H. Burpee, Robert Zitz, and other officials who did not wish to be named
at Space Imaging, Thornton, Colorado, December 9, 1999: Mark E. Brender, Frederick J. Doyle Jr., K. Bolling Farmer, Jeffrey Harris, Bryan McFadden, and Mike McGill

with Elizabeth Goldman
Frank "Buzz" Buzard, November 17, 1999, Rancho Palos Verdes, California
Ingard Clausen, January 8, 2002, Paradise Valley, Arizona
Vincent Ford, August 4, 2000, McLean, Virginia
Willis M. Hawkins, November 15–16, 1999, Woodland Hills, California
Bill Johnson, November 9, 1999, Arnold, Maryland
William King, November 18, 1999, Pomona, California
Roy Worthington, November 16, 1999, Air Force Village, California

Columbia University Oral History Research Office, Eisenhower Administration Project, New York, New York
Winthrop Aldrich, with David Berliner, October 16, 1972
George V. Allen, with Ed Edwin, March 7, 1967
Arthur C. Lundahl, with Peter Jessup, June 10–October 8, 1981
Nathan F. Twining, with John Mason, June-September 1967

Princeton University, John Foster Dulles Oral History Project, Princeton, New Jersey
Sherman Adams, with Richard D. Challener, August 15, 1964
Winthrop Aldrich, with Richard D. Challener, July 15, 1964
George V. Allen, with Philip A. Crowl, April 7, 1966
Dillon Anderson, with Richard D. Challener, June 13, 1966
Richard M. Bissell Jr., with Richard D. Challener, September 7, 1966
Charles Pearre Cabell, with Philip A. Crowl, May 22, 1965
Dwight D. Eisenhower, with Philip A. Crowl, July 28, 1964
William C. Foster, with Philip A. Crowl, August 30, 1966
Edward L. Freers, with Philip A. Crowl, May 21, 1966
Christian Herter, with Richard D. Challener, August 31, 1964

Curtis LeMay, by Gordon A. Craig, April 28, 1966
Neil H. McElroy, with Philip A. Crowl, May 6, 1964
Robert D. Murphy, with Richard D. Challener, June 8, 1965
Gerard C. Smith, with Philip A. Crowl, October 13, 1965
Nathan Twining, with Philip A. Crowl, March 16, 1965

Dwight D. Eisenhower Presidential Library, Abilene, Kansas
Richard M. Bissell Jr., with Ed Edwin, June 5, 1967, and November 9, 1976
Charles Bohlen, with Don North, December 17, 1970
Thomas S. Gates, with John T. Mason Jr., October 3, 1972
Andrew J. Goodpaster, with Maclyn P. Burg, June 26, 1975
Gordon Gray, with Paul L. Hopper, January 23, 1967
George Kistiakowsky, with Thomas Soapes, November 17, 1976
Harold Stassen, with Thomas Soapes, April 29, 1977

John F. Kennedy Presidential Library, Boston, Massachusetts
Robert Amory, with Joseph E. O'Connor, February 9, 1966
Roswell L. Gilpatric, with Dennis J. O'Brien, May 5, 1970
Roger Hilsman, with Dennis J. O'Brien, August 14, 1970
Walt Rostow, with Richard Neustadt, April 11, 1964
Theodore Sorensen, with Carl Kaysen, March 26, 1964

Lyndon B. Johnson Presidential Library, Austin, Texas
Bryce Harlow, with Michael Gillette, May 6, 1976

National Reconnaissance Office Oral History Program, Chantilly, Virginia, all interviews by R. Cargill Hall
James G. Baker, May 9, 1996
William O. Baker, May 7, 1996
Robert John DePew, May 7, 1998
Sergei Khrushchev, July 5, 1995
Robert S. McNamara, March 25, 1999
Stacy D. Naftel, December 27, 1997
Philip O. Robertson, December 29, 1997
Don H. Schoessler and Charles P. Spoelhof, May 16, 1997

ARCHIVES AND LIBRARIES

Dwight D. Eisenhower Presidential Library, Abilene, Kansas
Harry S Truman Presidential Library, Independence, Missouri
John F. Kennedy Presidential Library, Boston, Massachusetts
Library of Congress, Washington, D.C.
Lyndon B. Johnson Presidential Library, Austin, Texas
National Archives and Records Administration, Washington, D.C.

National Reconnaissance Office, Chantilly, Virginia
Polaroid Corporation, corporate archives, Cambridge, Massachusetts
University of New Mexico Health Sciences Library and Informatics Center,
Albuquerque, New Mexico

Books

Ambrose, Stephen E. *Eisenhower: Soldier and President.* New York: Simon &
Schuster, 1990.
———. *Ike's Spies: Eisenhower and the Espionage Establishment.* Garden City, N.Y.:
Doubleday, 1981.
Andrew, Christopher M. *For the President's Eyes Only: Secret Intelligence and the
American Presidency from Washington to Bush.* New York: HarperCollins
Publishers, 1995.
Arnold, H. H. *Global Mission.* New York: Harper & Row Publishers, 1949.
Bamford, James. *The Puzzle Palace: A Report on America's Most Secret Agency.* New
York: Penguin Books, 1982.
Beschloss, Michael R. *Mayday: The U-2 Affair.* New York: Harper & Row
Publishers, 1986.
Bird, Kai. *Color of Truth: McGeorge and William Bundy, Brothers in Arms: A
Biography.* New York: Simon & Schuster, 1998.
Bissell, Richard M., Jr., with Jonathan E. Lewis and Frances T. Pudlo. *Reflections of
a Cold Warrior: From Yalta to Bay of Pigs.* New Haven, Conn.: Yale University
Press, 1996.
Bottome, Edgar M. *The Missile Gap: A Study of the Formulation of Military and
Political Policy.* Rutherford, N.J.: Fairleigh Dickinson University Press, 1971.
Brian, Paul. *Nuclear Holocaust: Atomic War in Fiction, 1895–1984.* Kent, Ohio: Kent
State University Press, 1987.
Brugioni, Dino A. *Eyeball to Eyeball: The Inside Story of the Cuban Missile Crisis.* New
York: Random House, 1990.
Buderi, Robert. *The Invention That Changed the World: How a Small Group of Radar
Pioneers Won the Second World War and Launched a Technological Revolution.* New
York: Simon & Schuster, 1996.
Bulkeley, Rip. *The Sputniks Crisis and Early United States Space Policy: A Critique of
the Historiography of Space.* Bloomington: Indiana University Press, 1991.
Burrows, William E. *By Any Means Necessary: America's Secret Air War in the Cold
War.* New York: Farrar, Straus and Giroux, 2001.
———. *Deep Black: Space Espionage and National Security.* New York: Random
House, 1986.
———. *This New Ocean: The Story of the First Space Age.* New York: Random
House, 1998.
Byrnes, Donn A., and Kenneth D. Hurley. *Blackbird Rising: Birth of an Aviation
Legend.* Los Lunas, N. Mex.: Sage Mesa Publications, 1999.

Campbell, James B. *Introduction to Remote Sensing*, 2nd ed. New York: The Guilford Press, 1996.

Carmel, Hesi, ed. *Intelligence for Peace: The Role of Intelligence in Times of Peace.* London: F. Cass, 1999.

Clarke, Arthur C. *Voices from the Sky: Previews of the Coming Space Age.* New York: Harper & Row Publishers, 1965.

Coffey, Thomas M. *HAP: The Story of the U.S. Air Force and the Man Who Built It, General Henry H. "Hap" Arnold.* New York: Viking Press, 1982.

Colby, William, and Peter Forbath. *Honorable Men: My Life in the CIA.* New York: Simon & Schuster, 1978.

Crickmore, Paul F. *Lockheed SR-71: The Secret Missions Exposed.* London: Osprey, 1993.

Cutler, Robert. *No Time for Rest.* Boston: Little, Brown, 1966.

Day, Dwayne A., John M. Logsdon, and Brian Latell, eds. *Eye in the Sky: The Story of the Corona Spy Satellites.* Washington, D.C.: Smithsonian Institution Press, 1998.

Dickson, Paul. *Sputnik: The Shock of the Century.* New York: Walker & Co., 2001.

Divine, Robert A. *The Sputnik Challenge.* New York: Oxford University Press, 1993.

Donald, David. *Spyplane.* Osceola, Wis.: Motorbooks International, 1987.

Donovan, Robert J. *Eisenhower: The Inside Story.* New York: Harper, 1956.

Dulles, Allen. *The Craft of Intelligence.* New York: Harper & Row Publishers, 1963.

Eisenhower, Dwight D. *Crusade in Europe.* Garden City, N.Y.: Doubleday, 1948.

———. *The White House Years, 1953–56: Mandate for Change.* Garden City, N.Y.: Doubleday, 1963.

———. *The White House Years, 1956–61: Waging Peace.* Garden City, N.Y.: Doubleday, 1965.

Ferrell, Robert H., ed. *The Eisenhower Diaries.* New York: Norton, 1981.

Foreign Relations of the United States, Dwight D. Eisenhower, 1952–54, vol. 2 and 13; 1955–57, vol. 5, 11, 19, 20, and 24; 1958–60, vol. 2, 3, and 10. Washington, D.C.: U.S. Government Printing Office.

Freedman, Lawrence. *U.S. Intelligence and the Soviet Strategic Threat.* Boulder, Colo.: Westview Press, 1977.

Gaddis, John Lewis, et al., eds. *Cold War Statesmen Confront the Bomb: Nuclear Diplomacy Since 1945.* New York: Oxford University Press, 1999.

———. *The Long Peace: Inquiries into the History of the Cold War.* New York: Oxford University Press, 1987.

———. *We Now Know: Rethinking Cold War History.* New York: Oxford University Press, 1997.

Gates, Robert M. *From the Shadows: The Ultimate Insider's Story of Five Presidents and How They Won the Cold War.* New York: Simon & Schuster, 1996.

Gavaghan, Helen. *Something New Under the Sun: Satellites and the Beginning of the Space Age.* New York: Copernicus, 1998.

Gavin, James M. *War and Peace in the Space Age*. New York: Harper, 1958.

Gertz, Bill. *Betrayal: How the Clinton Administration Undermined American Security*. Washington, D.C.: Regnery, 1999.

Goddard, George W., with DeWitt S. Copp. *Overview: A Lifelong Adventure in Aerial Photography*. Garden City, N.Y.: Doubleday, 1969.

Godson, Roy, ed. *Intelligence Requirements for the 1980s: Analysis and Estimates*. Washington, D.C.: National Strategy Information Center, 1980.

Graham, Richard H. *SR-71 Revealed: The Inside Story*. Osceola, Wis.: MBI Publishing, 1996.

Greenstein, Fred I. *The Hidden-Hand Presidency: Eisenhower as Leader*. Baltimore, Md.: Johns Hopkins University Press, 1982.

Grose, Peter. *Gentleman Spy: The Life of Allen Dulles*. Amherst, Mass.: Amherst University Press, 1996.

Gunston, Bill. *An Illustrated Guide to Spy Planes and Electronic Warfare Aircraft*. New York: Arco Publishing, 1983.

Haines, Gerald K., and Robert E. Leggett, eds. *CIA's Analysis of the Soviet Union, 1947–1991, A Documentary Collection*. Washington, D.C.: CIA Center for the Study of Intelligence, 2001.

Halberstam, David. *The Best and the Brightest*. New York: Random House, 1972.

———. *The Fifties*. New York: Villard Books, 1993.

Henriksen, Margot A. *Dr. Strangelove's America: Society and Culture in the Atomic Age*. Berkeley: University of California Press, 1997.

Heppenheimer, T. A. *Countdown: A History of Space Flight*. New York: John Wiley & Sons, 1997.

Hersh, Burton. *Old Boys: The American Elite and the Origins of the CIA*. New York: Scribner's, 1992.

Historical Statistics of the United States. Washington: U.S. Bureau of the Census, 1975.

Hough, Harold. *Satellite Surveillance*. Port Townsend, Wash.: Loompanics Unlimited, 1991.

Immerman, Richard. *The CIA in Guatemala: The Foreign Policy of Intervention*. Austin: University of Texas Press, 1982.

Jackson, Robert. *High Cold War: Strategic Air Reconnaissance and the Electronic Intelligence War*. Somerset, U.K.: Patrick Stephens, 1998.

Johnson, Clarence L. "Kelly," with Maggie Smith. *Kelly: More Than My Share of It All*. Washington, D.C.: Smithsonian Institution Press, 1985.

Johnson, Loch K. *America's Secret Power: The CIA in a Democratic Society*. New York: Oxford University Press, 1989.

Jones, R. V. *The Wizard War: British Scientific Intelligence, 1939–1945*. New York: Coward, McCann & Geoghegan, 1978.

Khrushchev, Nikita, trans. and ed. Jerrold L. Schecter with Vyacheslav V. Luchkov. *Khrushchev Remembers: The Glasnost Tapes*. Boston: Little, Brown, 1990.

Khrushchev, Nikita, trans. and ed. Strobe Talbott. *Khrushchev Remembers*. Boston: Little, Brown, 1970.

———. *Khrushchev Remembers: The Last Testament*. Boston: Little, Brown, 1974.

Khrushchev, Sergei, trans. and ed. William Taubman. *Khrushchev on Khrushchev: An Inside Account of the Man and His Era by His Son, Sergei Khrushchev*. Boston: Little, Brown, 1990.

Killian, James R., Jr. *The Education of a College President, A Memoir*. Cambridge, Mass.: MIT Press, 1985.

———. *Sputnik, Scientists and Eisenhower: A Memoir of the First Special Assistant to the President for Science and Technology*. Cambridge, Mass.: MIT Press, 1977.

Kistiakowsky, George. *A Scientist at the White House: A Private Diary of President Eisenhower's Special Assistant for Science and Technology*. Cambridge, Mass.: Harvard University Press, 1976.

Klass, Philip. *Secret Sentries in Space*. New York: Random House, 1971.

LaQueur, Walter. *The Uses and Limits of Intelligence*. New Brunswick, N.J.: Transaction Publishers, 1993.

Lashmar, Paul. *Spy Flights of the Cold War*. London: Sutton Publishing, 1996.

Launius, Roger D., and Howard E. McCurdy, eds. *Spaceflight and the Myth of Presidential Leadership*. Urbana: University of Illinois Press, 1997.

LeFeber, Walter. *America, Russia and the Cold War, 1945–1996*, 8th ed. New York: McGraw-Hill, 1997.

LeMay, Curtis E., with MacKinlay Kantor. *Mission with LeMay: My Story*. Garden City, N.Y.: Doubleday, 1965.

Lewis, Jonathan E. *Spy Capitalism: Itek and the CIA*. New Haven, Conn.: Yale University Press, 2002.

Lindgren, David T. *Trust but Verify: Imagery Analysis in the Cold War*. Annapolis, Md.: Naval Institute Press, 2000.

Logsdon, John M., ed. *Exploring the Unknown: Selected Documents in the History of the U.S. Civil Space Program*, vol. 1 and 2. Washington, D.C.: NASA, 1995.

Manchester, Harland. *New World of Machines*. New York: Random House, 1945.

Marchetti, Victor, and John D. Marks. *The CIA and the Cult of Intelligence*. New York: Alfred A. Knopf, 1974.

McCullough, David G. *Truman*. New York: Simon & Schuster, 1992.

McDonald, Robert A., ed. *Corona: Between the Sun and the Earth—The First NRO Reconnaissance Eye in Space*. Bethesda, Md.: American Society for Photogrammetry and Remote Sensing, 1997.

McDougall, Walter A. . . . *The Heavens and the Earth: A Political History of the Space Age*. New York: Basic Books, 1985.

McElheny, Victor K. *Insisting on the Impossible: The Life of Edwin Land, Inventor of Instant Photography*. Cambridge, Mass.: Perseus Books, 1999.

Miller, Jay. *Lockheed Martin's Skunk Works*. Leicester, U.K.: Midland Publishing, 1995.

———. *Lockheed U-2*. Austin, Tex.: Aerofax, 1983.

Naimark, Norman. *The Russians in Germany: A History of the Soviet Zone of Occupation, 1945–1949*. Cambridge, Mass.: Harvard University Press, 1995.

Ordway, Frederick I., III, and Mitchell Sharpe. *The Rocket Team*. New York: Crowell, 1979.

O'Shaker, Mark. *The Polaroid Story*. New York: Stein and Day, 1978.

O'Toole, G. J. A. *Honorable Treachery: A History of U.S. Intelligence, Espionage and Covert Action from the American Revolution to the CIA*. New York: Atlantic Monthly Press, 1991.

Patton, Phil. *Dreamland: Travels in the Secret World of Roswell and Area 51*. New York: Villard Books, 1998.

Pedlow, Gregory W., and Donald E. Welzenbach. *The CIA and the U-2 Program, 1954–1974*. Langley, Va.: Central Intelligence Agency, 1998.

Peebles, Curtis. *Battle for Space*. New York: Beaufort Books, 1983.

———. *The Corona Project: America's First Spy Satellites*. Annapolis, Md.: Naval Institute Press, 1997.

———. *Dark Eagles: A History of Top Secret U.S. Aircraft Programs*. Novato, Calif.: Presidio Press, 1995.

———. *Guardians: Strategic Reconnaissance Satellites*. Novato, Calif.: Presidio Press, 1987.

———. *The Moby Dick Project: Reconnaissance Balloons Over Russia*. Washington, D.C.: Smithsonian Institution Press, 1991.

Pocock, Chris. *Dragon Lady: The History of the U-2 Spyplane*. Osceola, Wis.: Motorbooks International, 1989.

———. *The U-2 Spyplane: Toward the Unknown*. Atglen, Pa.: Schiffer Publishing, 2000.

Polmar, Norman. *Spyplane: The U-2 History Declassified*. Osceola, Wis.: MBI Publishing, 2001.

Power, Thomas. *The Man Who Kept the Secrets: Richard Helms and the CIA*. New York: Alfred A. Knopf, 1979.

Powers, Francis Gary, with Curt Gentry. *Operation Overflight: The U-2 Pilot Tells His Story for the First Time*. New York: Holt, Rinehart and Winston, 1970.

Prados, John. *Keepers of the Keys: A History of the National Security Council from Truman to Bush*. New York: Morrow, 1991.

———. *The Soviet Estimate: U.S. Intelligence Analysis and Russian Military Strength*. New York: Dial Press, 1982.

Ranelagh, John. *The Agency: The Rise and Decline of the CIA*. New York: Simon & Schuster, 1986.

Reeves, Richard. *President Kennedy: Profile of Power*. New York: Simon & Schuster, 1993.

Rhodes, Richard. *Dark Sun: The Making of the Hydrogen Bomb*. New York: Simon & Schuster, 1995.

———. *The Making of the Atomic Bomb*. New York: Simon & Schuster, 1986.

Rich, Ben R., and Leo Janos. *Skunk Works*. New York: Little, Brown, 1994.

Richelson, Jeffrey T. *American Espionage and the Soviet Target*. New York: William Morrow, 1987.

———. *America's Secret Eyes in Space: The U.S. Keyhole Spy Satellite Program.* New York: HarperBusiness, 1990.

———. *America's Space Sentinels: DSP Satellites and National Security.* Lawrence: University Press of Kansas, 1999.

———. *A Century of Spies: Intelligence in the Twentieth Century.* New York: Oxford University Press, 1995.

———. *The U.S. Intelligence Community,* 3rd ed. Boulder, Colo.: Westview Press, 1995.

———. *The Wizards of Langley: Inside the CIA's Directorate of Science and Technology.* Boulder, Colo.: Westview Press, 2001.

Rostow, W. W. *Open Skies: Eisenhower's Proposal of July 21, 1955.* Austin: University of Texas Press, 1982.

Ruffner, Kevin C., ed. *Corona: America's First Satellite Program.* Washington, D.C.: CIA Center for the Study of Intelligence, 1995.

Sagdeev, R. Z. *The Making of a Soviet Scientist: My Adventures in Nuclear Fusion and Space from Stalin to Star Wars.* New York: John Wiley & Sons, 1994.

Sakharov, Andrei. *Memoirs.* New York: Alfred A. Knopf, 1990.

Schlesinger, Arthur M., Jr. *A Thousand Days: John F. Kennedy in the White House.* Boston: Houghton Mifflin, 1965.

Smith, R. Harris. *OSS: The Secret History of America's First Central Intelligence Agency.* Berkeley: University of California Press, 1972.

Sontag, Sherry, and Christopher Drew. *Blind Man's Bluff: The Untold Story of American Submarine Espionage.* Thorndike, Maine: Thorndike Press, 1999.

Sorensen, Theodore C. *Kennedy.* New York: Harper & Row, 1965.

Spidle, Jake W., Jr. *Doctors of Medicine in New Mexico: A History of Health and Medical Practice, 1886–1986.* Albuquerque: University of New Mexico Press, 1986.

———. *The Lovelace Medical Center: Pioneer in American Health Care.* Albuquerque: University of New Mexico Press, 1987.

Srodes, James. *Allen Dulles: Master of Spies.* Washington, D.C.: Regnery Publishing, 1999.

Stares, Paul B. *The Militarization of Space: U.S. Policy, 1945–1984.* Ithaca, N. Y.: Cornell University Press, 1985.

———. *Space and National Security.* Washington, D.C.: Brookings Institution, 1987.

Statistical Abstract of the United States: 1954. Washington, D.C.: U.S. Bureau of the Census, 1954.

Steury, Donald. *Sherman Kent and the Board of National Estimates: Collected Essays.* Washington, D.C.: CIA Center for the Study of Intelligence, 1994.

Sturm, Thomas A. *The USAF Scientific Advisory Board: Its First Twenty Years, 1944–1964.* Washington, D.C.: USAF Historical Division Liaison Office, 1967.

Taylor, John W. R., and David Mondey. *Spies in the Sky.* New York: Scribner, 1972.

Thomas, Evan. *The Very Best Men: Four Who Dared: The Early Years of the CIA*. New York: Simon & Schuster, 1995.

Thornborough, Anthony M., and Peter E. Davies. *Lockheed Blackbirds*. Surrey, U.K.: Ian Allan, 1988.

Twining, Nathan F. *Neither Liberty nor Safety: A Hard Look at U.S. Military Policy and Strategy*. New York: Holt, Rinehart and Winston, 1966.

Van der Aart, Dick. *Aerial Espionage: Secret Intelligence Flights by East and West*. New York: Arco/Prentice Hall Press, 1985.

Welzenbach, Donald E., draft of unpublished manuscript.

Wensberg, Peter. *Land's Polaroid*. Boston: Houghton Mifflin, 1987.

White, Ken. *World in Peril: The Origin, Mission and Scientific Findings of the 46th/72nd Reconnaissance Squadron*. Elkhart, Ind.: K. W. White and Associates, 1994.

White, William L. *The Little Toy Dog: The Story of the Two RB-47 Flyers, Captain John R. McKone and Captain Freeman B. Olmstead*. New York: E. P. Dutton, 1962.

Wise, David, and Thomas B. Ross. *The Invisible Government*. New York: Random House, 1964.

———. *The U-2 Affair*. New York: Random House, 1962.

Wolfe, Tom. *The Right Stuff*. Thorndike, Maine: Thorndike Press, 1979.

Wyden, Peter. *The Bay of Pigs: The Untold Story*. New York: Simon & Schuster, 1979.

Yost, Graham. *Spies in the Sky*. New York: Facts on File, 1989.

———. *Spy-Tech*. New York: Facts on File, 1985.

Zachary, G. Pascal. *Endless Frontier: Vannevar Bush, Engineer of the American Century*. New York: Free Press, 1997.

Zaloga, Steven J. *Target America: The Soviet Union and the Strategic Arms Race, 1945–1964*. Novato, Calif.: Presidio Press, 1993.

Ziegler, Charles A., and David Jacobson. *Spying without Spies: Origins of America's Secret Nuclear Surveillance System*. Westport, Conn.: Praeger, 1995.

REPORTS

Clauser, F. H., et al. *Preliminary Design of an Experimental World-Circling Spaceship*, SM-11827. Santa Monica, Calif.: The RAND Corp., May 2, 1946.

Corona Program History, Vol. 1–4, Directorate of Science and Technology, Central Intelligence Agency, May 19, 1976.

Davies, Merton E., and William R. Harris. *RAND's Role in the Evolution of Balloon and Satellite Observation Systems and Related U.S. Space Technology*, R-3692-RC. Santa Monica, Calif.: The RAND Corp., 1988.

Davies, Merton E., and Amrom H. Katz, et al. *A Family of Recoverable Reconnaissance Satellites*, RM-2012. Santa Monica, Calif.: The RAND Corp., November 12, 1957.

George, Alexander L. *Case Studies of Actual and Alleged Overflights, 1930–1953, with*

Supplement, RM-1349. Santa Monica, Calif.: The RAND Corp., August 15, 1955.

————. *Diplomatic Aspects of Soviet Air-Defense Policy, 1950–1953*, RM-1347. Santa Monica, Calif.: The RAND Corp., October 15, 1954.

————. *Intelligence Value of Soviet Notes on Air Incidents, 1950–1953*, RM-1348. Santa Monica, Calif.: The RAND Corp., October 15, 1954.

————. *Soviet Reactions to Border Flights and Overflights in Peacetime*, RM-1346. Santa Monica, Calif.: The RAND Corp., October 15, 1954.

Greenfield, S. M., and W. W. Kellogg. *Inquiry into the Feasibility of Weather Reconnaissance from a Satellite Vehicle*, R-218. Santa Monica, Calif.: The RAND Corp., 1951.

Hall, R. Cargill. *A History of the Military Polar Orbiting Meteorological Satellite Program*. Chantilly, Va.: National Reconnaissance Office, September 2001.

Handler, Joshua. *Russian Nuclear Warhead Dismantlement Rates and Storage Site Capacity: Implications for the Implementation of START II and De-alerting Initiatives*, CEES Report No. AC-99-01. Princeton, N.J.: Princeton University, 1999.

Huntzicker, J. H., and H. A. Lieske. *Physical Recovery of Satellite Payloads—A Preliminary Investigation*, RM-1811. Santa Monica, Calif.: The RAND Corp., June 26, 1956.

Katz, Amrom H., ed. *Selected Readings in Aerial Reconnaissance: A Reissue of a Collection of Papers from 1946 and 1948*, RAND P-2762. Santa Monica, Calif.: The RAND Corp., August 1963.

Lipp, J. E., et al. *Reference Papers Relating to a Satellite Study*, RA 15032. Santa Monica, Calif.: The RAND Corp., 1947.

————. *Utility of a Satellite Vehicle for Reconnaissance*, R-217. Santa Monica, Calif.: The RAND Corp., 1951.

Lipp, J. E., and R. M. Salter, eds. *Project Feed Back Summary Report*, R-262. Santa Monica, Calif.: RAND Corp., March 1, 1954.

Polaroid Corporation Annual Report, 1952.

Polaroid Corporation Annual Report, 1953.

The RAND Corporation: 40th Year. Santa Monica, Calif.: The RAND Corp., 1988.

Reference Volume Three: Stereoscopic Photography, Polaroid Corporate Archives, 1984.

Richelson, Jeffrey T. *U.S. Satellite Imagery, 1960–1999*. National Security Archive Electronic Briefing Book No. 13, April 14, 1999; http://www.gwu.edu/~nsarchiv/NSAEBB/NSAEBB13/index.html.

Wohlstetter, A. J., et al. *Selection and Use of Strategic Air Bases*, R-266. Santa Monica, Calif.: The RAND Corp., June 1962.

————. *Vulnerability of U.S. Strategic Air Power to a Surprise Enemy Attack in 1956*, SM-15. Santa Monica, Calif.: The RAND Corp., April 15, 1953.

Articles

Aviation Week & Space Technology, 1950–2002.
The New York Times, 1950–2002.

"Eastman Kodak Company Designed the Camera that Delivers the Images."
Photogrammetric Engineering and Remote Sensing, January 2000.
"Fairchild Brings the CCD to Market." *Business Week*, March 24, 1973.
"Fighting the Feds Over Shutter Control." *Communicator*, December 1999.
"Is Russia Winning the Arms Race?" *U.S. News & World Report*, June 18, 1954.
"Land Satellite Information in the Next Decade: Plans for Thirty-Meter
Resolution or Better Land Observation Satellites." Collected for 1995 American
Society of Photogrammetry and Remote Sensing Conference.
"Leveraging the Infosphere: Surveillance and Reconnaissance in 2020." *Airpower
Journal*.
"Observing the Satellites." *Sky & Telescope*, April 1960.
"PFIAB: An Historical and Contemporary Analysis, 1955–1975." Congressional
Research Service.
"Polar Sky Spies." *Time*, December 15, 1958.
"Red Air Force: The World's Biggest." *Newsweek*, August 23, 1954.
"Taking a Look Back at Project Feed Back." *RAND Newsletter*.

Amelio, Gilbert F. "Charge-Coupled Devices." *Scientific American*, February 1974.
Austin, Harold. "A Cold War Overflight of the USSR." *Daedalus Flyer*, Spring
1995.
Behling, Thomas, and Kenneth McGruther. "Planning Satellite Reconnaissance to
Support Military Operations." *Studies in Intelligence*, Winter 1998–99.
Brugioni, Dino A. "The Art and Science of Photoreconnaissance." *Scientific
American*, March 1996.
———. "The Unidentifieds." *Studies in Intelligence*, Summer 1969.
Brugioni, Dino A., and Robert F. McCort. "British Honors for Lundahl." *Studies in
Intelligence*, Spring 1975.
Burnham, James. "Intelligence on Cuba." *National Review*, November 20, 1962.
Burrows, William E.. "Beyond the Iron Curtain." *Air and Space*, December 1998.
———. "The Coldest Warriors." *Air and Space*, December 1999.
———. "How the Skunk Works Works." *Air and Space*, April 1994.
———. "Imaging Space Reconnaissance Operations During the Cold War: Cause,
Effect and Legacy." http://webster.hibo.no/asf/Cold-War/report1/williame
.html.
———. "The Oxcart Cometh." *Air and Space*, February 1999.
———. "That New Black Magic." *Air and Space*, December 1998.
Cain, John W. "Technical Factors in Aerospace Photography." *Studies in
Intelligence*, Fall 1962.

Clark, Keith. "On Warning." *Studies in Intelligence*, Winter 1965.

Daso, Dik. "Origins of Airpower: Hap Arnold's Early Career in Aviation Technology, 1903–1935." *Airpower Journal*, Winter 1996.

———. "Origins of Airpower: Hap Arnold's Command Years and Aviation Technology, 1936–1945." *Airpower Journal*, Fall 1997.

Day, Dwayne A. "Big Black and Small Satellites: Comparing NASA and NRO." *Space Times* 38, no. 5, Sept.–Oct. 1999.

———. "Listening from Above: The First Signals Intelligence Satellite." *Spaceflight* 41, no. 8, Aug. 1999.

———. "Mapping the Dark Side of the World Part 1: The KH-5 ARGON Geodetic Satellite." *Spaceflight* 40, no. 7, July 1998.

———. "Mapping the Dark Side of the World Part 2: Secret Geodetic Programmes After ARGON." *Spaceflight* 40, no. 8, Aug. 1998.

———. "Medium Metal: The NRO's Smaller Satellites." *Spaceflight* 42, no. 1, Jan. 2000.

———. "Rashomon in Space: A Short Review of Official Spy Satellite Histories." *Quest* 8, no. 2, Summer 2000.

———. "Relics of the Space Race: Space Archaeology of Vandenberg Air Force Base, Part 1." *Spaceflight* 42, no. 2, Feb. 2000.

———. "Relics of the Space Race: Space Archaeology of Vandenberg Air Force Base, Part 2." *Spaceflight* 42, no. 3, Mar. 2000.

Dourgarian, Jim. "Test Pilot Seeks Beauty During Flight or at Home." *Daily Review* (Burbank, Calif.), Oct. 12, 1970.

Drell, Sidney D. "Physics and U.S. National Security." *Reviews of Modern Physics*, April 17, 1998.

Dulles, John Foster. "A Policy of Boldness." *Life*, May 19, 1952.

Eberhart, Jonathan. "The CCD: New Eye on the Sky." *Science News*, March 12, 1977.

Edwards, Philip K. "The President's Board: 1956–1960." *Studies in Intelligence*, Summer 1969.

Elliott, Richard G. "On a Comet, Always: A Biography of Dr. W. Randolph Lovelace II." *New Mexico Quarterly* 36, no. 4.

Fenton, Ben. "U.S. Spying Balloons Were Based in Britain." *Daily Telegraph London*, Aug. 10, 1998.

Flax, Alexander, and Ivan Getting. "Allen F. Donovan: 1914–1995." In *Memorial Tributes: National Academy of Engineering*, vol. 8, 1996.

Florini, A. M., and Y. Dehqanzada. "Commercial Satellite Imagery Comes of Age." *Issues in Science and Technology*, Fall 1999.

Garwin, Richard L., Kurt Gottfield, and Donald L. Hafner. "Antisatellite Weapons." *Scientific American* 250, no. 6, June 1984.

Glines, C. V. "Billy Mitchell: Air Power Visionary." *Aviation History*, Sept. 1997.

Grabo, Cynthia M. "Strategic Warning: The Problem of Timing." *Studies in Intelligence*, Spring 1972.

Greenwood, Ted. "Reconnaissance and Arms Control." *Scientific American* 288, no. 2, Feb. 1973.

Grundhauser, Larry. "Sentinels Rising: Commercial High-Resolution Satellite Imagery and Its Implications for U.S. National Security." *Airpower Journal*, Winter 1998.

Hafemeister, David, Joseph J. Romm, and Kosta Tsipis. "The Verification of Compliance with Arms-Control Agreements." *Scientific American* 252, no. 3, March 1985.

Hall, Keith R. "The National Reconnaissance Office: Revolutionizing Global Reconnaissance." *Defense Intelligence Journal* 8, no. 1, Summer 1999.

Hall, R. Cargill. "The Eisenhower Administration and the Cold War: Framing American Astronautics to Serve National Security." *Prologue* 27, no. 1, Spring 1995.

———. "From Concept to National Policy: Strategic Reconnaissance in the Cold War." *Prologue*, Summer 1996.

———. "Missile Defense Alarm: The Genesis of Space-Based Infrared Early Warning." *Quest* 7, no. 1, Spring 1999.

———. "The National Reconnaissance Office: A Brief History of Its Creation and Evolution." *Space Times*, March–April 1999.

———. "Origins and Development of the Vanguard and Explorer Satellite Programs." *Air Power Historian*, October 1964.

———. "Strategic Reconnaissance in the Cold War." *Prologue*, Summer 1996, p. 107.

———. "The Truth About Overflights: Military Reconnaissance Missions over Russia Before the U-2." *Quarterly Journal of Military History*, Spring 1997.

Handler, Joshua. "Lifting the Lid on Russia's Nuclear Weapon Storage." *Jane's Intelligence Review* 11, no. 8, Aug. 1, 1999.

Hersey, John. "Hiroshima." *The New Yorker*, Aug. 31, 1946.

Hillman, Donald E., with R. Cargill Hall. "Overflight: Strategic Reconnaissance of the USSR." *Air Power Historian*, Spring 1996.

Kennan, George P. "The Sources of Soviet Conduct." *Foreign Affairs* 25, July 1947.

Knebel, Fletcher. "Washington in Crisis: 154 Hours on the Brink of War." *Look*, Dec. 18, 1962.

Lawrence, R. E., and Harry W. Woo. "Infrared Imagery in Overhead Reconnaissance." *Studies in Intelligence*, Summer 1967.

Loeb, Vernon. "At CIA Tribute, the U-2 Flies Out of the Cold War's Long Shadows." *Washington Post*, Sept. 18, 1998.

Long, Lewis R. "Concepts for a Philosophy of Air Intelligence." *Studies in Intelligence*, Winter 1958.

Mathews, Charles W. "Technical Intelligence and Arms Inspection." *Studies in Intelligence*, Fall 1957.

McDonald, Robert A. "Corona: Success for Space Reconnaissance, a Look into the Cold War and a Revolution for Intelligence." *Photogrammetric Engineering and Remote Sensing*, June 1999.

McIninch, Thomas P. "The Oxcart Story." *Air Force Magazine*, Nov. 1994.

Orlov, Alexander. "The U-2 Program: A Russian Officer Remembers." *Studies in Intelligence*, Winter 1998–99.

Pinson, Ernest A. "A Tribute to Dr. W. Randolph Lovelace II." *New Mexico Quarterly* 36, no. 4, 1966.

Raloff, Janet. "CCDs: Astronomy's Superchips." *Science News* 114, no. 9, Aug. 26, 1978.

Richelson, Jeffrey T. "Out of the Black: The Disclosure and Declassification of the National Reconnaissance Office." *International Journal of Intelligence and Counterintelligence* 11, no. 1, Spring 1998.

Ruffner, Kevin C. "Declassification's Great Leap Forward: Corona and the Intelligence Community." *Studies in Intelligence*, vol. 36, no. 5, 1996.

Shulman, Seth. "Code Name: Corona." *Technology Review*, Oct. 1996.

Smith, F. Dow. "The Eyes of Corona: The World's First Satellite Reconnaissance Program." *Optics & Photonics News*, Oct. 1995.

Stanglin, Douglas, Susan Headden, and Peter Cary. "Flights of the Ferrets: Decades Later, Many of the Spy Missions Are Still Shrouded in Secrecy." *U.S. News & World Report*, Mar. 15, 1993.

Tarlofsky, Malcolm. "The Code War." *Washington Post Magazine*, May 10, 1998.

Tenet, George J. "The U-2 Program: The DCI's Perspective." *Studies in Intelligence*, Winter 1998–99.

Thompson, Tom. "Charge-Coupled Devices." *Computerworld*, Aug. 6, 2001.

Vick, Charles P. "Why the Soviets Never Beat the U.S. to the Moon." *21st Century Science and Technology*, Fall 1997.

Walsh, Maj. Gen. James H. "Strategic Thinking and Air Intelligence." *Studies in Intelligence*, Winter 1958.

Welzenbach, Donald E. "Din Land: Patriot from Polaroid." *Optics & Photonics News*, October 1994.

———. "Observation Balloons and Reconnaissance Satellites." *Studies in Intelligence*, Summer 1986.

———. "Science and Technology: Origins of a Directorate." *Studies in Intelligence*, Summer 1986.

Wheelon, Albert D. "Corona: The First Reconnaissance Satellites." *Physics Today* 50, no. 2, Feb. 1997.

Wheelon, Albert D., and Sidney N. Graybeal. "Intelligence for the Space Race." *Studies in Intelligence*, Fall 1961.

Wilson, Jim. "Skunk Works Magic: How a Handful of Men Broke the Rules and Created the World's Most Amazing High-Tech Weaponry." *Popular Mechanics*, Sept. 1999.

Wolfe, Frank. "NRO: Commercial, Military Satellite Gap Will Narrow." *Defense Daily*, May 26, 1998.

SPEECHES, CORRESPONDENCE, PAMPHLETS, VIDEOS

CBS Evening News, "Support to the Military," Feb. 2, 1998; "NRO: Eye on America," Feb. 4, 1998; "NIMA: Eye on America," Feb. 5, 1998.

"Corona Teamwork and Technology," video, National Reconnaissance Office.

Drell, Sidney. "Physics and U.S. National Security," presented at Stanford Linear Accelerator Center, Stanford, Calif., Apr. 17, 1998.

Eisenhower, Dwight D. "Chance for Peace," before the American Society of Newspaper Editors, Apr. 16, 1953.

"Fallout Shelter Surveys: Guide for Executives," Department of Defense, October 1959.

Franklin, Lewis R. "Recommendation of Dr. William Perry for the 1998 RV Jones Intelligence Award," Aug. 22, 1998.

Garwin, Richard L. "Corona: America's First Reconnaissance Satellite System, a View from the Land Panel," panel on "Developing Corona—Its Technical Problems, Improvements and Victories," at "Piercing the Curtain: CORONA and the Revolution in Intelligence," conference sponsored by CIA Center for the Study of Intelligence, May 24, 1995, Washington, D.C.

———. "Remarks for RV Jones Award Dinner," Mar. 12, 1996.

———. "Sidney Drell and National Security," July 31, 1998.

———. "Working Together in Intelligence: Can We Make the Whole More than the Sum of Its Parts?" SES Seminar on the Occasion of the RV Jones Award, Mar. 12, 1996.

Hallion, Richard P. "Aerospace Medicine Nears the Millennium: Adaptation, Anticipation and Advancement," before the Aerospace Medical Association, May 17, 1999.

Land, Edwin. Commencement address at the Massachusetts Institute of Technology, 1960.

Lashmar, Paul. "Spyflights of the Cold War," at Kingston University, Mar. 12, 1997.

Latell, Brian. "CIA and the New Era of Openness," at Harvard University, Dec. 2, 1994.

Leghorn, Richard S. "Objectives for Research and Development in Military Aerial Reconnaissance," at opening ceremonies of Boston University Optical Research Laboratory, Dec. 13, 1946.

McMahon, John. "Corona: The First Satellite Reconnaissance System," at "Piercing the Curtain: CORONA and the Revolution in Intelligence," conference sponsored by CIA Center for the Study of Intelligence, May 24, 1995, Washington, D.C.

Proceedings of U-2 History Symposium, National Defense University, Washington, D.C., Sept. 17, 1998.

"Secret Satellite," video, National Reconnaissance Office.

"Spies Above: National Photographic Interpretation Center," video, National Reconnaissance Office.

"Spy in the Sky," transcript of documentary aired on *The American Experience*, PBS.

Wheelon, Albert D. Correspondence, 1999.

———. "Strategic Reconnaissance," speech before the American Physical Society, Mar. 24, 1999.

Woolsey, James R. "Remarks in Honor of Dr. Albert D. Wheelon," RV Jones Intelligence Award, Dec. 13, 1994.

ACKNOWLEDGMENTS

A CONFLUENCE OF FORTUITOUS factors made this book possible, beginning with the government's declassification in the mid-1990s of voluminous materials related to the technological breakthroughs that vaulted American spying into the stratosphere and outer space during the early years of the cold war. That, in turn, freed the men and women who worked on these programs to talk about them publicly for the first time, ending decades of silence. I was fortunate to delve into these matters as a torrent of previously undisclosed information became available to scholars and journalists, illuminating a heroic and untold chapter in American history.

In doing so, I had the assistance of an extraordinarily dedicated and talented research assistant, Elizabeth Goldman. Elizabeth, who signed up for this project after graduating with a history degree from Stanford, worked alongside me for three years, gathering, organizing, and mining thousands of pages of recently declassified documents. She designed and maintained an electronic database to store and sort the information, spent weeks at a number of presidential libraries, produced countless reports on various pieces of the story, conducted interviews, attended historical conferences, checked hundreds of facts, and did a masterful job of managing the endnotes. She was my indispensable partner in this endeavor.

The gateway to this book was opened by the government's decision to unseal secret archives of the Central Intelligence Agency and the National Reconnaissance Office. The initial impulse for that decision came from Robert M. Gates during the time he served as director of Central Intelligence. It was advanced by those who followed him, including James Woolsey and John Deutch, and consummated in 1995 by President Bill Clinton and Vice President Al Gore when they ordered the declassification of the nation's first reconnaissance satellite system, the

Corona. There is nothing more important to the health of a democracy than letting sunlight pour into the inner historical sanctums of secret organizations like the CIA and NRO, and nothing that is more difficult to do because of the traditions of those organizations. George Tenet, the present director of Central Intelligence, continued the declassification process in September 2002 with the publication of imagery from the second generation of spy satellites. The CIA's Center for the Study of Intelligence has played a vital role in translating declassification decisions into reality.

Many of the people who played critical roles in the development and operation of revolutionary new spying tools like the U-2 and SR-71 spy planes and the Corona photoreconnaissance satellite system shared their recollections with me. Many of them were extraordinarily generous with their time, welcoming me into their homes for hours of interviewing that frequently extended over several days. For me, these visits were a journey back to an era—the Eisenhower presidency—that I had experienced as a boy, a time of high tension in the cold war that was condensed in my childhood memory as a series of scary crises in faraway places such as the Korean Peninsula and Berlin and more immediate realities like the fallout shelters that appeared in my neighborhood in New York City. In recent years, as I sat in the kitchens, dens, and living rooms of the spies, scientists, pilots, top government officials, and corporate executives who worked so hard to preserve American security in the 1950s, I was given a guided tour through an intricate and remarkable secret history of that period.

I am grateful for the patience and cooperation of these men and women. Most of them are identified in the list of interviews that accompanies this story. Some, who remain involved in government work or discussed operations that remain secret today, asked not to be identified. A number of actors in this story extended a helpful hand to me throughout this project, and I owe them special thanks. Sidney Drell, the former deputy director of the Stanford Linear Accelerator Center and a longtime government consultant on intelligence technologies, offered sage counsel, technical expertise, and even a place to stay during research trips to the Bay Area. Little did I know as a Stanford undergraduate in the late 1960s, when we first met, that Professor Drell was immersed in some of the government's most secret spy projects. Gen. Andrew J. Goodpaster, Dwight D. Eisenhower's staff secretary at the White House, repeatedly reached back into his encyclopedic memory on my behalf. Katherine Schneider, who helped organize the public unveiling of the Corona program in 1995, pointed me toward many of the pioneers who created the first satellites, and her enthusiasm for their story was contagious. Adm. Bobby Inman, a former director of the National Security Agency and deputy director of Central Intelligence, has explained innumerable matters to me over the years about the intelligence kingdom. He helped me decipher the institutional feuds that grew out of the development of powerful new espionage technologies.

I also benefited greatly from pioneering historical and journalistic work in this field. Long before most Americans had ever heard of a spy satellite, and years before government archives were opened, Philip J. Klass and William E. Burrows wrote exceptionally well informed books about America's secret intelligence programs. Jeffrey T. Richelson, a senior fellow with the National Security Archive, has produced a series of exquisitely detailed books about spy satellites and other intelligence matters, drawing on years of painstaking research and a sustained effort to obtain documents under the Freedom of Information Act. Dwayne A. Day, another resourceful scholar, has scoured the archives and played a vital role in assembling and analyzing the historical record. John Logsdon, director of the Space Policy Institute at George Washington University, Brian Latell, former director of the CIA's Center for the Study of Intelligence and now an adjunct professor at Georgetown University, and Robert A. McDonald, who edited a valuable compendium of information about the Corona satellite system, helped bring these records to light. Chris Pocock, a British writer, did groundbreaking work on the U-2. Donald E. Welzenbach, who worked for many years as a historian at the CIA and was coauthor of a secret history of the U-2 that was declassified in 1998, graciously shared information and insights with me. R. Cargill Hall, who has chronicled the evolution of overhead reconnaissance as a historian for the Air Force and more recently the National Reconnaissance Office, provided me with a steady stream of invaluable documents and interview transcripts as they became declassified. Mr. Welzenbach and Mr. Hall also reviewed the chapters on the U-2 and Corona, catching innumerable factual errors. I am solely responsible for any that may remain.

Elizabeth Goldman would like to thank the many librarians and archivists who made her work possible, including the staffs of the Harry S Truman Library; the Dwight D. Eisenhower Library, particularly Barbara Constable; the John F. Kennedy Library; the Lyndon B. Johnson Library; the National Archives and Records Administration; the Library of Congress; the National Reconnaissance Office Reading Room; the University of New Mexico Health Sciences Library; the Polaroid Corporation archives; the Columbia University Oral History Research Office; the John Foster Dulles Oral History Collection at Princeton University; the Space Policy Institute at George Washington University; the CIA Center for the Study of Intelligence; and the Washington bureaus of the *New York Times* and *Aviation Week & Space Technology*. Robb Hoover provided introductions to pilots at the annual birthday ball of the 55th Strategic Reconnaissance Wing. And thanks to Juan Perez-Mercader for checking our accuracy on technical points and to Joshua Handler for extracting Corona photographs from the voluminous collection at the National Archives and getting them to us in a usable format.

Critical financial support for this project came from the Carnegie Corporation of New York, thanks to the encouragement of Vartan Gregorian and David C. Speedie. David Hamburg, former president of the corporation, was one of the first people to urge me to tell this history. Ted Mitchell and John Bak at Occidental College kindly took me on as a senior fellow of the college. The Hoover Institution at Stanford University also provided research assistance under the direction of John Raisian and Thomas H. Henriksen. The Hertog Research Assistantships of the School of the Arts at Columbia University assigned Adam Beroud, an enterprising graduate student, to help me with research. Arianne Chernock also assisted with research.

My colleagues at the *New York Times* gave me constant support. I am especially grateful to Arthur Sulzberger Jr., Howell Raines, Gail

Collins, and Philip M. Boffey, who afforded me the time to work on the book, including a five-month leave from my duties at the editorial page. William J. Broad's knowledgeable reporting about many of the matters discussed in these pages first turned my attention to the declassification of the Corona program and informed my research. Christopher Drew, who with Sherry Sontag chronicled the story of America's submarine espionage in *Blind Man's Bluff*, spurred me on whenever my batteries started to run down. Jeff Gerth and Janice O'Connell opened their home to me during research trips to Washington, and Jeff peppered me with good suggestions and reporting tips, reminding me of the adventures we shared in the early 1980s when we were tracking the activities of a pair of renegade CIA officers, Edwin Wilson and Frank Terpil. Were it not for Bill Kovach, who unexpectedly assigned me to the spy beat in 1979 when he was the *Times*'s Washington bureau chief, I would never have traversed the path that led to this book.

Any book is in some fundamental way a collaboration between writer and editor, and I was fortunate to work with Alice Mayhew at Simon & Schuster, who is one of the best in the business. Alice and I first started talking about books in the mid-1980s, when I was reporting for the *Times* in Washington and preparing for an assignment in Moscow. She waited patiently for me to come up with a proposal that I could execute, and from our initial conversation about this project in 1998, she has provided wise advice, astute editing, and unflagging encouragement. Roger Labrie of Simon & Schuster walked me through the editing process with many fine suggestions about how to improve the book. Getting this project off the ground and bringing it to readers would have been impossible without the help of my agent, Amanda Urban, who has been both adviser and friend since we worked for Clay Felker at *Esquire* in the late 1970s.

My wife, Felicity Barringer, and our sons, Michael and Gregory, have every right to think of this book as a family enterprise. Their support and patience were invaluable. I long ago lost count of the weekends when I disappeared behind my desk to work on the project, not to mention the vacations sacrificed to research and writing. They accepted my obsession with grace and good humor. They were also excellent editors and critics. My brother, William Taubman, who was working in parallel on his own book, a biography of Nikita Khrushchev, helped to keep my spirits high and always made himself available to field my questions about the cold war. I regret that our parents, Howard and Nora, are not here to see the nearly simultaneous publication of our books. As people who were devoted to the written word, and taught us much about the importance of history, I'm sure they would have been pleased and proud.

New York City
December 2002

INDEX

Page numbers beginning with 371 refer to notes.

ILLUSTRATION CREDITS

Central Intelligence Agency: 9
Courtesy of Albert D. Wheelon: 18
Department of Defense: 20
Dwight D. Eisenhower Library: 3
Federation of American Scientists: 19
National Archives and Record Administration, courtesy of Joshua
    Handler: 16
National Park Service/Dwight D. Eisenhower Library: 15
National Reconnaissance Office: 4, 6, 7, 8, 10, 12, 13, 14, 17
U.S. Air Force: 5, 11
U.S. Navy/Dwight D. Eisenhower Library: 1, 2